The Great Lakes of Africa

The Great Lakes of Africa
Two Thousand Years of History

Jean-Pierre Chrétien

Translated by Scott Straus

ZONE BOOKS · NEW YORK

2003

I would like to thank Jean-Pierre Chrétien, Alison Des Forges, Michel Feher, Meighan Gale, Sara Guyer, Nelson Kaffir, Ramona Naddaff, and David Newbury for all their help with the translation. — S.S.

Originally published as L'Afrique des grands lacs: Deux milles ans d'histoire © 2000 Aubier.

Printed in the United States of America.

Distributed by The MIT Press, Cambridge, Massachusetts, and London, England

Library of Congress Cataloging-in-Publication Data

Chrétien, Jean-Pierre.
    [Afrique des Grands lacs. English]
The great lakes of Africa : two thousand years of history / Jean-Pierre Chrétien; translated by Scott Straus.
    p. cm.
    Includes bibliographical references and index.
    ISBN 1-890951-34-X
    1. Africa, Eastern – History. 2. Africa, Central – History. 3. Rwanda – History. 4. Burundi – History. 5. Uganda – History. I. Title.

DT365.5.C4613 2003
967.6–dc21   2002191001

Contents

To my former students, to my colleagues from the
University of Burundi, terribly afflicted by a History
that they try to overcome in spite of everything....

Preface

This work, first published in France in 2000, was designed to fill a gap. Over and over again, the Great Lakes region of Africa was on newspaper front pages and on the nightly news. But if the public wanted a better understanding of the historical background of the major crises in this region, it had only specialized monographs and very superficial, general takes to which to turn. Thus, this book had a clear objective from the start: to offer a synthesis of research contributions from various sources. This book is not an essay in political science or, strictly speaking, the result of a new inquiry, but rather the fruit of the author's thought and work for the last thirty years. To take stock of existing knowledge in this way is also to call for new research.

Addressing this issue required mobilizing old and new works scattered around the globe in periodicals of limited circulation or now defunct, in various archives, and in largely ignored academic writings in different languages.[1] An attempt at understanding the region's historical dynamics first encounters an absurd obstacle stemming from the colonial partition, which divided scholarship as much as politics into French-speaking and English-speaking zones. Until recently, the French-Belgian and English strands of research, focused on Rwanda and Burundi and on Uganda, respectively, existed side by side, often ignoring each other, as if they concerned distant regions without mutual relationships, even though they treated the same region, the same peoples, and the same cultures. Revolts that broke out in the early twentieth century in the mountains bordering Rwanda and Uganda gave rise to articles on the Ugandan side and on the Belgian side that left the impression they did not relate to the same movement; crucial elements of Burundi's deepest past implicate neighboring Buha, even though studies published in British Tanganyika on subjects that would shed light on this history were not read, and so forth. Over the last twenty years, things have changed little by little. Specialists read each other in their respective languages; works crossed borders; international conferences established ties between Congolese, Rwandan, Burundian, Ugandan, and Tanzanian scholars; and studies transcended linguistic divides.[2] One can imagine the holes, distortions, and intellectual myopia engendered by the depth of the divide born from the colonial partition and the primacy of Eurocentric frameworks. What needs to be thought anew involves spaces, temporalities, and themes.

Two geographic areas have received a lot of scholarly attention: Uganda and Rwanda-Burundi. Research largely left the northwest of contemporary Tanzania and the Kivu provinces of Congo fallow, as if the "peripheries" were less interesting. The Bukoba region has been almost forgotten since German colonial times.[3] The history of Lake Kivu's western shores did not figure in Belgium's colonial romance.[4] The linguistic family that strongly characterizes the culture of millions of people in the region has its poor relatives. Some languages are overstudied, with piles of dictionaries, grammatical studies, and anthologies, while other languages remain almost unknown for lack of political interest: what is known about the Fuliru in Congo or the Zinza in Tanzania? Until now, two "models" have been stressed: Buganda and Rwanda. But one might wonder if their remarkable organization, as well as the extreme events of the last few years, does not show these countries to be exceptions, some will say monsters. During the twentieth century, Apolo Kagwa and Alexis Kagame put their historical dimension on the map; their dramatic experiences over the last twenty years and the challenges posed to the international community, especially by Rwanda, launched that historical dimension onto the international scene.

Despite inequalities in documentation, I have tried to re-balance the picture and understand the region in its totality. This means it was impossible to treat each little political area in detail, period by period, or discuss all the chronologies and dynastic lists from each kingdom. It was also impossible to describe the role of every actor during the colonial period, of a given district administrator or mission head, of such and such a leader or catechist, however famous they remain (for better or worse) in their small area. Experts will surely find many holes or will deplore the allusiveness, to their eyes, of the discussion of a given situation. And the best-known countries (referred to above) have perhaps suffered the most from this necessary work of selection and synthesis. The importance of past realities cannot be measured by the power of present ones, be they political, emotional, or even academic. But the place of some of these countries and some of their problems is worthy of explanation, and I have taken that into account, as will be seen with regard to the "ethnic" question in Rwanda and Burundi and the importance of kingship in Buganda.

Above all, I wanted to avoid the myopia of monographs, though not by subscribing to the tradition of "interlacustrine" interpretations, with their exogenous comparisons (large invasions, feudalities, monarchies of medieval Europe, and so on). Instead, the emphasis had to be on comparative work bound to the geographic area in question. Comparing neighbors is a far more realistic approach than intellectually juggling concepts defined beneath

11

other skies. But this is certainly not a plea for the inexpressible singularity of the Great Lakes region. Its inhabitants have a banally human history that can be clarified through other situations, independent of language and race. What must be rejected here, as in the rest of African historiography, are hasty projections, familiar images that reduce specific situations to known models. Does not the historian's work always reside in this incessant dialectic between bringing out the particularity of given situations and integrating them into a shared understanding, one devoid of all exoticism? The Great Lakes region of Africa has recently been compared to hell, to the diabolical site of a genocidal obsession. Not long ago, it conjured up dreams of an earthly paradise, of an extended Solomonic Ethiopia — itself coming from "happy Arabia" — a region where the God of Christian monotheism would blow like a tornado. One forgot all the peasants sowing sorghum, maintaining their banana plantations, milking their cows, planting their beans; all the blacksmiths and salt workers, masters of their crafts for two millennia; all the religious quests confronting misfortunes; all the political inventiveness strewn with failure and conflict but also responsible for constructing public spaces where words triumphed over arms.

Even in the 1950s, written history began with the sons of Ham, sometime between the time of Genesis and the eighteenth century, stood still until the mid-nineteenth century, when white heroes, the explorers and missionaries, arrived, and then found a place on the international scene during the last half century. Thus it was not just a physical, human, economic, and cultural space that had to be reconstructed but also a long-term history, centuries of creating a mode of life and a vision of the world, a civilization. This ambition is legitimate, as much from the perspective of the historian's profession as from that of contemporary actors in this history, those who want to recover their past with its dynamics and its uncertainties, cleared of both obscurity and the false light of clichés imposed by colonial rule. Each period in this long journey depended on a specific level of knowledge, enriched over time with linguistic data, archaeology, oral traditions, and foreign and national archives. The limitations of different kinds of sources need to be recognized, as does the degree of imprecision in each period. Confirming my claim that "factual precision is not achieved before the eighteenth century" and that "political hypotheses only become reliable around the seventeenth century," Jan Vansina has recently remarked that "historical" narrations before Ruganzu Ndori's reign (in the seventeenth century) are essentially based on mythic composition. Political debates and social mechanisms in the seventeenth century cannot be reconstructed as those in the 1950s might be, though many authors who want to demonstrate supposed continuities devote themselves to this intellectual exercise nonetheless. Here as elsewhere, we must use historical method to carefully reconstruct qualitative breaks in time, in contrast to the continuities — and certainties — of "collective memory," which recurs or reconstructs itself based on the lived experience of each period.

Pedagogy informed by historical method is thus especially useful in the current ideological context. Following the region's explosion in the media since 1994, explanations have been furnished ad nauseam, but they are based on an old understanding, in general about a half century old, derived from "documentary" files lying around on the shelves of major media outlets and administration offices. More than ever, the "wise kings" of the sources of the Nile, the lords and serfs of "interlacustrine feudality," and the great Gobineauian confrontation between true Negro natives and the ancient Hamitic "white layer" became the formula that, whether out of naïveté or confusion, fueled fantasies where the past was described as "traditional" or "original" and considered extrahistorical fact. The famous layered pastry of races and its social schematization operated in full force, sustained again and again by the anthropologist Jacques Maquet's model from the 1950s, which had been widely disseminated in English and French. This would be the necessary picture, the permanent image, that preceded and explained the short film of recent history.

The effort to return to history has proved particularly difficult, intellectually and morally, because the "colonial library" has been internalized in African memory to the point of becoming politically operational, whether involuntarily or consciously. In this context, the work of historians has been perceived as a burden by various groups who want to revive the previous century's prejudices and orchestrate them politically. "Who has the right to change the history of the country?" wrote the editors of the racist organ *Kangura* in 1990. Historical critique appears as sacrilege to any group that maintains convictions about a past designed to justify its actions in the present. Spokesmen denounce "rereadings" of history and suggest existing works be thrown away and history be "rewritten." Indigenous tradition is invoked to bolster this claim, but exegesis of the proposed theses most often involves returning to sources from the colonial library mentioned above. This lends itself to the justification of the most antagonistic positions — the most extreme in light of their racializing foundations.[5] "Africanism" based on an early-twentieth-century anthropological model has become like a new African consciousness in several contemporary crises, but in the Great Lakes region the danger of this temptation has been the most virulent.

This merits reflection. It is fashionable today to stress the intensity of contrasting memories and political manipulations in order to relativize historical critique. Is the truth of historical narration that different from novelistic fiction? This is a question Hayden White has raised for the last thirty years.[6] A discussion that can be brilliant in the calm of Western campuses can turn piping hot and even devastating in societies or situations that require a search for reason and an exit from passion, the source of hundreds of thousands of deaths. Identification, critique, and reflection on sources, use of archives, and methodological investigations oriented more toward simple people than toward unofficial spokesmen of predefined positions — all this can arouse the discomfort of actors or observers riveted to the present. Historical research is enriched through questions about the present. But at the risk of frustrating a media in search of simplicity and eager to see clichés confirmed, historical research depends on a distancing, on a putting between parentheses, on *Verfremdung*, as Bertolt Brecht would say, which aims to shatter memory's false certitudes.

In the epistemology of change that all historiography represents, chronology, in the sense of identifying turning points and dynamics, is fundamental. But the landmark of "major dates" is often an illusion. The history of contemporary Africa transcends 1885 and 1960. People's lives did not suddenly change because diplomats met in a German capital or because new flags were hoisted in African public places. This does not mean that the impact of colonial rule should be neglected. The experience of this disciplinary modernization has inspired both idyllic nostalgia and intransigent denunciations. But the real debate concerns colonization's actual effect on the current course of events, a question that is posed dramatically in the Great Lakes region.

Two recent works have extended the debate since this book was published in French: Jan Vansina's synthesis on the history of old monarchical Rwanda and Mahmood Mamdani's essay on the 1994 genocide.[7]

The first returns to the progressive construction of the Rwandan kingdom between the seventeenth and the nineteenth century and the crystallization of the famous Hutu-Tutsi cleavage at the heart of this society. The work recalls that these historical processes stem neither from "great, continuous, and massive migrations" nor from "the ideas and actions of colonial masters."[8] Vansina shows how society's ethnicization along the lines of this antagonism, which today has become seemingly unavoidable, is above all the fruit of a sociopolitical dynamic that ultimately privileged the Tutsi both in reality, as far as a narrow ruling faction is concerned, and in the social imagination, to the point of lumping all the others under the pejorative rubric of Hutu "subjects."[9] However, the systematically negative description of this country's situation under Mwami Rwabugiri's reign in the late nineteenth century leaves open the question of this regime's role in the "Hutu-Tutsi polarization" and the role of the colonial system that in turn would "inscribe this quality on all sorts of census documents."

Mamdani reflects on the historical dynamic of the so-called ethnic cleavage, its political dimension, and the fact that the meaning of the terms "Hutu" and "Tutsi" varied over the course of centuries—ideas already present in my own work. But unlike Vansina, who focuses on signs of a precolonial antagonism, Mamdani underscores the role of "the poisoned colonial legacy" to explain how the country's ruling groups accepted this inheritance as part of a "nativist nationalist project that failed to transcend it."[10] Here the discussion relates not to the exact nature of the old monarchical regime but to colonial rule. Above all, Mamdani sees it as a regime of domination and exploitation where the colonized are divided into an "indigenous race" and a "subject race," setting up the Tutsi as a kind of second-tier colonizer, sort of like what the Indians were for the British colonizers in Uganda (and Mamdani is quite familiar with this subject!). Colonization's cultural dimension, including evangelization and missionary ideology — in other words, a form of paternalism whose moral influence deeply rooted the racial reading of society in thought and practice — seems, in his study, secondary to the purely economic calculation of domination. In particular, the internalization of racial obsession is limited to Kayibanda's regime, while his successor, Habyarimana, is exonerated, for unclear reasons, of this ideology.[11] Thus, according to Mamdani, it is as if the genocide of the Tutsi had been nothing more than a terrible episode — an enormous blunder — in the process of re-empowering the people who had previously been subjugated by both Belgian and Tutsi colonialism. In this Hegelian dialectic, it is up to the Hutu people, even the tenants of Hutu Power (whom the author distinguishes arbitrarily as promoters of the genocide), to realize a democratic synthesis that integrates the Tutsi minority. One could only subscribe to this hope if the 1994 genocide had been a social struggle run amok, if the culture of hate that it expressed had not involved a regime searching for a scapegoat precisely because it was incapable of thinking of democratization in truly social terms and because it was captivated by an ideology capable of tying up the country's past and future for the benefit of an exclusive ruling elite.

These latter discussions show how research on inheritance and continuity, legitimate in all historical reflection, can become a trap if the question of discontinuities — in light of contemporary reinterpretations and agendas — is not raised at every stage. The temptation to debate past responsibilities, imputed to actors of such and such a period, can make us forget that every generation tends to reshuffle the cards. Just as the present does not simply follow from the past, the past should not be reread in terms of the present.[12] The crucial problem lies in identifying the biases involved in stressing any set of continuities and discontinuities. The Great Lakes region no longer offers a "helpful" illustration of a "culture"; today it has become a laboratory for reflecting on history.

Jean-Pierre Chrétien
May 2002

Linguistic Note

Pronunciation Problems
The vowel e is always pronounced "ey" as in hay.
The vowel u is always pronounced "ooo" as in blue.

The consonant g corresponds to a hard g in English as in gift.
The consonant c is pronounced "ch" as in chew.
The consonant s is pronounced "ss" as in sat.
The consonant h is silent as in ghost.

For example: Gisenyi is pronounced Gissenyi and Maconco is pronounced Machoncho.

Bantu prefixes
The same root word is preceded by class prefixes that vary the meaning, for example:
Bu-rundi, the country or the Rundi kingdom.
Ba-rundi, the inhabitants of this country, the Burundians.
Mu-rundi, an inhabitant of Burundi, a Burundian.
Ki-rundi, the language of Burundi.

The same for Buganda, Baganda, Muganda, Luganda, and so on.

Writing History in Africa

"The Great Lakes of Africa, the vast heartland of East Africa, a place to vanish from history and geography, like Livingstone, Speke, Baker, and Stanley."[1] As recently as twenty years ago, this exotic image dominated the few written works published in France on this African region. The 1950 film *King Solomon's Mines* also evokes the hills of Rwanda as a mysterious Atlantis, a veritable world of *The Thousand and One Nights* somehow lost in the shadows of the Dark Continent.[2] Indeed, since Antiquity, the home of the legendary "sources of the Nile" has inspired a folklore peddled to Christian and Muslim worlds alike. But in recent years, French geographers, linguists, anthropologists, sociologists, and historians have produced many important studies. These works followed scholarship in Belgium, Britain, and Germany—the former colonizers of Rwanda, Burundi, Congo, Uganda, and Tanzania—and in the African countries themselves, independent now for a generation, despite the political and economic dangers of scholarship there.

Yet the region's recent tragedies, which have caused the international media literally to rediscover these countries, have provoked more "humanitarian" emotion than scholarly inquiry. There has even been a regression in several cases. Coverage of the 1994 massacres in Rwanda, then front-page news, revived the image of African barbarity as well as colonial-era racial stereotypes. The region's alpha and omega were reduced to an atavistic battle between the "shorts" and "the longs," between "Bantus" and "Nilotes," who were alleged to be as different as "Finns and Sicilians."[3] Popularization encourages, it seems, caricature, at least as far as this part of Africa is concerned.

For many years, the region was a paradise for colonizers, missionaries, and so-called development experts. In the early twentieth century, Uganda was known as the "pearl" of the British Empire. After 1945, the Congolese Kivu became a bucolic refuge for bourgeois Belgians haunted by the Cold War, and in the 1980s Rwanda was more than ever an "African Switzerland." Moreover, these verdant lands were inhabited by people described as wise and hardworking. But then the Holy Spirit "blew a tornado" (to quote a still-popular Burundian expression from the 1930s). Suddenly, in Uganda in the mid-1980s, in Burundi in 1993, in Rwanda in 1994, and in Zaire in 1997, mass graves and hundreds of thousands of dead evoked the image of hell in commentators' eyes. "Was God in Rwanda?" asked one Canadian journalist.[4]

In this context, a grounded approach, one that restores a concrete historical dimension to the people on the cusp of East and Central Africa, can seem difficult. Such an approach is further complicated because African societies were considered, from Hegel to Braudel, to have no place, or at best a peripheral one, in universal history.[5]

Interlacustrine Africa
The first question to ask is whether the "Great Lakes of Africa" even exists beyond the fantasies I have just evoked.[6] The term itself was forged by nineteenth-century Anglo-Saxon "explorers." After the publication of Richard Burton's *The Lake Regions of Cen-*

tral Africa, a series of travel narratives used the expression "Great Lakes of Africa."[7] The search for the sources of the Nile that drove these explorations involved the discovery of mountains and lakes — which conformed with the writings of Alexandrian geographers. Furthermore, late-nineteenth-century geography tended to revolve around finding and mapping water. In short order, the circle of lakes around the main flow of the White Nile came to define the region. The lakes included Lake Victoria to the southeast, Lakes Albert and Edward to the west, and Lakes Kivu and Tanganyika (which are part of the Congo basin) to the southwest.[8] In the early twentieth century, German specialists on East Africa introduced the noun *Zwischenseengebiet*, "the territory between the lakes," which later became the basis for the French adjective *interlacustre* and the English "interlacustrine."[9] These terms in turn were reprinted in volumes published by the International African Institute in London; the Musée Royal de l'Afrique Centrale in Tervuren, Belgium; and *Cahiers d'études africaines* in Paris.[10] During the last twenty years, the expression "Great Lakes" has come back into use, even before being popularized in the press.[11]

In fact, the region's most distinctive physical trait is its relief: a swath of elevated land, a table-like or rounded surface 1,000 – 2,000 meters high, situated in an equatorial zone between 5 degrees southern and 2 degrees northern latitude. A Massif Central in the tropics. The periphery's summits — Mount Elgon, the volcanic Virunga Mountains, and the Ruwenzori massif — reach 3,000 to more than 5,000 meters. The rest follows from there: in particular the heavy rainfall that the mountains trap. The heaviest rains occur around the equinox and are connected to the Indian Ocean monsoons. Average annual rainfall is at least 1,000 millimeters and reaches nearly 2,000 millimeters around the peaks near the western chain of lakes (an area called the western Rift) and along the northern shores of Lake Victoria. The dry season rarely exceeds two months. The driest zones are the middle-altitude plateaus (around 1,200 meters) in western Uganda and the border zones between Tanzania, Rwanda, and Burundi.

The other distinctive feature is human in nature: the demographic density of the region is of a type typically associated with Asian countries. Today, average density is nearly two hundred people per square kilometer. A century ago, a figure four or five times smaller than that was thought to outstrip the land's carrying capacity. Even if dispersed, human settlement has caused more deforestation here than anywhere else in Africa. The only remaining unpopulated zones are a few forested pockets on the highest peaks and reed and papyrus fields in the bases of several valleys. The region tends to contrast with surrounding areas: forest in the Congolese basin to the west, the more or less treed savannas of Kenya's and Tanzania's plateaus to the east, and a mixture of dry and marshy zones along the Sudanese border to the north, where human density is ten times less.[12]

When the first Europeans arrived in the second half of the nineteenth century, they were struck by these physical and human contrasts. After months of crossing dry forest and desert to the east and thickly forested areas to the west, they arrived in these cool, settled, and cultivated lands. The ancient mythology of the sources of the Nile had stoked their imagination. Now they found comfort in the enchanting spectacle of banana gardens, fields of cereal crops and vegetables, and cattle herds. Moreover, these highlands between the lakes seemed to have escaped some of Africa's most endemic scourges, notably trypanosomiasis. Idealized comparisons with different regions in Europe have a long history. In the heart of black Africa, the Great Lakes literally dazzled the whites.

The scholarly literature on this region has focused on several areas of study: the physical and human geography; an agrarian-pastoral complex and its social, cultural, and economic role; and the organization of powerful monarchies. Other areas of study, which are perhaps less explicit, more allusive, and sometimes confusing, even embarrassing, include oral traditions, their attendant rich myths and the refined languages in which they are told; nonfigurative and geometric art; the late arrival of Islam and its eastern commercial networks; the powerful impact that missionaries had in the countryside and on thought; and an ideology of races that posited distinct social groups structured by successive invasions. In the preface to a 1962 book published by the Musée Royal de l'Afrique Centrale in Tervuren, the Belgian anthropologist Marcel d'Hertefelt described it this way: "The interlacustrine region is distinguished ... by the juxtaposition or superposition of an Ethiopic race next to or on top of a Negroid race."[13]

In reality, the distinctiveness of the Great Lakes is not so neat. If an interlacustrine civilization exists at all, its outlines are blurred, owing to influences from and interactions with neighboring areas. Partial social, political, and religious analogues can be found in central Tanzania, eastern Congo-Kinshasa, and northern Uganda. Especially important to keep in mind is that the Great Lakes region is quite diverse. Its morphology includes escarpments that tower over the western chain of lakes and marshy valleys of the Malagarasi, Kagera, Katonga, and Nile-Victoria basins; these valleys cut the countryside into sectors, and access to each from the other can be very difficult during heavy rains. The region's languages are all Bantu, but they can be subdivided into at least four or five language families that are not mutually intelligible. The region has two main rural systems: banana gardens and fisheries in the low riparian plateaus along Lake Victoria to the east (and along the depression of Lake Tanganyika) and a mixture of cultivation and cattle herding in the western mountains (Rwanda, Burundi, southwest Uganda, and the Kivu plateaus).

Finally, the colonially drawn political borders remain. The Europeans dismantled old borders that were the legacy of a history rich in conflict between two expansionary states — Buganda and Rwanda. As we will see, over the last three centuries these two poles of power have played a leading role in the evolution of the region.

A Crucial Region for Africanist Scholarship

Since the 1950s, this area, whose complexity the reader is no doubt beginning to appreciate, has been a cherished land for Africanist political anthropology. The region offered exceptional examples of centralized powers, social hierarchies, sacred politics, and ties of dependence. Its isolated position in the heart of the continent and its relatively recent contact with the external world (hardly more than a century old) seemed to permit quasi-direct observation of an ancient way of being.

In the Belgian domain, the Institut pour la Recherche Scientifique en Afrique Centrale (IRSAC), based in Astrida (now Butare), Rwanda, became famous for Jacques Maquet's 1954 sociological synthesis, which was the bible of Rwandan studies for some twenty years. In the British domain during the same period, an American anthropologist, Lloyd Fallers, was the driving force at the East Africa Institute of Social Research (EAISR), based at Makerere University in Uganda. In 1956 and 1964, Fallers published two works that treated Busoga and Buganda as models of "Bantu bureaucracy." As early as 1940, the London-based International African Institute had published a collection of essays on African political systems, of which Ankole was a featured example. The classics of the 1960s applied a model of social stratification to the Great Lakes kingdoms. In Paris, the sociologist Georges Balandier directed a research team of anthropologists and political sociologists at the Centre d'Etudes Africaines at the Ecole des

Hautes Etudes, and the interlacustrine region was a favored zone in which to apply this model: in 1967, the team published a volume that introduced the much-debated notion of African feudalism. In 1970, Maquet, then a member of this group, published a work largely based on what he had seen in Rwanda. But Balandier's "dynamic sociology" had the distinct merit of emphasizing the need for a historical approach, a dimension often missing in the anthropology of "traditional societies."[14]

Nonetheless, the region quickly became and remained a site for theoretical debates on African political systems, with all the related misconceptions of tradition and modernity. These ideological battles often blacked out the region's concrete history, which was the pretext for the debate in the first place. Even if a Gobineauian-style racial interpretation had not completely disappeared, other analytic grids took center stage.[15] These new approaches included the "cultural areas" scheme, which came under the rubric of "the civilization of the spear and the cow" and was derived from German diffusionist ethnology; Weberian approaches to the exercise and legitimation of power in society; Marxist debates on class struggle in rural areas, which were dominant in France in the 1960s and 1970s (and led by orthodox Maoists); and structuralist rereadings of rituals and myths, notably those by the Belgian anthropologist Luc de Heusch.[16]

The intellectual excitement subsided in the 1970s and 1980s, perhaps because of the crises engulfing the region. The chaos, its unpredictability and violence — both periodic and sometimes years-long — discouraged field-based research. Discussions turned to the dramatic events and the attendant ethnic polarization, often eclipsing other concerns and at times discouraging analysis. Later, the major catastrophes of the 1990s spurred reflections on violence, humanitarianism, and conflict prevention but hardly reinvigorated questions on the region's past.

Still, historical research has made a small but real step forward over the last thirty years, largely because of the cultural and political expectations born of independence. Higher education in the African countries played a crucial role, even if universities in the former Belgian colonies were not established until after independence. Important research has been carried out at Makerere University (unfortunately squelched between 1971 and 1986 for political reasons), as well as at the universities of Rwanda, Burundi, Lubumbashi (Democratic Republic of Congo), and Dar es Salaam (Tanzania), not to mention the Nairobi-based British Institute in Eastern Africa. A first generation of real scholars liberated their countries' historiography from the clutches of specialists on the "customary" world — colonial collectors, missionaries, and educated elites. This effort was supported and reinforced by Africanist centers in Europe and North America, where members of this new group studied and then returned to universities in Africa. A number of dissertations were written in this way, notably at the School of Oriental and African Studies in London, at Cambridge, Oxford, Paris I (Centre de Recherches Africaines), Paris VII, Louvain-la-Neuve, the University of Wisconsin-Madison, and Quebec's Laval University, among others. These works appear throughout this book's bibliography.

These studies have relied on and benefited from collecting oral narratives, from a progressive opening of colonial and missionary archives, and from advances in the fields of archaeology and linguistics. Each source has its own issues and problems, all worthy of discussion.

The Search for Sources

The first written accounts of the Great Lakes kingdoms date from the mid-nineteenth century. It was in London that reports by British merchants and missionaries who frequented the Indian

Ocean littoral were first collected. Drawing on stories from Swahili and Nyamwezi traders who spoke of a land of kings and lakes, these accounts evoked mysterious "countries of the moon." Anglo-Saxon explorers soon replaced these "armchair geographers."[17] Financed by the Royal Geographical Society and voyaging by caravan, these travelers provided the first European eyewitness accounts of the Great Lakes kingdoms. Richard Burton first described Burundi in 1858; John Hanning Speke wrote about Buganda in 1862; Rwanda was only indirectly evoked, notably by Henry Morton Stanley at the 1885 Berlin Conference. Not until 1894 did a European — the German count Gustav Adolf von Götzen — penetrate Rwanda. Nonetheless, by the late 1870s, various missionary groups had firmly established themselves in the region and were regularly transmitting eyewitness accounts.[18] The Protestants belonged to the London Missionary Society and the Church Missionary Society (CMS), while the Catholics were members of Missionnaires de Notre Dame d'Afriques, better known as the White Fathers. The colonial occupations followed in the 1890s. The British took Uganda; the Germans seized the area between Lakes Victoria and Tanganyika; and the Belgians (assisted by others) occupied the area west of Lake Kivu as part of the Congo Free State (which became the Belgian Congo in 1908). After World War I, the Belgians and the English divided up the German territories, with the former acquiring the mandate for Ruanda-Urundi.

Some of these administrations left archives in the countries where the records originated. Today some archives operate as proper National Archives, notably in Entebbe (near Kampala), Dar es Salaam, and Bujumbura. But others are scattered all around the world: the Archives Africaines in Brussels; the Public Records Office in London; the Deutsches Zentralarchiv formerly in Potsdam and now in Berlin (not to mention Bonn, Koblenz, and Hamburg); the White Fathers Archives in Rome; and various Protestant missionary collections in Great Britain, Germany, and Scandinavia. Sparse documentation can also be found in France, the United States, Switzerland (which arbitrated the League of Nations, which handled the colonial mandates), and so on. For the most part, these sources became available only in the 1970s and sometimes even later. Moreover, because of statutes of limitations on these materials, we have access only to the period before independence.[19] I can give only a general idea of the state of the resources. However, I should note that these often criticized "colonial" texts, while requiring scholarly evaluation and interpretation, are surprisingly rich. The colonizers had their prejudices, but they were not necessarily poorly informed.[20] The independent countries conserved their files with less care, and of course many records disappeared or were destroyed during the recent crises.

Since the beginning of the twentieth century, the region has given rise to an extensive body of written material.[21] Foreigners and nationals alike have published books and articles; other publications also abound, including dissertations and memoirs, official reports and leaflets, domestic periodicals, including the *Uganda Journal* and *Tanganyika Notes and Records*, which began publishing in 1934 and 1936, respectively, and Catholic and Protestant publications written in local languages.

The region's administrative and political splintering poses a major problem for research. Except in Uganda, researchers often have to rummage through archives broadly labeled "East Africa" or "Congolese" in which material on Rwanda and Burundi is buried. A similar issue, pertinent to both sides of a border, may have produced documents with different titles, lost in some general file, and separated by thousands of kilometers. To reconstitute Africa's past in all its complexity, the historian must reconnect these broken paths and overcome these misleading but all too real divides.

The classical view links the development of history to the emergence of writing, and thus history in East Africa's interior started with the arrival of the first foreign conquerors. That, at least, was the view that the Oxford professor Reginald Coupland espoused in 1938. But for the last half century, in Africa and elsewhere, recourse to oral sources has not just been the prerogative of anthropologists. As the now-classic works of Jan Vansina and Claude-Hélène Perrot demonstrate, historians have also used this method, and notably so in the study of the Great Lakes.[22] Still, choosing the right informants and the best way to collect their stories requires an understanding of memory and the way communication works in oral cultures. All serious investigations today include such precautions as collecting divergent testimonies to cross-check information, using semi-structured interviews to balance the framework of a questionnaire with spontaneous expression, and making audio recordings to permit later re-examination of the form of the text.

The collected narratives are often quite varied. Some are true oral texts, "traditions" in the classical sense of the word. Their narrative form and quasi-poetic verbal rhythm guarantee a degree of linguistic stability over time. An excellent example is a dynastic poem titled *Ubucurabwenge* (The Source of Wisdom), which relates the succession of Rwandan sovereigns. Other information inherited from previous generations can take a looser form: stories heard at grandparents' homes; nonnarrative information concerning social, religious, and technical practices; explications of ancient terminology; and eyewitness accounts or descriptions of what parents remembered, especially about the colonial period. The main problem with this information is its fallibility, despite the care taken in collecting it. Nonetheless, experience enables one to challenge oversimplified criticisms of this approach. First, the idea that narrators would continually change their ancestors' legacies must be questioned; a more pertinent concern is that current events are interpreted in terms of the past, a seemingly integral part of the way history is conceived in these societies.[23] Second, the idea that informers would blithely mix up legend and fact must also be viewed with skepticism; in reality, legends are recounted as such.[24] Instead of excluding these sources, historians should appreciate what they have to offer (otherwise, wouldn't *The Odyssey* be off-limits for historians?).

Still, two questions remain: first on the work of memory in constructing traditions and second on chronologies. The crystallization of "things of the past" (*ivya kera* in Kirundi), of "that which is authoritatively established" (*amateka* in Kinyarwanda) — what we call history — is the fruit of a selection process that is not just a didactic summary but also the product of a then-predominant view of the facts in question, whether it is popular rumor or a government's or a lineage's official version. Oral traditions are not photographs of ancient times; they are settled discourses that reflect the "social conventions" at the time they were fixed. In periods of terrible crisis, the work of memory can take a fantastic turn whereby some marvelous hero emerges from a situation that is described as a catastrophe. That indeed is what happens in so-called origin stories. The older the traditions are, the more delicate their interpretations must be. More often than not, old narratives reveal more about ancient culture than about factual data, but that contribution is hardly negligible.[25]

For their part, chronologies are based on calculations derived from genealogical tables and dynastic lists, both of which pose significant problems. I will return to these questions in detail. But assuming an average generation of twenty-five to thirty years, one can backdate with reasonable certainty to the seventeenth century. Before then, the lists become unreliable given the symbolism in names.[26] Still, using astronomy and total solar eclipses (sometimes mentioned during certain reigns), some scholars have attempted to pinpoint dates with absolute certainty. Others have studied the Nile's hydrology. These scholars link narratives of regional famine and drought to flood dates, which, since the eighth century, have been recorded on Roda Island near Cairo. However, this is a risky endeavor, considering the various factors that might have affected the way the Nile was managed and considering the fact that, throughout history, floods and eclipses are among the most common clichés for scourges. It is therefore unwise for ethno-historians to attribute dates without a requisite "circa."[27]

Most of the misunderstandings about oral traditions come from an unequal exchange between the oral and the written, an unequal exchange sustained by a Western-educated group, the so-called elite traditionists.[28] During early colonial rule, a first generation of educated Africans emerged. Their ranks included aristocrats who studied at white schools, interpreters employed by administrators and anthropologists, and catechists. These so-called évolués (the advanced ones) wrote the region's first historiographies, but in so doing they had to balance several competing interests.[29] On the one hand, anxious to promote their kingdom of origin, they presented their communities as both civilized and ancient, older in fact than the kingdom next door. On the other hand, the Africans had to cater to their colonizers' demands and prejudices. In particular, the évolués conformed their narratives to the racial schemata of the day. Here the missionaries, in their ram-shackle Bible schools — where many évolués trained — had a major influence. To emphasize mankind's unity, the missionaries tied the region's different populations to various Ham lineages discussed in Genesis. Taught until just after independence, the évolué narratives were for a long time the sole historical accounts in their respective countries. As a consequence, sometimes contradictory and inconsistent dynastic lists became standardized.

33

In the early twentieth century, several authors were particularly influential. In Tanzania, Franzisko Lwamgira — first an interpreter for the German resident Willibald Von Stuemer in Bukoba and later an adviser to the English Native Administrations — oversaw several publications on the Buhaya kingdoms. In Uganda, Chief John Nyakatura championed the lost grandeur of Bunyoro, long subjugated by the Baganda. Also in Uganda, Ganda chief Apolo Kagwa compiled in 1901 *The Kings of Buganda (Basekabaka be Buganda)*, a national history written in Luganda; Kagwa was a leader of the Protestant party, his kingdom's "prime minister" under the British, and an insider at the CMS. In Rwanda, Abbot Alexis Kagame published that country's first dynastic history, *Triumphant Kalinga (Inganji Kalinga)*, in 1943 — the year King Mutara was baptized (Kalinga refers to the dynastic drum). A favorite of both the White Fathers and the king, Kagame became an ideologue for the Tutsi monarchy in the 1950s, a professor at the University of Rwanda (even, paradoxically, under the Hutu republic), and a member of UNESCO's International Committee on African History. He imposed a long-lasting Hamitic interpretation on Rwanda's ancient history.[30] Simultaneously source and historian, Kagame was convinced that he was both in the *biru*'s inner circle for knowing the "esoteric codes" of eternal Rwanda and part of a long line of classical medieval historians, like his teacher Canon Louis de Lacger.[31] An erudite priest from the clergy of Albi, Lacger began publishing a history of Rwanda in 1939 that adopted a Capetian version of French history.[32] This reconstructed account of Rwanda affected historical readings of Burundi (Rwanda's false twin and ruled under the same Belgian trusteeship), as can be seen in the 1930s work of Monsignor Julien Gorju, who was helped by several educated notables.[33]

In the debate over how much history and how much myth is in African traditional narratives, it is often forgotten that mythologies are frequently forged when the oral encounters the written. Marcel Detienne has convincingly shown that in ancient Greece "mythology" was forged through "the logographer's pen [conveying tradition] with subtle tattoos of verisimilitude ... intertwining the *muthos* and the *logos*, the writing and the telling." This is a matter more of graphics than orality. "Before being thought over, before being discussed, the Greek myth is written down."[34] This conclusion can be applied to the oral traditions in the Great Lakes kingdoms with one significant caveat: that the logographer's pen emerged under the shadow of foreign colonization. In 1920, Prince Gomotoka wrote in the Catholic journal *Munno* that the mythic founder of Buganda, Kintu, neither came from the sky nor quarreled with a serpent, as legend held. Instead, Gomotoka suggested, Kintu was a Clovis from a foreign invasion. This perfectly illustrates the peculiar game of writing, which passes on a culture's heritage while disguising it and extirpating its clan and religious roots, even if the new version is closer to historical reality.[35] It should not be forgotten that the White Fathers played a central role in this political-cultural reconstruction of history. They were present throughout the region; they first met and trained together in novitiates; they exchanged their observations and articles in congregational newsletters; they often spoke several languages, including that of the country in which they lived; and they moved between different parishes. Gorju, for example, was a missionary in Uganda before becoming the vicar apostolic in Burundi. Along with Upper Volta, the lakes region was the missionaries' darling child; they often were the ones who brought "modernization," for better and for worse.

Oral sources also can shed light on material references, natural and man-made objects, practices, rituals, and sites. Memory seems to cling to important places: boulders, mineral springs, watering places, ore deposits, and sacred forests.[36] Even if caution is warranted

35

about the factual aspects of these accounts, careful observation of the sites can yield new understanding of their significance, the role of belief and power, and the way human settlement developed.

In several cases, "sites of memory" offer historical insights that archaeologists, using scientific dating, can develop. This new horizon of African history takes its cue from oral sources, at least for the period prior to the seventeenth century. A good example is the work of Peter Schmidt, an American archaeologist who monitors an excavation site in Kyamutwara, south of Bukoba. Near a sacred forest associated with a seventeenth-century king, this site produced a stratum dating from the first Iron Age to at least the beginning of our era.[37] The discovery of an ancient blacksmithed anvil at this site suggests metallurgy has been present in the region since Antiquity. Archaeology might one day be able to specify a relationship between this finding and the more recent polities.

But it may be the task of the historian to propose hypotheses, because different sources only partially overlap and do not easily fit together. Indeed, the written, the oral, and archaeology operate according to their own logic. The archaeologist John Sutton has also warned of the potential dangers of interpretations, recalling one that, based on material culture found in excavation sites in western Uganda in the 1950s, led to the hypothesis of an "empire" that legends of so-called Bacwezi heroes were supposed to have supported.[38]

In sum, historical sources abound: legends and folktales recorded in the field; dynastic chronicles compiled by European and African scholars during the first half of the twentieth century; the sometimes hasty work of overenthusiastic archaeologists who dreamed of discovering a new Zimbabwe despite fragmentary evidence;[39] a mass of archives produced by foreign encounters; and an abundance of publications in which the wheat is far from separated from the chaff. But methodological doubt is a prerequisite for a reliable reconstruction of the past, despite objections from those who are certain they know the truth. Nonetheless, these old African polities have spawned a remarkable body of sources that require the historian's tools as much as other regions and other times do. This may mean juxtaposing customary ethnography with the study of royal and princely chronicles, in the style of Gregory of Tours. But in so doing, one can avoid the double trap of Basil Davidson's "liberal" history, which idealizes ancient states, and of "radical" history, which is so preoccupied with the impact of imperialism that it forgets the precolonial past or dismisses it as Third World feudalism.[40]

The Fiery Present

I cannot conclude these preliminary remarks without mentioning the most formidable obstacles to the progress of knowledge — namely, the power of passion and propaganda in the contemporary tragedies and the tendency to replace history with political sociology. The political and social stakes of the conflicts tearing the region apart are clear: control of land, money, and power. But what is new is the extent to which ideology is invested in these battles and the fervent desire to ground contemporary struggles in terms of the past. This has given rise to a malicious return to origins, both by local actors and by their external supporters — a fact that is abundantly clear in the media. In this regard, the Great Lakes crises resemble tragedies elsewhere, in Palestine and Ireland, for example, where fates seem sealed by a particularly fraught history.

In the region itself, the depth of what could be called ethnic fundamentalism is all too real. The past is ever present and discussed as inescapable. History is referred to at every level of politics, from a president speaking to an international audience and claiming five centuries of history for his country, to the resurgence of the Cwezi mythology in Uganda, to successive Rwandan presidents (first Habyarimana, then Bizimungu) manipulating historical maps to show a precolonial mega-Rwanda in order either to disqualify refugee demands or to evoke the need for a Berlin II conference, to the piercing return of history in political party programs, to the songs of militias sung as they massacre, and so on.[41] A recent study showed how much a nostalgic attachment to the past has become official ideology in refugee camps. Based on obsolete references to colonial ethnology, this nostalgia is part of a quasi-messianic desire to return to a purified ethnic state.[42]

This ideology, typical of "a time of scarcity," to quote the Cameroonian historian Achille Mbembe, is especially cultivated in extremist circles, and it flourishes in violent periods, when a spiral of fear and hatred is coupled with a scramble for gain.[43] This ideology also operates in a state of great intellectual confusion: ethnography, which is always cited in the African context, is insidiously mixed up with discourses on liberty, the nation, and democracy, which have been around since decolonization and are applied in Manichaean fashion. Thus, even though European ideals are manipulated through an ethnic lens, what we are witnessing today are undoubtedly late-twentieth- and early-twenty-first-century political debates and not the resurgence of an archaic past.

Confusion is also evident among the Western partners of these countries. History is invoked not just in ministerial cabinet meetings or Rwandan and Congolese nightclubs but also at the World Bank, the Quai d'Orsay, the offices of Médecins sans Frontières, and various Christian missions. At a time when funding for field research comes less and less from academia, strange debates on historiography take place in which economists, sociologists, political scientists, medical experts, and agronomists intervene. Unfortunately, their concerns lie less with understanding the specificity of long- and short-term historical processes and more with multivalent, "nongovernmental," or semiofficial expertise or even feverish political activism. In Paris, Brussels, and Washington, "the Great Lakes" are periodically the order of the day and on the front page. In this pragmatic context, history is frequently reduced to introductions in reports, where the past becomes a folkloric touch or at best one aspect of "social capital" in the global vision of macro financial and geostrategic equilibrium. The region's populations are viewed as pawns on a chessboard. Strangely enough, this cynicism is not dissimilar to a fashionable intellectual orientation, often called postmodern, namely, the primacy of representations or "perceptions" coming from the various communities. The already-cited study of Burundian refugees explicitly uses this approach:

> The "facts" it [mythico-history] deployed, true and false alike, were only the building blocks for the construction of a grand moral-historical vision.... [T]here exists no "God's-eye" view of history. The "worlds made" through narrations of the past are always historically situated ... and it is these that people act upon and riddle with meaning.... Different regimes of truth exist for different historical actors.[44]

Pushed to its logical conclusion, this reasoning militates against understanding remote groups and distant times, which is the foundation for historical work. And this is indeed what happens in the academic polemics and quarrels that infuse the writing on this part of Africa. History is incessantly invoked, but an essentially memorialistic and partisan view of the past has replaced historical critique. As Marc Bloch has observed about analogous medieval conceptions, the past is perceived "as the shadow of the future," but "through the very fact of their respect for the past, people came to reconstruct it as they considered it ought to have been."[45] What is at stake in this struggle for history in Africa is the preservation of the sacrilegious aspect of the historian's profession.

"Who has the right to change the history (*amateka*) of the country?" demanded the Rwandan extremist organ *Kangura*, a militantly racist publication, in November 1990. But this is exactly how the fetishized "that which is authoritatively established" justifies a strange return to the theories and fantasies of another age. Nazi theorists did this with mythologies of Atlantis.[46] I remember arriving in Burundi in 1964, when the country had not a single history teacher even at the secondary-school level, and finding a small missionary manual. "The first Bantu came from Asia during the diluvian era," it stated. "The Tutsi," it continued, "are Semitized Hamites whose birthplace is western Asia, from where they traveled to Africa by way of the strait of Bab el Mandeb."[47] Today, the international press again refers to "Hamites," to the "Hima empire," and to a "Bantu temperament."

In the following pages, I have tried to write a history that is neither genealogy nor a narrative of "natural" progressions. Rather, this is a history of ruptures and contradictions that are part of Africans' daily lives.

CHAPTER ONE

An Ancient Human Settlement

and Its Enigmas

Theories of population settlement, which are intrinsically linked
to the question of a supposedly timeless "ethnic" cleavage between "Bantu agriculturists" and "Nilo-Hamitic pastoralists,"
have today become eminently ideological. But the concerns of
physical and cultural anthropology, of disciplines that study environmental interaction, and of different scientific fields (biology,
linguistics, ecology, and archaeology) are quite distant from the
political fervor of the late twentieth century. As such, we need to
take stock of current scholarship. Moreover, we need to understand the specific human and physical environment from which
the political culture of the ancient kingdoms emerged. Even if
Vercingétorix has become a national myth, it would be surprising
to present a long-term history of France without discussing the
Celts. Permit me, then, this necessary return to the past.

Before examining remote periods, between the second millennium before Christ and around the fifteenth century, I must
make two observations. The first relates to the notion of a single
cultural zone, and the second relates to historical time. On the
various canvases of so-called traditional African civilizations, the
Great Lakes region seems to stand out for its high degree of cohesion. The region has centralized polities, common religious

references, intense human density, and similar languages, all of which underline a contrast with neighboring areas. These traits suggested a distinct cultural personality, at least in the state in which they were directly observed during the nineteenth century. Indeed, even if the region is today torn apart, its homogeneity is striking. The Great Lakes region is fundamentally different from the Congolese basin mosaic and the East African plateaus. But for the historian, interest lies in the rifts in this ensemble, including regional variations — notably between the western mountains and the riparian low plateaus around Lake Victoria — and in the socio-cultural cleavages at the center of each polity. If this zone's unity suggests its antiquity, then the lasting relevance of its internal contradictions and the virulent forms these can take in contemporary times presents a paradox. The existence of Rwanda, Burundi, or even Uganda is not surprising, in contrast to Congo or Cameroon, which were created by colonial partition. Rather, what is surprising is the persistence of profound internal conflict in such integrated countries. This is precisely where historical questions must be focused.

The scale of historical time should not be muddled up, as so often happens when it comes to African history. The task is to avoid reducing the long term of the "obscure centuries" to an ethnographic present, a practice that encourages all manner of oversimplification. Nor should we forget the depth of the changes that altered these so-called traditional societies during the colonial period and the preceding centuries. Having a historical perspective presupposes that History proper is not confused with considering humankind on the continent for the last million years. Nor should we confuse hypotheses about human occupation (of *Homo sapiens*) during the last tens of thousands of years with an understanding of a specific human settlement, one that over the last four millennia produced the contemporary configu-

rations. Nor should this history be confused with the political formations that date to just before the sixteenth century. Too often
one reads statements that would be laughable in a European context — if, for example, the foundations of the Capetian dynasty
were equated with the great Germanic invasions or the beginning
of the Neolithic period. The realities discussed in this chapter are
the fruit of a process that took place over a long period of time.
In particular, the phenomena called "migrations" should not be
thought of as huge, Boer-style treks, as if they were expeditions
spreading out over generations or even centuries.

The great human movements of this type were made up of an
infinite number of local dynamics, each with its own chronology.[1]
Social and political history is not analogous to the piling up of
sediment. Though often described as quasi organic in Africa, ethnic identities have, in their definition and characteristics, a historical dimension that resists categorization of the kind typical in the
natural sciences.[2] In the pages that follow, we will try to understand population settlement in the Great Lakes region from three
points of view: first, linguistics and archaeology; second, the natural environment; and third, the social structures recorded on the
eve of colonization. Following these discussions will be an interpretation of this ancient Bantu-speaking domain; a historical reconstruction of the region's forms of agro-pastoral management;
and, finally, some discussion of the hereditary cleavages (Hutu
versus Tutsi, and others) that are described either as castes or as
ethnic groups, depending on who is doing the describing.

The Archaeology of Human Settlement: Languages, "Races," and Pottery

The peopling of central and eastern Africa is generally summarized
in a single expression: "Bantu expansion." Nonetheless, we should
remember that the region was not empty before this event, which

is generally thought to have occurred at the dawn of the Christian era. Without delving into the mysteries of African prehistory, of different styles of rock engravings and pebbles marked with microlithic scrapes bearing traces of multiple kinds of flint, we can reconstruct some elements of the last three millennia B.C. with the help of certain archaeological methods, notably limnology (the study of lakeside sediment) and palynology (the study of fossil pollens, especially those found in peat bogs). Using the most recent research on climatic and vegetal change in East Africa and the Congo basin, as well as temperature variations reflected in glacial extension on the tallest mountains (notably Ruwenzori), we can observe great rainfall fluctuations during the last millennia.[3]

From around ten thousand years ago to about 3000 B.C., the continent experienced a long humid phase. We know that this period was significant for the development of the Sahara. At the time, lakes were at a much higher level than they are today, and the forests were at their maximum extension. But during the second and especially the first millennia B.C., the climate progressively dried; swamps and forests receded; and grasslands flourished. This can be seen in palynological diagrams, which show grasses expanding and trees and reeds declining. The change seems due both to less rain and to human activity. Indeed, we see the spread of plant species tied to secondary reforestation, which would have followed land-clearing activities. This all occurred earlier in the western mountainous areas than it did around Lake Victoria. Sometime around the dawn of the Christian era, between fifteen hundred and two thousand years ago, this biogeographic change accelerated: land clearing led to forest recession and to more open spaces — a change that undoubtedly was connected to keeping farmland fallow for long periods, to herding, and to wood-cutting for blacksmithing and charcoal burning. Around A.D. 1000, the region's countrysides began to look as they do now. Also evident is the advent of human settlement, which was spread out in various pockets but already relatively dense.

This progressive domestication, which began five thousand years ago both on the hills and in the lowlands, suggests a clear contrast between a "stone age" when human life was fragile and sparse and an "iron age" when some sort of civilization took hold. The existence of a "Neolithic period" thus remains an open question in the prehistory of the Great Lakes. Nonetheless, starting in the humid period, groups of sedentary fishermen using canoes and harpoons and decorating pottery in "dotted waves" lived on the shores of Lake Edward at Ishango and, much later, on those of Lake Victoria and in the Kagera valley (the Kansyore site). According to the archaeologist John Sutton, as the climate began drying, this "aquatic civilization of middle Africa" gave way to an agro-pastoralism that had developed on the high plateaus and that is known primarily through excavations in Kenya's Rift Valley.[4] From then on, a civilization at odds with fishing and fish, which became the subject of several dietary restrictions, developed in the area known as interlacustrine Africa. Still, the valleys and lakes continued to be areas of activities and beliefs that deserve to be better understood, even if for the last three thousand years they have been marginal to the dominant culture and often reserved for scorned groups.

The people of the Great Lakes speak various Bantu languages. The links between this cultural fact and technological changes in agriculture, cattle raising, and metallurgy will be explored later. But worth noting here is that the term "Bantu" is strictly linguistic. (For a linguistic map, refer to p. 481.) The Great Lakes are situated at the northern limit of the continent's Bantu speakers. The break is clear, contrary to what exists in Cameroon or Central Africa. The area is like a photograph of an ancient and complex entwining of migratory movements and influences that fanned out between

the first millennium B.C. and the sixteenth century. The Upper
Nile region is manifestly a long-standing human crossroads. Contemporary Uganda is cut from west to east by the demarcation
between Bantu speakers and those speaking different idioms who
are members of radically distinct groups.[5]

The latter, in fact, come from five linguistic families. Besides
isolated Cushitics in the east and some Kalenjins (Southern Nilotes)
along the Kenyan border (north of Mount Elgon), there are representatives of an ancient Central Sudanic population (the Lugbara and the Madi) in the northwest, more recently arrived Plains
Nilotes (related to the Masai) in the east (notably the Karamojong
pastoralists) and in the north (the more "aquatic" groups related
to the Bari of southern Sudan), and a last wave of so-called Rivers
and Lakes Nilotes, principally the Acholi and the Langi along
the northern banks of the White Nile. Although the Great Lakes
kingdoms emerged in a Bantu-speaking zone, there was no lack
of economic, political, and cultural interaction (even reciprocal
integrations) with their neighbors, who resided between Lake
Albert and Mount Elgon and were characterized by various types
of decentralized lineage systems.

The region's Bantu languages, which the Belgian linguists at
Tervuren considered a single group (Zone J) and Anglo-Saxon
scholars divided in two (Zones D and E), can actually be subdivided into several groups.[6] Despite their lexical and morpholog-
ical similarities, these languages are not immediately mutually
comprehensible. Traveling from Uganda to Burundi, one encounters languages as different (and similar) as Portuguese, Spanish,
and Italian, if such a comparison can be made.

Broadly speaking, the languages can be separated into five sub-
sets from east to west. North of Lake Victoria is Luganda, which
borders on two large Lusoga dialects. Then a long linguistic corridor stretches from Lake Albert to just southwest of Lake Victoria;

this corridor includes Runyoro and Rutoro in western Uganda, Ruhaya on the western shores of Lake Victoria, Runyambo along the plateaus east of Kagera, and Ruzinza. The groups' political division, such as it was in the nineteenth century, favored dialect variation, but it also makes one wonder about the historical grounds for a preexisting unity. In southwestern Uganda, near the Rwandan border, Runyankore has specificity and is similar to dialects in what is today the region of Kigezi (between Lake Edward and the volcanoes). From the Virunga volcanoes to the Malagarasi stretches a larger group of speakers who can easily understand each other. They speak Kinyarwanda, Kirundi, and Kiha (and to a certain degree Kivinza and Kishubi). The resemblance of these languages of Rwanda, Burundi, and Buha (Tanzania) is comparable to that of French in Marseilles and Liège or in Paris and Quebec. Finally, to the west of Lakes Tanganyika, Kivu, and Edward, a set of idioms stretches from south to north, more or less corresponding to this area's divisions: Kifuriru, Mashi, Kihavu, Kihunde, Rukonjo, and Runande.[7] All these regional differences thus coincide with a long-term cultural history, as well as with political cleavages. The poles of power established "classic" contrasting dialects, while falling within preexisting linguistic zones. Burundi, as we will see, overflows eastward into Kiha, while Rwanda never fully grouped together all Kinyarwanda speakers, notably those in the northwest. Here and elsewhere, these historical dialects caution against simplistic notions about "natural" borders or about language as a purely artificial construction of the state. But in this region, language and race became the subjects of perverse games, which took on specific importance that requires further attention.

The term "Bantu," whose application in the Great Lakes we have just seen, has entered contemporary discourse. In 1982, Gabonese president Omar Bongo founded the Center for Bantu Civilizations in Libreville, and the crises in the Congo familiarized the public with the term. Its African origin — in the plural, the word means "human beings" in many languages — lends it an air of exotic authenticity. In 1958, enchanted with theories of negritude, an Africanist called his book *Muntu*, as if the radical *ntu* lay at the heart of all African wisdom. But a Rhine philologist, Wilhelm Bleek, was the one who chose this term, in the nineteenth century, to characterize the cluster of central, eastern, and southern African languages. These languages were known through documents collected on the coasts by Catholic and Protestant missionaries beginning in the seventeenth century and compiled around 1850 by German orientalists and geographers.[8] In a thesis in Latin of some sixty pages, defended in Bonn in 1851, then in works he later published in German and English, Bleek defined the languages by their absence of gender: nouns were not masculine, feminine, or neuter but organized by a series of classes (sixteen, he wrote, including singular and plural) identified by prefixes. Located in front of adjectives and verbs that agree with the noun-subject, these prefixes serve a pronominal function.

Bleek's work primarily consists of grammatical ABCs. But worth noting are the cultural commentaries that accompanied the definition of this linguistic family, which, beginning in 1858, he labeled "Bantu." Opposing the Bantu languages to those that use gender, notably the Indo-European ones, he termed the system of classes "nonnatural." This system, he added, kept its users stuck at an incoherent stage, unsuited to accede to poetry or to philosophy. He wrote:

> The grammatical form of their languages does not offer their imagination the superior spirit that the form of gendered languages transmits, with irresistible force, to the thought of their speakers.[9]

According to nineteenth-century German linguists (from Jacob Grimm to August Schleicher), who dominated "Bantuist" studies with Carl Meinhof's *Grammatik* until the mid-twentieth century, these African languages were at an inferior level of evolution.[10] They were caught between the "insulating" and the "inflected" stages, defined as "agglutinative" and comparable to the "Malayo-Polynesian" family. In light of this classification, the analyses of Bleek, who, beginning in 1855, was based in South Africa, where he was the Cape governor's librarian, had a paradoxical dimension. The majority of blacks, then readily called Kaffirs, were considered more evolved than other "Negroes" and certainly more evolved than their "savage" neighbors, to wit, the Bushmen and Hottentots. But the presence of gender in the latter's languages prompted Bleek to see in them a lost southern branch of an original dialect of the high cultures and to claim having discovered distant cousins of Indo-Europeans or Semites!

From these historical-cultural hypotheses, the "Bantu" emerged with a pejorative image. The African ethnonym racialized observations made globally of this group, as if it were a single tribe. In fact, the denomination quickly acquired a racial connotation, simultaneously designating an ethnic group, an agro-pastoral social and economic lifestyle, and a physical type. The English anthropologist C.G. Seligman imposed this vision on his book *Races of Africa*, which was continually republished from 1930 to 1966:

> But although the Bantu are delimited on linguistic criteria, yet where Bantu and non-Bantu tribes are neighbors it may be found that certain physical qualities are to such a degree characteristic of each linguistic group that within particular areas a terminology based on language also serves to differentiate physical groups.[11]

For the last century, however, the Bantu image has fluctuated, given the Europeans' different experiences across so vast a territory. What do forest groups of the Congo basin, Zulus of southern Africa, and the kingdoms of the Great Lakes have in common? Eventually a general cliché served as a link, namely, the primacy of agricultural activity. The "Bantu peoples" are agriculturists, a number of encyclopedias tell us. As for the differences, they were interpreted according to the model in vogue among Africanists in the late nineteenth century, namely, as a function of migration and crossbreeding. The Bantu were configured as a mixed race that issued from the crossbreeding of an ancient wave of Pygmies from Melanesia with civilizing elements from the Horn of Africa or from the Nile valley.[12] The degrees of this mix were thought to explain the contrasts between "forest Bantu" in the west, "savanna Bantu" in the east, and "old" and "young" Bantu.[13] History was reduced to observing dosages, in which one searched for a sort of stratigraphy of waves of migrants.

The key idea, as we will see, was the Hamitic hypothesis: all features of civilization were attributed to Middle Eastern influences, either from a protohistoric period or from a more recent relay from the continent's northeast. Harry Johnston, the United Kingdom's first head of the Uganda protectorate, was the most influential spokesman of this "diffusionist" racial vision. The Bantu peasants, identifiable, according to him, by craniology, benefited from the immigration to East-Central Africa of a superior type of humanity, those of "semi-Caucasian" stock.[14] Seligman's classic put it bluntly: African civilizations, he claimed, are the work of Hamitic conquerors, "Caucasoids" who were superior to the "dark-skinned Negro agriculturalists." As we will see, this scheme found a favorite domain of application, even its very own experimental laboratory, in the Great Lakes region. In the eyes of many observers (even until the present day), social and political structure directly reflects the superposition of waves of people. In a relentless way, the population, especially in Rwanda and Burundi, was described in terms of sedimentation, with a base of leftover Pygmies, then a foundation of Bantu peasants, and a layer of Hamitic pastoralists on top. Fascination with these societies and with the racial interpretation they seemed to offer led to questions about how Bantu this Bantu-speaking culture really was. The interlacustrine region was essentially perceived as "Hamitic" or "Hamitic-Semitic."[15] In this perspective, the "Bantu as such" was described as a "Negro," for which all negative features were reserved, and the term was applied only to the peasant categories perceived as subjugated and inferior by definition, to wit, the Hutu and Iru as opposed to the Tutsi and Hima.

The debate on the "origins of the Bantu" went beyond this transcontinental alchemy of races. Starting in the late nineteenth century, classifications on linguistic maps inspired efforts to link various Bantu peoples to different geographic locations. On the one hand, scholars searched for an original departure zone, the birthplace of the "primitive Bantu" (Meinhof's *Urbantu*); on the other hand, they imagined migratory stopping places and highways that, after successive splits, produced the current configurations.[16] Various genealogical representations of languages accompanied by maps of the southern half of the continent, with arrows indicating diffusion, were published. Johnston, the premier from 1886 to 1919, proposed a theory of "Bantu migrations."[17] Their original homeland was around Cameroon, but for the most part, according to him, they subsequently left the Great Lakes region. Combined with the Hamitic hypothesis (as an explanation of this dynamic of expansion), this theory was practically repeated word for word in *Encyclopaedia Britannica* from 1903 to 1962.

Progress in linguistics and especially in archaeology, stimulated by the birth of nationalism on the continent, reopened the debate in the late 1950s, notably in Britain and Belgium (the former colonial powers most interested in the question).[18] But before that, the parallel work of two American researchers, the linguist Joseph Greenberg and the anthropologist George Murdock, re-established a historical link between the continent's east and west.[19] They argued that Bantu languages were integrated into a single whole called Niger-Congo; originating in the Chad-Benue area, expansion was rooted in demographic pressure born from the drying of the Sahara, a process that began around the third millennium B.C., and from the resulting southward agricultural expansion. Soon after, J. Desmond Clark, a student of African prehistory in South Africa, emphasized a link between Bantu people, pottery forms (those tied to agricultural settling), and iron metallurgy. Jean Hiernaux's archaeological sites in Kivu and Rwanda and Merrick Posnansky's in Uganda strongly show the connection between the start of metallurgy and a "dimple-based" pottery, which now became the calling card of a Bantu presence.[20] During the same period, the linguist Malcolm Guthrie, a former missionary affiliated with the London-based School of Oriental and African Studies (SOAS), launched a vast comparative study that resulted in his distinguishing fifteen Bantu-speaking groups (the Great Lakes being divided, as discussed above, into Zones D and E). Guthrie also identified a "common Bantu," which was best represented in the Katanga-Zambia area. In contrast to John-ston's and later Greenberg's idea of a Cameroonian Bantu home-land, Guthrie proposed the Katanga-Zambia area as the birthplace of Bantu culture.[21] Archaeology of the Iron Age, which had an early start south of the equatorial forest, seemed to reinforce Guthrie's hypothesis.

It was then that the London historical school intervened. Based at SOAS, this school was led by Roland Oliver, a founder, in 1960, of the *Journal of African History* and a specialist on East Africa, particularly Uganda. Oliver proposed a multidisciplinary synthesis, one that integrated Greenberg's and Guthrie's theories. In sum, a first emigration of iron-using hunter-fishermen leaves the Chad-Benue area sometime before the Christian era; they in turn climb the valleys that straddle the great Congolese forest. During the first millennium A.D., this process gives rise to a demographic boom in the southern savannas. There, the Bantu speakers, whose smithing capabilities give them a technological edge, expand their agricultural abilities by adding a "Malay" system that had spread from the eastern coast — principally the banana tree — to their African tubers and cereals. In this way, Guthrie's notion of a proto-Bantu homeland could be integrated into a comprehensible historical process. Subsequently, the evolution of pottery forms observed around A.D. 1000 led to distinguishing a late Iron Age, tied to the southeastern influence of the Katangese area.[22] What Jan Vansina called "the London paradigm" culminated in a 1968 article by Hiernaux, whose physical anthropology completed the new cultural portrait of the "Bantu" (agriculturist, iron worker, and dimple-based potter). According to him, physical kinship was evident, from the Cameroonian Basa, to the Tanzanian Nyamwezi, to the Katangese Luba. The only variations, he claimed, were due either to adaptation to a forest environment or to race mixing (the Great Lakes Tutsi were his example).[23]

For some ten years, Hiernaux's seductive synthesis dominated African history. In France, the historians Hubert Deschamps and Robert Cornevin promoted the theory. It offered a fresh look at the "Bantu" as innovators, land clearers, inventors of metallurgy, and spreaders of a novel civilization, fit to have been the builders of the fortresses of Zimbabwe. However, since this culture only reached the Great Lakes in the second half of the first millennium, the region was marginalized in this historical scheme.

But starting in the 1970s, it was apparent that reality must have been more complicated and that a longer time horizon was needed. Linguists criticized the shift from a comparative method to a genetic model as well as the fetishization of Proto-Bantu, which was reconstructed through a set of recent languages in which points of contact must have been as common as those of divergence. To that end, Greenberg ironically commented that Icelandic must have been the ancestor of Germanic languages. Emphasis was again put on the Bantu group's northwestern branch — justifiably, given its age — where linguistic variation was greatest (as evidenced in Gabon). The Great Lakes' languages were deemed members of an East African subgroup, at the same level as Guthrie's famous Proto-Bantu. This conclusion was based on several technical arguments, which, though impossible to develop here, include lexico-statistical analyses of base vocabularies, analyses of morphology and phonology, the role of loanwords, and contact with other non-Bantu families discussed above.[24] For their part, archaeologists, having collected a growing number of dates using carbon-dating processes, affirmed the antiquity of iron metallurgy in eastern and even southern Africa. They noted the diversity of pottery styles and proposed the possibility of autonomous inventions in the southern area.[25] In a general sense, this called into question the notion of a coincidence among language, culture, technology, and human type. Terms indicating metallic objects might have first described stone-cut tools, while names of plants that became typically Bantu might have been borrowed from non-Bantu neighbors.[26] In a grand history of Africa published in Cambridge in 1978, Oliver drew conclusions from these critiques: the ancient Bantu speakers, those who crossed the forest from the northwest, were still initially at a Neolithic level, and, according to the new dating, iron metallurgy would instead have been invented toward the northeast, notably in the Great Lakes region.[27]

For some twenty years, archaeological theories again emphasized the importance of this region.[28] The Iron Age appeared
there following the prehistoric evolution discussed above, and
from this region Iron Age technology spread southward, from
Kenya to the Zambezi and from Angola to the Transvaal. However, the relative role of local invention and external influence
remains subject to debate. Could, for example, Sudanic or Cushitic groups have brought coastal influences or Meroitic metallurgy
from ancient Nubia? Recent discoveries in Tanzania and Rwanda
suggest a regional invention during the first millennium B.C. — in
other words, much earlier than in Meroë (between the third and
the fifth century B.C.). In 1972, the historian Joseph Ki-Zerbo
had already warned against the habit of "scarring maps of Africa
with arrows representing theories of 'iron routes.'"[29] This point
also applies to the theory of a Bantu migration that brought technology from elsewhere, including the idea that everything that
reached the continent's south came from the lakes region.

In 1978, the American researcher Peter Schmidt published the
results of his excavations in Buhaya (to the south of Bukoba).[30]
Other than the ore quarry sites and slag buildups indicating long-
term metallurgic activity until the nineteenth century, iron-
smelting sites were found in Katuruka that date to between the
fifth century B.C. and the first century A.D. Early Iron Age activity was also discovered to the west: other low furnaces were found
in central and southern Rwanda (in Gasiza and around Butare)
and in central Burundi (in Mirama and Mubuga, near Gitega).[31]
They were in operation between the seventh century B.C. and the
seventh century A.D. This technology largely gave way to deep pit
smelting, which had more or less sophisticated ventilation and
stoking methods that were in use until recently.[32] Early Iron Age
low furnaces are remarkable. On top is a melting pot 20 to 75
centimeters deep and as much as 1.4 meters in diameter; the pot

contained crushed iron. Below that is a flattened furnace where charcoal was put; made from a clay tube, the furnace was about 80 centimeters to 1.3 meters high. And on the bottom, several inter-connected tuyeres on the bellows fed the fire. The combustible fuels used to fire the furnace suggest a treed savanna environ-ment, which corresponds to the general evolution under way during the first millennium B.C. and also to the role this activity played in clearing the forests.

At the beginning of the Christian era, an "intense human pres-ence" is already observable on the mountains of southern Rwanda. It is also seen on Lake Victoria's shores and islands and in the lower Kagera River valley.[33] This early Iron Age population gen-erally is associated with dimple-based pottery adorned with geo-metric decorations. Known as Urewe, this pottery style is named after the Kavirondo gulf (on Lake Victoria's Kenyan coast). In fact, the typology is more complex. In the Rwandan case, Francis van Noten noted the coexistence of a cluster on the shores of Lake Kivu that was similar to products found on the southeast shores of Lake Tanganyika and another cluster in the central mountains that resembled the Urewe type. But local diversity of techniques and materials does not necessarily translate into different "cultures."[34]

This point also applies to interpreting the technological changes (some call them a revolution) that occurred before A.D. 1000, that is, the emergence of the late Iron Age. During this period, new pottery styles emerged with the development of smelting, ob-tained by simple excavation. In particular, a form of pottery arose that was decorated with "plant roulettes" made from twisted, braided, or knotted fibers that left characteristic dots imprinted on the clay. It was, apparently, a less fine production. What is described as artistic decadence and technical regression seems to indicate the disappearance of furnaces — a change that prompted a theory of invasion. Scholars suggested that either a new wave of

Bantu came from the Katanga-Zambia area or coarser nomadic groups from the north or the east suddenly appeared. These latter groups were readily assimilated to Nilotic populations. A recent theory, for example, attributed the new pottery to Southern Nilotic groups, whom the author claimed are related to contemporary Kalenjins in Kenya and might be considered Tutsi and Hima ancestors.[35]

However, the chronology and styles suggest a different theory, one less concerned with the contemporary obsession with ethnicity. Roulette-decorated pottery has been found in southern Sudan, in the Kenyan Rift Valley, near the Uvinza (Tanzania) and Kibiro (Uganda) salt marshes, in western Uganda, in Rwanda, and in Burundi. The datings, however, invite caution: the seventh century for southern Sudan, only the tenth to the seventeenth century for Kenya, the twelfth century for Uvinza, the tenth through the sixteenth century for Uganda, and the eighth through the twelfth century for Rwanda. The break with the Urewe type is not always neat. Style comparisons are a more delicate process than they might initially seem: John Sutton argues that Southern Nilotic potteries of the Kenyan Rift and those of Uvinza and Bigo are distinct.[36] In a recent essay on western Uganda, he shows how this break in material culture does not reflect a new wave of immigration. Rather, he argues, it suggests an economic and social evolution marked by greater production of metallic tools and salt (which was used for an expanding human and livestock population).[37] The change in pottery, now more abundant and often entailing larger containers, would have been a response to increased demand. This discussion also extends to the so-called Cwezi culture, which is associated with a series of archaeological sites: Bigo from the thirteenth to the sixteenth century and Ntusi from the eleventh to the fourteenth century. Recognized in the 1950s, restudied more recently, these sites include large retrenchments, mounds, and artificial watering places. They also raise the crucial question of the relationship between cattle keeping and agriculture — a point to which we will return.

As I suggested at the beginning, human settlement is made from micro-migrations spread over time and not from massive invasions. We have seen the problems with the "Bantu expansion" thesis. Nor do archaeology and oral traditions suggest a "Galla conquest" originating from Ethiopia, which is the unfortunate cliché often found in popular literature.[38] To the contrary, the cultural continuities are striking. Archaeologists underline the lasting role of iron metallurgy in certain sites, even if these are reinvested with different cults and powers. Old iron objects (hammers, anvils) were often part of sovereigns' regalia.[39] The social importance of iron and blacksmiths, too often neglected, has lasted for more than two millennia. If we take into account spatial occupation and environmental relationships, the breaks between the Stone and the Iron Age need to be relativized. Ethnographic studies should also jettison the absurd, mechanical recourse to a theory of invasions: contemporary potters in Rwanda and Burundi are mainly Batwa women, the so-called pygmoid group considered the population's oldest members. Do we now need a theory of a "Batwa migration" that brought this new pottery style?

The ancient history of Africa requires a fresh approach. Many population movements certainly occurred, but, as elsewhere, they took several forms. When discussing migrations, we should not forget the alliances and interbreeding that accompany them, the technical or religious influences that follow or precede them, the coexistence on the same land of different groups who are bound by tacit or explicit accords, or mutual cultural effects. Vansina's recently proposed model for the Bantu phenomenon is particularly enlightening on this score.[40] Based on his research into forest

58

societies, Vansina argues against representing this "expansion" as a language family tree composed of births, successive splits, and emigration highways. Rather, he suggests focusing on groups that exercised centrifugal force on the peripheries. Born of dialectical divergences and external influences, these forces led to divisions over time. This cultural diffusion undoubtedly led to the gradual and successive whittling away of land, due to technical and demographic pressure. But as it progressed, this diffusion absorbed other populations who were already living in a more or less sedentary way in their respective environments. It was among these populations that the Bantu-speaking communities made themselves be accepted:

> Some groups may have consisted wholly of Bantuized autochthones. Be this as it may, eventually more and more migrants were physical descendants of former autochthones. Hence the input of even acculturated autochthones into the life-style of early Bantu communities may have been far greater than has hitherto been acknowledged....
>
> The whole conversion involved centuries rather than decades, and the largest numbers of agents involved were descendants of autochthones themselves. Thus major population replacements of autochthones by immigrant Bantu speakers may have never occurred.[41]

We can now make sense of the historian's image: this expansion happened in "waves" comparable to undulating, though not necessarily moving, ripples of water caused by a stone's throw. With this model, historiography can finally rid itself of the confusion between culture and biology. One begins to see that the ethnohistory that gave such credence to the Bantu expansion and the Hamitic invasions had less to do with African history and more to do with a particular European anthropology tainted by racial prejudice. The history of European societies has been freed for some time now from notions of "historic races," from *Völkerwander-ungen*, and from the Indo-European scheme.[42] The African Great Lakes has been the favored terrain for the same reading. Historical studies of this region can make headway today by grasping the specific regional realities and their material, moral, economic, and political management during the past centuries.

Archaeology of the Countryside: Plants, Cows, and People
Without revisiting the region's geographic facts in detail, we should keep two points in mind: first, that the region enjoys favorable climatic conditions and, second, that it lies at an eco-logical crossroads between large primary forests to the west and treed savanna plateaus to the east.[43] This position has much to do with the region's early agricultural stages, when several agrarian systems coalesced around the turn of the Christian era. Recon-structing this history depends on a delicate conjunction of several types of data, including carbonized seeds and fossilized pollens (with regard to cereals), artisanal objects used for production and consumption (millstones, for example), linguistics (while being conscious of semantic mutations), and paleoecological changes (discussed above). The region must be situated in the context of Africa's general agricultural evolution.[44] Agriculture appeared in the Sahelian band that stretches from the Niger to the Upper Nile during the second millennium B.C. This occurred conjointly with the drying of the Saharan area, forest retraction, and a human ebb toward more favorable zones. The shift from more or less selec-tive food collecting to true agriculture took place in several hu-man areas, but each time on the basis of different plants (grains, roots, vegetables, and trees). And, as we have seen, sedentariza-tion intensified during the first millennium B.C. through the com-bined action of collectors, fishermen, cattle raisers, cultivators of long-fallow fields, and blacksmiths.

The first European voyagers to the region during the second half of the nineteenth century left behind descriptions that allow us to imagine what the agricultural landscapes must have been like two thousand years earlier.[45] The situation changed again during the last century. But even before the colonial interventions and "development," the region was a hybrid of African, Asian, and American agrarian traditions. The African heritage can be divided into two parts: those that developed from the Sudanic savannas and those that came from the forest areas. The first principally includes sorghum, which was domesticated between the Nile and the Chad some three thousand years ago. Sorghum, in its kafir and caudatum varieties, was present in southern Africa, as well as in the Great Lakes region. Well adapted to rainfall irregularities, this kind of cereal could be complemented by garden and root crops, including gourds, a small haricot variety of the *Vigna* species (what is called *niébé* in West Africa), and *Coleus* tubers (the "Kaffir sweet potato" of southern Africa).[46] The second contribution, from the great forest, mainly includes propagation plants such as yams and other tubers (the so-called Hausa sweet potato), as well as *Vigna* haricot varieties, and palm oil, which extends as far east as Lake Tanganyika. A third group of African domesticated plants should be added to this list: those that come from the mountains. These include eleusine, a finger millet that can be found in Burundi, Rwanda, and especially southwest Uganda; a false banana called *ensete* in Ethiopia, a plant used during food shortages; a coffee tree called *Coffea eugenoides*, an indigenous small shrub developed notably in Buhaya that differs from the arabica coffee tree domesticated in Ethiopia; and, oddly, small peas, which have been grown in Ethiopia for years.[47]

The ancient Great Lakes agricultural complex seems to have emerged, in the context of relative climatic drying and forest recession, during the first millennium B.C.[48] This complex was

61

formed through the gradual integration of Bantu-speaking groups from the eastern Congo basin, Central Sudanic and proto-Nilotic groups from what is now Uganda, and southern Cushitic groups from areas south and west of Lake Victoria (as far as what is now eastern Rwanda and Burundi).[49] The Bantu speakers' tuber plantings (especially yams) and the other groups' cereals (especially sorghum), as well as legumes from both, were added to agriculture of the forest margins, which was common in the western Rift and in the areas bordering Lake Victoria. Developed by a group that we can for now call the Great Lakes proto-Bantu, the agricultural system slowly spread, largely thanks to this new resource diversification and its ability to adapt to seasonal variation, annual irregularities, and diverse microclimates. Cattle-keeping practices come from groups that were initially non–Bantu speaking, as we will see. Backed by a productive form of metallurgy from the same period, this agro-pastoral system goes a long way toward explaining the success of this ancient civilization in the Great Lakes. Crystallized around settlements of Bantu-speaking cultivators, the system could be adapted to diverse environments, including very humid ones on the western mountains and around Lake Victoria as well as the drier environments of the middle plateaus. At the turn of the Christian era, diversification in the model is also reflected in a western and eastern subdivision of the region's Bantu languages. David Schoenbrun, an American historian, could conclude:

> We can see that those non-Bantu peoples played a pivotal role in the adoption of cattle-keeping and grain farming by several of the Great Lakes Bantu communities, and a dry-land mixed agriculture in turn was to become a contributing factor to the further spread of Bantu tongue in later centuries.[50]

Several of the crops just discussed had practically disappeared or had become marginal by the last century. These include the *Vigna* haricots, the *Coleus* tubers, and the yams, which were replaced by plants from the Far East and Latin America.[51] The new plants were gradually adopted for their agronomic and nutritional qualities, and they in turn became part of the region's landscape, both in terms of agricultural practice and in terms of peasant mindsets, as reflected in the region's sayings and riddles, which are spoken as if they were timeless.

Two other plants — the taro and the banana — arrived years ago from Southeast Asia, due largely to ancient contacts that Malays and Indonesians had established with the continent's eastern shorelines. Taro (also called *Colocasia*) is a root vegetable that can be planted beside other root crops. The real revolution was brought by the banana tree, which penetrated the continent's interior at the Zambezi valley in the south and at the Horn, from where it went toward Lake Victoria.[52] Again, linguistics is instructive here. In the beginning, the terms employed to describe the plant were those that referred to the *ensete*. But by the end of the first millennium (between 800 and 1000, according to Schoenbrun), the banana tree was as plentiful on the shores of Lake Victoria as in the western ridge's forested highlands.[53] A special billhook, used to trim and cut bunches and also, it seems, to make "beer," or, rather, cider (which is still made today), accompanied the tree's diffusion. But banana gardens did not really develop on the western and northern shores of Lake Victoria until the fourteenth and fifteenth centuries. This is notably the case in Buganda, where about one hundred new terms appeared at this time to characterize banana varieties and farming practices. All this happened as if the banana tree had replaced the yam. The latter's yield was ten times less than the former's, and it quickly became a negligible product in the region.

The banana tree has many advantages, including simple propagation through cutting; flexibility in schedules and spacing of harvests; ease of cooking methods and preparation, thus freeing up time for other activities; multiple uses (leaves are used for matting and roofing); and the development, inside banana gardens, of a green-manure-based humus, which allowed highly fertile areas to be expanded and opened up the possibility of intercropping with such plants as taro near the homesteads. This year-round method of farming became synonymous with a good investment (the tree starts yielding a year and a half after being planted), and it reinforced a settled way of life. Buganda was the very model of this type of rural economy.[54] Care of the banana tree was above all women's work, which allowed men to engage in other activities like catching fish, which provided necessary protein. But the male labor freed up in this way could be mobilized for other tasks, the political repercussions of which will become evident below.

Judging from various vocabulary transfers, one can posit that a new agricultural revolution took hold between the seventeenth and the early nineteenth century with the arrival of high-yield crops.[55] Coming this time from the Atlantic coast, these crops included sweet potato, cassava, maize, and beans, which would supplant the ancient root vegetables and especially the ancient *Vigna* legumes. The chronology of this event is only approximate. Even though the plants came into daily use, the change as such did not leave traces in the traditions, as evidenced by the relative silence on these plants in oral literature and by their absence from legends and rituals (except for a couple of prohibitions). Paradoxically, some oral narratives about royal origins, which can be dated to between the fifteenth and the seventeenth century, evoke the introduction of sorghum and eleusine, whose presence is evident one thousand years earlier, and of the banana tree — which is a more plausible association. But these stories do not say a word about maize or beans, which must have appeared during the first reigns of the different dynasties. In the dicta, collective prosperity, seen as the deserved result of work, is tied to images of sorghum, eleusine (the plant of a thousand grains), and dough.[56] To find allusions to maize and beans, one must look to the more recently created riddles. The ancient written sources, which are mainly Portuguese, concern only the ocean littorals. These sources attest to the presence of maize, of Mexican origin, in Kongo country since the mid-sixteenth century and of sweet potato and cassava, of Brazilian origin, in Angola since the seventeenth century. Maize is mentioned in Zanzibar in 1643; cassava is mentioned in Mozambique around 1750. According to several linguistic indicators, the ordinary bean, *Phaseolus vulgaris*, also of American origin, seems to have penetrated the continent, going from west to east. Also evident is the arrival of groundnuts in less humid areas and of tobacco, which is translated in the archaeology of the last centuries by the appearance of pipes.

While cassava primarily spread during colonial rule, other crops in this group, notably maize and beans, were already present in the region when the first European travelers arrived in the mid-nineteenth century. Thanks to their rapid maturation, these two closely linked plants eventually dominated the crop rotations on the western mountains (in Burundi and Rwanda). They may even have led to the widespread adoption of two agricultural seasons, called *agatasi* and *impeshi* in Burundi, which produce a first harvest between January and March and a second one between June and July. Staggering, which had already been tried with other plants, given the brevity of the dry season, now became more structured, thus ensuring more intense soil exploitation and shorter fallow periods. Sweet potatoes were farmed primarily in the lowlands, which had been drained from the extensive marshy valleys. Several factors (including observations made in the last century and linguistics) point to knowledge of hydraulic practices in the mountains: man-made watering places, river diversions, hollowed-out tree-trunk pipes, irrigation on cultivated slopes, mounding in drained marshes, and irrigation of banana and palm tree gardens in the plains beside Lake Tanganyika. These modes of intensification all favored the logic of sedentary life, with its land implications. What one calls *itongo* in Burundi, *isambu* in Rwanda, and *kibanja* in Buhaya refers to restricted linear farming that forms an enclosure around a series of permanent crops (bananas or manure-fertilized gardens that produce gourds and vegetables), intensive seasonal crops (like the maize-bean pair), and regular annuals (cereals that grow around every seven months).

The agrarian success of the Great Lakes civilization accounts for its exceptionally high levels of human density. Social life also revolves around collective consumptions, in particular of alcoholic drinks made from bananas or sorghum. One might note here that the American plants furnished only a food surplus, whereas drinks originate in older forms of production: the pitcher of sorghum beer drunk with neighbors as opposed to the pot of beans served to the family. In this respect, another observation must be made: the intensity of the "American" system imposed greater demands on women.[57] Indeed, planting, weeding, and harvesting these crops were mainly women's responsibility, contrary to the situation with cereal agriculture and, in the western mountains, with care of the banana gardens. Nor should we forget pastoral activities, which were strictly male; it is to these that we now turn.

Despite their place in the social history of the region, cattle for a long time were the subject of only superficial studies. Even though cattle were domesticated in the Saharan area several millennia before Christ and have been present in southern African cultures and as far away as Madagascar for a long time, specialized academic literature stubbornly attributed to them a recent arrival in the Great Lakes.[58] Cattle were dated to some time between the thirteenth and the sixteenth century, if not later, according to when the Tutsi and Hima supposedly "arrived." Archaeology and linguistics are beginning to help us move beyond this misconception. The presence of bovines is traceable in East Africa, notably in the Rift Valley, to at least the first millennium B.C. Based on images found around Mount Elgon, these cows were long-horned and humpless, similar to those in ancient Egypt or Tassili. Early Iron Age sites in Rwanda have produced evidence, dated to the third century, of a bovine species whose morphology is debated.[59] The current breed of cattle, which is called Ankole, is a mixture of an ancient long-horned species and a zebu that came from Asia more than one hundred years before Christ.[60] These more or less long-horned, humped sanga-type bovines are found throughout the southern half of the continent. They were already known in southern Africa between the fifth and the eighth century. Vocabulary indicates an early domestication by populations speaking Central Sudanic, Nilotic, and Southern Cushitic languages.[61] Among the region's Bantu dialects, the radicals designating cows and dairy-cattle-keeping practices are most frequently derived from these languages. Therefore, the Great Lakes Bantu speakers were quite probably familiar with this type of cattle keeping since at least the beginning of the common era, thanks to the meeting of the different cultural traditions described above in the context of sorghum and eleusine. In fact, this integration was uneven: the populations on the western mountains seem to have mainly counted on agricultural resources, while cereal growing made cattle keeping essential for the populations on the eastern plateaus.

But archaeological attestations multiply from the eleventh century on, both in western Uganda and in Rwanda. In terms of linguistics, Schoenbrun believes he has discerned a change between the tenth and the twelfth century, which saw a multiplication of words for the color of cattle and for horn forms.[62] This phenomenon emerged in the region's "eastern" linguistic area and more precisely in the cultural space that is distinguishable from the populations along the northern bank of Lake Victoria. This "Rutara" zone (a term derived from the name of the future Kitara kingdom in western Uganda) was at the origin of a group of languages, whose commonalities were seen above, from Lake Albert to southwest of Lake Victoria. Then, around the fourteenth century, this pastoral culture spread to areas in the western mountains (Rwanda and Burundi). The emphasis on the aesthetics of sanga cattle (symbolized by the radical -gaju, which designates a reddish color) seems to indicate the social importance that this activity took as it expanded east to west during the late Iron Age (which also is coincident with the rise of roulette pottery). If this phenomenon ran parallel to the progressive expansion of the banana tree on the shores of Lake Victoria during the first centuries after Christ, we might wonder if the issue here is not one of competing uses of land. Schoenbrun theorized a combined demographic and social pressure that led youth to open new regions for pastoralism and extensive cereal cropping. In other words, this pressure led to the development of a different kind of specialization from that seen in the banana gardens in the area that later became Buganda. Moreover, the archaeology of west-central Uganda (the future Bunyoro) seems to confirm this process: in this very dry region, which is known for its pasturelands, traces of significant occupation are not apparent before A.D. 1000.[63] The excavations carried out notably at the Bigo and Ntusi sites, whose great retrenchments, as we have seen, occurred between the eleventh and the sixteenth century, have revealed an ancient civilization combining sorghum and eleusine crops (many millstones were found in Ntusi) with an expanding practice of cattle raising (with large watering places).[64]

Archaeologists and anthropologists have discerned an important rupture after the sixteenth century. The just-described abundantly populated large sites were abandoned. Several explanations for this rupture have been put forward, including a climatic crisis that required abandoning an area that became too dry, an ecological rupture with an overworked zone, and acute land competition between agriculture and pastoralism. Whatever the cause, this change led to other population movements and to political ruptures, which must be discussed.[65]

In any case, the hypothesis of an external Nilotic or "Hamitic" invasion is refuted. What we are seeing are internal movements at the center of a civilization, one that had been developing for two millennia. This discussion equally suggests there was Bantu pastoralism in the Great Lakes region, which might be compared with pastoralism in the heart of Bantu-speaking populations in southern Africa before A.D. 1000. From this point of view, one might also note a dialectic between agriculture and cattle keeping taking root at this early stage. Here, the interplay of exchanges and complementarities did not preclude competition and conflict, notably over the use of land and male time. Complementarity was primarily based on access to animal manure. But this was manifestly older and better managed with cereal agriculture than with the banana gardens and, later, with the American crops, which had two-season harvests.[66]

In summarizing the general evolution of these relationships, one can identify a meeting of two sectors of activity during the early Iron Age: a tendency toward cereal-pastoral specialization on the intermediary plateaus, as well as on the mountains of Rwanda and Burundi, during the late Iron Age, which caused a crisis in the middle of the second millennium that undoubtedly led to new relationships between agriculture and pastoralism; and a new period of tension caused by the diffusion of American plants and the accompanying demographic pressure, without, this time, the possibility of pastoralism opening up virgin territories as it did around A.D. 1000. And, of course, the issue of land competition is undoubtedly crucial in the contemporary social crises, given the current context of a demographic transition and high rural population growth. But this social history of the long term was eclipsed by a racial discourse.

The Socio-Ethnic Cleavage Question: Tutsi, Hutu, and Others

Before pursuing this history and in particular the emergence of monarchies, I want to focus on the nature of these famous groups, whose denominations return over and over again in the literature on this region. How does one define the Hutu, Tutsi, and Twa categories, or the Hima and Iru ones, in Burundi, Buha, Rwanda, western Uganda, and on the plateaus of Lake Victoria's western shores? European observers were immediately struck by the Hutu-Tutsi opposition and the Iru-Hima one. From the start, their impressions, at least those that have been recorded, mixed up physical cliché, political reference, and a theory of migrations. From the moment of his arrival in the Karagwe royal court in 1861 Speke observed:

> In an instant we both felt and saw we were in the company of men who were as unlike as they could be to the common order of the natives of the surrounding districts. They had fine oval faces, large eyes, and high noses, denoting the best blood of Abyssinia.[67]

During his time in Rwanda between the first of May and the middle of June 1894, Count Gustav Adolf von Götzen, already in-

fluenced by Speke's theories, commented on what he saw in Rwabugiri's entourage:

> Luabugiri and his closest relations surely must count among the
> largest people who exist under the sun and, if they were brought to
> Europe, would create an extraordinary sensation.... The color of
> their skin is of a very light brown, to which fat is carefully applied,
> giving off a luminous glow....
>
> The history of Rwanda is legendary and obscure.... We have
> heard discussion of great migrations of Hamitic peoples who came
> from Abyssinia and Galla countries, who dispersed in a southwest-
> erly direction with vast herds of long-horned cattle, and who con-
> quered the lands between the lakes. But one can only determine
> with great difficulty, if even at all, if these changes occurred two
> hundred, five hundred, or one thousand years ago....
>
> Beside this ruling class is the great mass of the local population,
> the agriculturist Wahutu, a tribe of Bantu Negroes who have been
> living here since time immemorial.

But he also noted, "In Ruanda proper, the lords and subjects
are already almost completely assimilated in their customs and
practices."[68]

The Hima and Tutsi groups, whose pastoralism is emphasized,
were subjected to intense ideological projection, which must be
discarded if the region's historical realities are to be found. Three
themes are evident: first, Hima and Tutsi are primarily described
by comparing their physical traits (physiognomy, stature, and skin
color) with those of Somali or the Galla from the Horn of Africa;
second, most of the time, those who were seen were attendants
of the sovereigns, whose courts were visited systematically by
the first voyagers, and thus all Tutsi and Hima were considered
powerful; and, third, these groups were repeatedly assumed to be

descendants of a relatively recent invasion from Abyssinia and, before that, from the ancient Middle East. The thesis of Galla origins that Speke launched (and that he also applied to the Buganda dynasty, even though these social categories did not exist there) became the ethnohistoric gospel for this region. Later the ideological and political context of this racial anthropology will become clear. Nonetheless, it has persisted. Several texts illustrate this continuity:

Did we not see Caucasian crania, admirably Greek profiles, beside quite pronounced Semitic and even Jewish countenances, and even true beauties with bronze-red faces in the center of Rwanda and Burundi?

— Johannes-Michael van der Burgt, Dutch missionary in Burundi, 1903

The Bahima or Bahuma are therefore of a Semitic race, whether or not that displeases our bairu Bahaya who claim that their hygiene and milk diet is the cause of their physical beauty. But clearly semito-hamitic crossbreeding...begot the Muhuma.

— Edmund Césard, French missionary in the Bukoba region, 1935

One calls them the Batutsi. In reality, they are Hamites, probably of Semitic origin.... In reality, they form a race of lords. The Hamites are 1.9 meters high. They are slender. They possess straight noses, high foreheads, thin lips.... One discerns in them a sense of treachery, masked by a certain refinement.... The rest of the population is Bantu. They are the Bahutu, Negroes who possess all the typical characteristics: flat nose, thick lips, low forehead, and brachycephalic heads. They have a childlike character, both timid and lazy.... They are the class of serfs.

— Dr. Jules Sasserath, Belgian doctor, 1948

The Tutsi shepherds, slender and graceful, warriors of Nilotic origin, arrived in Burundi sometime around the thirteenth century, according to some historians, and later according to others. They rapidly reduced the Hutu agriculturists, a population of Bantu stock, to servitude and installed a feudal-like system where the venerated cow served to guarantee serf contracts.
— *Le Point*, September 1988

People as different as Finns and Sicilians.
— *The Economist*, August 1988[69]

Readers will have noticed the aesthetic and even fantastic dimension of this vision. But starting in the early twentieth century, several more lucid observers focused attention on the dubious character of this hypothesis of two races:

We should not lose sight of the fact that Batutsi immigration rests on conjectures of an anthropological and ethnological sort. In terms of this migration, we still do not have a single authentic tradition.
— Jan Czekanowski, German anthropologist of Polish origins, 1917

Physical differences: yes, they exist, but they are not general or constant enough to allow us to conclude that there is a neat and always real racial differentiation.
— Albert Gille, Belgian resident in Urundi, 1937

One may however think of the strongly marked physical differences between the Bairu and Bahima as due to nutritional and social factors rather than necessarily inferring a folk movement from the Horn of Africa.
— Merrick Posnansky, British archaeologist, 1966[70]

We have seen how archaeological and linguistic research over the last thirty years has thrown into question the model of civilizing invasions. When one refers to the distant origins of the internal categorization that marks the region's societies, notably in the western part, two kinds of answers are possible: on the one hand, populations with different geographic origins and from different linguistic families encountered one another; on the other hand, a socioeconomic cleavage developed between largely agricultural groups and largely pastoral ones, each of which found a different ecological niche for itself. The first episode would have occurred more than two thousand years ago, and the second more than one thousand years ago. It is therefore impossible to hold fast to explanations tied to this distant past, which would mean neglecting everything that happened demographically, economically, socially, and politically during the last ten or twenty centuries. This would be comparable to an interpretation that treats the French Revolution as the final episode in an age-old conflict between Celts and Franks! The "interlacustrine" literature is itself laden — one cannot avoid returning to this — with this model of "historic races," which was fashionable in the nineteenth century. And the traditions on the origins of different kingdoms have been molded to fit this interpretation.

But what makes understanding this social structure difficult, to the point of turning it into a true enigma (except when one clings to ideological certainty), is that the definition of the different categories rests on two realities: patrilineal birth and a certain function or place in society.

One is a Tutsi because one is born to a Tutsi father, a Hutu because one is born to a Hutu father, and so on — a hereditary factor that lends itself to racial definitions. Frequencies of distinctive somatic traits were added to that. Indeed, colonial observers very quickly tried to complement their impressions with measuring-stick facts.[71] A series of anthropometric studies was carried out in Uganda, Rwanda, and Burundi. The most significant synthesis was done by Jean Hiernaux in the early 1950s in Rwanda and Burundi.[72] Based on measurements taken of 879 individuals from different regions, who were selected with the help of Belgian administrators and missionaries knowledgeable about the society, Hiernaux's conclusions were relatively nuanced: the three categories, Tutsi, Hutu, and Twa, then qualified as Hamitic, Bantu, and pygmoid, were distinguishable by their members' average height and by different indicators of bodily proportions but not by skin color, contrary to a constantly repeated position. Moreover, these differences were sharper in Rwanda than in Burundi, and a "crossbreeding" was evident between the two groups. This later led Hiernaux to write that "the Tutsi of Burundi are as biologically similar to the Hutu, among whom there are no Hamites, as they are to the Masai."[73]

Recourse to genetics founded on blood markers has partially revived the debate.[74] This approach reopened questions about environmental adaptation, which had already been formulated in relation to the role of food and lifestyle in trait selection. Indeed, one of the most widespread blood markers in Africa, sickle-cell hemoglobin, which takes on positive value in malarious environments, diminished with altitude as much among the Hutu as among the Tutsi. The relative rarity of this gene among the latter might be explained by long-term ecological selection tied to pastoralism. It might also be the result of marriage prohibitions, considering the dangers of unions between two carriers of this gene. In the same way, for the Twa, Hiernaux backed the hypothesis of a "pygmaean evolution" "in the great equatorial forest" over that of a "crossbreeding" with a "Pygmy race." One nonetheless might note a remarkable evolution, over the course of a few years, in Hiernaux's positions on this question. After having tried to confirm blood-group distribution using anthropometry, he ended with a question. In 1968 he wrote:

> The Tutsi of Rwanda and of Burundi have dark skin, frizzy hair, and small noses; they combine characteristics that for an old typological approach to anthropology would be considered both white and black. However, they have nothing to do with a mixture of whites and blacks. It is their biological history that makes them what they are.... It is a question of selection. Classificatory mania, which is peculiar to the human spirit and maybe especially so to European culture in recent centuries, for years obsessed anthropologists, who are only now beginning to extricate themselves from it.[75]

A study of blood groups in Uganda similarly shows a greater blood-marker frequency in the highest altitude regions in the west, but one cannot determine whether these effects are environmental or genetic.[76] In fact, different studies show genetic proximities between populations that are culturally far apart: for example, between a Kuba Twa group in southern Congo and Tutsi from the Itombwe Mountains (today's Banyamulenge), or between Bantu-language speakers and those speaking Nilotic languages in eastern and central Africa.[77] These findings support Vansina's hypothesis of an expansion of Bantu cultures by "waves" reshaping older populations. In fact, on the basis of maybe thirty thousand years that constitute the history of sub-Saharan Africa's "modern" settlement, change came from migrations, genetic derivations, and adaptations to different environments, all constantly interwoven by interbreeding. This brings into relief the fiction of positing various encounters between "Negroes" and so-called Hamitic pseudo Asiatics. To the contrary, the "elongated" East African human type seems to be particularly old in this evolution.[78]

The use of physical anthropology to answer historical questions raises an epistemological problem that is beyond the scope of this book. The issue pertains to how one defines a particular group and to how one treats "aberrant" cases, notably when the distribution of blood markers does not correspond to anthropometry, assuming that the sampling did not a priori exclude these cases. To speak of interbreeding is to suggest a past that can be considered "pure." The "real" Tutsi or Hutu will therefore be defined according to an ancient ideal type, which later produced bastardized forms. As Agnès Lainé observed, "Anthropologists believe they are allowed to reconstruct real populations in order to reconstitute theoretical ancestral ones," whereas historians "look for the dynamic by which these populations organize themselves to live together in a given environment and by which they become what they are." Each follows a course of time of his own devising, and the logic of history is not the logic of biology.[79] It is necessary to pay attention to the conception the societies themselves have of their different components. This conception is fundamentally tied to a social imagination and to political practice, and every imaginable interaction between them — but not heredity.

This brings us to the question of defining these social components. In Burundi, the term *ubwoko* (which in Rwanda is applied to clans) designates the ancient categories of Twa, Hutu, Tutsi, and Ganwa (a princely group to which we will return). It signifies "sort, kind, species" — in other words, all forms of classification and categorization. Relations between these categories can be seen in some cases (for example, in matrimonial alliances and forms of conviviality), but they also are subject to restrictions, especially with the Twa group. Oral culture reflects a belief in the existence of socioeconomic vocations: the Batutsi and the Bahima are associated with the cow, the Bahutu and the Bairu with the hoe, the Batwa with hunting and pottery. One tale, for example,

77

seems to have circulated throughout the entire region under different variants. It relates a test to which children of a mythic king at the beginning of time — Gihanga in Rwanda or Ruhanga in Bunyoro — are submitted.[80] The children must carry pots of milk without spilling the contents; or they must obtain the secret of agriculture from the master of time; or they are invited to choose between several foods and objects (sorghum, metallic or wooden utensils, and so on). At the end of this ordeal, during which some are more careful, some more attentive, and some more fortunate than others, their "father" allocates specific functions to their respective descendants: cattle keeping for the Gatutsi's sons, agriculture and forging for the Gahutu's sons, and pottery and hunting for the Gatwa's sons. In Uganda, where the Batwa are absent, the triad is formed of Kakama, Kahima, and Kaïru, ancestral eponyms of kings (*bakama*), of the Bahima, and of the Bairu.[81] Sometimes women are incorporated into the story. Other times the challenge consists, as per Abraham's sacrifice, in having to kill one of the brothers, and, for example, only Gatwa accepts, which would justify Batwa marginalization.[82] These narratives do not just legitimize one type of social order: they refer to respect for human life, the agricultural calendar, distribution of tasks, the place of women, royal power, and a hierarchy privileging the pastoral group. As such, justification of hereditary vocations often, but not always, goes hand in hand with inequality.

In a way, this myth lays the groundwork for castes that are comparable to blacksmiths or griot castes in Sahelian Africa. This notion is reinforced by the cultural role of bovines and especially by the respect that surrounds milk: from the collection of milk to its consumption, gestures are codified and prohibitions abound, notably relating to food. Only special wood containers can be used to store it. Guarding the herds and milking the cows are exclusively men's work, mostly young men's work. Only churn-

78

ing is women's work. In Nkore, prohibitions affecting women in particular are numerous: moving away from the herd a little girl whose first tooth just came in, abstinence from milk for menstruating women, and so on. All this occurs as if women and cows are two major sources of fertility and one must try to avoid their neutralizing each other. These practices support a veritable pastoral culture that is especially valued by the Nkore and Karagwe Bahima and is equally esteemed by Rwanda's and Burundi's Batutsi.[83] By contrast, the prohibitions relating to the Batwa, in terms of refusing to drink with them or enter their houses, seem to paint a picture of a society obsessed with a certain model of purity.

The relation between cattle keeping and agriculture would thus be a marker around which a social rationale pivoted. One might also refer to "ranks," or, in German, to *Stände*, when thinking about other archaic societies that codified relations around sections or quasi-ritualized "halves."[84] But when the anthropologist Jacques Maquet imposed the model of a caste society in his description of "traditional" Rwanda, it was rather in the sense of "orders" of the French ancien régime — that is to say, differentiated and hierarchal "conditions," in short, more a Dumézil-style orderly tripartition than a Lévi-Strauss–style game of structured roles.[85] Maquet settled on a "premise of inequality" between Batutsi and Bahutu, maintained through clientage relationships and rooted in an ancient conquest. His model was a "feudal" one, but it was quite similar to a racial one. The function of cattle in all social and political contracts (gifts, fines, dependency ties, and matrimonial compensations) apparently reinforced this concept of "pastoral feudalism." The identity of Tutsi or Hima seemed more "noble" than that of other groups. Did one not see Rwandan and Burundian Bahutu who could advance in their society by renouncing their initial status, that is, by "dehutuisizing" (*kwihutura*) themselves? Taking into account preferential marriages in aristocratic circles and certain aesthetic practices, a Canadian author even suggested that a racial vision had been part of pastoral domination before colonization.[86]

However, faced with these interpretations, reservations and hesitations began to emerge in the 1960s, and other ideological trails were blazed. The reference book published by the Musée Royal de l'Afrique Centrale in Tervuren in 1962 wavered between certainty and confusion.[87] On Rwanda, Marcel d'Hertefelt did not hesitate to comment on the "racial" origin of the "three castes." On Burundi, Albert Trouwborst extended the cliché: "different social and racial groups that one might call castes." On the Buha, J.H. Scherer began the same way by setting out "two more or less distinct groups from a racial point of view": "the true Ha of Bantoid origin" and "the Tutsi, of so-called Hamitic origin." But using a rubric of "cultural variations," d'Hertefelt claimed that regional variations are stronger between "castes"; Trouwborst underlined the relative importance of such and such a chief; and, without beating around the bush, Scherer wrote that differences related to "racial groups" were "of such minimal importance that they had become negligible."

To escape the contradictions born of racial dogma, research was oriented toward more concrete social and economic analyses. On the one hand, these analyses emphasized material complementarity between cattle keeping and agriculture in the region, and, on the other hand, they questioned the way in which inequalities were constructed. One study recalled that cattle keeping produced milk, meat, skins, and manure. Two Tanzanian sociologists observed:

> Because of the belief by some writers that it is only agricultural products which come out of labour, the other side of the dependency is rarely mentioned. In fact, so far, very few have seen the contribution of the livestock owners in the whole system.[88]

More recently, the agronomist Hubert Cochet also underlined the decisive role of animal manure in the ancient success of agriculture in this region.[89] But complementarity does not exclude inequalities and the emergence of genuine social classes. Samwiri Karugire, a historian of Nkore, could write at one point that "economic relations between the Bairu and the Bahima were based on mutual exchange... rather than [on] ethnic superiority or inferiority," and then several pages later write that "Nkore society was a class society in which the possession of cattle counted for much" and the "governing class was drawn from the wealthy section of Bahima."[90] Marxist analyses of the 1960s continued to emphasize this class phenomenon, either in effectively reproducing the duality of cattle keepers and cultivators or in identifying rich and poor categories at the center of these two groups. To quote Claudine Vidal, the "fetishization of the cow" culturally facilitated the success of Tutsi feudalism, even if all Batutsi were not powerful and even if some Bahutu also had access to cattle outside dependency ties. Jan Czekanowski had already made this claim in 1917: beneath a small aristocratic minority one can distinguish, he wrote, autonomous peasants and those forced to do corvée labor; yet this distinction did not correspond to the Tutsi and Hutu categories. I might add that, morally and materially, products like sorghum, iron, and honey also brought ease and prestige. Still, the specific potential of cattle for obtaining social and political success must be appreciated: this investment, both medium- and long-term, could be compared with that of the banana, but with the added advantage of mobility. In other words, cattle, as mobile capital, provided the capability for exchange and influence (one might even say credit).[91]

These debates too often err because they lack geographic precision. In fact, relations between cattle keeping and agriculture vary greatly from one region to the next in the heart of the Great

Lakes, and the existence of the corresponding statuses is not universal. For example, a Batwa category appears only in Rwanda, Burundi, Kivu, and Buha, the latter under the name Bakiko. Another anomaly: in Burundi, there is a separate category for royal bloodlines. In Bunyoro, a similar phenomenon exists in which the princely group is reputed to have Nilotic origins, going back to a quite real Lwo invasion during the sixteenth century. In Buganda, the land of bananas, all these categories were absent. The society was structured by clans, though that did not prevent explorers from detecting "Hamite" blood in them. In other cases, the coexistence of agriculturists and pastoralists was organized into distinct ecological niches, for example, in Nkore and Karagwe. In Burundi, the extreme east and the shores of Lake Tanganyika had almost no Batutsi; nor were there many in what is contemporary western Rwanda.[92] Here, local populations identified themselves not necessarily as Iru or Hutu but according to their clans or local place-names. What became the classic coupling (Hutu-Tutsi or Iru-Hima) only made sense in a framework involving the close cohabitation of two partners and their integration in a politically centralized tributary regime. No Hutu without Tutsi. Even the denomination Muhutu was ambiguous because, in a clientage relationship, it indicated the dependent, even if he was a Mututsi.[93] The number and situations of groups labeled pastoral varied considerably: the Batutsi represented 15 to 20 percent of the population in Rwanda and Burundi, according to estimates furnished by the Belgian administration in the 1950s, while the Bahima in what is today northwest Tanzania and even in Nkore hardly amounted to 5 percent. The former consisted of sedentarized groups, involved in agriculture (assuming one does not forget about the work of the vast majority of Batutsi women) and integrated in the social fabric of each country. By contrast, in the latter case, we can observe more mobility, transhumance, and even migrations, either to both sides of the Kagera (between contemporary Uganda toward the Buganda border, or from Karagwe toward Buhaya country) or from south to north (from Buzinza country).[94] From at least the eighteenth century, pastoral communities even migrated to the eastern Congo basin or toward the center of what is today Tanzania, as will be shown below.

Therefore, even if the composition of the Great Lakes region's societies is rooted in a history of human settlement, environmental management, and agro-pastoral systems that go back, in successive phases, two thousand years, the contours of the different categories and their relations consist of a history of breaks and ruptures that must be reconstructed. This history is largely political. A Rwandan historian, Emmanuel Ntezimana, courageously underlined this during a 1986 university meeting: the claim, by Hutu or Tutsi intellectuals, to the invention of iron, or the introduction of the cow, is ridiculous. In the traditions, he said, "references to the Abatutsi, Abahutu, and Abatwa appeared many times in the late eighteenth century. They only seem voluntarily omnipresent in the lineages that are precisely . . . those that are predominant."[95] Said another way, the cleavage, today called ethnic, was essentially introduced politically by the *imfura*, the people of value, and not by the *rubanda*, the simple people (all "ranks" together), before taking root in the heart of the society.

To be Tutsi or to be Hutu, in Rwanda and Burundi, did not have the same sense in 1994, at the time of the genocide, in 1894, when the whites arrived, in 1794, when the former kingdoms were almost at their apogee, and in 1594, when the kingdoms came into being. . . . And before then, when were these two terms first used? What kind of social archaeology can tell us when they were inscribed in the region's human landscape, before they were inscribed on identity cards?

83

CHAPTER TWO

The Emergence of Kingship:

Power and Religion

We have seen how the history of the Great Lakes region cannot be dissociated from the historiography that made it emerge, albeit in a roundabout way, from its soil, from its elders' speech, and from foreigners' writings. Scholars constantly face the task of having to make use of a copious literature that is loaded with traps that require careful deciphering. The region's political culture has fascinated every observer, largely because of the sophistication of the monarchies, which managed to control both sizable territories and especially populations, without writing, money, or the wheel. Everything functioned through verbal messages, personal ties, cow redistributions, and jug porters — in short, by emissaries endowed with strong legs, good memories, measured language, and, if possible, loyalty. In the "darkness" that was supposed to cover "the heart of Africa," this success was attributed to "Hamitic" conquerors, as we have seen, who came to civilize the "Negroes," who were a priori thought to be incapable of such achievements. What most impressed the first voyagers were the royal capitals, their complexity, and the affluence and etiquette that reigned before their dumbfounded eyes. There is much to choose from in this genre of descriptions. Let's take the cases of

Buganda and Rwanda, which, each in its own way, excited the most amazement and perplexity.

In September 1875, the American journalist Henry Morton Stanley was received in the court of Mutesa, the *kabaka* of Buganda:

> The curtain rolls up, and discloses a hill covered with tall conical huts, whose tops peep out above the foliage of plantains and bananas, and lofty fences of cane.... [People] crowd around the gates in social gossip, exchanging morning greetings.
>
> Suddenly the murmur of voices ceases, and the long rumbling roll of a kettle-drum is heard, announcing that the monarch is seated on the burzah.... At the farther end, by the light afforded by the wide entrance, we perceive the figure of a man clad in an embroidered scarlet jacket and white skirt seated on a chair, guarded on either side by a couple of spearmen and two men bearing muskets. The chiefs and the principal men now hastening through the gates ... after which they severally betake themselves to their respective seats in order of rank. Two long rows of seated men are thus formed along the caned walls of the hall of audience, facing towards the centre, which is left vacant for the advent of strangers and claimants, and the transaction of business, justice, &c.[1]

In June 1898, the future resident of Rwanda Richard Kandt visited the court of Mwami Yuhi Musinga, who had reigned over the country for two years:

> The sun was at its zenith above us and the thousands of spears barely cast more than a thumb's shadow.... I advanced toward the entrance alone: in front of and half hiding it stood a gigantic Mtussi, more than 2 meters tall, of light, almost reddish complexion, carrying a finely sculpted spear and a long stick in his taut right hand and a minuscule

shield in his left hand.... I went into the large court proper, I again passed through a standing human mass and I entered a minute later in a large hut: Ruhenankiko [Ruhinankiko, a major chief] welcomed me by the door. In the weakly lit entrance, a dozen major notables were seated tightly next to each other.... A clapping of hands in the audience apprised me that the Mtussi, who came from the rear of the hut supported on two servants' shoulders, was the king. Without looking at me, he sat down on the stool to my right.... He wore the king's emblem, a headband about 20 centimeters wide, made from white beads except for six jagged lines of pink beads. From the upper side of this strange headdress draped large tufts of long white marmoset hair that reached the nape of his neck. From the lower side hung about fifteen red-and-white bead strings sown with art.... He wore a finely tanned short loincloth.... A host of amulets covered his chest. They looked like little bottles wrapped in two colors of beads that were embroidered in a zigzag.[2]

Torn between surprise at the rustic exoticism of these courts and the desire to make historical comparisons, these authors underlined the foreignness of the courts' superstitions and fictively projected the scene onto their own past. The Great Lakes sovereigns became Clovis, William the Conqueror, even Louis XIV, Ramses, and Sesostris. But the film of history, according to the colonizers, only started with their coming: the past they discovered was presented as an unchanging photograph, something frozen in time. However, the process by which different kingdoms crystallized and monarchical powers formed did not happen in a day. Different factors contributed to this historical dynamic: besides the material and human environment seen above, there were structures of extended kinship, beliefs, military capacity, and means for political control. In tracing history from the sixteenth to the nineteenth century as best we can, we will see how power shifts from having half-clan, half-religious bases toward becoming true, state-like machines. The "kings" appeared as mediums before becoming reigning and governing monarchs.

Clans

Without subscribing to some simplistic evolution that would take us from "clans" to "empires," we must recognize that the groups known since the nineteenth century as clans are the oldest structures of society to go beyond the limits of family enclosures and limited lineages; they combine kinship, exogamy, shared symbols, and rules of solidarity.[3] They have remained at the heart of social life. In the 1930s or 1960s, when one asked a peasant, whether in Burundi, Rwanda, or Tanzania, "Who are you?" the immediate answer was mention of a clan.[4] However, the ways in which clan membership is indicated can seem vague: reference to a collective name, at least a formal conviction of having come from a common patrilineal ancestor, and sometimes a "totemic" marker described as a prohibition (most often a wild animal or a cultivated or undomesticated plant, but also a part of a slaughtered animal or a cow of a particular color). The concrete ties are very loose, in part because clan members are dispersed throughout the country. The Burundian historian Emile Mworoha cites the banal case of a hill in northwest Burundi where in 1971 one could count eleven clans with members in the country's other regions.[5] Clans thus do not consist of lineages that bear a true genealogical imprint, nor is there any residential unity. Rather, clans consist of social identities that allow one to be situated in relation to others, to find friends just about everywhere, and to benefit from their hospitality and support.[6] They also play a role in marriage, since in principle (except in the case of subdivisions) clan exogamy governs marriage choice. Ancient biographies all insist on the importance of this identity. The terminology designating it is revealing:

88

umuryango, which applies also to lineage, in Burundi; *ubwoko*, "category," in Rwanda; and *ruganda* in Bunyoro and Buhaya, *ishanja* among the Buhavu of Kivu, and *igise* in northern Buha, terms that apply more to social ties than to family lines.[7] Colonial interpreters in northwest British Tanganyika employed the Swahili (the lingua franca of East Africa) term *kabila* (derived from Arabic), which means "tribe," a term that missionaries in Rwanda willingly employed in French.

In fact, the structure takes contrasting forms in different countries in the region, if only because of the varying number of groups in each. Buganda's system is distinct, having a strong element of segmentary splitting: some forty clans (*ebika*), each named after its own protective animal, are subdivided into subclans (*masiga*), which in turn are subdivided into major lineages (*mituba*) and into minor lineages (*enyiriri*), with each subdivision being hierarchically characterized into elder and younger lines.[8] On the plateaus that stretch from Bunyoro (east of Lake Albert) to Buhaya and Buzinza country (west of Lake Victoria), as well as in Burundi, Buha, and the societies west of Lake Kivu, the number of clans is considerable, totaling more than two hundred in Burundi.[9] Each consists of an undetermined number of lineages. By contrast, in Rwanda and Nkore, the situation is more structured, with some twenty clans in the former and four in the latter, which themselves are subdivided into subclans (*mashanga*) that group together lineage units.[10]

Far from being accidental, these latter formations' limited segmentation points to their historical and social dimensions; namely, they seem to fulfill an integrating function. First, from Lake Kivu to Lake Victoria and from Lake Albert to the Malagarasi, that is, across nearly the entire region, identical names of clans (or subclans) can be found. This might indicate an ancient history of human settlement. Demonstrating this is difficult because origin stories vary according to the place where they were recorded, and each group tends to put itself at the center of the world or to assign itself marvelous ancestors taken from regional mythology — a point to which we will return. No "clan tradition" is so authentic as to escape reconstruction and reinterpretation. At best, each clan's geography, combined with elders' firsthand accounts, gives an idea of the clan's history over a relatively limited area (on the scale of Rwanda, for example) and for a maximum duration of three centuries.[11] It would surely be naive to claim a history that dated back to the beginning of the Christian era — an idea that was periodically proposed for ancient Kitara-Bunyoro.[12] More remarkable is the maintenance, care, and construction of these sorts of ties across areas that transcend modern political borders. Focusing on these processes shows how contacts, exchanges, and movements occurred over the long term. Even between Buganda and its western cousins, whose social organization is quite different, some equivalences have been found, for example, between the Grasshopper and Basonga clans.

These identities also transcend so-called ethnic cleavages. Some clans in Burundi include Bahutu and Batutsi or one of these two groups and Batwa. This pertains respectively to 10 percent, 50 percent, and 90 percent of the clans in each of these three categories. In Buhaya country, of the 122 clans observed during British rule, one-third either had mixed membership (described as "ennobled") or had both Bahima and Bairu members. The Basita clan, which is common in regional traditions, is sometimes described as pastoral and other times as agricultural and smithing. The Bajiji are considered Hutu in Burundi and Tutsi in Buha, where they constituted a dynasty. But the most remarkable examples are those of Rwanda and Nkore. Of the eighteen clans cataloged by d'Hertefelt in Rwanda (Antoine Nyagahene counted twenty-seven), the five largest (the Abasinga, Abasindi, Abazigaba, Abagesera, and Abanyiginya) account for more than half the population. Bahutu constitute 85–90 percent of each clan, except the Banyiginya, where the Batutsi are 40 percent. The same or almost the same percentages of Batutsi are found in seven other small clans. Batwa also are found in each of these clans. Two hypotheses have been proposed to account for this integration: Jan Czekanowski argued there was intermixing between Batutsi and Bahutu (by concubines or strategic alliances), while Fathers Léon Delmas and Albert Pagès invoked the *buhake* clientage relationships, claiming they led dependents to adopt their patron's clan.[13] Unfortunately, the history of recent centuries does not attest to mutations in clan membership along these lines, and in the two prominent cases of Rwanda and Nkore the Batwa would have remained unaffected. The problem with both hypotheses lies with an anachronistic privileging of caste over clan.[14] Indeed, as I emphasized at the beginning, for a very long time clans were the fundamental basis for identity in people's minds.

At this level, two social institutions are more revealing: blood pacts and joking relationships.[15] The former, often called *bunywane*, which means "to drink together," also known as a blood exchange (during which in Buhaya country, for example, one rubs two coffee grains from the same berry), can unite lineages after members take a solidarity oath.[16] But more significant, the so-called joking relationship, which is present between patronymic groups in Sahelian Africa, links two clans. The partners exchange mockeries and insults without physically striking each other; these verbal comedies create a fictive kin-like space. What one calls *ubuse* in Rwanda or *buswege* in Buha also entails — when a new house is constructed, someone dies, or a mourning period is over — a member of the allied clan carrying out the ceremonies. This function was performed by all three of Rwanda's largest and oldest clans: the Basinga, the Bagesera, and the Bazigaba. In Nkore and the other societies bordering Rwanda (southwest of contemporary Uganda), including the Bahavu of Ijwi Island (Lake Kivu), this relationship, called *bacumbi* or *bakumbi*, allowed a clan of one country to become linked to, or even integrated into, a clan in another country. This in turn facilitated migrations and new forms of social influence. This complexity amazed Father Félix Géraud, a regular visitor to Uganda's Kigezi:

> The Bahanda, who originated in Rwanda, are *bacumbi* of the Bagahe, who come from Mpororo. The Bakimbiri, the Bahinda's *bacumbi* in Nkole, are *bacumbi* of the Bashambo in Mpororo and *bacumbi* of the Beega of Kigezi (who came from Rwanda). The Bakonjo of Toro are *bacumbi* of the Basigi from Rwanda.[17]

We here see the strategies involved in the formation of overarching clan groups, whose different components can evolve into subclans. We also can imagine how the clan landscape observed in the early twentieth century covered up various events in which amalgamation was at least as important as fissuring.

In describing analogous networks on Ijwi Island, David Newbury concluded that this was not "descent groups from time immemorial," but the product of a history. After comparing the mutations he generally observed on the shores of Lake Kivu and the Rwandan model, Newbury insisted on the political dimension of these reconfigurations, in particular the political dimension of a system of "multiethnic" clans. He cited the example of the Banyambiriri and the Beshaza. A joking relationship, he argued, united these two clans, which were present on Ijwi and in Kinyaga, in southwestern Rwanda. Both clans claimed to have Rwandan ancestors from the Basinga clan, but indirectly, as if when they left Rwanda two hundred years earlier, the Singa "clan identity" had not yet been truly structured.[18]

92

In Rwanda and Nkore over the last two centuries, the central power in all likelihood manipulated the clan structures. But analogous political-clan configurations are found elsewhere. In the Buhaya-Karagwe area, for example, several clans might be grouped together around the same "prohibited" animal, a genuine emblematic figure for what became a superclan. In several cases, the networks formed in this way clearly had connections with the royal powers. For example, members of the Ngabi (Bushbuck) and the Nkende monkey (a *Cercopithecus*) groups, as well as the Mamba (Lungfish) ones, held many ritual and political positions: guardians of dynastic drums, diviners, palace builders, royal blacksmiths, iron keepers, important advisers, drummers during the new moon, the sovereign's cooks or shepherds, bodyguards, and even the sovereigns.[19] In this case, the totemic markers formed an expanded network that was organized around the functioning of the monarchy, because the members of these groups were permanently in the royal person's presence. The top positions in the Bugandan court also were automatically filled with these groups' members: for example, the canoe-fleet admiral on Lake Victoria came from the Mamba clan. But I do not want to jump ahead to the ways in which these powers were organized. Rather, the question to ask now pertains to the exact role these clan identities played in the crystallization of power, even independently of the notion of a monarchy.

The *kabaka*, king of Buganda, was called, among other names, the "father of the *bataka*," meaning the father of the clan chiefs. For years, these clan chiefs maintained an eminent role, especially in the center of the country. They served a protective function, in particular with regard to property. Generally speaking, as clans dispersed, lineages divided, and political authorities increasingly intervened, this aspect became less and less real. Still, a few dicta (for example, in Bunyoro) continued to affirm that "the clan

93

governed the land while the king governed the people."[20] Clans often appeared as the explicit or implicit managers of the past or the sacred. They might carry on ancestral vocations in production and environmental management (for example, honey making, care of the herd's sick, and forging). At this level, specializations are as prominent as they are in the hackneyed register of "castes" and were especially on display during court functions. King Mwezi said to young Bireme: "Your clan is reputed for guarding calves, so you will guard mine." This trait sometimes takes a historically rich anecdotal turn, whether real or reconstructed: in Nkore, every time a princess dowry was taken, a subclan received a cow as tribute for a gift it supposedly made to a king long ago.[21] The sacred, for its part, mostly arises in relation to sites dedicated to protective spirits or mythical founders. Patronage and care of the sanctuaries connected to the powers are essential to the prestige of clan leaders, as we are about to see. But the sacred woods or prominent natural sites (boulders, springs, marshes, rivers, lakes, and so on) that the clans manage also serve to mark out territory. This has remained a lasting practice in, for example, Buganda, but that is not the only country where clans depended on networks of memory sites inscribed in the soil.[22]

The supernatural, tradition, soil, protection, group solidarity — all these things can foster and shape a genuine political order, which is what one finds at the origins of the monarchies. This aspect has often been neglected in the historiography of the large kingdoms and has instead been discovered in the study of small principalities, such as the ancient micro-kingdoms of northwestern Rwanda.[23] In these cases, the familial model, which the clan institutions claim through lineage networks, can create territorial powers. These are distinct from kinship proper, since many dependents, who benefit from the "land-clearing" group's "hospitality," become part of this clan or at least fall under its authority.

Foundation Myths

The kingships that blossomed in the region during the eighteenth and nineteenth centuries were named as such because they possessed the standard attributes of this regime type: supreme power of one man, rules of dynastic transmission, religious references, and rule-based territorial control that had fiscal and military consequences and made recourse to jurisprudence. But this institution was not born fully formed on a particular date. Rather, the kingships matured over time and were the products of ruptures within clan networks. In medieval times in the West, a kingship could marshal the Bible and scattered memories of the Roman Empire, all the while benefiting from the support of a Christian Church network. In this region, neither the Bible nor Rome existed. We must therefore analyze the underlying social imagination in the region that could inspire such power, and we must explain how the kingships gained popular support. This is not to endorse the Marxist position of the state as a superstructure that reflects social relations or to reduce the state to forms of coercion. Rather, one must focus on the political culture that these kingships established.[24] This culture can be seen in foundation myths and major rituals.

Origin stories are primarily concerned with the memory of a marvelous rule that supposedly engendered the majority of kingdoms, as if the Carolingian empire had been the source of different Frankish monarchies. I am here referring to the Bacwezi myth, which is especially well known in southwestern Uganda but extends well beyond this area and has been reproduced in contemporary historiography. In the context of the racial ideology discussed above, a combination of ethnographic naïveté and the pro-tradition group's political interests allowed an African-style *Nibelungenlied*, or a regional *Odyssey*, to appear as a factual, eventful chronicle. For years, manuals and atlases have been published without discussing whether the "Bacwezi empire" even existed.[25]

In 1958, the young English historian Christopher Wrigley had the audacity to see it as a mythological pantheon of sorts.[26] However, even today, many observers in the region seem to need to believe in this empire's existence, which has become the pivotal vector for the racial explanation of the emergence of the Great Lakes kingdoms. Nonetheless, the richness of these traditions takes place on another level, one that we must try to understand.[27]

The myths are inscribed in various landscapes: sparse forests, volcanic lakes, swampy valleys, termite mounds, rocky islets that cover contemporary south-central Uganda around the Katonga valley between Lakes Albert and Edward and the Kagera. Only a few recorded versions exist. The corpus rests primarily on stories recorded by several Protestant and Catholic missionaries: principally Ruth Fisher, then the Reverend John Roscoe, and finally Fathers Julien Gorju and Nicolet.[28] The Bacwezi myth depicts various persons who are related over four generations. Five main episodes can be distinguished:

- There was once a king named Isaza. He let himself be lured into some other world, whose sovereign, Nyamiyonga, bewitched him by forming a blood brotherhood with him, offering him his daughter Nyamata, and giving him some especially beautiful cows. In Isaza's absence, his kingdom was managed by his "doorman" Bukuku.

- Isimbwa, born of this mysterious union, loved to hunt on earth. One day he passed the home of Bukuku, whose girl, Nyinamwiru, had only one eye and one breast and lived like a recluse. According to a prediction, she would give birth to a son who would kill his maternal grandfather. Isimbwa seduced this strange girl. The child born from this union, raised in secret by the potter Rubumbi, later killed Bukuku during a brawl with a shepherd. This young man in turn assumed the name Ndahura and reigned over his paternal grandfather's kingdom, whose capital was Mubende.

- Ndahura conquered lands in various directions and installed his sons Mulindwa, Mugenyi, Mugasha, and so on, in each captured zone. Then came the ordeals: taken prisoner and buried in a termite mound, he was saved by a half brother, Kyomya. Nevertheless, disqualified by these failures, he stepped down and went into exile with his mother in Busongora, north of Lake Edward.

- His successor was his son Wamara, who had been living near the Katonga valley in the Bwera region. He was more cow keeper and hunter than conqueror. Here, the epic poetic tragedy is transformed into a pathetic family drama. There is a litany of catastrophes: Mugasha unleashes a deluge, then drought sets in and starvation strikes his court; then his half brother Mugenyi threatens to kill himself after the death of his most beautiful cow, and his mother tries to kill another half brother, Mulindwa; some cow thieves (who come from either the north or the south, according to different versions of the story) ravage the royal herd; Kyomya's son, Kagoro, plays the role of savior (like his father). All this comes to a close when two diviners from Bukidi, that is, from the northern wild country (the land of the Nilotes), based on what they see in beef intestines, prophesy the end of the Bacwezi reign.

- The Bacwezi in turn leave their familiar land; they disappear in a lake (Victoria or Albert), or in the western extinct volcanoes, or in the Ruwenzori beyond. They leave emblems of

97

their authority in the new dynasty, born from Kyomya, the founder of which would be called Rukidi, given his northern origins. With the latter began the historic Babito lineage. Moreover, Wamara, with the servant Njunaki, was said to have had a bastard, Ruhinda, who is especially spoken about in Nkore and south of the Kagera.

Other variants were recorded, notably in Buhaya country, such as this one:

Mugasha, the master of the waters, has a dispute with his cousin Kagoro: the former becomes lame and the latter a stutterer. Then Wamara, accompanied by Mugasha and Irungu, descends into a grotto to visit Kintu's subterranean kingdom; Kintu gives them seeds and cattle, but later punishes them for their ingratitude and sends them to their death. All the Bacwezi subsequently disappeared in a well, from which they are supposed to emerge one day.[29]

A number of versions have been spun off this base of stories. These legends are tied to a strange family history in which the family is poisoned through deception, treason, and conflict. Half brothers fight; wicked mothers scheme; and bastards born of casual encounters (Isimbwa, Ndahura, Ruhinda) are decisive figures. The role of women is surprising, given the culture's patrilineal principle. All this brings to mind the romantic aspects of ancient Greek mythology. The projection of existential anxieties, including those about death, has a dreamlike dimension in the realist setting of these lands. Cattle, whose success on the plateaus has been apparent since at least A.D. 1000, are omnipresent, but so are cereals, iron making, fishing, hunting, and pottery. Ndahura is the grandson of Nyamata, "the lady of milk," and the son of Nyinamwiru, "the mother of agriculture." Moreover, the memory of heroes remains attached to specific locations, which are marked out by natural sites (wells, watering places, lakes, fords, strangely shaped rocks) or by sacred groves. Particularly noteworthy is that by the early twentieth century, a cult had been set aside for spirits named after this marvelous and vicious line. The largest sanctuaries were in Mubende (for Ndahura), Buyaga near Lake Albert (for Mulindwa), and Masaka (for Wamara) but also, much farther to the south, Itaba in Nkore, Bitoma in Kyanja, and Ruhita in Ihangiro, lands whose subsequent historical role will be seen shortly. In Masaka, near a ficus and dracaena grove, appointed guards keep watch over a drum, supposedly Ndahura's, and an iron spear. Priests who held the spear had the right to be possessed by Wamara's spirit. Throngs of pilgrims went to Masaka, notably during the new moon, to celebrate a cult of fertility.[30]

The traditions published in the early twentieth century concluded by evoking a mystical return of the Bacwezi and the establishment of mediums chosen from different clans and dedicated to reincarnating these so-called *embandwa* spirits. Mythological episodes reappeared in physiognomy and in the possessed's powers: Mugasha's spirit had to limp; Kagoro's had to stutter, and it sometimes cured rashes and eczemas, inasmuch as it was a specialist in "fire" (because Kagoro was supposed to have incinerated Wamara's body). In fact, each had his domains: Wamara was invoked for death and rain; Irungu for the bush, hunting, and voyages; Kagoro for lightning and cattle; Mugasha for rain, storms (he was supposed to have unleashed one against Wamara to get his daughter), the waters of Lake Victoria, and bananas; and Ndahura for epidemics (including smallpox starting in the nineteenth century). Wrigley's 1958 position makes sense: these legendary figures were deities, represented on earth by *kubandwa* religious mediums, either permanent or improvised, whose political importance and ambiguity will soon be apparent.

Since the mid-nineteenth century, several observers have made the same point. John Hanning Speke and James Grant in 1861, as well as Emin Pasha in 1881, described "itinerant singer-magicians" (often women) called Wichwezi in the Karagwe and Bunyoro courts. In 1910 in Kiziba (near Bukoba) Hermann Rehse noted, "One imagines the spirits in the form of ancient kings of the universe"; in Bunyoro in 1923 the Reverend Roscoe wondered, "No one can tell whether they really represent royal families... or whether they are purely mythic personages."[31] In 1945 in Buhaya Administrators Hans Cory and M.M. Hartnoll claimed, "The Bachwezi here are not known to have been living men, but are considered as purely supernatural beings."[32] But the reach of this cult is impressive: not only are these heroes, who are only a minute part of the spirit pack (their number is estimated at 350), invoked in this way, but they also have different regional expressions and are even relayed by secondary figures, who elsewhere play the central role. Among the venerated spirits in Buganda, especially around the sanctuaries on the Sese Islands, one finds Ndawula, Wamala, and Mukasa (names we recognize). The latter is the great god of Lake Victoria. Ryangombe, a hunting hero honored in Nkore and Karagwe, is present in Rwanda and Bushi, with Kagoro and Mukasa at his sides. In Burundi and Buha, the same figure is called Kiranga. As far away as Buha, he is known to come from *bicwezi* spirits.[33] What we are witnessing here is a vast cultural zone, crisscrossed by related beliefs. This brings to mind the world of the listeners, then the readers, of *The Odyssey*, a world of the Greeks, at the junction of the Bronze and Iron Ages. No one would speak about a Greek "empire" before Alexander; no one would claim the historical existence of Agamemnon or Ulysses, still less of Vulcan or Apollo. We must therefore understand the logics at work that led to the historicization of the "Bacwezi empire."

We will start with two claims about how this mythology took root sociopolitically: the involvement of clan networks and of a whole series of dynasties that reigned from the sixteenth to the seventeenth century. As discussed above, clans operate around Cwezi beliefs and cult. Some clans' influence depended on controlling sacred sites and on one of their ancestors' being represented in the myths. In Masaka, it was the Bamoli, a clan reputed for its metallurgy; in Mubende, it was the Basazima, whose priestess played a role during the enthronement of the Bunyoro kings. The myths' first-generation heroes — Isaza, Bukuku, and Nyamiyonga — were attributed to the Bagabu, the Baranzi, and the Basonga, respectively. The Bacwezi "kings" themselves, Ndahura and Wamara, as well as the Basita clan, shared the same totemic prohibition — namely, that of milk from a cow that had calved less than five days before (*obusito*). The Basita clan, present in most places, was the clan of Mulindwa's mother and also, more historically, of the guardians of the dynastic drums of Nkore and (at its beginnings) of Karagwe. The same *obusito* prohibition applied to the Nkore kings. The Basonga and Kimera's mother also are found in Buganda's origin myths. This prompted the historian Semakula Kiwanuka to interpret the Cwezi ensemble as a confederation of clan powers.[34] By linking these references to sites important in Cwezi mythology, some authors hypothesized a series of conflicts between powerful clans that resulted in shifting the political center of gravity from north to south and from west to east.[35]

Moreover, this mythical horizon is at the origins of the Bunyoro kingdom, which was founded by the Babito dynasty and has historically been dated to the late fifteenth century. The Babito dynasty is presented as coming from a Nilotic raid, more precisely from a southward descent of the Lwo group (the so-called Rivers and Lakes Nilotes).[36] This was the only real external invasion in the region, one affirmed in narrative and linguistic sources.

Episodic raids are mentioned on several occasions in the region's traditions: in the early sixteenth century, as far as Rwanda; in 1520, after a victory in Nkore (the date has been established by the coincidence of a solar eclipse); in the seventeenth century and especially in the early eighteenth century, as far south as Buhaya country and, to the east, as far as an area south of Mount Elgon and along the contemporary Kenyan shoreline of Lake Victoria. The first thrust thus took place north of Lake Albert, but the amalgamation with the Bantu-language culture of contemporary western Uganda apparently happened quite quickly. Only a few Lwo words remain in the Bunyoro language. The Babito constituted an upper princely layer, but many also became simple people, mingling with Hima cattle herders and Iru cultivators.

What is surprising is that those who guarded the ancestors in the official traditions were represented as "savages": even Rukidi's name can be seen in this way. But the cultural connotation must be taken into account. All the dynasties' founders, as we will see, appeared as adventurers who came from unknown places. What's more, the key to these Bunyoro traditions resided in the desire to demonstrate continuity between the Bacwezi heroes of the ancient "kingdom of Kitara" and the new Babito dynasty.[37] Rukidi, also nicknamed Isingoma (He of the Drum) and Mpuga (White and Black, as on cowhide or on the sides of an unevenly polished spear), was immediately situated in the cultural and religious universe of the conquered populations: he was thought to have descended from Kyomya, Ndahura's hunter half brother, and to have been led in his new kingdom by diviners, who held the Cwezi kingship's secrets. The Mugungu ritualist made him hand over the sacred drums, which their guardian (from the Basita clan) ceded in exchange for a basketful of eleusine and a set of regalia (spears, basketry, copper bracelets, and so on), which were added to those brought from the north. When the court's fire was

relit and the drums struck, Rukidi became *mukama* (king) under
the Lwo name Winyi. A capital was later established in Mubende,
Ndahura's holy site. Members of the region's influential clans
surrounded Rukidi and his descendants, and then matrimonial
alliances were made among them.[38] Bunyoro's official traditions
thus identify the Babito as a third dynasty, after the Bacwezi and
the Batembuzi, which ended with Isaza. Kitara is evoked, at least
in the early twentieth century, as a centuries-old empire that
engendered other kingdoms following successive conquests by
Ndahura and Wamara.[39] Though with other preoccupations, this
theory is also found in the traditions of the southern zone of the
Great Lakes countries, thus establishing a veritable genealogy of
kingdoms tied to the Bacwezi.

The Europeans who arrived in the second half of the nineteenth
century made this kingdom's decline — already in fact under way
(it had even lost the holy site in Mubende) — coincide with the
diffusion of the Hamitic scheme. The luminous and mythical
Bacwezi and the presence of white kaolin in some rituals dedicated to these "white spirits" (*embandwa zera*) were interpreted
through a racial lens: they were seen as manifestations of an ancient "Caucasoid" population in the region.[40] As we have seen, in
his 1863 book Speke the explorer set forth the hypothesis of an
ancient invasion by the Galla, the supposed ancestors of the Hima
pastoral groups.[41] The region's kingdoms thus were explained as a
function of Ethiopian influence. Speke believed that the traditions
relating to the Kitara kingdom, collected first in Karagwe and
then in Buganda, confirmed this theory. At the Bunyoro royal
court, Samuel Baker later obtained details on how this kingdom
had extended from Lake Albert to the Kagera until the eighteenth
century.[42] Kitara's past grandeur under the Bito dynasty was
therefore projected onto the fantastic empire founded by the

"Wawitu" (a deformation of Babito), taken for the Galla from "Omwita," the ancient name for Mombasa on the Indian Ocean coast. After assembling this etymological bricolage, Speke conjectured that they must be part of a remarkable "race...of the semi-Shem-Hamitic." In this context, the traditions left the door wide open for all kinds of fantasy: Rukidi's second nickname (White and Black) must have made him a mestizo; because the Banyoro nobles told Speke their ancestors came from the north, he concluded that "the Wahuma make themselves a small residue of the original European stock"![43]

However, until the end of the century, observers made a distinction between this hypothetical crypto-Galla or Hima state and the Cwezi culture of the region's black populations.[44] In his 1902 synthesis on Uganda, Johnston lent authority to the Galla-Hima-Cwezi equation. According to him, the legends of the Bacwezi — along with the "Kitwara empire," created by an "invasion of bands of Gala people" — illustrated "the heyday of Hamitic civilization" in this part of Africa. Decline would have coincided with the "negrification" of these leaders. However, Czekanowski and Gorju identified the recent Lwo origin of the Babito (quite distinct from the Bacwezi), thus disqualifying a fundamental element in Speke's hypothesis but not calling it into question. The then-current Gobineauian model was too seductive. Did not one believe that the queen of Sheba or the Phoenicians had created Zimbabwe? For Gorju, the Bacwezi remained "conquerors." For Fisher, who edited the corpus of myths, they were "evidently a migratory tribe that swept down from the north, and...taught the Banyoro to work the iron." All that was disputed was the date of this supposed immigration: before the Christian era according to Johnston, in the sixteenth century according to Gorju. The latter even offered a Portuguese hypothesis, inspired by Christopher de Gama's expedition to Ethiopia in 1541. According to Gorju, one must credit an "infiltration of whites" for waking up the "apathetic Bantu." Even thirty years later, Father Nicolet spread this theory among the Catholic teachers: the Bacwezi were of "Portugo-Abyssinian mixed blood [and had] descended from the Kaffa [sic] highlands."[45]

What is most surprising about all of this is the success of these Eurocentric theories among literate notables in the concerned countries. Seeing talk of empire as an opportunity to promote his small homeland of Bunyoro, Chief John Nyakatura rallied to the thesis of the "race of white people known to us as the Abachwezi": "It is probable," he wrote, "that they were not Europeans but they could have been Arabians, Abyssinians, or Egyptians [Abamisri] since they migrated into Kitara from the northern direction." He did not hesitate to describe Ndahura as a colonial proto-governor who developed cash crops such as coffee and cotton.[46] In the early twentieth century, the informants for the Cwezi tradition were principally Banyoro aristocrats, sometimes kings, even as their political domain was being restricted with Britain's benediction — to the benefit of the Baganda. Nyakatura was among the most outspoken activists for restitution of the "lost counties," which housed sites like Mubende and Buyaga, genuine places of memory in Cwezi tradition and in Bunyoro's major royal rituals. The ancient "Kitara empire" became fundamental in these demands and was invested with a political and civilizing mission for the entire Great Lakes region. Today, it continues to be the source of fantasy and irritation in Ugandan political circles.

What does archaeology have to say on this debate?[47] Administrator Eric Lanning and Pastor Mathew Gervase of Oxford University established the first archaeological sites in 1952 — first Bigo, then other sites south of the Katonga (Ntusi) and farther north near

Lake Albert (Kibengo and Munsa). These sites prompted enthusiastic comparisons between their large entrenchments and fortified mounds and the ruins in Rhodesia. The relative proximity of these "ruins" and the sacred woods of the Cwezi cult spawned claims of additional proof of the existence of an ancient pastoral empire, with cattle enclosures and watering places. The traditions recorded in Nkore and the comparison between this small kingdom's princely enclosures and Bigo's circumvallations caused some to see in this southern sector (Bwera in Nkore) traces of the "Wamara kingdom," which was in turn labeled a Hima proto-state. The northern sites posed more of a problem because the traditions recorded there evoked figures foreign to the Cwezi myth. The English historian Roland Oliver, whose role in the 1960s syntheses on Bantu Africa was seen earlier, here promoted the idea of a historical greater Kitara dating to the Cwezi period. As late as 1977 he wrote, "In purely archaeological terms, all these traits taken together do suggest a concentration of political power which perhaps encompassed ... several hundred thousand people, at a period ... between the late thirteenth and the late sixteenth century."[48]

More nuanced conclusions emerged from the research of Peter Shinnie and Merrick Posnansky in the late 1950s as well as the later work of Peter Robertshaw, Andrew Reid, and John Sutton, whose insights into the late Iron Age were seen above. Specifically, the link between the Hima population and this history was shown to be not so simple. As we saw earlier, authors wavered between viewing this pastoral group as the founders or the destroyers of Cwezi civilization.[49] In fact, pastoral activity preceded and followed the period to which these archaeological sites are testament. No tradition confirms the migrations in question, and we must look elsewhere to understand the relationship between cattle raising and agriculture in the ways kingdoms emerged. The archaeology of these Ugandan sites points to a period between the eleventh and the sixteenth century. The ruptures that mark the beginning and the end of this period can be better analyzed by looking at internal logics rather than at exogenous forces. This period is characterized by the central role of cattle keeping, combined with land clearings linked to cereal growing and iron metallurgy; it also saw increased production in various areas (grains, but also salt in Kasenyi and Kibiro, near Lakes George and Albert, pottery, iron, and so on); and it had a seemingly high population density. At the time, six or seven centuries ago, according to Sutton's formulation, "Kitara can perhaps be still imagined not as a single united kingdom but as a vaguer *system* of political organization and economic exploitation."[50]

Then came a global crisis, either of an ecological nature (soil erosion, excessive deforestation) or of a demographic and social nature. This crisis inaugurated heightened competition between cattle-keeping and agricultural interests, which in turn inspired searches for new lands but also new relationships. Since then, the intermediate plateau region, where the Bigo and Ntusi communities prospered, has never witnessed such activity or such human occupation. Political realignments probably accompanied this crisis, ones involving both religious and clan networks. As will be shown below, we can hypothesize a link between this global situation and the emergence, about five centuries ago, of a new generation of kingdoms — kingdoms with precisely this genealogical depth whose history can be traced into the twentieth century. Moreover, this form of structuring seems to have succeeded in the region's different geographic sectors, from Lake Victoria to Lake Kivu. More than seeing the explosion of an empire or new conquests, we are witnessing a contagious effervescence, a mushroom-like proliferation, of political poles. This effervescence depended on a culture of power that was at least partially sustained by lived experience on the western Ugandan plateaus.

The Cwezi world thus functioned as a quasi-initiatory model. Many kingdoms, in the south and the east, refer to it explicitly. The thematic analogies in myths collected from narrators who lived quite far apart are astonishing. The story of a future king disguised as a shepherd, who overheard the secrets of a neighboring potentate, is found in Burundi and Rwanda as well as Nkore, where Kyomya is supposed to have recovered Wamara's dynastic drum in this way.[51] That said, dynastic traditions, often modeled on the standard version of the Cwezi tradition, and popular accounts can diverge substantially. Each country mobilizes — in ways that must be deciphered — its own cultural and social resources, clan realities, and religious imagination. We will see, successively, the Ruhinda legend, which takes us from Nkore to Buzinza; the foundation myths for Buganda, Rwanda, and Burundi; and the particularities on the periphery (Busoga, Buha, Bushi, and Buhavu). These peripheral countries, mentioned only in passing so far, can be seen in this book's maps. We will delve into these issues now, though without exploring the full details of each corpus of traditions, which oral inquiries from the 1950s to the 1980s have considerably enriched.

The Ruhinda gest is apparently totally in keeping with the Bacwezi one, at least when referring to Nkore traditions.[52] In these stories, Ruhinda is the bastard son of Wamara and the servant Njunaki. He is supposed to have been born during the reign of an Nkore king named Katuku, a friend of his father's. He later seized power in this country with the help of a diviner, who made him hand over the Bagyendanwa dynastic drum and other regalia that Wamara had entrusted to the Basita clan.

The dynastic traditions of four or five kingdoms that appeared around the sixteenth century west of Lake Victoria treat Ruhinda as a single conqueror who came from Nkore, where he had bequeathed power to his son Nkuba (Lightning). Ruhinda is described simultaneously as shepherd, hunter, and warrior. In Karagwe, he eliminates King Nono through magic, and then seizes the royal Nyabatama drum. Elsewhere he imposes himself by guile and magic as much as by force:

> In Kyamutwara (between Karagwe and Lake Victoria), the official version claims that the founder was Bwogi, a son of Ruhinda, while a more popular version explains how King Kashare, from the Basita dynasty, lost power through a male descendant: his daughter had an illegitimate child with Ruhinda's son, and this son killed his maternal grandfather.

The same family intrigues can also be found in the Cwezi myth, notably an equivalent story about Ndahura and Bukuku.[53] But in Ihangiro and Buzinza, Bacwezi ancestors are totally absent: Ruhinda is described as a companion, even the son, of Kayango, a blacksmith who called him to power.

A synthetic model was imposed in all these countries: Ruhinda was at the beginning of the legitimate dynasties. According to this model, after various peregrinations (by land and lake), Ruhinda distributed the drums and founded the oldest capitals. When he died, his body was divided among Karagwe, Ihangiro, and Buzinza. In fact, the myth pertains to two main areas: the riparian regions at the elbow of the Kagera, Nkore, and Karagwe and the plateaus southwest of Lake Victoria, renowned for years for their iron production. This myth combines two clan configurations: the Bahinda and the Bayango, both united around the same totemic taboo, the *nkende* monkey. In each kingdom, Ruhinda and his relatives — in particular, his children or grandchildren, who most often appear as the true founders — occupy the origin period for some time. We have already seen this reduction of foundations in the Bacwezi case, and we will find it again in other origin stories: the syncretism in the myth corpora glosses over many ruptures and divisions as well as an unbridled quest for the oldest possible origins.

Ruhinda, then, became a regional symbol establishing the legitimacy of the Bahinda sovereigns. The diffusion of power linked to this name is undoubtedly quite ancient. Even other dynasties in one way or another placed Ruhinda in their origin stories: for example, in Kiziba (a small kingdom at the mouth of the Kagera), where the kings are of Bito heritage; in Gisaka (east of what is now Rwanda), whose former kings were from the Bagesera clan; and, still farther, in Bukerebe (a peninsula in southwestern Lake Victoria), where the founder came from Ihangiro in the seventeenth century.

Ruhinda was emphasized all the more in the eighteenth and nineteenth centuries when usurpers and secessionists violated his memory. Indeed, the region's traditions often were collected in the context of acute political frustration: Kyamutwara was divided in three; Buzinza was equally split; Karagwe had broken down; and Nkore was squeezed by Rwanda on one side and Buganda on the other. A similar situation in Bunyoro was noted above: forced to retreat in the face of the Ganda's expansion, Bunyoro's leaders skillfully seized on the Hamitic myth to impress the European masters. In Buhaya and Buzinza, local elites used the vision of a "Ruhinda empire" in the same way. In 1931, the British administration reported that missionary students knew more about Ruhinda than about the people of the countryside.[54] The diffusion of traditions by "literate elites" prompted dating the foundation of a fantastic "Bacwezi empire" — described as more vast than Kitara proper and encompassing the whole Great Lakes region — to Wamara and even to Isaza: Ruhinda would have been only an epigone.[55] His name was at the same time interpreted as the sign of a new southward Hima invasion. However, as we have seen, the chronological depth of human settlement and the multiplicity of pastoral movements undermine such a simplistic perspective. Moreover, the autochthons clearly distinguished between the Bahinda and the simple Bahima, notably when some tried to supplant the legitimate dynasties in the eighteenth century. As for the "Nilotic" theory, which made the Lwo not just the developers of Bunyoro's and Kiziba's Bito dynasties but also creators of Cwezi culture and the carriers of "Ruhinda's conquest," this stimulated ethno-historians to search more for strata of invasions than for local actors.[56]

A discussion of the Cwezi tradition's exact role can be found in Buganda, where the monarchy was split between two founding heroes, Kintu and Kimera.[57] The first, whose name primarily means "human being," is the subject of a story transcribed in Christian circles in the late nineteenth century:

> Kintu descended from the sky with all the elements of civilization (bananas, grains, cattle, poultry, iron, barkcloth, the holiday of the new moon, and so on). But his wife Nambi, daughter of Gulu, the sky king, returned to the sky to search for the millet she had forgotten. This prompted reprisal attacks on the couple by Walumbe, the brother-in-law, who rained death on the land. However, Kintu succeeded in destroying the power of the serpent Bemba, thanks to a trick by the tortoises, who were accomplices of our heroes. Leading the serpent to believe, based on their example, that a head can disappear and then reappear, the tortoises convinced the reptile to let itself be decapitated.

Here again, myth reflects universal preoccupations: death, marriage, and relations with in-laws. It also reflects the cultural and material foundations of an "eternal" Ganda culture. Kintu is placed at the head of a list of about twenty sovereigns and is therefore situated historically in about the thirteenth century. But right after him, the situation becomes confused:

> One of his descendants, Kalemera, hounded by a dignitary named Walusimbi, must leave for exile in Kitara's court. There, he seduces one of the king's spouses, and a potter secretly raises his child. When he grows up, this son, named Kimera, returns to his father's country. He marries Nakku, daughter of Walusimbi, who had welcomed him, and he founds a sanctuary for Kintu in Magonga, where the latter had disappeared.

This is a narrative framework with which we are familiar: that of the hidden child recognized as true king. In terms of the kingdom as such, Buganda begins with Kintu, but the dynasty starts with Kimera. Because some Nyoro traditions made him Rukidi's twin, several authors have proposed a Babito conquest of Buganda. But, besides problems with chronology, this hypothesis fits poorly with the independence Kimera embodies in backing up the worship of Kintu. Therefore, if the foreign origin were real, this person, by virtue of his belonging to the Locust clan, would have been related to a marginal group that came from the western part of the Cwezi territory. But the external origin of these two founders — the sky for Kintu, and Kitara for Kimera — instead affirms the superiority of kingship, at the *kabaka* level, over the powers of clans. In the nineteenth century, the sovereigns and their entourages gave a new "historical" twist to these "foreign" origins by taking up the Hamitic theme. Under the influence of Zanzibari Arabs, relayed by European missionaries, the Buganda court even claimed Kintu might be Ham himself, whose grave could be found in Magonga!

In fact, in Buganda, even more than in Bunyoro and Buhaya, kingship emerged through a compromise between a new authority, of a strongly religious nature, and a network of influential clans. Comparison of Bugandan traditions with those of other principalities, including Busoga, its eastern neighbor, confirms this process.[58] In Busoga, Kintu and Walumbe embodied the Lion and Lungfish clans, associated with Mount Elgon and Lake Victoria, respectively. Kintu's tomb would be in Buswikira in southern Busoga. In Buganda, one finds an accord riven with tension between the Lion and Leopard groups and the Genet group. Walusimbi, the Genet clan's eminent member, welcomed Kimera and gave him his daughter Nakku: this gesture was repeated ritually at the beginning of every reign. The enthronement ceremonies also assign roles to the clans of the Lungfish, the Colobus Monkey, the Pangolin, the Mushroom, and the Cercopith Monkey. As for the Lion and Leopard groups associated with Kintu, they were somehow out of the loop. As shown above, every new *kabaka* is proclaimed "father of the clan chiefs."

However, in the traditions, Kimera is presented as Kintu's heir, and he founds a lineage of sovereigns who become increasingly autonomous in relation to the clans. In linking all this to the Cwezi political experience, of which he was a carrier, Kimera attests to Buganda's independence. One has here moved from a proto-kingship coordinating a clan confederation to an increasingly monarchical form of kingship, if it could be called that. But since each *kabaka* belonged to his mother's clan, despite the society's patrilineal structure, the system reflected an initial compromise. By alternating queen mothers, different clans at least symbolically shared the exercise of supreme power.

Even if the structure of the monarchy is quite different in Rwanda, the symbolism in the origin stories conveys, through a dialectic between the exterior and the interior, a logic of compromise involving a complex of large clans. This kingdom also refers to two successive founders, Kigwa and Gihanga:[59]

> The first, born from a sterile woman and the heart of a sacrificial bull, falls from the sky with all the domesticated animals, cultivated plants, and professions (including blacksmithing). His lineage stems in part from incestuous unions, because also "descending" with him were a half brother and a half sister, and in part from an alliance with the lineage of the Kabeja king (from the Bazigaba clan), who welcomes them in Mubari (northeast of what is today Rwanda). The latter is later ousted, despite the diviners' warnings.
>
> Several generations later, this matrimonial alliance produces Gihanga, who is presented as both a blacksmith and a conqueror. Everywhere he goes, he marries local princesses. He appears simultaneously as the heir of the ancient principalities, as the precursor of greater Rwanda, and as the ancestor of nearly every dynasty in the region. One of his daughters discovers the use of cows. He dies in the north of the country after having divided his "empire" among his sons, each equipped with his own special drum.

We have to wait for seven generations in the list of Gihanga's successors, until about the fifteenth century, to find a true historical figure. The two original figures, whom contemporary ideology turned into symbols of a Tutsi conquest "coming from the north," are, to the contrary, associated with clan history. The stories pertain to nearly half of the Rwandan *amoko* described earlier. We have mentioned the modern dynasties of Rwanda (Banyiginya), Bugesera (Bahondogo), and Ndorwa (Bashambo) and those of the Rwandan queen mothers (notably the Bega, who have dominated this function since the eighteenth century). Also discussed have been the so-called found-on-earth clans, the Bazigaba, Bagesera, and Basinga, to which the ancient dynasties reigning over the northern and eastern third of what is contemporary Rwanda belonged.[60] Each of these three groups is represented among the leaders of the great royal rituals, called the *biru*, through the respective Batsobe, Bakono, and Basinga clans. In the "origin stories," nineteenth-century Rwandans (those who delivered these traditions) amalgamated the previous three centuries of their country's history. Clan alliances, religious powers, and warrior conquests all were integrated into a single narrative. Rwanda's expansion in the nineteenth century is described as if it were a timeless calling, akin to a Bayeux tapestry presenting William's conquest of England as a foretold and deserved event. The so-called ethnic dimension — a dimension that both Hutu and Tutsi political leaders have been quick to valorize since the 1950s — is marginal in these traditions. Ethnicity even seems an afterthought in the theme of Kigwa's Tutsi half brother, who appears as the ancestor of the queen-mother clans.

In Burundi, the traditions reveal still another political-cultural space.[61] The kingdom's founder was Ntare Rushatsi, literally Lion the Hirsute. The story begins in the south of the country:

> The child Cambarantama (Clothed in Sheepskin) is the bastard of a small king (Jabwe) and of the latter's sister-in-law (King Nsoro's wife). He is hidden in the court of a Buha king named Ruhinda, where he guards cattle. Diviners come from Burundi to reveal to him his true identity. He flees with them, and after arriving on the Nkoma massif, he sacrifices a bull and spreads its skin over a termite mound, but the skin resounds under the blows of a serpent who is trying to escape. This is the debut of Burundi's dynastic drum. Called Ntare from then on, the new sovereign makes his way up toward the crest, founding the kingdom's capitals as he goes.

This tale is the best-known tradition of origin across the country; over one hundred versions have been recorded. However, another cycle, for which around a dozen stories exist but only in the north, has benefited from almost official promotion since the 1930s. This version constitutes what one might call the Kanyaru cycle, because this time the events take place not in the southeast, as in the Nkoma cycle, but farther north, near the Rwandan border:

> Young Cambarantama is a shepherd and wood gatherer in the estate of the Rwandan magician-king Mashyira. But his aunt, the queen, helps him recognize his future. He crosses the Kanyaru and, arriving at the Nyamigango boulder, he kills a wildcat that controlled the region. The people proclaim this hirsute hunter their king.

In both cases, the new king brings rain and breaks the famine. But in the latter, he is attached to Rwandan traditions, not Buha ones. More precisely, he seems connected to the memory of Bugesera, a great ancient pastorally dominant kingdom that covered the southeast of contemporary Rwanda and the north-northeast of contemporary Burundi. Working closely with Prince Pierre Baranyanka, the main chief during Belgian rule, Bishop Julien Gorju backed this version.[62] In fact, he connected Burundi's historiography with that of Rwanda and thus situated it in the context of a "Hamitic" conquest from the north. Even if one admits that a first Ntare might have reigned in the country's north around the sixteenth century before a new, more southerly dynasty was founded a century later, these traditions have no evident relationship to the history of human settlement per se. Here as elsewhere, they establish the legitimacy of the Baganwa dynasty and of several allied clans responsible for managing the main religious sites, notably the Hutu clans of Bajiji and of Bashubi.

The countries near Burundi and Rwanda, to the south and west, have specific traditions, but these are set in their large neighbors' past. Along Burundi's eastern border, the Baha are divided into three distinct dynastic zones: the Bahumbi to the north and east, the Bakimbiri to the south, and the Bajiji (like Burundi's sacred domain of Nkoma) to the far south.[63] In the beginning of both Bahumbi and Bakimbiri, the brothers Nkanza and Kimenyi are said to have shared the country. But the names Ruhinda and Ntare also can be found in Bakimbiri's royal nomenclature. And both the name Mugasa (the water god) and the *nkende* prohibition (that of the Bahinda) can be found among the Bajiji on the banks of Lake Tanganyika and among the dwellers around Lake Victoria. In the same way, the small kingdom of Bushubi, threatened by Rwandan expansion, attributed its foundation sometimes to Karagwe and sometimes to Burundi. Though definitively part of Rwanda by the early nineteenth century, the ancient kingdom of Gisaka was also oriented toward Karagwe.

Names, rituals, beliefs, and symbols all circulated in this region, giving rise to different versions that apparently had a decisive impact on the political imagination four centuries ago. Analogous crossings of influence can be seen in what is today eastern Congo (the Kivu region).[64] The Bafuriro and the Bavira on the Rusizi plain, the Bashi southwest of Lake Kivu, and the Bahavu on the lake's western shores and on the large island Ijwi share origin stories with one another and with their Rwandan and Burundian neighbors. The western regions of these two countries were annexed late, and they have their own histories, ones oriented more to the west. In the Rwandan-speaking area, for example, the two small kingdoms of Busozo and Bukunzi, southwest of Lake Kivu, had historical ties with Burundi and Bushi.[65] Farther north, a swelter of political entities existed between Lakes Kivu and Edward on both sides of the Virungas: Bushiru, Cyingogo, and so on, in northwestern Rwanda, and Igara and Buhweju in contemporary southwestern Uganda.[66] Only recently has historiography made an effort to put the contemporary borders in perspective. Moreover, the politically divided populations near the great Congolese forest and the "monarchical" world in the lakes region share cultural ties, in terms of clan organization and religious conceptions.[67] Though these ties are often neglected, the origin stories of the different principalities on the western Rift intertwined. Bushi's two principal states — Ngweshe and Kabare, on the one hand, and Kaziba farther south, on the other — have distinct histories. In the past, Havu kingdoms, particularly the one on Ijwi, seem to have had more ties with the Barundi and the Bafuriro than with their Bashi neighbors. The diviner Lubambo, the maternal grandfather of Mwendanga, the founder of the eighteenth-century Basibula dynasty, has the same name as the spirit of a Burundian initiation cult, the guardian of diviners. Kabwika, father of the same Mwendanga, is evocative of the Bafuriro sovereigns who have the same name. But all the local dynasties claimed their origins lay farther west, near the Itombwe Mountains or near Lwindi, in contact with the Barega, Babembe, Banyindu, and Batembo traditions. Deciphering legends can be puzzling. But their main theme is clear: the kingdom came from somewhere else. Here as well, colonial literature is not shy about seeing evidence of an invasion from the Upper Nile area.[68] In particular, the Baluzi princely milieu (in Bushi) was likened to that of the Batutsi, and again the region's educated class quickly considered this racially rewritten history more legitimate than their ancestors' rustic traditions. In the latter, the kingdom comes not from Egypt but from the bush, the result of exploits, magic, and the generosity of hunter-heroes:

Accompanied by his hunting dog, Kangere, the distant ancestor, left in search of salt needed for an initiation ritual. Clothed in leopard skin and carrying a huge reserve of meat, he was hailed as king in Lwindi. His descendants acted in the same way in several directions, creating different kingdoms.

In another version, Kangere discovered two children in the forest, a girl and a boy, whose incestuous union later produced the dynasties' founders.[69] This theme of royal incest, which can be found in other legends from the region, is taken up in several rituals: in defining the crown prince by choosing his mother from among the sovereign's half sisters and nieces and in educating the future king in a secret place from where he will suddenly appear at the appropriate moment.[70]

The kingship's founder thus has the face not of a conqueror but of a clever, lucky, and initiated man who possesses the means and powers that allow him to unite several clan groups around him, notably those who later will occupy the *bajinji* (or *bagingi*) ritual functions. In his study of the Sibula dynasty on Ijwi, David Newbury noted in relation to the founder discussed above:

> What distinguished Mwendanga . . . was his success in breaking away from reliance on a single narrow kin group for political support. . . . Mwendanga was more successful, over time, in incorporating himself within a widening alliance pattern, and thus in widening the perceptions of political action. His status was essentially the product of his ties to — and ability to mobilize — people outside his own kin group.[71]

To the eyes of a society beholden to clan logic, it was this miracle that the above origin stories tried to make marvelously explicit. The stories' contents are probably not very "factual," but they matter in the way that they convey change. Indeed, it is now clear that the principal narrative motifs recur again and again:

the hidden child-king, the secret of his stolen destiny, and the intervention of diviners who use trickery to reveal the truth. The founder-hero comes from a "non-civilized" elsewhere, that is, from a rupture with the social and lineage order of his time. He is a shepherd, a hunter, a charcoal burner, someone familiar with forests, marshes, and grottoes, an unrefined bushman, one ready to kill his father, marry his sister, or inherit his mother (in a patrilineal society). In the Burundian case, he can be compared to the ogre in popular tales, whose environment and customs are identical to those of the founder-hero, but with one crucial difference: the ogre devours those who stray from their homes, whereas the king protects them and brings them into his service.[72] As we saw in each case, even though kingship is tightly connected to clan constellations, it is at odds with the clan order. Kingship expands the order.

To succeed in this political revolution, a strong mental support was necessary, one that could only have been religious. As the Bito and Hinda traditional states and Buganda show, the Cwezi model undoubtedly represented as much a religious idea as a political one. But this is not the only example of this kind: in the west, Burundi, Rwanda, and Kivu country also were witness to these events, a point to which I will return. In other words, change came not from conquests but from internal ruptures on a regional scale. If displacements occurred, they probably involved small, if not marginal, groups and at least some adventurers who were later absorbed. But, as with the "Bantu" cultural model seen earlier, the displacement was at the level of waves of influence, of new models of social management, and even of inspired propaganda. The legends' beautiful images poorly conceal crises and breaks that surely lasted longer and were more frequent than the foundation scenarios suggest. The human and material environments that might have provoked or rendered indispensable these changes will be returned to later. But the relationship between cattle keeping and agriculture and between the corresponding social categories does not appear to constitute the critical, and certainly not the sole, stakes of these crises. The origin stories are particularly quiet on these subjects — which today are the object of obsessive interest — so much so that a single legend can be interpreted in totally contradictory ways, as the case of the myth of the two brothers, ancestors of the Balisa dynasty in Buhweju, shows.

Royal Rituals

The political culture of the royal innovation shows through in the origin stories. But this culture also was maintained and reproduced in the monarchy's major rituals: funerals, enthronements, and other ceremonies. Rituals in different countries are broadly similar in words and gestures.

The death of the king is the occasion for assessing the nature of his person: sacrifices, body-preservation practices, the management of dynastic cemeteries and of funerary functions, and commemorations — everything refers to this.[74] It is blasphemous to speak of the king's death: the deceased "drank the mead" (the drink that poisoned him when his time had come); "milk was spilled"; more positively, "he ceded" the drum; or "he left to fight" for his country. His remains are coated in butter (sometimes milk or blood) and in the fat of sacrificed animals (a bull, a ram, and so on), then they are cured in a low fire, sometimes placed on a shelf, sometimes in a wooden trough (a divining instrument, besides its use for brewing banana cider or for dispensing salt to cattle). The body is generally enveloped in a bull's skin of a chosen color. In Bunyoro and Buganda, the jaw is removed and deposited in a different place. The last residential palace of the deceased is often destroyed.

The specialists in these funerary tasks belonged to specific lineages. They collected the deceased's insignia, jewelry, and amulets, and then they attended to the curing either at the court or on their own land, to which the cadaver was solemnly transported (this is the case in Burundi, for example). Located in sacred woods where an annual worship was conducted, dynastic necropolises were often in peripheral regions, as if to guard a contested border or memorialize an ancient site of power: on the forest's edge in northwestern Burundi and in Buganza (near Lake Muhazi); in the eastern part of Rwanda; near the Rwandan border in Bushi; in Kitara for the first Babito kings of Kiziba; in various sacred woods in southern Buha; in a cave in northern Buha. These domains were autonomous and inaccessible to the royal family, by virtue of the double connotation — venerable and fearful — of sacred. In these places, the dead king's body pursued its destiny in a festive atmosphere. In Burundi, where this special place has been baptized the "site of triumph" (*inganzo*), four branches of the same Bajiji major lineage share in the management of the four dynastic names (Ntare, Mwezi, Mutaga, and Mwambutsa). They play the role of the kings in the beyond, or they become permanent incarnations of the *mwami*'s four figures. The king's spirit survives in a strange way: it escapes through the hole that the first worm makes in the cadaver, then is fed in a pot of milk or honey, and finally transforms itself into a lion, a leopard, or a python.

The rest of the country mourns his "departure" for several months. The chaos created by his disappearance is staged: agricultural activities as well as arts and crafts (especially those requiring iron tools) are completely halted, and sexual relations among humans and among cattle are interdicted. The successor's enthronement marks a "return to normal." Offerings are then regularly brought to the necropolis. Sometimes the remains, watched over in a special hut, are moved after a given period: for example, after four reigns for kings with the names of Mutara and

Cyirima in Rwanda, where the code of royal rituals is particularly sophisticated.

Enthronement was designed to ensure a return to normal by symbolically transmitting specific royal powers to the prince who is chosen heir, according to precise rules, from among the king's sons.[75] This choice is made jointly by the family and religious dignitaries from certain clans. In Burundi and Bushi, it is said that the prince was born with grains (from sorghum, eleusine, or squash) in his hand. The queen mother, whose role at least symbolically endured, belonged to a specific lineage: for example, Tutsi lineages from one of the three "matridynastic" clans in Rwanda. In Buganda, nearly every major clan had its turn insofar as the new *kabaka* belonged to his mother's clan. In Kaziba, the queen mother, among the last to be married, had to be a daughter of the king of Burhinyi (a small neighboring state). In principle, the heir had to be raised outside the court without seeing his father. After the king dies, the enthroners (parents, diviners, and ritualists) bring the heir to a waiting place. The heir plays an important role by lifting the mourning period and then immediately expressing the social and religious dimensions of his power. In Burundi, a procession of priests and princes accompanies the future *mwami* across two rivers near their confluence in the center of the country. A German officer who attended the accession of young Mwambutsa in December 1915 described this scene:

> He was followed by small cattle herds, which were escorted by a number of Watutsi; these cattle were delegations from every herd that the king had given by fief. There were people carrying hives, caged bees, people with bananas, with all sorts of fruits of the earth, with milk pots, and with hoes and spears. Everyone had a white mark on his forehead and nose, a festival symbol of this joyous day. Cattle

owners and important shepherds were adorned in paint of a yellow-ocher color. The Muhutu who carried the young king clasped two sacred spears that had been passed from king to king for generations. The style of these spears is no longer in use: a short staff, a thin blade with a protruding band, and a very sharp point. They were painted white on all sides.[76]

Enthronements are fundamentally initiatory and are marked by a series of rites: a river crossing, a sacred bath, or the digging of a new spring; sacrifices, including human ones; tree plantings (of ficus, erythrinas, and such); expulsion of a scapegoat; a ritual hunt for a specific animal, usually an antelope or hare, using a dog; a session on a termite mound (as, for example, in Buhaya); the installation of a throne or the erection of a new palace; the inscription of a royal name into a list; the presentation of the dynastic drum, which has been rubbed in butter or blood and which the new sovereign touches, lifts up, or beats as a sign of his taking possession of the country; his marriage to a first wife after having been treated like a child at the beginning of the ritual; and the presentation of various regalia. Among the latter one finds iron or copper spears, copper bracelets, iron tools (a pruning knife, a knife, a hatchet, a hammer, and so on), leopard or lion skins, as well as bull or ram skins, fabric made from ficus bark, sacred diadems (like a genet-skin *ishungwe* decorated with cowries in Bushi or a bead diadem in Nkore).[77] These objects bore history: they said something about metallurgy, but also about long-distance trade. Equally, royal treasures became richer with time: for example, glass beads, that came from central Europe via a series of intermediaries only date here to the eighteenth century.

The ceremonies are organized as a journey from one sacred site to another, and each is led by a particular dignitary of the sacred. During these journeys, the royal person, at first treated delicately like a child, visibly becomes an adult and a master of the situation. "The kingship captures the king," to take up a famous phrase.[78] He appears not as a god or as a priest, according to James Frazer's "Golden Bough" model, but as an intermediary slowly infused with the force that lived in his father — a force that is managed by the ritualists and clans endowed with these responsibilities. He is a kind of medium that guarantees the return to normalcy, that is, production, harvests, cows who calve, and newborn babies. He becomes "father" of the country. This passage from fragility to strength is accompanied by popular joy, which is expressed in song and especially in the exuberance of the dancer-drummers.[79] The drum merits some commentary.[80] The folklore surrounding this instrument since colonialism has obscured its symbolic richness. The drum resembles a large mortar on which a cow's skin has been stretched; the names of its parts conjure up birth and fecundity; it is played in alternating rhythms that convey dicta, and its name, *ingoma*, signifies kingdom. Only the king and his religious dignitaries can make it "speak." In other contexts, beating the drum signaled rebellion. Enthronement therefore puts into play a dialectic whereby the kingmakers — the priests and clan dignitaries — are stripped of their power by the one to whom they have just given the dynastic drum. In Burundi, the main initiates of the Kiranga cult accompany the king to the river, and then he proceeds without them. In Kiziba, he removes a diviner's headgear and proclaims dominance henceforth over this profession. In Buhaya, as told by a missionary, the new *mukama*, perched on a termite mound, swears to the power to kill even his father, his uncle, and his blood brother if they are found guilty of a crime, thus indicating a break with an order based entirely on lineage.[81]

In fact, the king enters into a contract with his country: prohibitions are imposed on his everyday life, and in return the population must give him absolute respect. In this way, political loyalty, religious prescriptions, and taboos are linked. His decisions must be obeyed, but one must not look him in the eye. Before a crowd gathered from all around the country, the king makes a proclamation, which serves to recall this non-written constitution. All sorts of objects and commodities (cultivated plants, hoes, cattle) are handed over to the sovereign. He in turn contacts specialists in these types of production so as to demonstrate that he is the king of all and that he protects all activities, including hunting, agriculture, cattle raising, blacksmithing, and pottery. In Nkore, the new *mugabe* gives a hoe to an agriculturist and a thong (one that ties the cow's legs during milking) to a cattle keeper. In Rwanda, on this same day, the new *mwami* participates in blacksmithing, churning, and sowing, before simulating a tribunal and even a war. In some cases, the new king tours his country, to "be seen" there, as one says in Bushi, and feasts in his honor are organized in the villages, as in Ihangiro. In these rites, political geography combines with a geography of the sacred and a taking control of territory.

More than the funerary ceremonies, which are really an amplification of family mourning, the enthronement ceremonies reflect the history of each dynasty. They reproduce founding episodes and are embellished with episodes from the regime's evolution. In Nkore, the master of ceremonies belongs to the Bayangwe subclan, an equivalent of the Bayango, whose totemic tie with the Bahinda in Buhaya was seen above. At one moment, this man takes the king's bow, and then, in his name, shoots it in different directions, as if to return to the Hinda sovereign a country that his people had controlled long ago. In Kiziba, a messenger leaves in search of new fire on the Sese Islands, another searches for sorghum and salt in Nkore, and a third chooses the site of the first palace. Each action symbolizes the new horizons of this small state, which is situated at the junction of Cwezi territory and the world of Lake Victoria. Each kingdom, as we have seen, is embodied by a principal drum: Rusama in Bunyoro, Timba in Buganda, Nyabatama in Karagwe, Bagyendanwa in Nkore, Kalinga in Rwanda, Karyenda in Burundi, Rugabo and Buhabugari in Buha, and so on. But if one lists the regalia, including the secondary drums, the sacred spears, and the royal bulls, one discovers identical names from one country to the next, reflecting the common culture and crossings of influences underlined above. For example, a copper spear in Buha and a drum in Rwanda are called Kalinga; similarly, the Bushubi drum is called Muhabura, as is the sacred bull that always accompanies Burundi's king.

The most interesting interaction is that between the monarch and the ritualists who represent influential clans. In Buganda, liturgical evolution is particularly revealing from this standpoint.[82] After five months of mourning, the new *kabaka* participates in a ritual gazelle hunt. Then he is installed on a throne covered in lion and leopard skins; reclothed in ficus fabric; and given two spears, a shield, a pearl bracelet, a copper bracelet, and two drums, one inherited from Kintu and the other from Kimera. Nearly every sacred object was attributed to Kimera and given by dignitaries from specific clans. But the latter still had to "confirm" the new king, called Sebataka, the father of the clans. This ritual therefore underlined the character of the *primus inter pares* in which the sovereign becomes enmeshed. However, the ceremonies stopped in the eighteenth century, under Namugala's reign. An initial ritual was added, one that invoked Kintu, the hero who came from the sky and the vanquisher of the serpent Bemba (the clan compromise that he had undoubtedly embodied is thus forgotten). This rite takes place on a hill in Naggalabi called "the house of the Buganda," which is managed by members of the Lungfish and Pangolin clans. From this point on, the *kabaka* was Buganda's master

127

before being confirmed by the clan, thereby denoting the extension of monarchical power into the rites themselves. This site, with its large trees and termite mound, came into use again in 1993, when the monarchy was restored.

A third type of major ritual governed life in each country. Held monthly or annually, these rituals staged heavenly time and that of the earth under the kingship's control. In the northern and eastern kingdoms (Bunyoro, Buganda, Nkore, Karagwe, and the Haya states), the new moon is marked by festivities primarily dedicated to the drums, under the dual responsibility of the king and the drums' guardians. The radical -ezi designating the moon strongly suggests a tie with the Bacwezi spirits, whose priests also take part in the rituals.

The area farther to the west — Rwanda, Burundi, Buha, Bushi, and Buhavu — is distinguished by large annual agrarian rituals associated with sowing and harvesting sorghum and eleusine, the region's two age-old African crops. The best studied is *muganuro* in Burundi, celebrated around December (until 1929) in the four major royal "capitals."[83] The *mwami* consumes a sorghum dough, whose flour (called *isugi*, "the pure") comes from a special field. The flour was cultivated in the Nkoma massif by a ritualist called Ntare — the name of the founder-king who supposedly sprang from this region of the country. Other lineages that specialize in the kingship's "secrets" are based in their own southern and central domains. During *muganuro*, they furnished various products (cereals, bananas, mead, salt, and so on) and replaced the drums destined to be struck at the court. These "drumming" lineages thus were both makers and beaters. The holiday itself unfolded in several phases: once the king "ate the year" — that is, once he consumed the first fruits of a harvest from six months earlier, in order to bring good fortune and to authorize seeding for the following year — he was united with the "vestal" of the dynastic drum, Muka Karyenda; then a cult was rendered to Kiranga's spirit; a ritual hunt was organized in a special marsh; and hoes and cattle were distributed. This preliterate national holiday each year reactivated the *mwami*'s strength in the presence of delegations from every region. It demonstrated the support of a network of ritualists, whose sacred woods formed the country's borders and who notably belonged to the major Bajiji and Bashubi Hutu clans. It also quite probably was designed to make the sidereal calendar, that of the seasons and harvests, coincide with the lunar calendar, allowing diviners to choose a date to account for a delay in the lunar month roughly every three years (by adding a thirteenth month called "the black").

Rwanda's *muganura* was organized around a sorghum harvest carried out around April in a ritual field in the north, in Bumbogo, and was led by ritualists from the Batsobe clan.[84] The *muganuro* of the Buhavu from Ijwi Island and the *ndolegwa ya mpeshi* of Buha were celebrated on the standard date of the sorghum harvests. By contrast, Kaziba's *mubande* and the central Bushi's *mubandampundu* coincided, as in Burundi, with sorghum plantings, but at the beginning of the rainy season around September, not in December.[85] Moreover, in this Kivu area, the king consumed a brew, made from plant and soil, called *mubande*. Everywhere drums and regalia were involved, cattle were slaughtered, and eleusine was combined with sorghum. On Ijwi, fish also had a part in the ritual.

Both mystical and popular, these holidays were rooted in old lineages. In Burundi, for example, an ancient holiday was held for the first fruits of eleusine. This was called "eat the year" and was celebrated with one's family in April. It was once described to me as "the year of the Bahutu and the Batutsi," in other words, ordinary folk, whereas *muganuro* symbolized "the year of the king" and focused on a late date and thus was best suited for sorghum plantings.[86] West of Lake Kivu, the term *mubande*, which refers to a mixture consumed in these ceremonies, also was applied to a sacred rock relating to old lineage circumcision rituals that took place among the forest Banyanga, for example.[87] Accompanying the human practices, these agrarian rituals clearly made the king a medium between nature and culture, a mediator between the drum of monarchical power and the authority of a set of ritualist clans (*biru* in Rwanda, *banyamabanga* in Burundi, *bajinji* in Bushi, *bagingi* in Buhavu, and so on) who managed the rites, and a mediator of predynastic logics. At the heart of each festival is a dialectic between the country's unity, which is forged by royal symbolism, and the country's clan, socioeconomic, and ecological diversity. The rites even embodied the spirit of kingship to which the population adhered.

Kingship in the Shadow of Religion

In European languages, we entitle a person "king," *roi*, *König*, and so on, on the basis of historical experience that involved King David, the Greek *basileus*, the Latin *rex*, and the Capetian "miracle-working" king. In the Great Lakes region, this same figure has its own names. Four terms predominate: *kabaka* in Buganda; *mukama*, literally "the milker," in the Nyoro-Haya linguistic area; *mugabe*, meaning both gift and command, in Nkore and Buzinza; and *mwami*, which suggests fructification and fertility even if the etymology is not known for certain, in the western cluster (Rwanda, Burundi, Buha, Bushi, and Buhavu). The king's body itself is imbued with a triple vocation: of natural strength, cultural capability, and power. The body is named through stylistic devices: in Burundi, his feet are called "hammers"; his belly is called a "churn"; and he himself is a "life-source amulet" (*biheko bizima*), an expression that also applies to Kiranga's spirit. His daily life, as well as the lives of those related to him, including parents and palatines, is regulated by gestural, food, and sexual prohibitions. He must abstain from eating sweet potatoes, he must drink milk only from cows that never had a calf die, he must only eat the meat of young bulls, and he must spit in a horn specifically earmarked for that function. His cooks and milkers must abstain from sexual relations. After the king's death, as we have seen, his body is split into one spirit that is embodied in an animal and will reinhabit his successor, and another spirit that is embodied in a mask that his reigning name represents in the dynastic list, which continues to live with protection from the dynasty's ritualists.[88]

A royal court is a true sanctuary where particular drum beatings govern everyday life. In addition to the dignitaries responsible for domestic tasks requiring trust (with the same rough ambiguities of a Merovingian court), there are agents of the supernatural who have daily functions or have functions linked to the major rituals discussed above. Let's take the example of the Burundi court on the eve of the colonial conquest. This court was under Mwami Mwezi Gisabo's rule and has been extensively studied by the historian Emile Mworoha, whose grandmother was a lady-in-waiting.[89] Two vestals lived nearby, that of the Karyenda drum and that of Kiranga, the latter of which was chosen from the Bashubi clan. Other women had other functions of this kind: Nyenumugamba replaced the queen mother when the latter died; Mutwenzi (Dawn) held the post of ritual sister; Inabamataramuka watched over rain and storms; and Inamukomacoto watched over the sacred fire. Another vestal, Jururyikagongo, guarded a python called Bihiribigonzi (Of a Thousand Coils) on a nearby hill. Other sacred animals were allotted to the court: the Semasaka (Father of Sorghum) bulls were connected to a dynastic drum; the Muhabura (Guide) bulls were connected to the king himself; a ram and a billy goat (each of these males with his herd of cows, sheep, or goats); and a dog confined to a repulsive woman called Mujawibwami (Servant of the Royal Court). Renewed with each reign, a drum accompanied the *mwami* everywhere he went: called Rukinzo (Shield), it was managed by a clan (the Basengo), which also furnished the appointed jester. All these were considered lucky charms (*ibimazi*), which were chosen according to their clan origins (for the humans) and colors (for the animals).[90] But one would be wrong to see them only as magic toys.

In fact, the royal institution was everywhere embedded in a network that controlled the supernatural, managed from generation to generation by clans whose history went back to an immemorial past and whose involvement appeared fundamental. The court, itself mobile, was situated in an enlarged sacred space, whose boundaries were groves attributed to various founder-heroes and to cults based on these figures. In Burundi, it consisted of the necropolis region and of Ntare Rushatsi's itinerary, which is replayed, as we saw earlier, at each *muganuro*.[91] Elsewhere, memory is attached to Gihanga, to Ruhinda, or to the Bacwezi, whose large shrines we cited above. The kings of the earth echoed the kings of the beyond, whether they were ancestors of a dynasty or spirits from the initiatory cults, themselves credited with fantastic empires.

This leads us, in conclusion, to focus on the close but delicate relations between kingship and the religious. Religion in the region does not consist of the vague belief in an omnipresent but impersonal supreme divine principle (Katonda in Buganda, Ruhanga in Bunyoro, Imana in Rwanda and Burundi, and so on), even if the missionaries and their flocks wanted to see it as an equivalent of Yahweh.[92] Nor does it consist in worshiping ancestors, whose spirits (*imizimu*) are more feared than venerated. It consists even less of the activity of diviner-healers (*abapfumu*), a profession in its own right, which is inherited along with specific techniques. The latter include divination practices through, for example, augury of bull or chicken intestines, knowledge of plants, and "rainmaking." Rather, religion is more about the initiation cult devoted to the Cwezi spirits, notably Wamara, from Bunyoro to Buzinza; or, by extension, to Ryangombe or Kiranga (a hero whose spirit survived after he was killed by a buffalo or an antelope during a hunt) in Rwanda, Burundi, and Bushi; or even to Buganda's *lubale*. In other words, one is referring to the religion of the *kubandwa*, one of the essential cultural characteristics of the entire region.

All start with a mystical revelation: some believers might be possessed by one of these spirits and become capable of presiding over adoration ceremonies (with chants, dances, and drinks) dedicated to handling the anxieties of people facing illness, the death of a loved one, sterility, the birth of twins, or lightning or the obsessive fear of the sorcery that accompanies these misfortunes. Certain symptoms (illness in the digestive system, skin ailments, mental disorders) were thought to require recourse to the *kubandwa*. These threats were experienced as coming from ancestors, who are not comforting figures in this region of Africa — in fact, quite to the contrary. The cult sites are marked by sacred groves (composed, among other things, of ficus and erythrinas), supplemented by bunches of grass and sometimes votive huts. Members of the neighborhood gathered there, men and women, of all clans and all categories (Hutu and Tutsi, and so on). This religion also was a factor in social integration, an answer to kinship divisions, through neighborhood solidarity. Its extensive diffusion on the hills was observed primarily in the western part of the region. In Buganda, Bunyoro, and Buhaya, this form of worship was more concentrated around shrines, which were the destination of pilgrimages. But in Rwanda and Burundi, one also finds major initiates, called *bishegu*, who played the role of mediums.[93]

The affinities between kingship and the *kubandwa* go beyond syncretism in the origin stories that mix up gods and kings. In Burundi, Kiranga is described as a "brother" of the king. Moreover, Kiranga is the only one who cannot be initiated. The cult itself is present in every major monarchical ritual, as will be shown below. Some insignia (leopard skins, cowrie diadems, and even drums in Buhaya country and in Bunyoro) and vocabularies assimilate royal authority and that of the *embandwa* priests: in Nkore, *kagondo* designates a royal funerary site and a Cwezi shrine; among the Bahaya, *kutendekwa* means both to be enthroned and to be initiated; in Burundi, *kuvumera* is applied to the king's speech, the sound of drums, and the muttering of the Kiranga initiates; in Buha, the spirits called *biyaga* or *bicwezi* in the cult of Kiranga are applied to the name of the *mwami* and control the drums, which are based in sacred places.[94] Esoteric language common to these two forms of the sacred feeds on terms that circulate from one country to another. The terms shift slightly in meaning, but with a clear cultural affinity.

Interpretations vary between two extreme positions: religion as instrumentalization by the powers that be, or religion as the ultimate site of contestation, reflecting the oppressed's aspirations and the former elites' nostalgia.[95] In fact, as we will see, the relations between these religious beliefs and the monarchy varied infinitely, from a total stranglehold, with the court responsible for ordaining priests (as in the cult of Kiranga in Burundi or that of Ryangombe in Rwanda since the eighteenth century), to the most uncontrollable effervescence, notably in periods of crisis and revolt. But opposing the terms "kingship" and "initiatory cult" in this way is simplistic: royal authority itself is a product of mysticism and revelation, and the cult, even in its more anarchic forms, can create new powers, as happened a century ago with the Nyabingi movement on the Rwanda-Uganda border.[96] In fact, a permanent tension existed between the monarchy as governmental order and the religious ideology in which it was immersed; indeed, excesses of power were condemned and opposition was born in the name of origin myths and cult enthusiasm. I have often emphasized this, and even the works most taken by the "contest" interpretation have remarked on this knot of contradictions. Was not Dionysus both wild exuberance and the inspiration for catharsis at the heart of the Greek city?[97]

A combination of obsessive fear and strategy has governed relations between kings and the major initiates or priests of the Cwezi-Mbandwa religion; this has punctuated the known political history since at least the eighteenth century. The Bunyoro and Nkore kings increasingly depended on the Bacwezi; indeed, they closely tied the Bacwezi to the memory of their ancestors, and they venerated, at least from afar, these heroes' shrines (for example, that of the great Ndahura priestess in Mubende). But among the Bahaya or the Bazinza, one sees a contradiction in the sovereigns' preference for their supposed Ruhinda grandparent over one related to Wamara's spirit, which they believed was subversive. In reference to Wamara's shrines, they emphasized the secondary status of the unrefined bastard who appeared at the beginning of these dynasties. This led some *bakama*, in Kyamutwara, for example, to valorize some of their ancestors but also to pit the cult of Mugasha against that of Wamara. In 1879, the White Fathers described Mutesa, the *kabaka* of Buganda, as trembling before the medium of the Mukasa *lubale*, which supposedly had made him ill and had ordered a three-month blockade of the lake. The king finished by soothing him and welcoming him to his court. Especially in Buganda, the Christianized elites' political calculations prompted them to retain a "secularized" vision of royal power, which for many years eclipsed the religious dimension of this institution.[98]

135

In the entire region, from the shores of Lake Albert to the area around the Malagarasi valley (in contemporary Tanzania), this dimension is vividly present in the Cwezi imagination, a veritable unwritten Genesis of the plateau kingdoms. But Victoria's lacustrine horizon, that of Kintu and the Sese Island shrines and those of Buvuma, has kept its originality. And on the western mountains, around Lakes Kivu and Tanganyika, how can one not wonder about the relationship between the institution of the *mwami* and the nearby cults of the Congolese forest bearing the same name — the *bwami* of the Balega and the Babembe?[99] In these so-called segmentary societies, initiation societies with this name offered a space of arbitration, authority, and solidarity that was situated above the lineages. In fact, one finds there the same dialectic of association and marginalization among the clans as one finds in the emergence of kingship. The *bwami* vocabulary has other analogies with vocabularies in the small western kingdoms around Lake Kivu and the Rusizi valley. For example, one finds there the *ishungwe* insignia, but in this case it is made with iguana skin, leopard teeth, and copper. We saw the same shifts in the case of the *mubande* circumcision ritual, which is also performed in the agrarian festival of kingship among the Bashi and Bahavu.

In fact, the move from clan networks to centralized powers — the shift that produced the monarchies — was not made in a day, nor did it happen in one fell swoop. Rather, the common point is the intimate relationship between a religious type of support and political submission. The logic of kingship is identical with that of initiation. That is why kingship was fast in competition with religion: the terrestrial medium up against the mediums of the beyond. Among the Ijwi Bahavu, the *bagingi* ritualists in a sense have a "social power ... greater than that of the king," because, as David Newbury puts it, "as a corporation they represent kingship in its abstract formal essence."[100] The clan strategies played themselves out in this rift; indeed, in the nineteenth century, the relative marginalization of clans was much like that of priests. It is possible now to analyze the history of the last three to four centuries, whose scope and stakes have been set out.

CHAPTER THREE

The Formation of Monarchical States

The dynastic lists to which we have access, along with supporting genealogical tables, claim to bring us back to at least the fifteenth century.[1] But political hypotheses only become reliable around the seventeenth century, and factual precision is not achieved before the eighteenth century. Such is the constraint of oral sources — one we must know how to recognize. Before the first-person written accounts by foreigners in the nineteenth century, the only available dates that we know in absolute terms are two solar eclipses. These eclipses occurred in 1520 and 1796, and in the traditions of several countries they are referred to in relation to political-military events.[2] The first is supposed to have coincided with the battle of Biharwe (in Nkore) between Ntare Nyabugaro, king of Nkore, and Olimi Rwitamahanga, king of Bunyoro, and was contemporaneous with other specific events in Buganda and Rwanda. The second would be the eclipse mentioned in relation to Mwami Mibambwe Sentabyo's enthronement in Rwanda and contemporaneous with the beginning of Ntare Rugamba's reign in Burundi.

In fact, choosing the right eclipse date is not obvious, because this phenomenon has happened several times over the last four centuries. The one seen at the end of the afternoon on December

22, 1889, left vivid and precise memories and is backed up by astronomical data. But the conditions of the older ones (season, time of day) left no traces in the stories. Among different possibilities, genealogy-derived approximate chronologies provide the best information. On this subject, contemporary authors rely on a European tradition: that of Greek logographs of the fifth century B.C. that had developed a computing method founded on "a generational average." This notion is extended in the works of the genealogist Otto Forst de Battaglia, who, based on European dynasties, proposed the figure of thirty-three years per generation. Alexis Kagame applied this statistic to Rwanda. Comparative studies on the region's dynasties converge on a figure of twenty-seven to twenty-nine years. The problem is complicated by the uncertainty of dynastic lists, which were contradictory when first transcribed, before certain variants — the longest — became official. But these lists often only give names without providing other factual data that would allow a richer picture of different reigns to emerge. From this point of view, Buganda, since Apolo Kagwa's writings in the early twentieth century, and Rwanda, since Kagame's in the 1950s, have become standard references, considering their subregional strength. In his Kinyarwanda-language work *Inganji Kalinga* (Triumphant Kalinga [the dynastic drum]), Kagame fully endorsed the official genealogy called *Ubucurabwenge* (The source of wisdom).[3] Between this chronicler and the Belgian historian Jan Vansina, the chronological differences for the most remote reigns diverge by a century.

Moreover, the royal appellations periodically recur, and they were not numbered in the traditions (before they were written). Though personal names were used, their attestation is fragile: this facilitates confusion and even manipulation. In eastern Burundi, for example, "Ntare the ancient," founder of the kingdom, is often confused with Ntare Rugamba, who conquered the region in the nineteenth century. A last point might be noted: a dynastic list is not a genealogy, because the sovereign's heir is generally a son whose age depends on that of the most influential queen mother at the time of her husband's death. The heir might also be a brother or a nephew, or a usurper. Some kings die young, others live a long time. All these difficulties have been underlined in recent studies. In an article, I ventured to calculate the date of the emergence of the Burundian kingship's founder, Ntare Rushatsi, which one narrative associates with a solar eclipse that — insofar as it is not an imaginary natural catastrophe, so common to origin stories — could have been the eclipse of 1680 or 1701.[4]

Breaks between eras are difficult to establish. However, two transitions might be distilled. First, a move from a "clan" situation to "kingdoms"; the shift is progressive, has different speeds in different areas, and defies dating. But then, what the traditions call "king," for example in the sixteenth century, did that word designate the same authority as it did in the nineteenth century? The logic of these traditions, as I noted in the introduction, is that of loyal continuity with the past, even if this past is reorganized. In fact, the idea that the institution suddenly sprang up one fine morning is the result of a totally anachronistic illusion. Historical analysis is preoccupied with finding fault lines and changes. From this point of view, a second transition must be made clear, that which brought a kingship founded on compromises, linked to networks, and wrapped up with beliefs and prohibitions to a true monarchical state, one more or less evoking political formations of ancient, medieval, or modern Europe. In fact, this moment was spread over the eighteenth and nineteenth centuries. It will be the main subject of this chapter.

The Control of Space: Ecology and Power in the Eighteenth and Nineteenth Centuries

For the most remote periods, one might trace the major lines of a regional geopolitics, given the landscapes, ecology, and farming methods described above. Until the eighteenth century, political dynamism took place on the intermediary plateaus, from Lake Albert to the Katonga, Kagera, and Malagarasi valleys. These relatively dry regions are characterized by pastoralism, cereal growing (eleusine and sorghum), and their resources in iron and salt. Relatively homogeneous linguistically, these regions are also the privileged horizon of Cwezi political-religious culture.

On several occasions, I have mentioned the ecological crises that seem to have destabilized this area, already made fragile by moderate rainfall levels. These crises and their effects are evidenced through archaeology, in its interpretations of the disappearance of Cwezi culture, and through the origin stories. This atmosphere of an economic and demographic dead end and human calamity (drought, famines) seems to mark the turn of the sixteenth century, often identified as the *terminus a quo* of the kingdoms' history. This situation calls to mind the Sumerian expression "After the deluge came, kingship descended from the sky." In the traditions, this climate of catastrophe increases until the eighteenth century. It also weighs heavily on the region's settlement and political organization. J.B. Webster's hypotheses based on Roda Nilometer marks and the traditions, which speak of immense brush fires and famines, support the idea of a long period of disturbances between the seventeenth and the eighteenth century.[5] Droughts seem to have occurred in the early seventeenth century (around the 1620s) and in the decades 1720–1730, 1750–1760, and 1780–1790. Not until the 1890s did the region experience another calamitous period.

In the face of the incapacity of the oldest form of organization, the so-called clan, the emerging kingships were left with the task of managing the situation and with responding to the ordeals and conflicts that followed. What were the stakes? They consisted in managing a periodically disrupted population; internal migrations in search of food, better land, and the wettest areas; and the lineage schisms linked to these displacements. Relations between agriculture and pastoralism in the areas afflicted by the crises or in the newly colonized territories were redefined. Toward the east, the banana trees around Lake Victoria were a world apart, which we will come back to later. But toward the west, the more humid and more wooded highlands dominating the western Rift, peopled and cultivated since the first millennium B.C., still offered many opportunities for land clearing. Agricultural potentialities were also more important, given the brevity of the dry season: cereals were supplemented, even rivaled, by tubers and legumes, an ensemble that the American plants (especially the maize-bean complex) reinforced in a revolutionary way in the period we will discuss now. Therefore, the old complementarity of cattle and sorghum, milk and dough, pasture and laying land fallow was confronted with a more intensive agricultural logic of two harvest seasons, not to mention the benefit of the proteins in bean stew. This agriculture also benefited decisively from animal manure.[6] Thus this pioneering front was occupied and farmed more and more intensively and was simultaneously filled demographically, while consistently driving land-clearing activity toward the border zones of the Congolese forest. This occurred well into the twentieth century. The problem of the relationship between agriculture and cattle keeping was therefore reproduced from generation to generation not on the basis of a cohabitation of distinct "ecological niches," as might have been the case between the Bahima and the Bairu in ancient Nkore, but as a form of integration: the Batutsi of Rwanda and Burundi were cattle raisers/agriculturists while the

Bahutu were cultivators who also knew how to raise cattle, goats, and sheep. This reality is too often eclipsed by what one might call the Masai imagery of pastoralism in eastern Africa. Complementarity and competition between the two activities were the order of the day, notably in land management.

Kingship thus emerged in these societies as a political institution that could arbitrate and further — more concretely than the initiation cult — the coexistence and blossoming of all. The major rituals emphasized activities tied to the sovereign. Some regalia link iron and cattle: in Karagwe, Nkore, and Rwanda, royal hammers were endowed with different kinds of horns, echoing the alliance between the Bahinda and the Bayango blacksmiths.[7] The *muganuro* in Burundi valorized sorghum and cattle, and, moreover, the date fixed to sowing this cereal (December and not September at the beginning of the rains), which is a priori strange, reflects both a more eastern agricultural calendar (that of the Buha) and an optimal integration in the bi-seasonal cycle of the other products, at the moment of the first bean harvest. All this happened as if this ritual had been developed on the eastern plateaus before it took root in the mountains of Burundi.[8]

The monarchy supported and inspired an order that, in return, involved respect and material prestations. A political aristocracy managed these services, and it profited from this form of subordination. In other African regions, the state met its needs by resorting to slavery. But this was not the case in the Great Lakes region. Here the establishment of monarchies corresponded to the implementation of tributary regimes, whose forms we will discuss below.

But first we must note the apparently critical role of possessing cattle. Owning cattle was important even on the western highlands, where cultivators' hoes and coalman-metallurgists' hatchets were more responsible for clearing forests than were bovine teeth.

Beyond its material products (milk, meat, skins, manure, and such), the cow occupied an eminent place in these cultures and in the symbolism that governed their human relations (from dowries and gifts to dependency ties and fines). This does not amount to an a priori fact. Even in this region, there are counterexamples of conquered or marginalized pastoral communities: groups of Batutsi from Gisaka, Bugesera, Buha, and other parts of the same linguistic cluster, as well as groups of Bahima from Karagwe or elsewhere, transhumances to the lightly forested areas of central Tanzania, where they were under the thumb of Nyamwezi chiefs.[9] Other Batutsi left, also as victims of eighteenth- and nineteenth-century conflicts, for the high plateaus of Itombwe on the western side of Lake Tanganyika, where they lived as simple cattle raisers near Bembe and Fuliru populations.[10] The historian Edward Steinhart, who worked on Nkore, proposed seeing the eighteenth-century "ecological crises" as the decisive moment when dependency relationships between agriculturists and large-scale cattle keepers were established, a point to which we will return shortly. Indeed, during droughts and famines, herds were able to search for pastures in faraway areas, whereas the fields had to stay put: cultivators looking for food and protection found themselves in the weaker position; negotiating social relations favored the holders of this mobile form of wealth — cattle.[11] Still, the cow's becoming the mark of power — even if this was inflected differently in each country — was also the function of a political play by the ruling aristocracies. The situation at the end of the nineteenth century stemmed not from a "premise of inequality," as Jacques Maquet claimed, but from a historical construction.

These hypotheses merit a last word about the general chronology of human settlement. The movements we have discerned, notably in an east-west direction, over the last four centuries are part of a much longer history, that of a gradual human "filling up" of different areas in the region. This was not a sudden occupation of empty lands. Just as the "great land clearings" in western Europe between the eleventh and the thirteenth century did not eviscerate the Roman period, the "great invasions" of the fifth century, or the pre-Christian "Celtic migrations," this region's social history from the seventeenth to the twentieth century — marked by multiple shifts within lineage groups and the whittling away of land — did not represent a completely new beginning. But scholars often err on this point because the maximum time span of traditions and lineage genealogies is five or six generations, depending on the case. This means that the "origin" period is dated to 1650–1750. In Rwanda, for example, this inspired something of a caricature:

> If the era's warrior traditions are especially preoccupied with power relations among military chiefs and with cattle raids, this is because the settling of fields and of populations on territories where agriculturists and herders had established their respective rights had not yet taken place. We must wait until the eighteenth century before the chronicles mention a new figure: the land clearer.[12]

In the same vein, Claudine Vidal, forgetting that human settlement took place during the Iron Ages,[13] suggested characterizing the eighteenth century as the "era of land-clearers." Vidal rightly emphasized the phenomenon of human densification, which distinguished this period, and insisted that it affected every population category, including Hutu and Tutsi. And the term "sedentarization" that she proposed for designating the gradual shrinking of available lands and the tendency to delimit and control them is certainly appropriate. This term moved away from imagining a widespread nomadism (on the basis of transhumances, itinerant cultures, and warrior raids) for the earlier period. The

146

experience of Rwanda and Burundi over the last century is surely clarifying: grasslands whose ownership was in question gradually receded as high human density spread. And there was movement toward areas that had been forest, bush lands, or marshes for a long time.[14] In fact, this region's societies are marked by a permanent tension between various forms of internal mobility and lineage or especially political control. The play of interests in the different activities is part of this tension, which was a daily concern in these states.[15]

The Intermediary Plateaus: Decline and Division

Let us return to the kingdoms' historical geography.[16] Despite the collapse of the so-called Cwezi culture around the sixteenth century, this zone, which we have called the intermediary plateaus and where human activity dates back to the later Iron Age, continued to dominate the region's evolution for at least another century. A change in location from north to south might be discerned, though not without difficulty: between the time of the origin myths (of Wamara, Rukidi, Ruhinda, and so on) and the eighteenth-century political-military chronicles, there are several obscure decades. In the north was Bunyoro (or Kitara), which remained the most powerful kingship for many years. We have seen that a Lwo invasion did not just give rise to a Babito dynasty; the latter terrorized the region for years by launching southward raids that reached as far as Rwanda in the sixteenth century. Then, in the seventeenth and eighteenth centuries, the Babito episodically raided areas south of the Kagera. The first raids seem to have followed the victory of Biharwe in Nkore in 1520: a prince named Cwa, son of the *mukama* Nyabongo, supposedly led two expeditions into Rwanda. In the traditions, these missions are remembered as horrifying because first Mwami Kigeri Mukobanya and then Mwami Mibambwe Mutabazi were forced to flee west, the latter as far as Bushi. Farther south, Nsoro Sangano, king of Bu-gesera, also was a victim of this invasion. Then, after Cwa's death, the Banyoro seem to have retreated. In the mid-seventeenth century, near the mouth of the Kagera, Kiziba submitted to their assaults despite being a Bito dynasty. So did Karagwe. In the early eighteenth century, a *mukama* (undoubtedly Kyebambe) is said to have ravaged Buhaya for many years before being defeated and killed by Nyarubamba Kicumbu, king of Ihangiro. Later, other Nyoro groups were defeated in Karagwe and Nkore, each time by a king named Ntare Kitabanyoro (Killer of the Banyoro).[17] These raids (this is indeed how we must see these "wars") likely kept a belligerent spirit alive in the region and inspired different sover-eigns to take military measures, which quickly became an impor-tant dimension in the monarchies.

Despite its reputation, Bunyoro seems to have lacked powerful organization.[18] Nonetheless, it had many advantages. For example, it controlled the principal Cwezi sanctuaries. Given its external origins, the dynasty was above local rivalries, even while shoring up ties with the key clans. Besides engaging in agro-pastoral activ-ities, the country had considerable economic resources, including the Kibiro saltworks (near Lake Albert) and renowned metal-lurgy. But its political administration was decentralized, with autonomous peripheral principalities in Bwera, Koki, Buddu, and even Kiziba to the south and Busoga to the east. A series of suc-cession crises foretold dynastic breaks and secessions to come. Neighboring countries proceeded to exploit the difficulties in this undoubtedly too-vast cluster, which was managed very loosely. Buganda occupied Koki and Buddu in the late eighteenth century, cutting off Bunyoro's access to Lake Victoria. Then, around 1830, Toro, in the southwest, seized its independence under Prince Kaboyo's leadership: this new kingdom controlled the key salt-works in Katwe and Kasenyi, north of Lake Edward.[19]

In the south, other political entities quickly benefited from the decline of Bunyoro in the eighteenth century. First, Mpororo or Ndorwa, the kingdom of the Murorwa drum inherited from the mysterious queen Kitami, covered an area from the north-northeast of contemporary Rwanda to the Ugandan Kigezi. Only vaguely understood, a Bashambo lineage (which was pastoral) lasted only two reigns; its two kings were called Gahaya. Mpororo collapsed in the late eighteenth century, leaving behind dispersed clans and principalities (notably Igara) as well as an open door for the expansion of Nkore and Rwanda. Nonetheless, clan chiefs (more so the agriculturists than the pastoralists) conserved the memory of this ephemeral kingdom. According to the logic of initiation, with which we are now familiar, these chiefs became mediums of a "queen" Nyabingi, somewhat similar to Kitami: that is, they constituted a monarchy, as it were, without a kingdom, one that reappeared as a clandestine anticolonial resistance society in the early twentieth century. Indeed, this is a good example of kingship's possible avatars.[20]

For its part, Nkore overpowered the area that stretched from the northern bank of the mouth of the Kagera to the mountains towering over the lowlands around Lakes Edward and George. This kingdom emerged in Isisingiro, near Karagwe, under a dynasty that is claimed to be Hinda and had important alliances with the Bayangwe and the Basita, the respective guardians of the Ishange necropolis and the Bagyendanwa drum; the kingdom also allied, through marriage, with the Bashambo. The Bayangwe and the Basita were from subclans that date back to the world of Wamara and Ruhinda; the Bashambo spawned the Mpororo dynastic lineage. Nkore first lived in Bunyoro's shadow, as did other neighboring principalities, including Buzimba, Buhweju, and Kitakwenda. Then, starting at the end of the eighteenth century, Nkore, benefiting both from the weakening of its "protector" and from the collapse of Mpororo (under the reigns of Rwebishengye, Gasyonga, and Mutambuka, who died in 1867), established a political and military system equivalent to the one later found in Rwanda. Some groups of Hima shepherds who had frequented the court and guarded the royal herd were sent during each reign to different regions to form armies (*emitwe*). This military system was thus combined with the key social and political role of cattle. On this basis, a tributary system was organized, one that encompassed both Hima cattle keepers and Iru agriculturists but mainly benefited the Hima aristocracy. In the nineteenth century, Nkore, following the Nyoro model, established a protectorate over the surrounding principalities (Igara, Buhweju, and so forth). It even extended to Toro and attempted to gain control over the salt-works. But by the end of the century, Nkore had begun to have problems that stemmed from Rwanda's expansion, which threatened the grandson and successor of Mutambuka, the *mugabe* Ntare (1867–1895).[21]

Farther south, on the grassland plateaus on both sides of the Kagera valley, three ancient kingdoms collapsed or disappeared in the nineteenth century; these kingdoms typified pastoral states. Karagwe, which was central in the Ruhinda myth and had submitted to Bunyoro pressure, emerged in traditions of the seventeenth century: victorious forays and alliances with Rwandan kings were attributed to the kingdom's Hinda sovereigns, nearly all of whom were called Ntare or Ruhinda.[22] Indeed, it has been said that Mwami Ruganzu Ndori of Rwanda might originally have been from Karagwe and might have been a Muhinda. Sometime in the early seventeenth century, he was supposed to have returned from Karagwe, where, according to a common cliché in this type of narrative, a paternal aunt raised him.[23] Nonetheless, Karagwe only achieved a true regional presence in the nineteenth century under the reigns of Ndagara and Rumanyika; this came largely through the kingdom's position on the caravan routes linking Buganda with Nyamwezi country. This new dynamism was followed by ecological collapse at the end of the century, tied notably to the great rinderpest epidemic of 1891 that decimated the area's livestock.

On the left bank of the Kagera, two other kingdoms, Gisaka and Bugesera, present an analogous profile. Gisaka was governed under a Bagesera clan dynasty, with Kimenyi frequently as the ruling name, and had the same totem as the Bahinda, the *nkende* monkey. It also has a strong presence in Rwandan traditions: it supposedly exploited the Banyoro invasion in order to establish itself in the heart of ancient Rwanda (in Buganza and Bwanacyambwe, where Kigali is located today); farther north, in the mid-eighteenth century Gisaka is reputed to have allied with Ndorwa against Rwanda before being annexed by the latter between the late eighteenth and the mid-nineteenth century.[24]

Bugesera seems to be more an ancestor of the kingdoms in the Kagera basin. There are many ties between Bugesera's Bahondogo dynasty and the Banyiginya dynasty in Rwanda: alliances and marriages punctuate their history from the sixteenth to the eighteenth century. In fact, many indicators suggest that the small Rwandan principality was initially an annex of Bugesera. Like Gisaka, Bugesera seems to have taken advantage of the Banyoro expedition to consolidate its hold over what is today eastern Rwanda. Back in the seventeenth century, the Rwandan *mwami* Mutara Semugeshi is said to have been called Nsoro in his youth; this name is common in the Bugesera dynastic list. This *mwami* is thought to have inaugurated a "watering places" pastoral ritual, which came from Bugesera. Similarities can be seen in Burundi: According to Rwandan versions, the diviner Mashyira helped a Bugesera prince to found a new dynasty in Burundi under the name of Ntare Karemera (in the

version I have called "the cycle of Kanyaru"). But Burundian traditions refer to Bugesera royal sites throughout the north and northeast part of the country, as far as the edge of the Kibira (in the
west) and the mouth of the Ruvubu (in the center). For the two
future large mountainous kingdoms, Bugesera seems to have represented what Etruria had been for Rome at its beginnings. But
making this point became taboo: in Burundi, the word *mugesera* is
a sobriquet for bandits and the name of an ancient "foreign" sovereign, Nyabarega; the word also refers to abysses, grottoes, and
pits where trash is thrown. The key here, though, is the strong
pastoral element in this powerful kingdom, which existed between the sixteenth and the seventeenth century. By the late eighteenth century, Bugesera had been divided between Rwanda and
Burundi: on both sides of the border lakes, its ancient domain
was sprinkled with wells and watering places (*mariba*), where formerly cattle had received their necessary salt.[25]

In the extreme south of the plateaus region, we find two more
polities, Buha and Buzinza, whose histories are quite enigmatic.
Buha is part of the Rundi-Rwanda linguistic zone, Buzinza part
of the Nyoro-Buhaya zone. But their ecology is similar, and they
control important salt and iron resources, which are key to a network of regional exchange between Lakes Tanganyika and Victoria. From the get-go, the Baha seem divided between northern
Buha, which stretches from the Ruvubu (in contemporary Burundi) to the Muyovozi valley (in Tanzania), and southern Buha,
which covers the large mouth of the Malagarasi.[26] These two zones
correspond to distinct dynasties: the Bahambi and the Bakimbiri,
respectively. The totem of the former is a black cow; its kings are
named Nkanza, Gihumbi, and Ruhaga. The totem of the latter is a
bird; its kings are called Kimenyi, Ruhinda, Gwasa, Ntare, and
Kanyoni. The former are in closer contact with Karagwe and Bu-

zinza; the latter are more tied to Burundi, whose original homeland in the Nkoma massif is nearby. On Lake Tanganyika, Bujiji, or
Nkalinzi, has its own peculiar history, with its Bajiji dynasty, whose
totem is the *nkende* monkey. These countries are reputed for their
salt (indispensable for cattle; humans often content themselves
with vegetable-based brine): both salt marshes and access routes to
Buzinza's salt springs, not far from the lower course of the Malagarasi, which were controlled by autonomous powers.[27] In the
mid-nineteenth century, Buha experienced a new round of division, which followed from Burundian pressure and the unexpected
aggression of the Batuta (or Ngoni), who represented the farthest
northward thrust of the Zulu. Northern Buha was cut in two
(Buyungu and Muhambwe), while southern Buha was cut in three
(Ruguru, Heru, and Bushingo). Later, when the Zanzibari caravans
arrived, Bujiji had a new destiny, a point to which we will return.

To the east, the Bazinza had as much difficulty as the Baha in
establishing political coherence. In contact with various populations of contemporary central Tanzania, including the Bantu-
speaking Banyamwezi and the Nilotic Tatoga from the Rift Valley,
they were coveted because they included large communities
of renowned blacksmiths (notably the specialized group of Ba-
rongo). As noted above, the dynasty presented itself as Hinda, but
its real founder-hero was Kayango, a blacksmith. The genealogies
furnished by the missionaries, nearly the only ones to have written about this region, are contradictory and date the kings named
Ntare or Kabambo to a period before 1700, which is doubtful.[28]
At the turn of the eighteenth and nineteenth centuries, this
"greater Buzinza" split into three parts: an interior Rusubi, Buzinza, and Kimwani around Lake Victoria. The first later played a
role equivalent to that of Karagwe on the caravan route after the
mid-nineteenth century.[29]

The Shores of Lake Victoria: The Rise of Buganda

If we now return northward around Lake Victoria's western littoral, we encounter different landscapes, banana trees, and fishermen's canoes. This is the land of the Bahaya, a people who had gained a great reputation on Lake Victoria by the late nineteenth century.[30] But each of their small countries is subdivided according to the same logic of schisms observed among the Bazinza and Baha. The borders of each kingdom spread over two ecological zones: plains and fertile valleys on the one hand and grassland plateaus on the other. This duality was partly responsible for the fall of Kyamutwara in the nineteenth century.

On the southern bank of the Kagera is Kiziba, an odd kingdom whose traditions and rituals are connected to Bunyoro and the Sese Islands; it had a Bito dynasty. Kiziba conflicted with all its southern and western neighbors. In the late eighteenth century, Mukama Burungu Kakindi, threatened by a rebellion, called on Kabaka Semakokiro for help. This became one of the first Baganda interventions in Buhaya land: from then on, the large neighbor to the north repeatedly raided the Bahaya lands and meddled in their internal quarrels.

Here and elsewhere, family myths cloud the ancient history of Kyamutwara, which seems to emerge in force in the mid-seventeenth century under Rugomora Mahe's reign. This king also established ties with Kitara and the Sese Islands (that is, with both the Cwezi and the lacustrine sphere). But quarrels and wars of succession plagued the kingdom in the eighteenth century. King Bwogi Mpangukano eliminated his predecessor with the help of the Baziba and the Baganda, and starting at the beginning of that century, some Bahima from the Bankango clan (who are reputed to have come from Buzinza) became very influential in the court via matrimonial alliances. These "trust men" exploited the rivalries at the heart of the royal family. In the early nineteenth century, the kingdom split into four parts. Two principalities remained in the hands of the legitimate line of Bahinda: Kyanja and minuscule Maruku.[31] The Bankango took over the other two: small Kyamutwara at the edge of the lake (where the Germans founded Bukoba in 1890) and Bugabo. The major beneficiaries of this far-reaching explosion (because Kiziba continued to be torn apart by chief quarrels) were the Baganda, who intensified their presence under the reign of Kabaka Suna. Indeed, it was during an expedition to Kiziba and to Bugabo, in 1857, that this sovereign died from smallpox.

The same scenario played out in Ihangiro: divisions at the heart of the Hinda princely milieu, wars with Kyamutwara, and, in 1882, Baganda intervention, which had been requested by King Nyarubamba, who was threatened by a rebel chief.

Nothing, then, could federate the corridor between the Kagera valley and Lake Victoria. This region experienced the same negative trajectory, in terms of decline and division, that hobbled the other pastorally dominant kingdoms of the intermediary plateaus. The only unifying force came from the outside, and it rested on a different economic logic, that of banana production, canoeing, and commerce.

This political success from the well-watered plains around Lake Victoria was above all that of Buganda. We have seen that this region was under Kitara's cultural influence, either in replicating the Cwezi political-religious model or in coming under Babito pressure. But in contrast with the Haya lands, these forces, both material and symbolic, came from the lacustrine area, in particular from the Sese Islands. These forces clearly gained the upper hand starting in the mid-sixteenth century, a turn marked by the reign of Nakibinge. The history of this king is so dramatic and rich that Christopher Wrigley, who had a critical view of the region's legend, recently suggested reading this history as a mere trope.[32] There was once little Buganda: betrayed by a rebel prince, Buganda was invaded by the Banyoro, despite help from the king of the Sese Islands, who sent his famous warrior, Kibuka, to the rescue. Nakibinge and Kibuka were killed, and the queen secured the regency. From then on, the Kibuka hero became the god of war.... Still, according to tradition, the next *kabaka*, Mulondo, came from the Sese Islands and founded a new dynasty with Lake Victoria as its center of gravity.

Starting in the seventeenth century, this kingship was distinguished by a logic of territorial expansion.[33] First, toward the west, Kings Kimbugwe and Katerega conquered Gomba, which gave them pastureland and access to fords on the Katonga. Then, in the eighteenth century under the reigns of Mawanda, Kyabaggu, and Junju, after several decades of internal crises, expansion began again in all directions: toward the east, Kyagwe on the banks of the Nile was annexed, and the penetration of Busoga began; toward the north, Bunyoro's influence was curtailed, and there was expansion into Singo and Bulemezi; and toward the south, Buddu was conquered. At the beginning of the nineteenth century, Buganda replaced Bunyoro as "protector" of Bwera and Koki; it made use of new resources, in cattle, ivory, and iron; it launched canoe fleets on Lake Victoria, putting this force in the service of its commerce; it launched expeditions to the south of the Kagera, at least starting with the reign of Semakokiro (whom we have seen in relation to Kiziba); and by the middle of the century, it had gone on to control the Nyamwezi caravan route that linked the kingdom to the Indian Ocean coast. Buganda also intervened in Karagwe and Ihangiro in the mid-nineteenth century. In the southern parts of the lake, it competed with the commercial activity of Bukerebe Island, a small kingdom in the Hinda tradition.[34] Numbering more than a million, Buganda's population ended up being ten times greater than that of Bunyoro, while the banana economy freed up male labor for fishing, exchange, and war.[35]

This expansion was due to a gradual institutional overhaul, which started in the late seventeenth century. This reform consisted in elevating the *kabaka*'s authority, to the detriment of clans, *lubale* mediums, and princes. Clan chiefs (the *bataka*) were progressively, but not easily, brought under control by according them court posts, intervening in their succession struggles, and, from Mutebi's rule on, subjecting them to the new territorial chiefs (the *bakungu*). Their marginalizaton in the enthronement ritual began with Namugala's reign, as we have seen. Tension with the priests of the major shrines was a permanent feature through the end of the nineteenth century, as we have also seen. However, since Tebandeke, the mad king turned medium of the great god Mukasa, the royal function and that of the priest were neatly dissociated. Last, because the monarchy was transferred between brothers born from the same mother, who represented a predominant clan according to the matrilineal rule imparted to the *kabaka*, managing the princely milieu raised a fraternal problem. The absence of a dynastic clan, which on the one hand was favorable to the clans' political integration, was a source of constitutional instability because it sustained much personal jealousy and rivalry during successions. When Kyabaggu died, for example, a civil war broke out between two brothers, Junju and Semakokiro, who were to reign successively. But from this point forward, a new practice was instituted: systematic elimination of the crown prince's brothers. This aspect reminds us that the crystallization of a state does not exclude cruelty, according to what one might call an Ivan the Terrible syndrome. Each accession, including that of Kabaka Mutesa in 1854, sparked a confrontation between several "king-making" dignitaries, who manipulated clan interests, and resulted in the execution or exile of the losers. Political centralization therefore went hand in hand with military expansion, and it continued, as we will see, until colonial conquest.

The Western Mountains: The Emergence of Rwanda and Burundi

To find sizable state constructions, we must travel westward, where, by the late nineteenth century, Rwanda and Burundi had succeeded in controlling a human mass of almost two million inhabitants each. At the start, Rwanda was an apparently small principality, born in Buganza (near Lake Muhazi) and in Bugesera's and Gisaka's shadow.[36] Moreover, the Banyiginya dynasty was attributed to ancestors who came from Mubari, which is between Ndorwa and Karagwe. In the sixteenth century, a rival from Gisaka supposedly killed the best known of these ancient kings, Ruganzu Bwimba. But Ruganzu Bwimba's son Cyirima Rugwe in turn benefited from Bugesera's support and enlarged his domain by taking over the principalities of Bumbogo, Buriza, and Rukoma, which later kept a ritual role (sorghum for *muganura* came from Bumbogo). The installation of the royal necropolis in Buganza also attests to the founding role of this eastern region. But a series of catastrophes broke up the first Rwanda. Banyoro invasions destroyed it and forced the *bami* Kigeri Mukobanya and Mibambwe Mutabazi to flee westward.

A new center of gravity subsequently took root on the Nduga highlands. This second Rwanda was stuck between the power of its two large eastern neighbors (Gisaka and Bugesera) and encountered resistance from the Bashi and Bahavu (whose organization during this period one tends to ignore). After an internal princely quarrel and pressure from western competitors, Rwanda seemingly collapsed again under Ndahiro Cyamatare's reign in the early seventeenth century. The king's brothers allied with a certain Nsibura, king of the Bahavu or the Bashi, and the dynastic drum Rwoga (attributed to the legendary Gihanga) was seized and the *mwami* killed.[37] According to tradition, a son of the latter, hidden in Karagwe and raised by a paternal aunt, later returned to reclaim the kingdom of his ancestors. This pious imagery poorly disguises a dynastic break: the new founder was Mwami Ruganzu Ndori. Expeditions in every direction are attributed to him, in particular ones that reunited two cradles of the kingship, Buganza and Nduga. During the seventeenth century, his four immediate successors (from Mutara Semugeshi to Yuhi Mazimpaka) expanded their power in the direction of Kanyaru and Lake Kivu, and retook Bwanacyambwe in Gisaka. But, as we saw earlier, the region's major power during this period was Bugesera.

Faced with vague traditions concerning these seventeenth-entury *bami*, who are thought to have led fantastic expeditions even west of Lake Kivu, some authors have asked: were these imaginary kings, or were they adventurers always dependent on neighboring powers?[38] It is curious that the dynastic list (a Mutara or a Cyirima, "cowherd" kings, followed by a Kigeri and a Mibambwe, "warrior" kings, and a Yuhi, "ritualist" king) was formalized during this obscure period, as if the reconstruction of an eternal Rwanda had been continuous.[39] In the early eighteenth century, when Yuhi Mazimpaka went mad, his son Rwaka ruled until the true heir, Cyirima Rujugira, took power. Only after this reign in the mid-eighteenth century does Rwandan historiography become precise. The main event seems to be the crystallization of a political-clan space, under the aegis of Kigwa and Gihanga myths and under the protection of neighboring Bugesera: the concerned clans are the Bazigaba (in Mubari), the Basinga (from an ancient dynasty of the Barenge, whom Gihanga destroyed), the Babanda (in Nduga, with its diviner-king Mashyira), the Bongera (Bumbogo and other entities surrounding Buganza), and the Bagesera.[40] The Nyiginya dynasty had as little continuity as that of Kintu in Buganda;

the "kingship" reconstructed itself several times while negotiating with the clans. The religious dimension of the *mwami* moreover tended to multiply among the ritualists of Bumbogo, for example, and northwest (Bushiru, Cyingogo, and Buhoma) and southwest (Bukunzi and Busozo) of the Rwandan cultural zone — in what were "kinglets," according to official historiography.

Not until the mid-eighteenth century did the monarchy really take shape, linking military expansion with political centralization. Cyirima Rujugira and Kigeri Ndabarasa expanded their control eastward and southward: Burundi, whose King Mutaga was killed during a battle, was driven back to the Kanyaru; Ndorwa was dispersed (Mutara was incorporated); Mubari was occupied; and Gisaka was partially taken.[41] The westward expansion was more a matter of incursions. At the very end of the century, Bugesera was shared between King Mibambwe Sentabyo of Rwanda and King Ntare Rugamba of Burundi. In the nineteenth century, the expansion continued eastward with occupation of the remaining parts of Gisaka under Mutara Rwogera, and the expansion moved northward beginning with the reign of Yuhi Gahindiro through that of Kigeri Rwabugiri (around 1860–1895). The latter even penetrated Bufumbira (north of the volcanic mountains) and attacked Nkore. Under his reign, the Rwandan monarchy firmly established itself to the west on the shores of Lake Kivu and the banks of the Rusizi (from Bugoyi in the north to Kinyaga in the south). The Bahavu of Ijwi Island and the Bashi were more or less subjugated. In the east, Rwabugiri also intervened in Bushubi. Rwanda achieved its maximum extension, and the kingdom was feared throughout the region. However, many enclaves, especially in the west, escaped the central power's direct control, a situation that did not change until German colonization.

Two observations must be made on the modalities of this expansion: first, it rested on military organization, equivalent to what we observed in Nkore; second, it operated, more informally, through westward migrations of Tutsi or Hutu in search of new lands (the famous "land clearers"). Mwami Rujugira structured the armies by installing them in permanent camps near the most threatened borders. Two-thirds of these armies were created between his reign and Rwabugiri's, roughly between 1750 and 1895. These armies were corporations of young warriors loyal to the sovereign. They integrated Batutsi and Bahutu from differ-ent regions, who in turn were allocated herds. This, curiously, prompted Alexis Kagame to call these formations "social militias" or "bovine armies."[42] A new monarchist culture developed in this milieu, one that was expressed through historical poems (the *bitekerezo*). Territorial control that reached the borders gave rise to a new conception of the state embodied by the *mwami* and his representatives, the army chiefs (*batware b'ingabo* or *b'imiheto*: "chiefs of the warriors" or "of the bows"). Standardization of rit-uals and control of the cult of Ryangombe in the court also date to this period.[43]

On the peripheries, the expansion of Rwandan power was car-ried out more informally. More or less adventurous lineage groups infiltrated and carved out a new future for themselves in the zones to which they had migrated in search of greener pastures for their cattle and which they opened to farming. New lineages were cre-ated, but in these distant lands they commended themselves to the central authority in such a way that it could be useful to them, while, in return, they became agents of that authority's influence. Once again, the image of the center was constructed in the border zones, because the peripheral populations who had lived there longer were perceived pejoratively as not very "Rwandan." They served as a foil to the image of central civilization, which was defined in counterpoint. On the southwest frontier, for example, "others" were quickly qualified as "Bashi" or "Banyabungo" and scorned as such, even if they did not come from a Bushi principality. In another case, the Bagwabiro lineage, which originally came from Ndorwa, was integrated into "Rwanda" under Rujugira. Later, having fallen out with the powerful, the lineage went into exile in the northwest as far as Bugoyi, where, in the nineteenth century, this lineage, generally considered Hutu, redefined itself as Tutsi and tied to the court. A kingdom's construction is thus also a society's, in line with a particular political culture.[44]

Burundi had at its disposal less sophisticated traditions than the Rwandan dynasty: not the "source of wisdom," or historical oral literature such as the *bitekerezo*, or kingship "codes," but dispersed traditions carried on by families who played a political, religious, and economic role around the most powerful.[45] As we have seen, if one accepts the reliability of story fragments about Ntare from Kanyaru, a first kingdom had supposedly been established in the sixteenth century in the north, under Bugesera's protection. But by the late seventeenth century, a Baganwa dynasty had genuinely taken hold in the south with the support of clans who later became managers of this kingship's holy sites (primarily Bahutu clans — the Bajiji, Bashubi, and Bahanza — but also Batutsi ones like the Babibe). The founder, Ntare Rushatsi, established his capital on the eastern foothills of the Congo-Nile crest, reuniting under his authority, as in the Rwanda of Ruganzu Ndori, grassy areas and wooded zones more suitable for agriculture, as well as important areas of iron and salt production in the south. During the eighteenth century, Burundi asserted itself against its northern neighbors, Bugesera and Rwanda. In particular, King Mutaga Senyamwiza fought against the armies of Cyirima Rujugira and perished near the upper Kanyaru, on the edges of the Kibira forest. His successor, Mwambutsa Mbariza, seems to have been plagued by internal quarrels and by a major drought and went into exile or committed suicide. He left few traces, unlike Mutaga, who left behind many sacred woods and descendants.

Ntare Rugamba, who ruled for the first half of the nineteenth century, profoundly transformed the kingdom. He inaugurated a new dynastic cycle (the four names in the funerary ritual) and even a new dynasty. He doubled the country's surface area through a series of conquests in the north, west, and east: first he acquired the southern half of Bugesera. An accord with Rwanda did not prevent several wars between the two kingdoms from later breaking out. These wars served only to confirm the Kanyaru border. A series of expeditions to the west of the crest (as far as what is today eastern Congo, according to some stories) attached the Imbo plains to the country. Last, in 1840, a war with Ruhaga, king of northern Buha, led to the annexation of the Buyogoma region, east of Ruvubu, substantially augmenting the amount of available pastoral land.

The conquered regions were administered in different ways: local chiefs were maintained, as in Bugufi (in the far northeast); families allied to the monarchy were installed in the new provinces (as with the Babibe and Banyakarama Batutsi in northern Imbo, the Badaha and Bahanza Bahutu along the northern edge of Lake Tanganyika, and Mutaga's princes in the northeast and far south); or sons of the king were installed in the provinces, including Rwasha in Buyogoma and Ndivyariye in the northeast. The "Ganwa system" was structured in this way — that is, the sovereign's sons were placed on the periphery of the kingship's domains and then, during subsequent reigns, nephews were gradually removed to the benefit of the heirs in direct line to the throne. By the late nineteenth century, the Batare (the lines descended from Ntare) were in the north, east, and south of the country, while the Bezi (the line of sons of Mwezi Gisabo, Ntare Rugamba's successor) were closer to the capitals, for example, in Kirimiro (Gitega

region). All the princes of royal blood (the Baganwa) were supposed to be demoted and become simple Batutsi after a cycle of
four reigns. Thus it seemed as if distance in space (in relation to
the capitals) was proportional to distance in time (in relation to
the *mwami* ancestor of each lineage). Concretely, geographic marginalization and strategically opposing generations neutralized
the threat to royal power — which the princely milieu represented.
In Rwanda, the army-chief system played the same role. In Buganda, as shown above, the solution was to annihilate every princely category by matrilineal rotation of the clans that managed the
supreme function.

By the late nineteenth century, Burundi's expansion had been
blocked: in the north by the Rwandans; in the east by new threats
from the Banyamwezi, who had unified under the war chief Mirambo, and from the Ngoni; and in the west by Arab-Swahili
traders who had established themselves on the shores of Lake
Tanganyika. Internal tensions worsened under Mwezi Gisabo's
reign (roughly 1850–1908): there were princely vendettas in the
east; dissidence among the northeast Batare; repulsion of the
southern Batare by one of the king's sons; Tutsi chiefs' personal
strategies in the north and west; and the appearance of anti-kings,
such as a certain Rwoga, who rallied crowds in the southeast to
slaughter cattle for huge meat feasts around 1870, and Kibango,
then Kilima, who in the northwest in the 1890s combined magic
and firearms, which had been obtained in eastern Congo.[46]

West of Lake Kivu and the Rusizi valley, which goes all the way to
Lake Tanganyika, we find schisms similar to those in the corridor
west of Lake Victoria. Without delving into the details of the
innumerable small wars recounted in the traditions, we can nonetheless describe the region, from south to north.[47] In the mid-
nineteenth century, under the influence of Swahili traders from

Ujiji, the Bavira (literally "palm oil people") seceded from the Bafuliro in the Rusizi valley: a dynasty of usurpers, the Banyalenge, rebelled against the legitimate line of Bahamba. Later in the nineteenth century, the Bashi divided into seven or eight principalities, each managed by a *mwami*. The two oldest principalities on the plateau southwest of Lake Kivu — Kabare and Ngweshe (or Buhaya and Bishugi) — claimed to date back to the sixteenth and seventeenth centuries. But the principalities also included Kalonge and Irhambi (or Katana, created around 1860) farther north; Ninja, Burhinyi, and Luhwinja in the west (next to the forest); and Kaziba in the south. In addition, the Bahavu have a continental contingent, Mpinga (near Kalehe), and an island contingent, Ijwi, which was ruled by a Basibula dynasty. As was the case for Lake Victoria's Bahaya, hostility between neighbors prompted counter-alliances and external interventions, from Burundi (which controlled a territory run by chiefs from the Banyakarama clan on the right bank of the Rusizi) and especially from Rwanda: Mwami Rwabugiri succeeded in annexing Ijwi Island, but eventually failed, around 1894, in his attempts to conquer Bushi.

The Functioning of the Monarchy: The Political Capitals
The geo-historical journey that ends here was necessary. It clarifies king lists and kingdoms' maps, both of which offer only an ossified picture of a reality that is far more complex and fluid. Throughout these stories, we have perceived contrasts and analogies among and between different states, which were fashioned mostly from the eighteenth century on. We also have seen their organizational strengths and weaknesses, as well as the multiple social issues at stake. It is useful now to recap the essential points of their structures before analyzing the ruling aristocracies at the moment of their first contacts with the external world.

The first European descriptions, as we have seen, concerned

the kings' courts. The nature of these "capitals" is indeed revealing. The number of permanent and transient residents in each in
the late nineteenth century was impressive: according to sources
from this period, there were five hundred in Bunyoro, two thousand in Bukeye in Burundi, two thousand in Nyanza in Rwanda,
but twenty thousand in Mengo in Buganda.[48] Under Mutesa, the
kibuga (the residence of the *kabaka*) encompassed one thousand
houses, five hundred of which were in one royal enclosure. These
certainly were not cities,[49] but rather rustic palaces, both princely
residences and sites of political decision making, complete with
military camps, granaries, cattle enclosures, and workshops, all of
which had the look of an open market on certain days. But this
grouping did not amount to a special economic milieu distinct
from the surrounding agro-pastoral countryside. A royal capital
was both a reflection and a recapitulation of the country. "The
lugo [enclosure] of Kisabo is quite large, but not very beautiful.
Even the royal square, though preceded by a peristyle, had nothing distinctive and certainly nothing august about it," observed a
missionary visiting Mwami Mwezi Gisabo in Burundi in November 1904.[50] Even in the more open economic context of Buganda,
the royal settlement was distinguished only by its height and by
the size of the roads that brought one there. According to the
description of another White Father who frequented this court:

> One recognizes the king's house as the tall one, with a height of
> more than 20 meters. It is round like all the houses in Uganda. The
> roof is made from reeds and covered with grass that descends all the
> way to the ground; in the interior, the house is supported by a very
> large number of posts, which are arranged more or less in line.[51]

Each residence appeared as an interlocking of pathways; each was
surrounded by plant hedges (reeds, ficus, euphorbia, bamboos);

each included several dozen dwellings, arranged in a circle and made of braided plant material (reeds, papyrus, branches, grass, and banana leaves).[52] All this was surrounded by huts, where subjects who were supposed to complete their duties or who were in search of favors lived. Images of a maze or a labyrinth came often to the pen of European visitors: for example, two Germans present at the beginning of the century in Rwanda, Lieutenant von Parish and the future resident Richard Kandt, saw "a conglomerate of round straw courtyards" surrounded over a long distance by "huts of all kinds, large ones for notables and small ones for vassals . . . miserable shacks for brief visits."[53] In Kiziba and Buganda, this interlacing of dwellings was attached to banana gardens. These fragile constructions, which were periodically rebuilt, were designed to be functional.[54]

At the center of each complex were the sovereign's homes and those of his immediate family, in which partitions separated several rooms. Around these were reception and decision-making rooms, sacred sites, service quarters, granaries, and cattle enclosures. On the outside, vast esplanades were flooded with visitors seeking an audience, with the residences of notables in transit, and with the huts of young people who had been forced to perform domestic work or who had come to render their military service. The areas where the king led his social and political life were situated on several levels. Take the example of Burundi: the most secret receptions were held in small private enclosures next to the central palace; discussions with principal advisers (princes and palatines) took place in a forecourt directly overlooking the palace entrance (this forecourt was called the *rurimbi*, from which the name *banyarurimbi*, given to notables who acceded to this role, comes); judicial arbitrations unfolded in a room called *sentare* (from the founding king's name), which was situated in an interior court; and the quickest and least formal meetings might take place when the *mwami*, at the end of the afternoon, went to see his cows on their way back from their watering places or when he went to observe young warriors practicing archery on the surrounding grasslands (*ku nama*). In Buganda in the nineteenth century, public audiences with the *kabaka* took on the allure of an institution: official delegations and simple subjects flocked to him, and everyone was regulated by strict etiquette, which European visitors at this time often described. In the religious domain, one might cite huts throughout that housed diviners, vestals, sacred animals, royal drums, and other regalia, as well as open-air sites for sacrifices.

The royal courts mobilized a permanent staff. Court tasks were generally considered honors, which families hereditarily carried out by sending their unmarried sons or daughters to do them. Some of these servant-dignitaries were granary managers, cooks, and managers of sorghum or banana beer; others (notably girls) were responsible for ficus clothes, jewelry, palace care, mats, and containers made from wood, calabash, or clay. The royal herds required many shepherds and milkers. And then there were the more humble roles: watchmen and guardians, firewood collectors, water carriers, and palanquin carriers for the sovereign and his wives. In the kingdoms where a cleavage between pastoralists and agriculturists existed, it was particularly manifest at the court: only Batutsi could be milkers, and only Bahutu could be in charge of granaries or be cooks.

Thousands of people flooded the periphery of the sovereign's enclosure, as did delegations from remote regions, which added to the daily traffic of persons in the environs. Some basic huts housed many young people wanting to try their luck in the government's entourage: in this case, the "process" might last years because the time waiting for a favor from the king (a cow, land, or protection) was spent doing military exercises. It was from among these that elite warriors, who formed a sort of permanent guard, were recruited. This reality should focus attention on an often-misunderstood dimension in ancient social and political life: the monarchy, even if it constantly referred to its followers' clan and other memberships, also appealed to individual loyalties, and these "king's men" were youths. When the means of power multiplied thanks to new commercial resources — mainly in Buganda — a court society developed around prestigious commodities (such as cotton). This period was later termed the middle "chapter" of the *kabaka*.

These crowds posed logistical problems. The court's permanent residents had to eat. Of course, after leaving home, delegations and young warriors found a way to obtain provisions, but the sovereign also had to distribute a great deal, notably drinks. A royal court was not a "closed city" isolated from the rest of the country, even if it was generally located at the summit of a high hill, on a cleared site that towered over the countryside. At the heart of the sovereign's estate was a reserve land, which was administered by faithful directly dependent on him (this is practically the meaning of the term used to refer to them in Burundi, the *bishikira*, a majority of whom were Hutu). This reserve land was cultivated by peasants liable to corvée labor, or it was allocated for royal livestock. But these domains cannot be described as a verdant Versailles or a permanent manor. Indeed, the capital was itinerant. Being polygamous, the sovereign had wives in several enclosures; each enclosure was managed, both to prepare for one of the king's periodic visits and to supply provisions to the one he had left. In Rwanda, there were about one hundred *mwami* estates. In Burundi in the late nineteenth century, there were about fifty, of which about twenty housed a queen and might welcome the *mwami* one day (the others were purely economic). Mwezi Gisabo himself had a dozen wives. Nonetheless, it seems that the trend was toward sedentarization of power, at least in well-defined regions such as Muramvya in Burundi, Nyanza in Rwanda, and what is now Kampala in Buganda.[55] More broadly, each capital was situated in relation to the entire kingdom: it was defined as "the high one" (*ruguru* in Kirundi). I now want to turn to the question of how power was delegated in the rest of the country, in an administration that had neither salaries nor offices.

Managing the Kingdoms: Territories, Commands, and Prestations

For a century, assessments of the delegation of power were based on a comparison: a government founded on personal ties in a rural setting could only be "feudal." In 1882, English Protestant missionaries held that "the Government of Uganda is a very perfect form of the feudal system." In 1905, a German officer in service in Rwanda and Burundi explained that a pastoral clientage relationship "can be compared with the fief of our Middle Ages [because] the Watussi, beneficiaries of concessions from the sultans [the *bami*], in turn concede fiefs to their people by way of several or a single bovine." In 1918, a French White Father noted, "The governmental regime in Burundi greatly resembles feudalism of the Middle Ages.... The major lords or *baganwa* are vassals of the king; a certain number of simple chiefs, who recognize their suzerainty, are their vassals. All, big and small chiefs, have Bahutu for vassals." In the early twentieth century, another Catholic missionary in Burundi claimed that King Mwezi Gisabo was a myth, that Burundi was in the hands of "more or less powerful barons and dukes," and that the chief of the Buyogoma was a "palace mayor."[56]

Medievalists have rightly instructed us not to employ the vocabulary of feudalism (lord, serf, fief, suzerain vassal, privilege) outside the historical context of western Europe from the tenth to the fifteenth century. Nonetheless, feudal theorizing was ardently pursued, notably in the 1960s and 1970s, largely because of the laxness of this formulation in Marxist analyses. In an Africanist journal's special issue devoted to Rwanda, Claudine Vidal informed us in 1974 that the objective of research must be to revisit "methods closer to those of the historian than to those of ethnography" and to criticize, thanks to "peasant know-how," "knowledge trapped in the feudal elite's own ideology." Then, on this basis, she described "the economics of the Rwandan feudal society," one of the pillars of which was "lordly exploitation."[57] Rightly reacting against the "fetishism of the cow" omnipresent in the anthropology on this country, Vidal emphasized the importance of the land problem, and she described this subject in a far more nuanced way than the medieval veneer of her title seemingly indicated. But in moving to universal History, it seemed that Rwanda had to be situated at the medieval stage. During the same period, a leading light in Third-Worldist history, Walter Rodney, however attentive he was to the effects of imperialism on dominated societies, also thought ancient Rwanda could be defined as eminently feudal. The same type of interpretation dominated 1960s scholarship on the ancient kingdoms in Uganda. John Beattie's work, for example, compared old Bunyoro to England under Norman feudalism.[58]

However, warnings about the dangers of such approaches were not lacking. As early as 1936, a Belgian historian sent to Burundi to analyze "living feudalism" there had the honesty to recognize publicly, once he was back in Brussels, that his search had been in vain. He collected remarkable testimonies from the monarchy's former political and religious officials, but his papers were swept under the rug for the whole colonial period.[59] More recently, several studies have been done on the use of the concept of African feudalism, including its application in the Great Lakes region.[60]

We will return to this subject. For now, let us revisit the central aspects of a feudal regime as they emerged in relation to the European model: different types of power, land, and personal ties. Political power was monopolized by private networks and constructed through face-to-face loyalty. A minority of rulers monopolized land, while the peasant mass was both deprived of property rights and enslaved. The society was caught in a pyramid of personal ties, which both created an aristocracy of "vassals" and attached "serfs" to their masters. Instead of addressing each element in detail, I want to focus on the system of administration, on the constraints imposed in rural areas, and on the nature of the region's clientage relationships. I also intend to discuss the historical factors that led to the crystallization of the aristocracies, which will include a reflection on the famous Tutsi-Hutu phenomenon.[61]

Each sovereign had recourse to two circles of followers: his relations and his friends, "princes and palatines."[62] The first were also rivals, because they shared a royal bloodline; they "come from the drum's belly," as a Kirundi expression puts it. Nonetheless, they were key, and their role is everywhere manifest, as were ways of neutralizing their influence. The example of Burundi, as we have seen, is clarifying: the Baganwa furnished the majority of provincial chiefs, but the more distant their family relationship with the king, the farther away they were placed, to the point of being repressed and "demoted" after several generations. The *mwami* both used them and divided them. The same, often convoluted power games were evident in Bunyoro and the Haya kingdoms, with, respectively, the Babito *b'ebingoma* ("the Babito of the drum," in contrast to those of the same category who had lost all memory of a blood tie with the monarchy) and the Barangira of Kiziba and neighboring kingdoms. In Bushi, the Baluzi represented a category of this type. In Rwanda, the aristocracy, which can accurately be called princely, was made up of the sovereigns' descendants — namely, the Banyiginya Tutsi, notably since the reign of Gahindiro in the early nineteenth century, and the Batutsi from the Bega clan, who had furnished two-thirds of the queen mothers since the seventeenth century. The rivalry between these two groups was manifest at the beginning of the twentieth century after the major Bega chiefs plotted against Mwami Rutalindwa, who was deposed in favor of Yuhi Musinga in 1896. In Buganda, as we have seen, with every new reign the clan of princes was new, because the latter was produced by the queen mother. In addition, starting in the nineteenth century, the *kabaka* began the practice of eliminating his brothers.

Except for the sovereign's close relations (such as uncles at the start of a reign or eldest sons at the end), the most listened-to advisers were people of humbler origins. They belonged to appointed families that regularly furnished their young for service at the court. These youths literally made their careers by distinguishing themselves before the king for their bravery, wisdom, and loyalty; when they grew to maturity, they became notables, whom the sovereign consulted regularly and who constituted the monarchy's real government. The king gathered their advice before making major decisions, or he sent them to the provinces for special assignments.[63] This group formed the first delegations to meet the European conquerors. I have already cited the Burundian *banyarurimbi* ("the people of the court at the palace entrance"), who came from the group of notables on the hills (the *bashingantahe*, to whom we will return). In their youth, these grand advisers had been shepherds, cooks, or milkers at the court, or they had made a name for themselves in war or on a special assignment. In Bunyoro, the equivalent were the *basekura*, "those who speak honestly"; in Bushubi, there were the *bahanuza*, "the advisers"; and in Buhaya, there were the *baramata*, the specialists in law. In Bunyoro and Nkore, some were the king's messengers. In Bunyoro, the emergence of the state in the late eighteenth century was clearly tied to forming this group of chiefs and advisers, which included Iru, Hima, and Bito elements, around a "mode of Nyoro thought."[64] In Buganda, a genuine centralized administration took shape in the nineteenth century: a series of dignitaries, recruited from specific clans, functioned as grand servants in the court. But these functions were coupled with political responsibilities, which made these dignitaries appear as ministers in the eyes of the British protectorate. These included the *katikiro*, a court superintendent referred to as a "prime minister"; the *kibale*, master of ceremonies; the *kisekwa*, the supreme magistrate, the *kimbugwe*, the political and religious adviser; the *sabakaki*, the commander of pages; the *mujasi*, charged with military questions; and the *seruti*, in charge of banana cider.[65]

Outside the capitals, the "country," controlled both militarily and mystically by the king, consisted of both populations and lands (the two meanings of the term *igihugu* in Kirundi). These were organized territorially, with borders varying according to relations with local forces and possibly to strategies of crosscutting districts. One is often ironic about political or administrative borders in old Africa, but the absence of customs officials, road signs, and, more important, bureaucratic-style spatial homogenization (which was established in France with the creation of departments) does not mean that responsibilities were not territorialized.[66] People knew when they left a chief's or a king's jurisdiction. In terms of land and politics, natural and man-made landmarks mapped out rights: rivers and swamps, rocks, termite mounds, trees or sacred woods, and so on.

Territorial division and methods of determining officials introduced a variety of situations. Two general levels can be distinguished: the small province (what was called a chiefdom under colonialism) and the locality (a hill or a group of banana gardens). For example, in Burundi, one distinguished chiefs (*batware*) and their "delegates" (*vyariho*). Among the Bashi, the Bahaya, and the Baha, the same hierarchy existed. The Bugandan kingdom was divided into *saza* (translated as "counties" during colonialism), which were subdivided into *gombolola*. The Rwandan system observed in the nineteenth century was quite particular. Three local authorities, dependents of the *mwami*, shared tasks: army chiefs, pasture or cow chiefs, and land chiefs (*batware b'ingabo* or *b'u-muheto, batware b'imikenke* or *b'inka*, and *batware b'ubutaka*). The borders of their respective jurisdictions did not coincide, and in the majority of cases a single chief performed all three functions. The "system of intermingled fingers" (to cite the definition of Kandt, the German resident) was complete only in the center of the country. Thus, in Kinyaga, there were no pasture chiefs. Some persons combined responsibilities in several regions. Below them, starting with Rwabugiri's reign, were "hill chiefs," who tightly controlled the population.[67]

Local power holders could obtain their position in one of three ways: they could rise up locally and then be confirmed by the monarchy, which wanted to remain close to the local population; or they could inherit the position from a chief, who had been appointed either by a ruling sovereign or by one of his predecessors (these generally were princes of royal blood or notables from other lineages); or they could be named by the monarch, who could revoke their power at will.

The first type of authorities primarily involved powerful ancient lineages and clans, who stayed in place with territorial responsibilities. In Buha and Bushi, the sovereigns had to respect local authorities who presided over religious practices and land rights, the *bateko* and the *bajinji*; the sovereigns would use them as diviners and as agricultural officials.[68] In Burundi, the scenario was different: other than the lineages of influential ritualists, present in different regions of the country, the most original institution was the *bashingantahe* (literally "those who plant the staff of arbitration," or hill judges), who were chosen locally among different Hutu and Tutsi lineage groups. The choice was made on the basis of their moral authority, their wisdom, their linguistic mastery, their skill in social relations, and their experience in jurisprudence. They were appointed during a great festival, and they judged in the *mwami*'s name.[69] However, their decisions were autonomously made after a public hearing of the opposing parties and collection of testimony. It was from among these people, representatives of the population, that the chiefs and even the king chose their permanent advisers, as we saw above. Some also were chosen as managers of royal domains or as the chiefs' delegates. These men on the hills were essential to gaining popular support for the royal institution.

Other examples show a clash between monarchical logic and clan authorities. In Nkore, Bairu lineage leaders in the west succeeded in defending their autonomy in exchange for periodically paying tribute to and recognizing the supremacy of the Hinda dynasty. In Buganda, the *saza* were modeled on clan territories: for example, the chief of the "county" of Bulemezi possessed the hereditary title Nabugwamu and was head of the Lungfish (Mamba) clan. But starting with Mawanda's reign in the eighteenth century, the *kabaka* intervened in these commands by appointing new chiefs, superiors of the ancient leaders, who came from either the same or a different clan, and by creating new *saza*. The sovereigns thus marginalized, reinforced, or reused the *bataka*, "the clan chiefs": the latter still had their hereditary authority, but it was now under the monarchy's control. When they became the king's chiefs, they became *bakungu*, "the powerful."[70]

The same combination of hereditary notability and state hierarchy can be found throughout. Bunyoro's *mukama* and Nkore's
mugabe also had their *bakungu*, chosen preferably (but not exclusively) from certain clans (Bito for the former and Hima for the
latter). In Bushi, the *mwami* had at his disposal a *barhambo* network, whose members were princes (*baluzi*) or diviners (*bajinji*).
In Burundi, Buha, and Rwanda, a *batware* network stood behind
the monarchy. The complexity of the Rwandan system was described earlier. In Burundi, the situation was clearer, at least at
the territorial level: the majority of chiefs (*batware*) were of royal
blood, and the term *muganwa* (prince) also meant chief, in the full
meaning of the word (a usage that the colonial regime standardized). But some Tutsi or Hutu chiefs, called *nkebe*, were also in
charge of peripheral territories. Finally, Hutu and Tutsi notables
(the *bishikira*) managed royal lands in the center of the country,
as we have seen, and had direct access to the king. As in Rwanda,
the sovereign played off rivalries between ruling groups, and he
sometimes encouraged a prince or loyalist to establish himself in a
region, much to the detriment of the preexisting lineage. In the
long run, this practice eroded the power of those privileged during previous reigns and laid the groundwork for "demoting" them,
often starting with princes of remote ancestry.

Numerous methods enabled a sovereign to maintain an umbil-
ical cord with his chiefs, despite the distance and the hereditary
system. These included requiring chiefs to keep permanent representatives at the royal court (in Bunyoro) and to visit periodically.
In Burundi, a chief who did not appear, notably at the annual *muganuro* festival, was suspected of rebellion: this was how the Batare
princes of the northeast expressed their dissidence during Mwezi
Gisabo's rule. Evidently, intrigues were rife, and the central power
thus sooner or later learned all. But in the nineteenth century,
as we have seen, this control was structured through installing

officials in the provinces with personal ties to the sovereign. The newly conquered regions of Buganda are exemplary: military colonies were created there, the *bitongole*, under the responsibility of the *kabaka*'s right-hand man. Under King Mutesa, these new chiefs, or *batongole*, dependent on the goodwill of the king, multiplied. Their status might be compared with that of the commissions in contrast to the offices in the French ancien régime.

As we have seen, to secure their essential ties, the ancient states, lacking writing and money, relied on kinship, trust, and personal relationships, which were periodically rekindled by direct contact and exchanged words. This does not mean that power was privatized, as the Weberian interpretation of patrimonialism suggests. The state certainly did not benefit from the legacy of an ancient City. Still, it could rely on royal mystique, that is, on an authority superior to the obligations of blood, a notion that was reinforced by the territorial aspect of power. Without doubt (to take up Edward Steinhart's claim), "in any small scale agrarian society virtually all social and political relations will be personal in the simple sense of face to face. However, [this] does not mean that relations of political dependence are 'personal' in the sense implicit in the vassalage relationship." These African kingdoms can be compared to the kingdoms of the very late Middle Ages, when, in the Carolingian and even the Merovingian period, land benefices were effectively precarious remuneration for the functions performed by a *nobilitas* of imperial origin.[71]

The chiefs' main responsibilities were in rural settings and primarily concerned peasant subjects. These responsibilities included collecting prestations, arbitrating disputes, and organizing military mobilization if need be. Given the importance of the rural setting, the nature and weight of prestations and of the landowning system merit attention. Unfortunately, despite the volume of ink spilled over theories of feudalism, concrete studies on these aspects are rare. The "taxes" of these states were strictly in kind, which limited their scope. "Taxes" took the form of collections of agricultural, pastoral, or artisanal products as well as requisitions of workdays, that is, of corvées. In the Haya kingdoms, for example, each year subjects owed five large banana bunches and several kilos of coffee, plus a certain number of corvée days per family.[72] Hunters owed one tusk of each elephant killed as well as leopard skins. In Burundi, peasants (*bakopi*) paid taxes in bananas or beans; blacksmiths furnished spears; specialists in threshing ficus bark from Buddu brought clothes, and so on. In Nkore, the Bairu delivered food and artisanal products, while the Bahima brought cows.

The prestation system in late-nineteenth-century Burundi has been studied in detail.[73] Annual deliveries mainly consisted of sorghum, baskets of grain called *marari* (the "collected") that filled the king's and princes' granaries, and jugs of beer "showing" the delivery, of which intermediaries received "sediment" (that is, a share). This operation took place notably during *muganuro*, which inaugurated the dispatching of delegations to the royal court. For their part, cattle keepers provided "the family business cow." Additionally, though irregular, demands were made during walks, marriages, and when chiefs were changed; on other occasions, goods were collected to settle a fine or to mollify a somewhat nasty official. These consisted of heads of cattle called *ingorore* or jugs of beer called *biturire*. Moreover, some families had specific obligations called *inkuka*: hoes from blacksmiths, mats and basketry from the plains or forest border areas, salt from salt workers in the eastern and western valleys, jugs of honey from lineages engaged in apiculture, and milking cows from shepherds who had been given a royal bull for their herd (these cattle keepers were called *batongore* and were numerous in the southern parts of the country). These specialized prestations were considered an honor.

179

Moreover, the *mwami* had his own fields (a sort of land reserve), cultivated by peasants who resided within the jurisdiction of the royal estate and whom their respective *bishikira* sent for a tour of work for the sovereign. These teams rotated according to the required tasks and were composed of representatives of different lineages from each hill. In the end, this activity consumed only a few workdays per year for each cultivator. In the vicinities of the king's courts and of the major chiefs resided very poor landless peasants; their existence was precarious, and they were subject to corvée almost at will.

These forms of prestations (baskets of sorghum and beans, and so on) were found in Rwanda, where chiefs collected them on an ad hoc basis. It is possible that Rwanda's multiple local powers, which were both useful to the sovereign and usable by subjects in case of trouble with one or the other, did not lead overall to heavier "fiscal" demands. This is what emerges in Catharine Newbury's precise study on the "cohesion of oppression," which was conducted in Kinyaga, southeast of Lake Kivu.[74] Newbury shows the tax sum due to those of *muheto* (army) title and that due to those of *butaka* (land) title; the taxes included food products, heads of cattle, cows, mats, and bracelets. What is more, by the late nineteenth century under Rwabugiri's rule, a new corvée system was introduced. This new system was called *buletwa* and consisted in porterage and in performing agricultural tasks on the rulers' estates. First introduced in the center of the country, this requisitioning spread little by little to the peripheries, but it encountered so much resistance that it was only fully adopted under colonialism. The origin of *buletwa* is debated because it had existed for years as an obligation of two out of five days, five days being the ancient Rwandan week. But if the week (which is not an astronomical unit) existed in old Rwanda, other sources suggest it was only four days long. In addition, the term *buletwa* is not related to other words in Kinyarwanda and seems derived from the Swahili verb *kuleta*, "to recruit" porters or "to solicit" workers. All this suggests an external borrowing, which might be tied to the commercial caravans sent by King Rwabugiri to Rusubi. The so-called traditional institutions can sometimes be quite recent.[75]

It is difficult to evaluate the exact toll these taxes took on the peasant economy. How much pressure, in other words, did these ancient states put on the societies they controlled? Qualitatively, the question is tied to how land rights are defined.[76] We are certainly outside the field of Roman law. But this does not mean that land control was anarchic; rather, it was the stake in an ongoing tension between lineage rights and those claimed by the political powers. Without getting lost in a maze of infinitely different situations, we shall consider the main principles of this jurisprudence. In Burundi, for example, when a family had inherited rights acquired by the first land clearers (or those supposed to be first), one said that it lived on "grandfather's property."[77] This was in contrast to land granted by a chief as "vacant land" or claimed as such ("bow property"). As far as the lineages were concerned, the many agricultural activities — perennial and seasonal, pastoral and cultivated — in principle justified the widest rights possible and legitimized large estates, which were called *ubukonde* lands in northwestern Rwanda. But demographic growth as well as the general shift toward migration and increasingly intensive methods of working the land (notably with multi-seasonal harvests) gave the arbitration of royal power its very meaning. This included arbitration between rival lineages, between agricultural and pastoral interests, and between the rights of first comers and the demands of new arrivals. The landgrabs by the monarchy (real or perceived as such) were followed by remittances. The right of descent was all the stronger when it manifested itself in the effective exploitation of land.

In these countries of scattered settlement, it is possible to speak of a spectrum of land control, from the enclosure and banana garden to seasonal and annual fields, to pastures and surrounding long-fallow lands. Political control was established primarily on vacant lands, brush areas, pastureland, and abandoned farm fields. Demographic pressure thus rendered the sovereign's and the chiefs' intervention decisive. All this was inevitably accompanied by the development of privileges. By the late nineteenth century, a landless peasant class had emerged, that is, young people whose families could not decently house them and who lacked an influential backer.[78] These peasants became either domestics or day laborers at the homes of the more wealthy, notably the powerful (the *bashumba* of Burundi, the *bacancuro* of Rwanda), or tenant farmers with precarious tenures who were forced to perform work obligations (the *bagererwa* of Burundi and Rwanda, the batwarwa of Buhaya). This category remained a minority. Still, in order to appreciate social change during the nineteenth century, we must not forget its expansion.

The land regime is therefore not exactly feudal. Though the king, the guarantor of the country's fertility, claimed to be "father" of the country and the owner of everything (even babies), neither he nor chiefs delegated in his name actually exercised this right. They were not "lords" in the medieval sense of being chiefs of villagers and proprietors of their tenures. Rather, we should speak of a "tributary" regime functioning from poles of domination represented by the chiefs' enclosures: in these centers of power, land and herds accumulated; prestations filled granaries; teams of people performed corvée labor; gifts from those requesting favors were collected, and so on. This "little world" of "masters" and their "intendants" is undoubtedly what Claudine Vidal, when describing Rwanda in 1974, termed "lordship" or what Pierre Gravel, when describing Gisaka (east of Rwanda) in 1968, called a "nuclear feudal cluster." In Burundi, this was the atmosphere on the royal estates.[79] These poles of power spread as land was cleared and as agro-pastoral activity was intensified, but without a widespread appropriation of lands. The sophistication of taxation systems was proportional to military expansion, to territorial annexation, and to the capacity to administer the kingdoms. But this exploitation was limited: calculations made in Rwanda and Burundi put the taxation level at 4 to 10 percent of production, which is surely higher than in the West African states, which depended more on external tributes and slavery, but less than in the fields of the West at the height of the lordly regime.[80] In 1917, Jan Czekanowski analyzed, quite well in my estimation, the determinant factors of this situation, at least before modern commerce had made its effects felt:

> In a primitive and non-differentiated society, the possibilities for exploitation are limited. As long as there are direct deliveries of foodstuffs to a relatively small number of masters, even the biggest appetites can be satisfied. This reduced possibility of exploitation is what provides the foundation for social equilibrium without norms being juridically established. Arbitrary exploitation is further limited by permanent internal battles, which are germane to an unorganized state entity, where support of the mass of subjects matters a great deal. The powerful must take their subjects into account. If they fail to, they risk being abandoned by their followers and their subjects and being subjugated by their rivals.[81]

"Pastoral Feudalism": The Historical Dimension of a Mirage

These observations have not been read as much as they deserve to be. Did the Treaty of Versailles devalue everything that had been said in German on the region? The theme of the pastoral clientage relationship eclipsed all other analyses, especially in relation to

the western kingdoms. Jacques Maquet's 1954 work only synthesized an already dominant idea: that the *buhake* tie was the primordial way that the Tutsi had forged their rule centuries ago. In
1939, keen on the Middle Ages, Canon Louis de Lacger, the principal historian before Alexis Kagame, saw a "fief" in the cow that
the patron (*shebuja*) gave to the "vassal" (*umugaragu*), who in turn
"committed himself" to the patron. A distinction was not made
between the *mwami*'s political domination and the appeal of the
bovines, on the pretense that the sovereign strategically manipulated this socioeconomic stake.[82]

Cultural proofs of these social premises are not entirely absent: linguistic richness regarding pastoral activities and rules of
decorum for milk consumption; the aesthetic primacy of cows in
the designation of colors and in references to female beauty ("heifer
eyes"); the much-sought-after shape of horns, partly reproduced
in body movements in many dances; the importance of cattle in
heroic stories and their place in the monarchy's rituals; the power
symbolized by a large herd (even if wealth and prosperity were
also attached to sorghum and honey); the reference points offered
by pastoral life in the division of time, including hours of the day
indicated by moving cattle between the enclosure, meadows, and
watering places and years of life marked by the period when children could only watch over calves and when they were allowed to
guard the cows; all cultural experience (games, jokes, physical
exercises, knowledge of nature) that pastoral life represented for
boys, who all participated to greater or lesser degrees. This vision
of the world must have seemed to legitimate an oft-heard dictum
in Rwanda: "Nothing surpasses the cow." Before fascinating anthropologists, the "fetishism of the cow" had lived in the hearts of
the Banyarwanda and those of their neighbors.[83]

The problem here is that this cultural fact is taken to be an eternal reality. Let us recall what we have observed in this chapter: the

penetration or gradual intensification of a pastoral economy from east to west, and the western mountain states' takeover, in the late seventeenth century, as the intermediary plateau states failed from ecological and military problems. Certainly, the general evolution since this period, as much around Lakes Tanganyika and Kivu as toward Victoria, also shows that the better-watered and the more agricultural regions provided a more solid and durable foundation for monarchical constructions than did the pastoral savannas of the Nyoro-Haya-Zinza-Ha axis. Starting in the eighteenth century, the expanding kingdoms owed their demographic and economic force to sorghum and bananas as well as to beans and maize. In the western parts of the region, the integration of agriculture and cattle keeping therefore achieved new successes, coming after the much older successes of the so-called Cwezi culture on the banks of the Katonga. At the same time, the myths attached to different reigns and the history of institutions allow one to detect, starting in the eighteenth century, an increasing tendency to emphasize society's pastoral side. This can be seen in southern Buha and Bushi, as well as in Burundi, where the pastoral image of the *mwami* is much more pronounced for Mutaga Senyamwiza than for his ancestor Ntare Rushatsi and where Ntare Rugamba's wars in the early nineteenth century were often tied to expansion into the grassland areas. This evolution has mainly been analyzed in relation to western Uganda's and Rwanda's political formations.[84]

After the fall of Mpororo, the takeover of the Nkore dynasty on the western highlands was accompanied both by installing armies and by reinforcing the power of Hima lineages over the rest of the population, labeled Bairu. One observes the same process in small neighboring principalities, like Buhweju and, in the nineteenth century, Toro. By separating from Bunyoro, Toro could have counted on the support of the leaders of the Bakonjo population, who lived on the Ruwenzori slopes and partly controlled the saltworks, which were the basis of the entire region's fortunes. The power of the Babito, of which Bunyoro was the model, did not depend as much on pastoral contracts as did the Nkore and Rwandan monarchies. As we have seen, the eighteenth-century crises (droughts and famines) were likely quite propitious for cattle keepers and for implementing or hardening pastoral dependencies, which gave these two kingdoms their respective Hima and Tutsi faces.

The study of the role of bovines in Rwandan society by the Rwandan historian Jean-Népomucène Nkurikiyimfura confirms this assessment.[85] The army system dates back only to Rujugira's reign in the eighteenth century; so too does the systematic allotment of herds to those under the control of the "bow chiefs," giving rise to what one called the "bovine armies." The selection of *inyambo* cows at the court began only with Mazimpaka, his predecessor. Undoubtedly originating in Mpororo, these cows were distinguished by their very long horns and a particular grace that contributed much to the "fetishization" of cattle. Then, during Gahindiro's rule in the early nineteenth century, the land institution of *gikingi* appeared — that is, landed property was transformed into a pastoral reserve assigned to a cattle raiser whom the Court regarded highly. The *bikingi* multiplied in the center of the country, but not in the agriculturally dominated west or in the east, where grasslands were sufficiently abundant. Thus this institution was created in response to increased scarcity of lands and to newly acute competition between agriculture and cattle keeping. During the same period, notably under Rwogera, the subdivision of local power between land chiefs and cow chiefs spread. Agriculturists might be admitted onto a *gikingi*, but only precariously and in exchange for special fees. This practice strongly evokes the medieval fief and, moreover, can be found in kingdoms outside the pastoral context. An example is the so-called *nyarubanja* estates that the king allocated to his followers in Buhaya country: peasants living on these lands became simple tenant farmers.[86]

In any case, the consequences for Rwandan society were decisive because the government's growing encroachment on land rights was combined from then on with a clear discrimination between Batutsi and Bahutu, which in turn became part of everyday rural life (and not only in court functions). The conjunction with the introduction of *buletwa*, an agricultural corvée, reinforced this situation in the center of the country. Finally, starting in the seventeenth century, the relations of reciprocity that had functioned in pastoral settings under the name of *buhake* since time immemorial evolved more and more into unequal relations between cattle keepers and agriculturists, especially in the eighteenth and nineteenth centuries (the apogee, from this point of view, being reached during the colonial period). *Buhake* looked more and more like a political-administrative relationship linked to the network of powers.

Parallel observations can be made on the evolution of clientage relationships in Burundi (*bugabire*) and Nkore (*okutoisha*). It is striking to see how much "public" taxes are both reproduced and handled on a personal basis. In terms of vocabulary, this includes telling confusions between "gift" and "contribution" and between service and corvée.[87] In Rwanda, episodic requirements of "giving one's time" (*gufata igihe*) to chiefs and "building walls" (*kwubaka inkike*) for them became standard practices, with each patron playing the role of a small chief.

Backed by government practices, the Hutu-Tutsi cleavage thus penetrated social life decisively. Catharine Newbury showed this quite well in the Kinyaga case. The "Tutsi arrival" in this peripheral southwest area is represented in the late nineteenth century as the arrival of "Ndugans" — the royal court's men, who generally were considered Tutsi (the majority were). It was in relation to this that Kinyagans became "Hutu," except for the notables integrated into the system, who became "Tutsized":

> The introduction of central Rwandan chiefs in Kinyaga during the reign of Rwabugiri had an important impact on ethnic differentiation. With the arrival of these central Rwandan authorities, lines of distinction between Hutu and Tuutsi in the region began to be altered and sharpened. Since the new chiefs were almost invariably of Tuutsi status, the category Tuutsi assumed hierarchical overtones which heretofore in Kinyaga had been of minor significance. As the political arena widened and the intensity of political activity increased, these classifications became stratified and rigidified.[88]

One might wonder whether the central model was not forged in being defined, even if in a caricatured way, on the peripheries — a role the peripheries often play in "border" situations, as we saw above. Indeed, this type of evolution was gradual and initially imperceptible: it consisted of a shift from a logic of reciprocity, one of gifts and counter-gifts (according to the spirit Marcel Mauss defined), to a logic that, at least in principle, was redistributive and increasingly hierarchical to the point of perverting the personal ties that were central in this pyramid of power.[89] In countries less touched than Rwanda by this logic of discrimination — Burundi and Buha, for example — the logics of exchange remained more visible in the nineteenth century.[90] The *bugabire* combined simple Bahutu and Batutsi in various configurations. Exchanges of beer, sorghum, and bananas were central to social life. "In Urundi one gave gifts extraordinarily frequently, for friendship and for respect, for politeness and as a sign of submission."[91] Neighborly solidarities brought everyone together: during a fire, when lightning struck cattle, for notables' activities on the hill, for guarding herds, and in the cult of *kubandwa*. Clan memberships ranked higher than Hutu or Tutsi categorizations.

In fact, these realities persisted despite the discrimination we just saw. Even in Rwanda. Claudine Vidal shows that, again in Rwanda, wealth and poverty do not correlate to the Hutu-Tutsi divide. And Pierre Gravel observed, "The difference between classes is mostly a difference in emphasis. The richer Tutsi do less work in the fields and more herding." The great rinderpest epidemic of 1891 helped standardize the social situation at the grassroots of society, while creating a gulf that separated this base group from a privileged minority, which benefited from top-down redistribution. In Burundi, in 1904–1905, during the famines that ravaged the center of the country, missionaries described starving Batutsi in search of food. In Nkore, the mass of poor Bahima were as exploited as the mass of Bairu.[92]

Clearly, the notions of lord and serf, often applied to all Batutsi and Bahutu, do not correspond to the ancient reality — despite government intervention that since the eighteenth century increased privileges benefiting the Batutsi, notably in Rwanda (as well as the Bahima in Nkore). In fact, the words "Tutsi" and "Hutu" have not always had the same meaning. Sometimes they referred to being born as such, as a function of ancient sociocultural and familial heritage (having had or not having had a strong tie with cattle at some time). Again, this identity goes without saying and often is not expressed. At odds with the court, a group of autonomous pastoralists called Bagogwe, who lived in northern Rwanda at the foot of the volcanic mountains, were relabeled "Tutsi" within the kingdom, a label that persists in modern politics. In Rwanda, clan membership for a long time prevailed over so-called ethnic membership. Cultivators in western Rwanda, and those in western and eastern Burundi, around the Imbo and Kumoso depressions, were defined by their lineages, but in the context of the kingdom they became "Hutu." In the same way, cultivators in western Nkore became "Iru" in relation to Hima power. At this level, the connotation of these memberships became hierarchical, as we saw in Kinyaga. The term "Hutu" meant, in the clientage relationship, the subordinate position of the recipient: even if the recipient was Tutsi, the donor spoke of him as "my Hutu." In Rwanda, the term "Tutsi" little by little was perceived as an identity closely related to power, so much so that one had to "de-Hutuize" oneself if promoted (in Burundi, this occurred only under colonial rule). For years, foreigners missed this confusion of meanings, which was tied to political-cultural shifts. Indeed, foreigners saw the "Tutsi" only as a small minority in the courts: "I think there are hardly more than 20,000 Batutsi in Ruanda," wrote Father Léon Classe in 1916. A Belgian doctor estimated the Tutsi population of Ruanda-Burundi to be 7 percent in 1954. Not until the 1956 demographic surveys did the statistic of 13–18 percent come into use.[93] The simple Batutsi were almost invisible.

This leads us to conclude with the "aristocracies," such as they appeared before the colonial takeover. "Two dozen" major chiefs controlled 80 percent of Rwanda, according to Resident Kandt in 1906; "about 20 major chiefs," according to Claudine Vidal in 1974. Somewhat enlarging the field of the fortunate, we'll say there were several hundred, even several thousand people, including families: the major Tutsi lineages, the Banyiginya and the Bega, in the late nineteenth century in Rwanda; the upper layer of a group of Hinda princes and several allied families of Bahima, those who possessed large herds in Nkore; roughly a hundred chiefs of princely rank, as well as several influential Tutsi and Hutu lineages in Burundi; and the same for the Bahinda princes and the Babito and their allies in their respective kingdoms.

In Buganda, the factions witnessed when the Europeans arrived were composed mostly of persons from lineages relating to queen mothers from previous reigns; members of the Otter, the Lungfish, the Elephant, and the Locust clans; others who had distinguished themselves before the *kabaka*. The emergence of "new men" in the royal entourage was inscribed in client networks, which some major dignitaries made the most of. This was the case for the *katikiro* (prime minister), who became increasingly powerful at the end of the century, notably when he held on to his functions over several reigns (like Mukasa did between 1874 and 1888).

Political centralization thus was decisive in crystallizing the aristocracies. Their members knew how to use a country's economic forces, the prince's favor, heredity, matrimonial alliances, and, in the final analysis, a specific kind of pomp, which was maintained by etiquette, clothing, lifestyle, and marriages calculated, in the spirit of caste, to create "ideal" physical "types."[94]

The Regional Dynamic of Commercial Networks

However, if cattle were the nerve of an economy of social exchanges in the ancient mountain states of the Nkore-Rwanda-Burundi group, other resources depended on more commercial logics; this was particularly the case on the peripheries.[95] Certainly, the region was familiar with short-distance seasonal bartering of food and cattle products, as a function of complementarity between ecological sectors. Some food products won greater renown: palm oil from the shores of Lake Tanganyika (in Burundi and Buvira), dried bananas from Buganda, coffee from Bunyoro and Buhaya, dried fish from Burundi and Bujiji or from Lakes Edward and George, and, of course, livestock (goats, bull calves, and sterile cows) and butter from Rwanda and Burundi. Let us add tobacco from northern Rwanda and Nkore. But three products gave rise to truly regional trade: salt, iron, and jewelry.

Salt could be obtained from the ashes of certain reeds or from briny mud, but better-quality, intensive production that yielded standardized packets was developed on three saltworks sites: Kibiro on Lake Albert's shore (in Bunyoro), the salty springs near the confluence of the Malagarasi and the Rutshugi in Uvinza, and Katwe and Kasenyi on the volcanic sites (therefore producing year-round) between Lakes Edward and George.[96] The first supplied the north and east of contemporary Uganda; the second supplied Buha, Burundi, and the Nyamwezi countries; and the third supplied western Uganda and Rwanda. Kibiro was controlled by the *mukama* of Bunyoro; Buvinza was divided among three principalities that, during each dry season at the end of the nineteenth century, welcomed around ten thousand workers who came to "boil the salt"; Katwe and Kasenyi were managed by two local clans (the Bagabo and the Bakingwe), who exploited and transported salt in canoes on the small neighboring lakes. They would sell it at docks to foreign hawkers who came to stock up at these markets. Goats frequently had an exchange value in this commerce, both for Rwandans who traveled to procure packages of Katwe salt and for Burundians who went to work on the Uvinza saltworks. They returned with twice as many heads as they had brought.[97]

Some iron "melting" and forging was done throughout the area. But certain regions were distinguished for their abundance of minerals and their blacksmithing: southern Burundi, northern Rwanda, southern Kigezi, Bushi, Buhweju, Bunyoro, Buzinza, and Buyungu (northern Buha). Each sector had its specialties: quality of the metal, shape of the hoes, production of arms or bracelets made from braided material (the *nyerere*), and so on. Blacksmithing is also, by definition, a dry-season activity, because smelting in pits required dry weather.[98] Commerce in salt and iron objects, the root of mid-range trade networks, often brought together partners from two kinds of production: for example, the salt workers of Katwe and the blacksmiths of Kayonza or, in Burundi, the blacksmiths of Kangozi and the salt workers of Kumoso. Salt packages, heads of cattle, and hoes served as currency during bartering.

As for jewelry, at the regional level it only concerned commodities made from plant material such as threshed bark cloth, which was a specialty in Buganda (even if it was known in other countries, next to cow, antelope, or leopard skins), and braided raffia bracelets called *amatega*. The Batembo, who neighbored the Congolese forest in western Havuland, were the primary producers of *amatega*. To the Rwandans, these bracelets were a much-valued ornament and animated trade in the country's northwest. Farther south, notably in Burundi and Buha, the well-off placed more value on copper rings, which probably came from contemporary Katanga, and on shells from the Indian Ocean (small cowries or large crescent-shaped or half-cone-shaped pendants).[99]

Hawkers transported these products to rulers' courts or across the countryside. They circulated in small groups, utilizing cross-border clan relations or blood brotherhoods to find hospitality and to guarantee their safety. In some areas, either near royal residences or, especially, in the regions bordering complementary economic zones, true markets developed in the nineteenth century: for example, on the littoral of Lake Tanganyika, in Heru (southern Buha) near Burundi, in southern Bushi (notably in the Kaziba kingdom, in Mulengeza, where a five-day week was built around this activity), in northwestern Rwanda (some twenty markets are reported), on the southern border of Bunyoro, and on the shores of Lake Kyoga, in Kyagwe (the crossroads between Buganda, Busoga, and the Buvuma Islands).[100] These markets helped to crystallize an increasingly merchant sector: the canoeists on Lakes George, Edward, Albert, and Kyoga; the Bajiji on Lake Tanganyika; the Bahavu on Ijwi in Lake Kivu; and the Basuba and the

Bakerebe, who respectively lived northeast and south of Lake Victoria. In this regard, it is significant that in Burundi, as in Rwanda, a former word to indicate market was *icambu*, which meant ford or lake docking.[101] In addition to noting these waterways, one should cite the Batumbi between Toro and Kigezi, the Parombo north of Lake Albert, the Baziba in Buhaya, the Bazibaziba of southern Bushi, the Bayangayanga of Burundi, the Basubi of western Buzinza, and so on.

These groups, apparently, had a very different lifestyle from that of the agro-pastoral circle, which has largely been described here. They appear to be almost marginal, but they were nonetheless integrated into their societies. They simply carried out their activities in the dry season; they visited the powerful; and they delivered prestations. In Rwanda, the "armies" of the northwest had *matega* obligations that they collected from hawkers. In Burundi, the eastern and Imbo chiefdoms had to furnish salt to the court. In the markets — in Bunyoro and Bushi, for example — collectors representing the monarchical state, the *bahoza*, levied taxes. In the late nineteenth century, the saltworks of Katwe and Kasenyi were the subject of unending rivalry between Toro and Bunyoro, each of which tried to impose its tribute there.

In several cases (Bushi, Buhavu, Buhaya, Buha, and Buzinza), the dynamism of these exchanges did not coincide with political power. Bukerebe, a small kingdom based on a peninsula and on an island in southern Lake Victoria, dominated lake navigation in the mid-nineteenth century. One might also note that even Bunyoro, whose decline started in the eighteenth century, as we have seen, remained an influential commercial hub in the nineteenth century: it had iron, salt, and cattle, while controlling networks that reached from Lake Albert to Busoga. It could sell all that Buganda lacked. On the other hand, Buganda and Rwanda were rather predatory states that wanted to lay their hands on these trade circuits: Buganda, under the *kabaka* Suna and Mutesa, conducted raids into Busoga, on the western banks of Victoria (as we have seen), and on the Bunyoro plateaus; under Rwabugiri, Rwanda devoted itself to gaining control of Lake Kivu.[102]

In the mid-nineteenth century, the region was split into four trade zones: the Bunyoro-Busoga circle from Lake Albert to Mount Elgon, via the banks of the Nile and Lake Kyoga; the Kivu circle, incorporating the salty lakes of western Uganda and Rwanda and reaching the edge of the Congolese forest; the Tanganyika circle, from the Rusizi valley to the Malagarasi valley, including the Kaziba marshes, the Uvinza saltworks, and Burundi; and the Victoria circle, including Buganda, the Bahaya, the Bazinza, and the Bakerebe. But beginning in the second third of the century, the Tanganyika and Victoria zones received a new influx from the eastern coast. First, in several waves, caravans of Banyamwezi hawkers, "the people of the moon" in Swahili folklore, brought new products to the region: colored-glass beads from central Europe (notably the small red *sam-sam*), copper and brass bracelets, porcelain crockery, white cotton from New England (called *merikani*), and English "printed calico" of varied colors (such as navy-blue *kaniki*).[103] In exchange, they looked for ivory. Elephant herds having been decimated on the East African plateaus, the hunter-merchants now looked for them in the Great Lakes region, where they were still abundant on the Upper Nile, east of contemporary Congo and in Bunyoro.

In the 1830s and 1840s, clients from the Indian Ocean coast and Swahili and Arab merchants from the Zanzibar sultanate, among other places, reached the region. They began using the Banyamwezi not as intermediary hawkers but as simple porters (*pagazi*); these were the first salaried positions known in the region. They created permanent trading posts in Tabora and Ujiji on the caravans' central axis. People from the interior, those connected to this commerce, learned Swahili, a Bantu language that combines Arab and Persian vocabularies and that later became the region's lingua franca; coastal clothing and housing styles were imitated, though the people did not necessarily convert to Islam. Swahili culture thus spread, through assimilation, as it had done along the Indian Ocean coastline. Starting in 1844, Arabs, such as the Wahhabite Ahmed ben Ibrahim, frequented the *kabaka* Suna's court in Buganda. Expelled in 1852, immediately after Suna's succession, they returned in the early 1860s and their influence seems to have peaked again in King Mutesa's court. Mutesa feigned converting to Islam around 1867: Ramadan was respected; a new calendar was adopted; Eastern greetings were used; Eastern clothes were worn; and he exchanged delegations with the sultan of Zanzibar in 1869–1870. The Arab-Swahili merchants soon established control over the two access routes to this country. On the caravan route around Tabora, they were assured the collaboration of local powers: in Karagwe, they helped Rumanyika come to power in 1855; and they backed the secession of Rusubi at around the same time. Some permanent markets were installed around two small sovereigns' courts: Biharamulo in Rusubi and Kafuro in Karagwe, extended by Kitangule at a ford on the Kagera. South of Lake Victoria, they founded the Kageyi post, from which dhows in the 1870s were launched, which in turn posed a major challenge to local canoe boatmen.

The fundamentals of this long-distance commerce were ivory, slaves, and, in exchange, firearms (piston rifles). The ancient networks were grafted onto this new axis, which itself created growing demand for local products, notably foodstuffs. New monetary tools also came into use: rows of cowries and beads replaced the hoe, the goat, and the salt bundle.

The primary local beneficiaries of this external commerce were the sovereigns and their aristocratic entourages. They reinforced their control over markets; their physical proximity to capitals, as well as their being the ones foreign traders were obliged to visit, yielded taxes and "gifts." Toward the end of the century, predatory politics developed, in particular in Buganda: spoils were collected from peripheral regions using firearms. Despite the risks in obtaining it, ivory, the main export commodity, provided traders with profits of at least 200 percent. This was a genuine royal monopoly: half the tusks had to be given to Bunyoro's *mukama* or Buganda's *kabaka*. The kings moreover had their own elephant-hunting troops who hunted north of the Nile and around Mount Elgon. One can understand why Buganda attempted to establish control over Lake Victoria and to start a veritable economic war with Bunyoro by trying to break the Zanzibari circuit. In response, Mukama Kabarega, in power since 1869 — simultaneously being antagonized by Khartoum traders along the Upper Nile — moved his capital south (from Masindi to Mparo) and set out to retake control of the salt lakes region and to reconquer Toro. Securing firearms was essential; they became indispensable for hunting and war and gave their owners incommensurable power. Mutesa and Kabarega reorganized their armies by creating permanent bodies of infantrymen, which became despotism's new tool.[104]

However, this new economy also favored factional rivalry and the emergence of "big men" capable of breaking traditional rules. Small states were logistical stopping points along the caravan route, and they took on the role of brokers, as the Karagwe and Rusubi examples have shown. Even here, one saw secessions of local powers directly connected to foreign networks. In Bujiji, a *muteko* (a political-religious authority in the villages) from a trading-post district on the lake's shores made the most of a succession crisis in 1845; using a Swahili administration, he became practically independent of the *mwami*: this was the start of

Ujiji town. An analogous secession took place north of the lake, where Uvira hawkers created a broker principality at odds with the rest of the Fuliro country. Slowly a new human landscape emerged, in which coastal dress, the white Swahili gown (*kanzu*), predominated. This became the virtual national outfit of Buganda. In 1894, Count Gustav Adolf von Götzen described King Kasusura's court (in Rusubi) as having a guard equipped with piston rifles, courtesans clad in cotton, and the sovereign dressed in Turkish-style clothes with blue pants, a red tunic, and a gray jacket.[105] This recalls Stanley's description of the Buganda court cited at the beginning of the previous chapter.

Slavery was another innovation. The slave trade, organized by the "Turks" of Khartoum or by the "Arabs" of Zanzibar and their Swahilized auxiliaries (the Wangwana), mostly afflicted the politically divided populations on the Upper Nile and in what is today eastern Congo. The kingdoms' political and military organization protected their inhabitants from this scourge. The Barundi resisted attempts to penetrate their country by Zanzibaris who lived on the banks of Lake Tanganyika, in particular in the 1880s (under Mwezi Gisabo's rule). They were only one example of the effects of the region's political-military structuring. But this did not prevent some states from participating in the slave trade at the expense of their neighbors. This was the case in Buganda as well as Rwanda from the 1880s to the early twentieth century. In Rwanda, the slave trade mostly affected young girls. It was carried out not in markets but in enclosures set up for this purpose, of which the best known were in Kavumu (in Nduga) and Rukira (in Gisaka); toward the east, it was practiced around Rusubi and Unyamwezi, via the Gisaka route.[106] The traders were merchants from these countries and Rwandans protected by Rwabugiri, who in turn demanded that captives be taken from west of Lake Kivu, among other places. Elephant hunting was tied up with this activity. The famous trader Mulinzi, who was a rich Muhutu and the son of an arrow trader, is an example. In business with the Swahili since 1887, he sold slaves for copper bracelets and beads. This government-controlled opening toward the external world is little known. Even so, in the late nineteenth century, all the European visitors (Count von Götzen in May 1894 and Captain Hans Ramsay in March 1897) commented on the diffusion of cotton clothing in ruling circles.

Inequality is not therefore made in a day, or according to a single explanation, or with immutable contours across the whole region. This runs contrary to the idea that "Rwandan studies" for years imposed an idea, diffused notably through Jacques Maquet's work, which is endlessly commented upon and cited, in French and in English.[107] A social model that was thought to apply to the entire region, aestheticism, and the prejudices of an ending colonial mandate were combined in this work. The result maintained an ultimately racial vision, a "true essay on the inequality of ethnic groups," that gave a gloss of legitimacy to every extreme political attitude witnessed recently in these countries. To the contrary, what should be noted is the complexity of a social and political history that, in the nineteenth century, saw the rise of different aristocracies — political-landowning, pastoral, warrior, and political-commercial — whose actions played a determinate role in the context of European conquest.

CHAPTER FOUR

Colonial Trusteeships and

Reconstructions of Tradition

The Europeans who arrived in the 1860s saw, above all, aristocracies in power. As we already know, the Europeans later racially classified these formations. But despite (or because of) the immediate importance of religious objectives, they primarily missed the cultural dimension, that of beliefs and rites involved in kingship. What escaped them, in other words, was how this institution ultimately took root in the popular imagination. The abuses of the powerful were revealed, but not the motives for why people supported them. The colonizer, of course, was more interested in division and moralizing than in trying to understand. And this is certainly not the first time a conqueror's vision has been spelled out in this way. Indeed, the colonizers exercised their power through their superior science and technology and through claiming to have the true God. Little by little, the ancient logics lost their meaning, and by the end of the period the monarchies had vanished: what remained were empty shells. This was true in every case except, paradoxically, Buganda, where modernity was most precociously experienced. In the pages that follow, I will analyze these different contemporary trajectories and try to understand how different political cultures resulted in change being managed in varying ways.

The Search for the "Sources of the Nile": A British Endeavor
For Europeans, the motives to first encounter this part of Africa
largely stemmed from their imagination. Before the mid-nineteenth century, this region had been known only as the land of
the Mountains of the Moon that towered over lakes from which
the Nile somehow sprung. This was a vision based on cartography inherited from the second-century Alexandrian geographer
Ptolemy. For a very long time, one had to be content with this
image, since six cataracts upriver from Aswan followed by the
immense Bahr al-Ghazal swamps blocked a 6,000-kilometer valley ascent to the sources of the White Nile. These sources were
at the drainage of Lakes Albert and Victoria, which themselves
were respectively fed by the Semliki and the Kagera, which drained
from the snow-covered Ruwenzori massif and mountains in
Rwanda and Burundi. It is clear that as soon as sailors and missionaries arrived on the eastern coast and were told by Swahili
traders about large lacustrine expanses near the equator, European geographers became obsessed with the idea of physically
verifying the truth of Ptolemy's scheme. Had not the Swahili
themselves, raised on the culture of *The Thousand and One Nights*,
nicknamed the petty traders of the interior "the people of the
moon" (the Banyamwezi)? Moreover, the presence of navigable
waters in the heart of the continent inspired economic projections sufficient to justify subsidies.

London took the initiative. The economy of the world's then-
leading power, scientific curiosity, and philanthropy — which,
since the start of the abolitionist campaigns in the early nineteenth century, had focused public opinion on Africa — converged
to support this adventure. In the 1840s, two Germans of the
Church Missionary Society (CMS) who were living in the Mombasa region had discovered Mounts Kenya and Kilimanjaro and
had collected information about a great lake that tallied with lakes

reported in the same period by London's "armchair geographers," who had based their claims on reports from Zanzibar. After this, the Royal Geographical Society, with government support, organized a series of expeditions between the mid-1850s and the late 1860s. Responsibility for these "explorations" was given to men who had experience in faraway worlds, notably former officers of the Indian Army who were familiar with the Orient.[1] This was how Richard Burton and John Hanning Speke came to be sent, in 1857, to search for the famous equatorial lake. With guides from the region, they followed the ivory caravan route from Bagamoyo to Ujiji. They "discovered" Lake Tanganyika and, in 1858, heard of a powerful Mwezi, king of Burundi. In disagreement with his fellow Nile-source traveler, Speke set off again in 1860 with James Grant. Between 1861 and 1862, they established contact with the sovereigns of Karagwe, Buganda, and Bunyoro: Rumanyika, Mutesa, and Kamurasi. Standing before Ripon Falls, north of the lake, which he named after Queen Victoria, Speke declared, "I have seen the ancient Nile come out of Victoria Nyanza.... This great lake gives birth to the sacred river on which the child Moses floated." Elsewhere, enraptured by the royal courts he visited, Speke inaugurated, as we have seen, the Galla hypothesis, which was rapidly taken up by other explorers.[2] In the eyes of the Europeans, this region became a second Ethiopia.

The Royal Geographical Society also had sent Samuel Baker by way of the Nile, starting in Cairo. Baker (traveling with his wife) crossed paths with Speke and Grant on their way back from what is today southern Sudan, and then he discovered Lake Rwitanzige, which he named Albert after Her Gracious Majesty's deceased spouse. These voyages did not end the polemics over the region's hydrography: Burton hung his Nile-source hypothesis on a link between Lakes Albert and Tanganyika. Speke's dramatic death in 1864 was perceived as an admission of failure. Two strong personalities continued the debate. The first was the famous David Livingstone, who, before circling the shores of Lake Tanganyika, had worked in southern Africa on behalf of the London Missionary Society (LMS) and was inspired by two passions: Nile geography and anti-slave crusading. The second was an American journalist of Welsh origin, Henry Morton Stanley, who, financed by the *New York Herald*, left specifically "to search for Livingstone" and ended up "finding" him in Ujiji in 1871. The visit to the north of Tanganyika by the two men did not dispel uncertainty: a rise in the lake's waters prevented them from advancing to the Rusizi delta and thus from resolving the direction of its flow. But four years later, Stanley crossed the continent from east to west, which led to his systematically visiting the entire network of lakes in western Uganda — and by consequence resolving the question of the sources of the White Nile — before he headed down the Congo River. The 1890s debates concerned the question, as absurd as it is fascinating, of the "southernmost source" of the great river; that is, they made a detailed survey of the Kagera basin. In 1892, the Austrian Oskar Baumann, dispatched to the region by a German antislavery committee, chose the Ruvubu in Burundi as the source; but in subsequent years, Richard Kandt, Hans Ramsay, and other German agents debated the lines and flows, proposing the Kanyaru or the Nyabarongo in Rwanda.[3] In the 1930s, the Mining Union of Upper Katanga built a pyramid in Rutovu, in southern Burundi, above the source of a rivulet. Today, it is a tourist attraction.

During his voyage, Stanley lent the names of the English royal family to these lakes (Edward and George were added to Albert and Victoria). Upriver from Lake Albert, the falls of the Victoria Nile earned the name of the Geographical Society's president, Murchison. Central Africa suddenly resembled a London suburb. Elsewhere, Stanley, very favorably impressed by Mutesa, to whom he had paid a visit, published in November 1875 in the *Daily Tele-*

graph a letter in which, praising Buganda, he launched an appeal to the missionary societies to come to this country. The Anglican CMS soon became interested, as did Monsignor Charles Lavigerie, as we will see below. What is interesting in this mélange of racing to the moon and of humanitarian emotion, which characterized European attitudes toward Africa in the second third of the nineteenth century, is also what it foreshadows. "Media coverage" filled with political misunderstandings is not a recent phenomenon in the Great Lakes region.

At the turn of the 1870s–1880s, when the region's major sovereigns were Mwezi Gisabo in Burundi, Kigeri Rwabugiri in Rwanda, Kabarega in Bunyoro, and Mutesa in Buganda, the threat of foreign expropriation and the shadow of international ambitions over the region took shape in two domains: the Upper Nile and the Indian Ocean littoral.[4] The most brutal external irruption came from Khartoum, founded in 1824 by Khedive Mohamed Ali.[5] His son and second successor (between 1863 and 1879), Ismaïl, decided to expand into southern Bahr al-Ghazal, where the Gondokoro trading post had been established in 1841. This expansion translated into many raids on cattle, slaves, and ivory, items that subsequently were stored in fortified posts (*zariba*) where steamers came to collect them. Even Bunyoro was reached under Kamurasi's rule. In fact, the so-called Khartoum Turks' imperialism had its sights on all of what is today Uganda. The name "Turks" was used even though the traders and soldiers who constituted this predatory state's staff were Egyptian, Levantine, and European.

In 1872, Sir Samuel Baker reappeared as the governor ("Pasha Baker") of Equatoria Province, which was created by the khedive to reorganize the southern part of this Egyptian-African empire. But this effort failed due to resistance from the new king of

Bunyoro, Kabarega. Colonel Charles Gordon replaced Baker between 1874 and 1877. He launched two steamships on the Nile, which were added to the many sailboats, and he dispatched the Italians Romelo Gessi and Carlo Piaggia to explore Lake Albert and create a chain of fortified posts on the northern Bunyoro border. Then, with backing from Ruyonga, a rebel prince of this country, Gordon tried to gain control of the road leading to Buganda via Mruli along the left bank of the Nile, and he sent several delegations to the capital of Kabaka Mutesa in Rubaga, including the American colonel Charles Chaillé-Long in 1874, the French Linant de Bellefonds in 1875, and the German Eduard Schnitzer in 1876.[6] Schnitzer became governor of the province under the name Emin Pasha after Gordon was nominated head of Sudan. A skilled diplomat, Pasha set out to reassure Mutesa and Kabarega about Egypt's intentions. The sudden Mahdi uprising in 1881 separated Equatoria from Egypt, and three years later it forced Emin Pasha and his Sudanese troops to withdraw to the shores of Lake Albert. There, along with the explorers Wilhelm Junker and Gaetano Casati, Pasha lasted for five years before being "saved" by Stanley's new expedition, which this time came from the Congo under the auspices of Leopold II and the businessman William Mackinnon, whose Imperial British East Africa Company (IBEAC) had just been established in Mombasa. One is now in the midst of imperialist fever. Emin Pasha was later recovered by his compatriots.

In fact, the Mahdi movement cut short Egyptian ambitions in this region. The European expansion was launched from the eastern coast, at first through the Arab-Swahili commercial network, which had been expanding since the sultan of Muscat moved his capital to Zanzibar in 1840 and linked his country's economy into the world market through three products: cloves, ivory, and cotton.[7] The paradox of this "village race" between the two access routes to the Great Lakes is that it ultimately involved the British on both sides. In 1882, they occupied Egypt, ousting the rival French. But, starting in 1873, they also intensified their humanitarian, economic, and military presence around the sultan of Zanzibar. The slave market was closed; Indian bankers took control of the country's finances; Consul John Kirk became the most important person on the islands; and in 1877 the sultan's army was entrusted to an Englishman, General Mathews. Virtually the only remaining competitor was the Belgian king, Leopold II. He had been promoting the African International Association (AIA), created at the end of the International Conference on Geography, which was held in Brussels in 1876; he envisaged making use of explorers' skills from the Atlantic to the Indian Ocean. Finally, aroused by Stanley's 1875 appeal, missionaries played a crucial but complicated role, given the nasty rivalry between the French Catholics and the British Protestants. The time was not one of ecumenism, even and especially in missionary country.

The Christian Missions: Dreaming of a Second Ethiopia
The White Fathers and the Protestant preachers arrived more or less simultaneously, in the late 1870s — in other words, twenty years before the colonial partition — on the shores of Lakes Victoria and Tanganyika. In both cases, their dream was to find pagan societies that would be susceptible to accepting the Christian message and escaping from the Muslim grip. The hypothesis of the Ethiopian origins of the region's kingdoms allowed them to reactivate Prester John, a mythic figure who, it was hoped, would serve to confront Islam from behind (that is, from the south).

This project was primarily attempted in Buganda, an effort that spawned a veritable religious war for some fifteen years (notably between 1889 and 1893), articulated as a crusade against Islam. In June 1877, the reverend C.T. Wilson of the CMS arrived in the Bugandan court. Other British members of this Protestant

missionary society followed. Created in the late eighteenth century, the CMS united Anglicans with rather evangelical tendencies; since the 1840s, it had been established on the coast, near
Mombasa.[8]

Then, in February 1879, Father Siméon Lourdel arrived, and
he and three other French White Fathers settled in Rubaga.
Founded in 1869, this congregation was marked by the strong
personality of its founder, Monsignor Charles Lavigerie.[9] From
his headquarters in Algiers, Lavigerie dreamed of restoring and
enlarging Saint Augustine's ancient "Church of Africa":

> Before me lies a continent of 200 million human beings. I ask myself
> every day if we must make them into men, into Christians, or if we
> should leave them in their centuries-old state of savage bestiality.[10]

Stymied by Islam in North Africa, Lavigerie became interested in
equatorial Africa at a time when Vatican propaganda harped on
the English Protestants' grip there as well as on the AIA's free-
thinkers. In January 1878, he addressed a "Secret Memorandum"
on evangelizing this part of the continent: one had to "liberate the
poor sons of Ham" from slavery and ignorance. The battle against
Arab slave trading and the formation of African Catholic communities had to go hand in hand. The following February, the
new pope, Leo XIII, entrusted Lavigerie with the responsibility of
the Central Africa missions in the name of an apostolic delegate.
The barely known lakes region passed to the White Fathers, who
bypassed three competting projects: the African Missions of Lyon
and the Spiritains, both of which worked on the eastern and western coasts; and Father Daniel Comboni's Italians, who were in
Sudan.[11] Thus, from the start, evangelization of this region involved multiple power games deep in the Catholic Church, between different denominations, against Muslims, and in light of

the existing monarchies. The White Fathers responded to these challenges by maintaining strict internal discipline, as the Jesuits did; by keeping their society regularly informed of everything they observed in the field; and by adapting their strategy to local political conditions.[12] On this subject, Lavigerie, who was known as a pragmatist (he had "rallied" to the Republic), wavered among three positions that can be observed throughout his congregation's history: converting African chiefs into Christian princes, creating a "Christian kingdom" around neophyte communities, and collaborating with the colonial authorities. The latter occurred after 1890, but not without tension with the other two agendas. The hope to witness the Constantine or the Clovis of future Christianized Africans coincided with protecting missionary autonomy when the latter dealt with the local population.

If the Great Lakes region appeared to be the White Fathers' favorite land, the main reason was their success in Buganda, which was at least four years ahead of Rwanda and Burundi in terms of results.[13] In 1880, seven Baganda were baptized; in 1882, 440 were catechumens. In 1883, an apostolic vicariate called Nyanza (the Swahili name for Lake Victoria) was established; this vicariate covered contemporary Uganda and every one of this large lake's shores. Protestants with the CMS achieved similar successes among the king's pages, a veritable breeding ground of neophytes. For them as for the sovereign, the new religion, like Islam, brought an ideological opening to the world, one that was experienced as more potent than the former *lubale* cosmology.[14] Moreover, this religion offered them a means to escape the encircling traders from Khartoum and Zanzibar. The rapprochement with the Europeans was lived as a defensive alliance. After Stanley's passage, King Mutesa retained at his court one of the explorer's interpreters, Muftaa Dallington, who served as an informer and a scribe. Mutesa and his court expected from both denominations' missionaries new knowledge, training in reading, more effective medicine, technological progress, new clothing, and arms. One could say that "in Buganda, the Abrahamic religions became the protector cult of writing and firearms."[15] Conversions corresponded to political and social ambitions. The *kabaka* broke with Islam in 1876, but he expected too many tangible benefits from Christianity. This misunderstanding led to conflicts in which the converted — young aristocrats who were called "readers" — were both hostages and actors.

The first crisis occurred in 1882: the White Fathers, trapped by the rivalry between the Baganda catechumens and the foreign-born freed slaves who surrounded them, fled to an area south of Lake Victoria. They returned to Buganda in 1885, after Mutesa's death, and found a community of six hundred who had succeeded in caring for themselves without them. In the same year, tension rose between the Protestants and the court after the Anglican bishop James Hannington was murdered. Hannington had traveled via Busoga, that is, via a prohibited eastern route. Then, in 1886, several dozen Catholic and Protestant pages were burned alive on orders from Mwanga, the new *kabaka*. The Catholics became the most famous: beatified in 1920, canonized in 1964, they were "the martyrs of Uganda."[16] These executions did not spell the end of missionary activity or of conversions. The victims were apparently paying for having put the biblical God above loyalty to their king — notably, by balking at satisfying the king's homosexual demands while he, newly enthroned, was trying to demonstrate his authority. However, in 1888, the king was overthrown in a Christian- and Muslim-led military coup d'état, and he fled to an area south of the lake. In 1889, a Muslim minority alone controlled the government and chased out the missionaries and the Christian chiefs. Having taken refuge in Nkore, those who had been expelled organized a crusade on the western border; this movement was led by Honorat Nyonyitono, a Catholic chief and a survivor of the persecutions. In the meantime, Mwanga, who had become a cate-chumen of the White Fathers, benefited from Charles Stokes's backing. Stokes, an Irishman and former member of the CMS who had become an arms trafficker, helped Mwanga regain power at the start of 1890.

But the Christians' victory sharpened the rivalry between Catholics and Protestants, a political-religious polarization that lasted for a century. At the time, they were respectively nick-named the "French" and the "English." Indeed, from then on, the two religious parties politicized their conflict by drawing on international rivalries: the Protestants won support from the Imperial British East Africa Company, and the Catholics were supported by the Germans, who started showing interest in the region in 1887 and benefited from the grudging support of the White Fathers. The British company definitively took the lead in December 1890, and with that so did the Protestant party led by the *katikiro*, Apolo Kagwa. Short of a Clovis, Kagwa proved a faithful palace guard for the English. An open civil war broke out in 1892, and the Catholic forces were pushed south: the vicar apostolic, the Alsatian Jean-Joseph Hirth, took refuge in the Bu-koba region under German control with thousands of Baganda. In 1894, Rome conferred on him the apostolic vicariate of southern Nyanza, separate from Uganda and having jurisdiction not only over Buzinza and Buhaya but also over Rwanda.[17]

On Lake Tanganyika, Protestants again were the first to arrive, with missionaries from the London Missionary Society. This soci-ety, of Congregationalist inspiration, was very open, at least on the doctrinal level. Especially active in southern Africa, where Livingstone worked on its behalf, the LMS first wanted to estab-lish posts on the lakes and develop means of transport. Working with Scottish missions, the LMS focused on navigating Lakes Nyasa and Tanganyika as its major project. A steamship was launched on Tanganyika's waters in the early 1880s, thanks to a donation from a Quaker manufacturer from Leeds. In 1878, a station was created in Ujiji under the responsibility of a sailor, Edward C. Hore, but it was abandoned in 1884.[18]

Less ephemeral was the presence of the White Fathers, who arrived in Ujiji in 1879. An apostolic vicariate was established in Tanganyika in 1880; it was subdivided in 1886 into three ecclesiastical entities: from east to west, Unyanyembe, Tanganyika (including Buha and Burundi), and the Upper Congo (including Kivu). However, the situation was quite different from that in Uganda. In these parts, as in southern Nyanza, missionaries were wedged between military-commercial networks of the Zanzibari Muslims (who controlled the Tabora-Ujiji and the Tabora-Kagera axes) and the monarchical powers, which were hostile to all foreign penetration. For the monarchs, the White Fathers, with their gandouras and beards, moving along the slave-trading routes or on the Swahili dhows, were a new variant of Arab slavers. These misunderstandings made the first contacts particularly difficult. The majority of converts would be "children" of missions, slaves originally nabbed from other regions, such as in the Nyamwezi countries (south of Lake Victoria) or Maniema (west of Lake Tanganyika).[19] Lacking local support, the White Fathers adopted the strategy of creating "Christian villages" under armed protection, notably on the lake's western shore.

A first attempt was made in southern Burundi, in Rumonge, between 1879 and 1881. Faced with the hostility of the Ujiji-based Wangwana traders and with the mistrust of King Mwezi's local representatives, French missionaries fell into a trap: three missionaries and a former papal Zouave of Belgian origin, who served as an "armed auxiliary," were massacred. After two new attempts

north of the lake in 1884 and 1891, the White Fathers entered
Burundi from the east. The first definitive foundation was established in Muyaga in 1898, followed by Mugera in the center of the
country in 1899, and Buhonga above the German post of Usumbura (the contemporary city of Bujumbura) in 1902. In the meantime, in 1895 this country had been placed under the leadership
of the Unyanyembe vicariate, whose headquarters was in Ushirombo, in Nyamwezi country. Rwanda was also penetrated from
the east: the Episcopal headquarters was in Kashozi (or Marien-
berg) in the principality of Bugabo, north of Bukoba; in 1897, a
mission was created in Katoke, in Rusubi, near the Biharamulo
trading post, and thus on the Swahili commercial axis. But not
until 1900 was a foundation established in southern Rwanda, in
Save; four others had been set up by 1903.

In the early twentieth century, missionary activity, which had
preceded colonialism proper, became inscribed in a colonial logic.
The boundaries of the apostolic vicariates corresponded to those
the colonial powers laid down, and the missions were created
with the administration's and the military's blessing. In Uganda,
for example, Catholic missions were established in different kingdoms — in Toro in 1895, Bunyoro in 1901, Nkore in 1902 — which
paralleled the British consolidation of control. In Rwanda and
Burundi, the White Fathers, confronted by local leaders and agents
of the Congo state on the shores of Lake Kivu, settled where the
German authorities wished.

But the gap between the northern and the southern half of the
Great Lakes region remained enormous.[20] In 1914, in terms of
total equivalent populations, the Catholics numbered more than
100,000 in Buganda (the Protestants a little less) but only 10,000
in Rwanda and 3,000 in Burundi. In Uganda, Christianity, represented by the two major denominations, in a sense was a victor's
religion, that of the Baganda chiefs who had European backing and

later made themselves into indispensable intermediaries for the British protectorate. In the region's southern kingdoms, Catholicism faced practically no competition until around 1910, but it only influenced marginal minorities, ones who were at odds with their kin. At first, the White Fathers' catechists and auxiliaries were mainly Baganda in Rwanda and Basumbwa (from western Unyamwezi) in Burundi. One can understand why, for years, the missionary enclosures were perceived as foreign, even strange, by the societies in which they were found.[21] Not until the 1930s did the missions play a central role in reconstituting politics and society.

The Colonial Partition: Diplomacy, Cartography, and Local Politics

For twenty years, between the early stages of conquest (1890) and the regularization of borders at the 1910 Brussels Conference, territory was divided evenly among the region's three colonizers, the British, the Germans, and agents of Leopold's Congo state.[22] Within Africa, the Great Lakes region is an exceptional case: its contemporary borders largely reflect ancient political boundaries, but the cultural, economic, and political unit it had largely been was broken into three zones connected by Léopoldville (Kinshasa), Dar es Salaam, and Mombasa. These borders were the result of a compromise between a chorus of powers and historical constraints.

In Europe, in the chancelleries and embassies thousands of kilometers away from the scene — a distance requiring three months for exchanging information — experts in African geopolitics believed they could bring the situation under control by making pencil marks on relatively approximate maps. Today's borders were not established at the Berlin Conference, contrary to what one often hears. Rather, behind the scenes, the king of Belgium, Leopold II, paved the way by establishing a domain for which his

214

International Association of Congo would be responsible. In 1885, he had this domain recognized as an independent state (the Congo Free State). He negotiated, according to his representatives, using one of Stanley's particularly fanciful maps, variously referring to waterways and relief. In the end, for the eastern border he obtained an oblique line connecting the northern point of Lake Tanganyika to the intersection point of 20 degrees southern latitude and 30 degrees eastern longitude, extending northward along a vertical line on this longitude. This geometric line intersected the Rusizi plain in western Burundi, the crest dominating Lake Kivu in western Rwanda, and the southwest of contemporary Uganda (including the Lake Edward saltworks). But at the time, neither the region nor its inhabitants were known in Europe. Even the existence of Lake Kivu was poorly understood. Not until "effective occupation" were rights given concrete expression in these "lands without masters."

In the eyes of the then-major powers, which became involved willy-nilly in the colonial melee, Leopold II was the lesser evil. In the 1880s, rivalry increased among the British, who occupied Egypt and ruled Zanzibar and Mombasa, the French, who had established themselves in western Africa and were active in the Indian Ocean, and the Germans, who forced their way onto the East African scene from Dar es Salaam. A tense moment came when Colonel Jean-Baptiste Marchand confronted Horatio Kitchener's expedition in Fashoda in 1898, an event that has remained in French political consciousness ever since. Less well known are the clashes in the Great Lakes region during the same period.

For the English, a clash took place on the "red road" from the Cape to Cairo. In 1887, London was recognized on paper as controlling a sphere west of Lake Victoria. That same year William Mackinnon founded the IBEAC. Stanley subsequently left to "liberate" Emin Pasha, who had taken refuge near Lake Albert. On this trip, Stanley made an Nkore prince and other Lake Edward notables "sign" treaties. On his return to London in May 1890, he claimed that, thanks to him, the IBEAC's sovereignty was recognized in the entire region, from Lake Victoria to Lake Tanganyika. At the same time, a missionary from the Lake Nyasa post of the LMS planted a British flag in Burundi, near contemporary Bujumbura. And the trans-African lobby, coordinated primarily by Cecil Rhodes in southern Africa, failed before the superior interests of British diplomacy.

That same year, following the repression of the Swahili revolt called Bushiri, the Reich retook control of German interests, which had been represented on the eastern coast by the Deutsch-Ostafrikanische Gesellschaft of the adventurer Carl Peters. The imperial commissar Hermann von Wissmann entrusted Emin Pasha, who had returned to his motherland, with a large expedition to Lake Victoria, and he began a project to launch steamships on the lake. Emin and his assistant, the naturalist Franz Stuhlmann, went on to found military stations in Mwanza and Bukoba. Oskar Baumann's 1892 "antislavery exploration," which resulted in a German flag's being flown north of Tanganyika, was also part of this program. Berlin specialists described the *Zwischenseengebiet* space as both a natural border of "German India" in Africa and a trading crossroads that would allow, according to Friedrich Ratzel's geographic model, Germany to govern the continental mass: the "interlacustrine" region represented a "second shore." These dreams of navigating the interior lasted until 1914. They can be seen in the famous film *The African Queen*.[23] Back in Berlin, Chancellor Leo von Caprivi sought a rapprochement with London in the face of the Franco-Russian threat. Uganda and Rwanda were the stakes of this high-flying bargaining. Germany gained control of the small island Heligoland, at the exit of the Kiel Canal, in exchange for concessions in eastern Africa. The resulting July 1890 accord allocated Uganda to Britain and the countries south of 1 degree southern latitude, including Rwanda, to Germany. Rwanda was very nearly made part of Uganda.[24] Stanley later wrote that Germany had sacrificed new pants for an old trouser button! In fact, naval interest and diplomatic equilibrium had taken precedence over colonial fever on both sides: as late as 1890 the mountain kingdoms (Burundi, Rwanda, Nkore, and other principalities) remained unknown.

The situation changed drastically in 1894: Count von Götzen's expedition discovered that Lake Kivu was situated west of the "oblique line" recognized by Leopold II ten years earlier and that the Rwandan *mwami*'s authority extended to the shores of Lake Kivu. In light of these hydrographic and ethnopolitical facts, Germany called for border regularization in January 1895. Leopold II refused. Like the Germans, he was interested in these mountains with healthy climates, areas that would be propitious for European colonization. But the agents of the Congo Free State were primarily concerned with maintaining their monopoly over the ivory trade, and they set out to dismantle the Arab-Swahili network that had been active in eastern Congo for thirty years. They did so in the name of the "antislavery crusade," which Cardinal Lavigerie had launched in Paris in 1888 and which the 1890 Brussels Conference made official. At the time, elephant tusks were the main stakes in the race to the Great Lakes. In this sense, the Tanganyika-Kivu axis played a key role. In 1884, an Ujiji-based Arab leader, Mohammed ben Khalfan, nicknamed Rumaliza, created a chain of slave-trading posts north of Lake Tanganyika, from which he launched caravans and raids.[25] An attempt to penetrate the mountains of Burundi failed in the face of resistance from Mwezi Gisabo's armies, and in 1891 Rumaliza's armed bands climbed the Rusizi valley and reached an area south of Kivu. In

1894, the Congolese police destroyed this military-commercial power, and Rumaliza was forced to flee to Zanzibar. Nonetheless, some Swahili traders remained active in Ujiji and on the lake's Burundian littoral under German protection.

Starting in 1896, the Germans and Belgians from the Congo Free State clashed along this border. Opposite the Belgian-built Uvira post, the German captain Ramsay established a military station in Ujiji in 1896, then a post in Usumbura in 1897. At the same time, expeditions from two camps reached the area around Lake Kivu. Still, this military maneuvering never went as far as open confrontation, given how isolated these European posts, far from the railroad network and telegraph lines, were. In the end, the local impact of African initiatives was often decisive. A Belgian captain created a post southwest of Lake Kivu, but he encountered strong Rwandan armed resistance. The resistance persisted despite the crisis that contemporaneously struck the monarchy: Mibambwe Rutalindwa, the successor of the formidable Rwabugiri, who died in 1895, was overthrown at the end of 1896 following a defeat, to the Belgians, and a plot that brought young Yuhi Musinga to power. In March 1897, the royal court openly welcomed Captain Ramsay and accepted the German flag: the Rwandan aristocracy manifestly played the card of one European camp against the other, and it sought the support of those considered the least dangerous and the most respectful. In fact, from then on, Berlin demanded ethnically and politically coherent borders that respected the unity of the Rwandan kingdom. In the same year, a mutiny broke out in the Congolese army, and thousands of rebels, led by Canguvu, one of Rumaliza's former loyalists who proved to be a brilliant war chief, swept from the Upper Nile to the Kivu region: a Belgian captain was killed, and Uvira was taken. On several occasions between December 1897 and June 1898, the Uvira garrison had to take refuge in Usumbura with the Germans, who apparently remained neutral in this affair. Berlin exploited this situation. Toward the end of 1898, Captain von Bethe, the new head of Usumbura station, was charged with seizing positions along the Rusizi-Kivu "natural border." Posts were established in Cibitoke (Burundi), and in Shangi and Gisenyi (Rwanda). In November 1899, a provisional compromise was negotiated between Bethe and his Belgian counterpart, Hecq: Congolese posts could be established near former ones to symbolize the existence of a dispute, but they had to be quickly evacuated. Here again, German authorities knew how to manipulate Burundian and Rwandan local authorities; indeed, through intimidation and cajoling, the Germans had turned the Rwandan authorities against the people of Congo. To finish, a compromise was signed in Brussels in April 1900: Leopold II ceded the Rusizi plain, and in 1901–1902 mixed border commissions were charged with drawing cartographic layouts of the contested region in Rwanda. Between 1902 and 1904, the English did the same for the volcanic mountains. As in 1890, European diplomacy had the last word: the rapprochement sketched out between Berlin and London in 1900, and again in 1907 and 1912, penalized Leopold II. Leopold died in 1909; his Congo had become Belgian the year before; and the general desire in Brussels was to escape this hornet's nest. The German authorities established a residency in Kigali in 1907, which they entrusted to Richard Kandt, an expert on Lake Kivu since 1898. The Germans also wanted to stabilize the running of Rwanda, and they insisted that these tergiversations among Europeans would threaten public order in the country. In the end, a May 1910 conference in Brussels resulted in accords that fixed borders in Uganda, German East Africa, and the Belgian Congo. Germany ceded certain regions demanded by King Musinga, notably Bufumbira in Uganda and Ijwi Island (where the Bahavu lived), to Congo.

This small border war was punctuated by sometimes-absurd episodes, but its outcome demonstrates something else: the dialectic that had been unleashed when the region entered onto the world stage. Europe's technologies and strategies clearly affected the fate of the ancient powers, but these powers were not entirely absent; they influenced the solutions that were eventually adopted. Still, the nature of political borders changed after this crisis: the former "frontier areas" on the kingdoms' borders, characterized by a range of powers and fluid identities, were replaced by linear territorialization. The centuries-long Rwandan expansion (and the Burundians' expansion) westward, at the clan and monarchy levels, was interrupted. From then on, one could speak no longer of migrations but of emigrations, and new eastward and northward orientations appeared. The nineteenth century's historical dynamics were blocked. The same point might be made for the Baganda's expansion on the shores of Lake Victoria: the 1890 border had been definitively crushed, to the great satisfaction of the small Haya kingdoms, which now had cast off their burdensome protector.

Opening to the World and an Ecological and Demographic Crisis

At the turn of the century, between 1890 and 1905, the European takeover was perceived in the region in a very confused way: white soldiers and their infantrymen appeared as a new wave of intruders, adding to the missionaries and Zanzibar's Arab-Swahili people. Each group was somewhat distinctive, but they all shared an incontestable mastery in firearms. After several last-ditch efforts in the late nineteenth century, resistance seemed impossible, but, as discussed above, the ruling aristocracies adapted their political strategies to this new external challenge, a fact of which the fragile administrations in this far west of colonial imperialism were always keenly aware. However, for the mass of the population, the irruption of these strangers, often described as monsters, was experienced with much anxiety. The Bazungu (the Europeans) were just one of the calamities afflicting the region during this period. The opening to the world, begun by traders' caravans, also unleashed access to a "common market" of microbes. Indeed, a complex chain of events led to a true ecological and demographic crisis between 1890 and 1930.[26]

The list of scourges is evident in the region's oral traditions. In 1891, a rinderpest epidemic, which had originated in Ethiopia, decimated cattle. This translated into social shock, but one with contradictory effects: in Rwanda and Burundi, the so-called *muryamo* (the great sleep) pest led to a concentration of cows in the hands of the most powerful; they in turn reserved this form of wealth — much coveted for reasons shown above — for restricted groups of loyalists. By contrast, in Karagwe the Hima cattle keepers were ruined, and the government was definitively weakened. In 1892, smallpox — which had already been found on the southern shore of Lake Victoria in the early nineteenth century and in Ujiji, on Lake Tanganyika, in the 1870s — penetrated the mountains, which until then had been spared, from the eastern coast. The first microbial shock ravaged the area: the majority of sick died, and dispersed habitats were all that prevented further contagion. No milieu was spared: the royal court in Nkore was decimated. Also in 1892, a parasite from South America, which had propagated little by little across the Congo basin along the main commercial roads, reached the region: in boring under foot skin, these "chiggers" (*Sarcopsylla penetrans*) created wounds and multiplied the number of infirm, given the initial ignorance of the nature of the problem. Then, between 1893 and 1897, waves of migratory locusts devastated crops in many areas.

Very early in the twentieth century, an epidemic of *gambiense*

221

sleeping sickness ravaged the plains around Lakes Victoria, Albert, Edward, and Tanganyika. After World War I, an analogous epidemic, this time *rhodesiense* sleeping sickness, spread across the plateaus of what is today northwestern Tanzania.[27] The spread of venereal diseases and recurring fevers, a sort of typhus, on the commercial routes should also be mentioned. And the colonial period's military episodes — from the initial expeditions of conquest to World War I and World War II, with their succession of constraints and requisitions — led to terrible shortages, even to famines, as in 1904–1905 in central Burundi and in 1916–1917 and 1943–1944 in Rwanda and Burundi. A veritable regional famine nicknamed *Gakwege* swept across these two countries in 1925–1929.[28]

The demographic effects of these crises were enormous: sleeping sickness killed more than 200,000 people in Uganda, and it overcame at least half the population on the Rusizi plain (in western Burundi) between 1905 and 1914. After undergoing a slow but real crisis during the nineteenth century, the region was characterized by a palpable population decrease between the 1880s and the 1920s. A fragile resurgence took place between 1930 and 1940 as the economic and health effects of colonial policy slowly shrank mortality rates. But growth only really resumed after 1950. From then on, the region began its contemporary "demographic transition," which was marked by a sharp fall in mortality rates and a continuously strong birthrate, which was driven by the memory of the crises that afflicted the preceding generations. In Burundi, which has been well studied in this domain, the growth rate went from 1.5 percent around 1950 to 2.5 percent in the 1960s. But not until 1950 did the size of the total population (about two million) reach what it had probably been in 1880. The same changes occurred in the Bukoba region, west of Lake Victoria, where the 1948 census indicated statistics equivalent to those estimated for 1890. In Buganda, the population diminished by around 60 percent between 1870 and 1920, and the number of deaths remained greater than the number of births until the 1940s. Depopulation also occurred in Bunyoro and Nkore into the late 1930s.[29]

The traumas experienced by these populations during this period have too often been neglected in discussions of the conditions under which the colonial-era social and political restructuring took place. The European conquerors at first managed societies that had undergone a profound crisis for more than a generation. The disorder induced by their arrival was inserted into a panorama of catastrophes, which began with the spectacular decrease in Lake Tanganyika's waters (about a dozen meters between 1879 and 1896), at times transforming its shores into an unhealthy mess, and was followed by a total solar eclipse in December 1889 and by the eruption of the Nyiragongo volcano in May 1894. This sort of millenarianism can make one smile, but it is true that the ecological disorder had some relationship to the political problems: the simultaneous increase in traffic and insecurity favored both the spreading of disease and a new encroachment of uncontrolled bush (what the Germans called *Grenzwildnisse*) into the inhabited areas, leading to a withdrawal for security reasons. Equilibriums between population and environment were ruptured; economic activities (notably on the lakes) were disturbed; and political-mystical boundaries were blurred. The place of the Sese Islands in the Ganda political complex was broken; Karagwe's pastoralism was ruined; the prosperity on the Imbo plains in Burundi was destroyed; and the caravan routes were infested by contagion and violence. The new contacts could incite withdrawal or resistance as much as opening and submission.

•

223

The Ugandan Model: Indirect Rule

The countries north-northwest of Lake Victoria had been in contact with Europeans (explorers, missionaries, businessmen, and
soldiers) for some thirty years when Great Britain proclaimed its
protectorate over this region in 1894. In the previous four years,
since the July 1890 accord, the region had been British only
on paper. The kingdom of Buganda was a notable example of the
colonial combination of economic calculation, missionary activity, and political strategizing. In this process, the African actors
ultimately played as decisive a role as the European imperialists.

Kabaka Mwanga, whom Christian factions returned to power
in February 1890, was quickly confronted with the attempt to
establish the IBEAC as a chartered company. This company dispatched Captain Frederick Lugard to the field, and, with a contingent of infantrymen and a machine gun, he handled the job
brilliantly. Arriving in Kampala in December 1890, Lugard established a fort there, and he obtained a commitment from Mwanga
not to negotiate with other powerful nations. In exchange, Lugard
offered his support to Buganda and to a Protestant party. In 1891,
he signed a treaty with representatives of Nkore's King Ntare, and
in Toro he reinstalled King Kasagama, who had been driven from
power by Kabarega, his rival in Bunyoro. Finally, he rallied hundreds of Sudanese mercenaries to his side; since Emin Pasha's
departure, they had been running rampant in areas south of Lake
Albert. Lugard used them to occupy military posts along the
southern border with Bunyoro, then in a state of rebellion. In
early 1892, he crushed the Catholic party, as discussed above. After
that, the first arrangement was denominational: every Bugandan
region was returned to a Protestant chief, except Buddu (in the
southwest), which was left to the Catholics, and three chiefdoms,
which were left to the Muslims. Ten thousand pounds were paid
to France in 1898 to compensate its expelled missionaries. The

IBEAC's financial difficulties nonetheless risked ruining the whole enterprise, but in London the imperialist lobby, led by Lord Rosebery, who had replaced William Gladstone as prime minister in March 1894, marshaled every patriotic, economic, and religious argument so that the Crown would live up to its "civilizing" mission. The chambers of commerce and the Church Missionary Society inspired press campaigns that invoked the struggle against slavery — still an effective theme, even though the British slave trade had already ended. Dispatched on a mission, the diplomat Gerald Portal wrote the favorable report expected of him: he advocated establishing an official protectorate over Buganda and launching a railroad from Mombasa to Lake Victoria. In April 1894, Parliament agreed, and the following August a new statute was announced at Mengo's court before an assembly of all the Bugandan chiefs. The protectorate did not formally spread to Nkore, Toro, and Bunyoro until 1896.

In 1895, the administrator George Wilson set out to regularize Bugandan court practices. He transformed the *kabaka* and his advisers' more or less regular hearings into regular sessions called *baraza* in Swahili and *lukiko* in Luganda; this institution went on to become the "Parliament" of Buganda a half century later. Arriving in 1899, Commissioner Harry Johnston put the finishing touches on his major plan to remodel the local political system by negotiating the Uganda Agreement, which was concluded on March 10, 1900. In the meantime, Mwanga, who had joined a mutiny of Sudanese soldiers, had been arrested with Kabarega, his Bunyoro counterpart. In 1899, the two kings were deported to the Seychelles. The new *kabaka* was a child, Daudi Chwa. He was assigned three tutors, of whom the most important were Apolo Kagwa, a Protestant, and Stanislas Mugwanya, a Catholic.

The fundamental compromise that Johnston brought about in 1900 perfectly illustrates the ambiguities in "indirect rule."

Buganda's powers were "respected," but they were substantially reorganized along the lines of a modernized feudalism, as if the England of the Magna Carta or the Domesday Book had been restored on the equator. Had not the Baganda negotiators themselves insisted that they not be confused with the Masai and other "savages"? The "agreement" had four rubrics: political, administrative, financial, and land-related. Though now under British protection, the Bugandan kingdom kept its autonomy, with its king, the *kabaka*, its justice system under colonial supervision, and its "Parliament," the *lukiko*. In reality, the *lukiko* was a chamber of peers with three regents, twenty "county" chiefs, and about sixty notables chosen by the sovereign, and it had largely consultative powers. The country was divided into counties (*saza*), subdivided into subcounties (*gombolola*), which themselves were divided into parishes (*miruka*). The only taxes were supposed to be those on guns and huts. Ganda authorities would be salaried, which represented a revolution in the way revenue functioned.[30]

But land reform showed best both the capacity of the Ganda aristocracy to make itself heard and the skill of the colonizer in remodeling supposedly customary law in the name of making it more rational. After having considered recognizing the rights of smallholder farmers, even while planning to create a land reserve that could be distributed to colonial settlers, Johnston agreed to recognize the political authorities' eminent rights. After a quick land inquiry — a delicate endeavor given the country's troubles of the previous twenty years or so — the facts furnished by the chiefs, with the aid of CMS missionaries, resulted in partitioning the territory into two more or less equal parts: on the one hand, state lands that were considered fallow and, on the other hand, lands that could be fully owned. The fully owned lands would be allocated through the so-called *mailo* procedure (a term derived from "mile," which became the base unit in the new cadastral method).

These were then distributed in the following way: 914 square miles were given to the king and his immediate entourage; 92 square miles were distributed to the missions; 50 square miles were given to the administrative centers; and 8,000 square miles went to a thousand chiefs and other notables. This "thousand" was discovered to be four thousand in 1921: they included *ba-kungu* chiefs, many former *batongole* chiefs, and a number of clan chiefs (*bataka*).[31] These authorities, who previously had been only administrative and judicial arbiters of land possession, were now in the position of proprietors in the feudal-lord sense of the word (or in the sense of British India's zamindars). The mass of peasants was reduced to the status of simple tenant farmers (*bakopi*) and stripped of their former lineage rights. Reform laid down the principle of private property, but this was reserved as a monopoly for the oligarchy — a veritable class of African landlords who were rewarded for their openness to colonial and missionary projects. The "customary" corvées were appreciably worsened, at least until 1928–1938, when they were transformed into monetary payments.

At the political level, recognizing the Bugandan monarchy as a partner in colonization coincided with a significant weakening of its real power. This benefited the oligarchy of chiefs that, under the leadership of the regents and especially the Protestant "prime minister" (*katikiro*) Apolo Kagwa, collaborated with the new regime. The conception of power remained autocratic, but government was now put under European control, and it benefited a class that became independent of the *kabaka*, in particular at the economic level (salary and land). However, the *kabaka*, even the child Daudi Chwa, continued to have an emotional value; he was even the very symbol of uninterrupted national Ganda identity.[32]

The 1894–1900 period thus proved decisive in the history of this ancient kingdom, at least until Uganda achieved independence more than half a century later. The period also was determinant for the other territories in the British protectorate. But, quite significantly, the overall territory was named after the state that was its founding nucleus: "Uganda" is the Swahili form of "Buganda."[33] Certainly, the British takeover marked the end of Buganda's expansion and of its military initiatives on the shores of Lake Victoria, both of which had characterized the kingdom's "sub-imperialism." From now on, Buganda's influence stopped at 1 degree southern latitude, that is, where the German sphere began. Buganda also renounced its suzerainty over Busoga in the east, even if a Muganda war chief, Semei Kakunguru, ran this territory from 1906 to 1913. The *kabaka* no longer had an army. Still, the Ganda political system and administrative staff were spread to the other kingdoms and districts that had been grouped together in the protectorate.

The three western kingdoms — Nkore, Toro, and Bunyoro — illustrated this process of "Gandaization," but the process varied according to each territory's heritages and initiatives.[34] Nkore's collaboration slowly took root after a major crisis that marked the end of Mugabe Ntare's reign. Rinderpest ripped apart the pastoral economy in 1891; then smallpox struck the population. No one was spared, not even the royal court: the only direct heir of the king died in the epidemic. Then the wild quest for cattle to compensate for the losses sparked a war with Rwanda, which invaded Uganda in 1894. English help was again sought, and a new accord was signed the same year. Still, a European did not arrive in Nkore before 1898. In the meantime, in 1895 King Ntare died, sparking a war of succession that lasted for more than thirty years: two princely factions squared off, and eventually a nephew of the deceased was enthroned under the name Gahaya, surrounded by two regents. In this atmosphere of crisis, one person progressively made his presence felt: Mbaguta, a thirty-year-old minor Hima chief from ancient Mpororo who had been the army chief responsible for King Ntare's dirty work. In 1888, he had welcomed the Christians refugees from Buganda's civil war and later organized them into a mercenary militia. Mbaguta also negotiated the 1894 accord with Major Cunningham: he was given the title *enganzi*, which referred to a brother in arms of the king. Soon thereafter, he forced out the king's father, Prince Igumira, and seized control of the wealthy agricultural chiefdom of Shema, which Igumira had controlled. In reality, his force was part of the Anglo-Ganda connection, and he acted as Nkore's *katikiro*. In 1899, a colonial post was established in Mbarara, with a Baganda police staff and Baganda clerks; the royal court was set up nearby. Mbaguta is an example of a leading commoner coming to power thanks to his understanding of the new world opened by European rule. Nkore became Ankole: it was a small name change but a large territorial expansion. The ancient kingdom encompassed, in a structure that had a federal appearance, the western neighboring principalities: Igara, Buzimba, Kajara, and Buhweju. In general, the small local potentates were replaced by one of their sons, who were surrounded by regents connected to Mbaguta and by Baganda advisers. Every succession crisis and internal quarrel thus became an occasion to install new governments that subscribed politically to the idea of collaboration with the whites. In 1901, an "agreement" was concluded along the lines of the one in Buganda. And in this transition, local Banyankore and Baganda actors played as decisive a role as the English colonizers.

In Toro, the sovereign himself collaborated. Indeed, Kasagama owed to the English his restoration as head of the country, a position his Bunyoro neighbor, Kabarega, had twice tried to dispossess him of, before 1890 and in 1893. In 1894, Kasagama obtained the same type of statute as in Ankole: his kingdom was enlarged with neighboring principalities (Mwenge, Busongora, Kitagwenda, and Kyaka). This sort of federation benefited from an "agreement" in June 1900. From then on, Kasagama was both chief of Toro and *mukama* (king) of the new territorial cluster. The chiefs who were his brothers in misfortune during the wars with Bunyoro supported him, and he chose as *katikiro* a young Protestant warrior. But Kasagama secured contacts with the English and their Baganda agents. Indeed, he combined the royal function with the role of "arch collaborator," a position Mbaguta held in Nkore: he moved his capital near the post of Fort Portal; he befriended Protestant missionaries; and his powers were reinforced in 1906.

Bunyoro faced an entirely different situation because it consistently resisted foreign conquest. In 1893, Mukama Kabarega was about to be confronted by a large expedition, led by the IBEAC and supported by significant contingents of Baganda auxiliaries. The king fled to the north. There was a last hope when Sudanese mercenaries mutinied in 1897, but the king was seized north of Lake Kyoga along with Mwanga, with whom he had joined forces. Deported to the Seychelles, he died there in 1923, and his country lived under foreign occupation until 1933. In 1896, several chiefdoms south of the Kafu River were ceded to Toro and Buganda. These territories, which sheltered the royal funerary sites and the sacred woods associated with the Bacwezi legend (including the Mubende site, which had been occupied since the early part of the century), were now considered "lost counties," a real "place of memory" for Nyoro nationalism, which was sustained around this irredentism.[35]

Disputes over Ganda claims sustained Bunyoro's political life for forty years. After conquering the kingdom, the English sought the support of notables, who submitted themselves in 1895 at the post of Hoima. But they wavered between Rwabudongo, a former chief of Kabarega's elite troops (the *barusura*), and Byacabwezi, a former territory chief. Both men were of common birth (neither from the princely Bito group nor from the Huma group), and both had great prestige among the masses, who had been waiting for Kabarega's return. In 1898, Commissioner George Wilson planned to enthrone in Masindi a young son of the king in exile, Kitahimbwa; the young king would be flanked by a regency council (as in Nkore and Buganda). But the system never got off the ground. Rwabudongo's death in 1900 prompted a new series of measures: Wilson named James Miti, a Muganda who had served as an interpreter, to the head of local government. A chief hierarchy, each member of which bore titles taken from the Ganda system, was put in place. Only some were Banyoro, like Paul Byacabwezi, but none came from the princely Bito group and many were Baganda. The Baganda language became quasi-official, with the support of the CMS missions. In the end, young Kitahimbwa, considered incompetent, was replaced in 1902 by his eldest brother, André Duhaga, a former aide to a Protestant mission who agreed to accept Miti's permanent supervision. Five years later, a crisis broke out: peasants in the "lost counties" and in Bunyoro agitated against the new prestations imposed by the Baganda. In March 1907, the Banyoro chiefs, with Byacabwezi as their leader, used this discontent to unleash a campaign of resistance against these foreigners, who were accused of monopolizing power, conducting various kinds of funny business, and displaying unacceptable arrogance: the movement was called *Nyangira Abaganda* (I refuse the Baganda). Some emissaries were sent to Toro and Ankole to generalize the protest. The CMS suspected the White Fathers, and the only Catholic chief was dismissed from his post. The administration sent reinforcements to Hoima, arranged the arrest of the ringleaders, and deposed several chiefs. Order was reestablished, but the impasse remained until 1924: Kabarega's death in exile and Duhaga's allowed the much more diplomatic Tito Winyi to be enthroned. Moreover, the region was loyal during World War I. In 1933, the English thus signed an "agreement" with Bunyoro. However, distrust persisted between this former kingdom and the British-Ganda complex imposed over the region.

These initial experiences in Uganda led to varying assessments of the political meaning of "indirect rule" for a colonizer's African partners. Some saw indirect rule as colonial manipulation and considered the preservation of ancient powers, which had become the whites' puppets, an illusion. Others emphasized the local actors' room for maneuver and the ability of those who had only been theoretically colonized to control the colonial experience. The status difference between Buganda and the other kingdoms from 1900 and the Ganda elite's grip over the rest of the protectorate also produced different assessments of the new regime's effects.[36] Here, a given author's origin came into the picture; the Baganda, for example, were most likely to claim that their ancestors were more England's partners than its subjects.

Despite variations in the ancient sociopolitical configurations, bureaucratic homogenization of administrative structures began to take place in the early part of the twentieth century. Significantly, in 1905 Ugandan affairs passed from the Foreign Office to the Colonial Office. The protectorate, whose capital was Entebbe, on Lake Victoria, was split into different, supposedly homogeneous territories. The southern Bantu-speaking half, where one found the ancient kingdoms, consisted of three provinces (in the 1950s): Western, Buganda, and Eastern, each under the responsibility of provincial commissioners. For example, Ankole formed a district, whose headquarters was Mbarara. Buganda comprised three districts (Mengo, Mubende, and Masaka). Then, at the lowest levelAfrican administration, there was everywhere the Ganda-style hierarchy described above: counties, subcounties, and parishes. The administrative vocabulary itself was copied from Luganda. The status of local chiefs (five to twenty per kingdom according to its size) was defined in 1919 by a Native Authority Ordinance: the maintenance of order, the collection of taxes, and the requisition of corvée labor were put under the district commissioner's direct control. In 1930, Bugandan local authorities were given greater autonomy, with the commissioners becoming "residents." But supervision of the districts returned following the 1945 disturbances. Not until 1955 did elected district councils appear throughout; that same year saw a real transition to self-government in Buganda. New stakes for representation and for the exercise of power were emerging; these were a priori different from those of the kingdoms' ancient political culture.

Nonetheless, a simple opposition between this administrative modernization and the logics of traditional politics is misleading, especially if it overshadows the complex dynamics of African governments confronting the challenges of their time. Edward Steinhart rightly emphasized the superficiality of the supposed antagonism between collaboration and resistance in the ancient ruling circles.[37] He showed how the issue was a question not just of ideology but of economic and tactical judgments linked to power relations. The "collaborationists" sought to create a sphere of autonomy at the heart of "the empire," while the "resisters" sought recognition from "the empire"; both groups quickly realized that they could not drive the Europeans away. They had to make the most of a situation in which they had everything to lose. Moreover, the region's politics tended to reward indirect approaches more than open confrontation. European observers called this "African lying," but they forgot that Machiavellianism is not the only way to maneuver.

In short, the specific characteristics of this transition period must be explained, in Uganda under the British as elsewhere under German and Belgian rule. In other words, we must examine the nature of the projects and the social and cultural identity of the actors. As we have seen, original political strategies were forged in this period; factions defined themselves using new parameters and new solidarities, overlapping (rather than annulling) the ancient lineage, regional, and other forms of group membership.

In the 1890s, binary cleavages crystallized in the ancient kingdoms that were made part of the Ugandan protectorate.[38] These cleavages could be defined more exactly, as in early-nineteenth-century France, in terms of "change" or "resistance," which here correspond to more or less intense relationships with the foreign occupying power and to denominational differences. In a general sense, a new generation of leaders was coming into being throughout. This generation was rooted in the ancient power networks, but these networks now belonged to another time, and they were more or less infused with Christianity. Their members often were bilingual (they spoke the local language, Luganda, and Swahili); some were literate. And they all knew how to communicate with British administrators, with missionaries, notably the CMS Protestants, and with the Bagandan auxiliaries. The Reverends Fisher, Lloyd, and Maddox, for example, elsewhere authors of several anthropological monographs, played active roles in Bunyoro's and Toro's politics. In Buganda, Bishop Alfred Tucker (head of the Anglican Church for the protectorate from 1890 to 1908) exercised strong influence, and he established an autonomous diocesan structure in which laypeople and African pastors held top positions, hence offering a completely new space for political experience. For example, Ham Mukasa was a preacher before becoming chief of the important county of Kyagwe in 1905. In the western kingdoms, the former Bito and Hinda aristocrats were marginalized. Throughout, the kings became Protestants.

Faced with this informal "party," which was viewed as a force for progress, as a friend to the British, and as intimately tied to Protestantism, another camp took shape. The latter consisted of those who were reluctant to collaborate or to change and who found support from Catholic missionaries, who in general were French. In 1899, in the Busoga principality of Bugabula, the English deposed the sovereign, who had remained pagan, and replaced him with a Protestant. In reaction, the chiefs partial to the former government converted to Catholicism in the 1920s and 1930s. Young Basoga organized themselves into rival denominational associations, which represented different interests; the ruling and wealthy circles were on the Protestant side, and the more humble rural groups were on the Catholic side.[39] In Nkore, after the White Fathers arrived in 1902, Mbaguta's opponents tended to become catechumens of Catholicism; this was notably true for the Iru chiefs: this is how the categorical cleavage between Hima and Iru (what one today calls an ethnic cleavage) found new political life, even if an exact equation between "ethnic group" and religion cannot be established:

> The class system began to take on new coloration in the early days of colonial rule as Bairu began to assert themselves as part of the Catholic and royalist opposition to the Protestant establishment led by Mbaguta and the child king, Kahaya.[40]

But this regime of factions at the heart of the political class — factions that dovetailed with autonomous denominational organizations — was most prevalent in Buganda. Foreign missionaries were only their advisers and intermediaries with colonial authority. The Catholics had use of one of the first journals, *Munno*, which was started in 1910. The crucial stake for these religious parties was control of the political posts craved by young graduates of the Catholic and Protestant establishments: elite rivalries were played out at the scholarly level (and later at the level of sports). The most prestigious secondary school was the Protestant King's College Budo, near Kampala, itself a symbol of "equilibrium" that the British maintained until just before independence.[41] When, in 1925, the *kabaka* rejected a remarkable Catholic candidate for the Buddu chiefdom, the tension was palpable, but everybody understood that the Protestant order was a mainstay of the system.

Uganda: "The Pearl of the Empire"?

Indirect rule seemed so ambiguous because its discourse was applied to a society thought to be immutable. At the same time, however, it had an entirely direct effect in terms of economic transformations induced by the colonial "opening." The changes that took place over several decades in people's daily lives make the idea of a "preservation of tradition" particularly illusory. Three things drastically changed Ugandan societies, even before World War I: the railroad, cotton, and schools.[42]

As shown above, the establishment of the protectorate went hand in hand with a decision to open a pathway between the sea and this enclaved region. Begun in Mombasa in 1896, the railroad reached Lake Victoria (in Kisumu, Kenya) in 1902; significantly, it was called the Uganda Railway. The Kenyan territory initially was considered less valuable than the rich, densely populated lands of the countries around the sources of the Nile.[43] At first, four steamships were launched on the lake to attract traffic from different shores. The railroad reached Kampala only in 1931.[44] In the 1950s, it was continued westward as far as the copper mines of Kasese, while a huge electric power plant was constructed on the Nile where it emptied out of Lake Victoria (Owen Falls).[45] This railroad was the privileged access route to the Great Lakes region until 1914, before the German "central railroad" was built con-

necting Dar es Salaam to Lake Tanganyika. This in turn was de-
throned by autoroutes. Trucks began proliferating in the second
decade of the twentieth century. From the very start of the century, transcontinental portage by porters collapsed in favor of
modern transport systems.[46] The time of the trip from Mombasa
to Lake Victoria was reduced from more than two months to just
over two days, and freight costs fell by 90 percent, making the
goods imported from the eastern coast competitive — much to the
detriment of local production: Kibiro's salt was replaced by Aden's,
bark cloth by cotton goods, the hoes of Banyoro blacksmiths by
those from England or Germany.[47] Commercial expansion and
monetization went hand in hand, but the single highway between
the Indian Ocean and Lake Victoria supplanted the ancient regional
trade networks, which had over time become entwined with one
another.[48] With the Berlin Act, Uganda was made part of a free-
trade zone, called for by the Congo Basin Convention, that ran
across the center of the continent.

The major vectors of this new economy were foreigners, mainly
Indians, who were plentiful in commercial activity, from kiosks
to import-export business.[49] Veritable merchant dynasties arose,
including those of Muslim Gujaratis and Bombay Hindus. The
firm Allidina Visram was based in Zanzibar and had some thirty
agencies in the interior, in both German and English territories,
until 1916; the Mehta and Madhvani families owned sugar refiner-
ies around Jinja in the late 1920s; and the company Narandas
Rajaram exported a large share of cotton in the 1930s.[50] Nationals
from different kingdoms became less and less common in the
markets, and they increasingly became clients of the nearest
Indian *duka* (shop, in Swahili).

Development could take two forms: investing in production, to
the point of making the protectorate profitable, or investing in

the agents of this process. The Ivory Age had ended, given the strict closure of the Leopoldian state. Agriculture then appeared to be the most promising sector: different cash crops were tried, including robusta coffee (in Buganda), sugarcane (in Busoga), tobacco (in Bunyoro), tea (in Toro), and cotton (primarily in Buganda before spreading to the eastern and northern parts of the protectorate), which eventually became the country's white gold. In 1904, Kristen Borup, a Danish agent of the CMS, distributed Egyptian cotton seeds to some thirty chiefs. The first results were disappointing qualitatively, but demand for this raw material was strong in the early part of the century. In 1908, the British Cotton Growing Association, a recent creation of Lancashire industry, convinced Governor Hesketh Bell to regulate production methods by passing the Uganda Cotton Ordinance. Cotton production rose from 1,000 bushels in 1906, to 22,000 in 1916, then to 180,000 in 1926, 316,000 in 1936, 364,000 in 1956, and nearly 380,000 bushels right before independence: Buganda's share of the total varied from a third to a half, the rest mainly came from Busoga. In value, cotton represented almost 94 percent of exports in 1925, and 60 percent in 1945.[51]

The period when production took off coincided with a social choice that the colonizer made in favor of African producers. The initial option — inspired by the spirit of the 1900 Uganda Agreement and promoted by Governor Bell and the director of agricultural services from 1911 to 1929, S. Simpson — was to lend support to Baganda peasants, who would be supervised by their chiefs. But others backed a process like the one unfolding in Kenya, where land was alienated to European settlers. This latter option had the support of William Morris Carter, for many years the protectorate's first judicial authority in his capacity as chief justice and as head of an important land commission; between 1918 and 1922, Governor Robert Coryndon, who was originally from South

Africa, also backed the land-alienation option. These two men in turn had the support of the successive secretaries for the colonies Lord Alfred Milner and Winston Churchill. But economic logic proved stronger: the crises of the 1920s and 1930s struck the European plantations with full force; these plantations were much more vulnerable than those of African farmers. The Africans contented themselves with smaller revenues; their dietary consumption was assured by their own food production; and supplementary labor needs were covered by seasonal workers from, among other places, Rwanda and Burundi. Chief supervision, peasant financial motivation, and control of colonial agronomic services combined to obtain the results seen above. The supporters of the White Highlands position bowed to evidence of profitability; Uganda remained a Black Man's Country. Starting in 1915, was not the protectorate able to cover its financial needs, thanks to the direct and indirect taxes whose base depended on the efforts of the African peasantry?[52]

Little by little, during the first third of the century, the region's human landscape changed, especially in Buganda: permanent rectangular houses, covered with corrugated iron, replaced round huts made from plant material; bark loincloths were replaced by white cotton clothes for men (combined with very British jackets among the most well off) and gaudy Victorian dresses with puffed sleeves for women; bicycles appeared on the roads; and enameled dishware, consumption of sugar and tea, and lighting by oil lamps (and, in the 1950s, the introduction of radios) changed the atmosphere in homes. In the cotton fields, these new modes of consumption created a situation resembling that in the Deep South of the United States during the same period (except here the white planters were absent). If one sketched a comparison with western Europe in the spirit of Braudelian syntheses, in fifty years southern Uganda passed from an eighth-century age of scarcity with its Syrian dealers (here the Swahili caravaners) to the euphoria of the sixteenth-century world economy.

Social change also manifested itself in education. Mission-school students totaled thirteen thousand in 1920.[53] The state did not intervene until 1922–1924: a Department of Education was created; some fifty establishments were selected and subsidized; and the Phelps-Stokes international commission (strongly influenced by the black leader Booker T. Washington's ideas in the United States) traveled to East Africa and supported the idea of adapted education.[54] Founded in 1922, the Makerere school first dealt with technical subjects (carpentry and mechanics), then spread to medical and pedagogical areas, before it became a real college that in 1949 established ties with the University of London. This was an effort to retain young Ugandan intellectuals tempted to pursue their studies in India or South Africa. The first Ugandan university students graduated in 1953, ten years before their counterparts in Belgian territories.

The Baganda's initiative in this takeoff, their appetite for money, and their dynamism led many observers at the time to compare them to the Japanese during the Meiji Restoration. But there was a considerable difference: the investors and promoters were not Africans (the kingdom's authorities or private individuals) but British and Indian foreigners.

In addition, the society was not homogeneous. Cleavages and antagonisms were even aggravated during this period. Peasants had to deal with as much coercion from European administrators and Indian merchants as from their own chiefs. Colonial agronomy replaced the disciplinary system inherited from the ancient monarchy. As we have seen, the land system in Buganda favored the creation of an oligarchy. Certainly, not every kingdom had the same system; a strategy of sharing inheritance taxes and sales (which was prohibited for non-natives) led to about fifty thousand landlords in 1950. Generally, cash crops consolidated the rights of those who occupied the land. But agriculturists suffered under the weight of several superimposed taxes: the poll tax; the colonial corvée (*kasanvu*), which was abolished in 1922; and prestations due to chiefs (in Buganda, the corvée of twenty-four days called *busuju* and a tithe called *envujo*), which were limited and slowly monetized after 1928.[55]

At the economic level, competition between merchants and owners of ginning factories declined; in 1938, truck owners began handling deliveries, according to an official zoning system. These monopolistic conditions contributed to gutting the amount paid to producers. From the 1920s to the 1950s, many conflicts erupted between peasants and industrialists (mainly Indians). In 1945 and 1949, distrust took a brutal and political form as the battle for better revenues was joined with youth demands for more democratic participation in local councils (notably in the *lukiko* in Buganda).

In 1921, this current of protest was expressed in the formation of "the party of the *bataka*," named for the ancient clan chiefs. Its two principal leaders were Joshua Kate, a former chief of Busiro county and the chief of the Gray Monkey clan who was forced to step down in 1919, and Semei Kakunguru, a war chief in the late nineteenth century, once a head of Busoga, and a rival to Apolo Kagwa. Their action was directed more against the Ganda oligarchy than against the English administration: nonetheless, the party refused to question the 1900 pact.

Social contestation could not escape religious involvement. As we have seen, the Anglican establishment backed the oligarchy. In Buganda in 1950, out of 1.3 million inhabitants, 41 percent were Catholic, 7.5 percent Muslim, 27.5 percent non-baptized, and 24 percent Anglican. Those at the top of society thus were only a quarter of the population.[56] Despite their number, Catholics held a marginal position among potential opponents. But in 1914, a sectarian current emerged from Anglicanism: the Bamalaki, a group that refused modern medicine and catechism before baptism and was quite close to the *bataka* party (both groups had the same leaders).

A new society transformed by monetization, trade, school, and every kind of individual mobility did not really emerge.[57] Certainly, the fact that acculturation did not lead to total uprooting delighted the backers of progressive and adapted modernization, which in principle was incarnated by indirect rule. But this colonial modernity closely combined British bureaucratic power, neo-traditional supervision by chiefs (themselves trained according to new values, even if they inherited the precolonial oligarchy), half-interventionist economic policy that benefited from crises and isolation, practical schooling founded on racial considerations, and, finally — the keystone — the unwavering authority of the churches and especially quasi-official Anglicanism. Christianity, however glorified with the blood of the 1886 martyrs, was integrated into local society as if it had always been part of Ganda values. R.C. Pratt summarized it very well:

> The introduction of Christianity did not lead to the creation of a believing minority alienated from the whole tribal society. Rather, Christianity became in a real sense the new religion of the tribe, with the missionary societies and the ruling chiefs and ministers [of Buganda] each strong supporters of the other.[58]

The "traditional" powers that the protectorate maintained represented a new form of power, as different from the former monarchical states as from the British liberal model, which was thought to influence and guide them. Social, economic, and technical modernization reached an impasse in the late 1930s, with a touch of totalitarianism that characterized all colonial modernity. The ancient hierarchies were neutralized politically, but they were preserved socially, with a new face: sons of former chiefs had become civil servants charged with agricultural, medical, and other questions, all of which was supervised by district commissioners. This transmutation of elites was symbolized in 1926 by Apolo Kagwa's departure from his *katikiro* post, and it was reinforced by the purge that followed the 1945 disturbances.

The legitimacy of African rulers, whose ancient religious, military, and lineage foundations were shaken, endured through the collective identities they incarnated, those of different kingdoms that continued to compete with one another under colonial "protection." In Buganda, the elite played up a sentiment of the entire population's superiority vis-à-vis neighboring peoples, from whom their agricultural workers came.[59] And in Bunyoro, Toro, Busoga, and Ankole, the elites leaned on popular discontent stemming from the abuses and arrogance of Baganda aides installed in their regions by the English and on the frustrations of the young, who faced inequalities, which were seen as the product of discrimination. This sentiment was particularly strong in Bunyoro, which was wounded by the memory of the lost counties. What were then called tribal rivalries, far from subsiding, coalesced in these battles over power and dignity during the century.[60] Social and political disputes were channeled — some would even say diverted — by these cleavages in the political arena. Both the colonial government and African actors discouraged all supra-ethnic movement. Very significantly, in 1931 Ugandan elites successfully militated against both a federal East Africa (the project was called a "closer union" with Kenya and Tanganyika) and the use of Swahili as an official lingua franca. Even today the country's two official languages are English and Luganda. By the mid-twentieth century, the sovereigns of the Ugandan protectorate undoubtedly had retained less room to maneuver than their Nigerian counterparts, but the dream of independence for their former states remained more alive, especially in Buganda.

German Conquest Between Lakes Victoria and Tanganyika

The zone southwest of Lake Victoria allotted to Germany in 1890 did not include a modern pole of power analogous to Buganda. With the exception of those in the area north of Lake Tanganyika, the first real contacts with Europeans happened between 1890 and 1896; not until about a dozen years later did the political-military grip become effective. In 1891, German East Africa became the Deutsch-Ostafrika "protectorate" (*Schutzgebiet*), run by its colonial army, the *Schutztruppe*. What first preoccupied the Germans, as we saw above, was securing the borders that touched British Uganda and Leopold's Congo. The first initiative in the region was launching an expedition headed by Emin Pasha. He planted the German flag at the trading post Tabora, created Bukoba, and then ventured into Congo south of Lake Albert, where he disappeared in 1892. For several years, the region remained a soldiers' domain; indeed, soldiers had been Imperial Commissioner Hermann von Wissmann's companions.[61] Later called "civilizing heroes" (*Kulturhelden*), they effectively combined raids, economic initiative, and scientific knowledge — for example, in the 1891–1892 expeditions carried out around Victoria in the name of the German Anti-slavery Committee.[62] "Military stations" representing Dar es Salaam's governmental authority were set up in Tabora and Bukoba in 1890, in Mwanza in 1891, and in Ujiji in 1896.

German control first took hold in the small principalities of Buzinza, Buhaya, and Buha, before spreading to the two large mountainous bastions of Burundi and Rwanda. As the English did in Uganda, the Germans sought to manipulate internal conflicts by playing one faction against another, notably during succession quarrels. But the Germans primarily presented themselves as liberators in relation to the three external rules that had been rivals in the region since the mid-nineteenth century: the Banyamwezi hawkers and warriors, who, even after the fall of the Mirambo "empire," made their pressure felt in Buha and in the saltworks of Buzinza; the Baganda, who, under Kabaka Mutesa, had moved unstoppably west of Lake Victoria as far as Ihangiro, Karagwe, and Rusubi; and the Arabs and the Swahili, who had built an Ujiji-based military-trading network that incontestably controlled Lake Tanganyika in the late 1880s under Rumaliza's forceful leadership.[63]

Emin Pasha and Franz Stuhlmann's rapid success west of Lake Victoria mainly depended on the support they received from sovereigns in the region. These rulers were glad to be separated from the Ganda yoke. Mukama Mukotani of Kyamutwara offered land for the Bukoba post. Bugabo subsequently accepted the Kashozi mission, founded by Monsignor Jean-Joseph Hirth. Only Mukama Mutatembwa of Kiziba, allied to Buganda, refused German "protection" for any length of time: he repeated that his master was Kabaka Mwanga and not Bwana Mzuri (Mister Things-Are-Fine), Captain Wilhelm Langheld's nickname. Prudent with regard to the English, the Germans dispersed thousands of Catholic refugees who had come from Buganda in 1892 and later were found in the entourage of the White Fathers' mission. Nonetheless, the authorities in Bukoba quickly found themselves involved in local rivalries between the "legitimate" sovereigns from the Bahinda line and the "usurpers" from the Bankango Hima clan. The leader of the first, Mukama Kahigi from Kyanja, established friendly ties with the Germans that lasted until their departure in 1916: his kingdom was enlarged to the detriment of his neighbors, and he received the trusteeship of Ihangiro in 1901 and of Karagwe in

1904; he even earned the title *Obersultan* of Buhaya. Only Kiziba kept its autonomy by collaborating with Bukoba starting in 1903 with the accession of a new king, Mutahangarwa.[64]

In the south, in Buzinza, the king of Rusubi, Kasusura, also adapted: he controlled a commercial crossroads between Tabora and the Kagera, and he knew how to use Bagandan support to expand, but he also understood the importance of making use of the region's new strongmen. He sent presents to the Bukoba and Tabora posts, and in 1894 and 1895 he received the explorer van Götzen and Captain Langheld, who gave him a "letter of protection" (*Schutzbrief*) and a German flag, respectively, and he distinguished himself by his attire in the fashion of the *kabaka*'s court.[65] In 1903, a military post was established at the Biharamulo site.

Toward Lake Tanganyika, the Germans practiced the same strategy with the local potentates. At the same time, they neutralized — to the potentates' benefit — the Banyamwezi and Zanzibari threats.[66] Captain Hans Ramsay founded a military station near the Swahili trading post of Ujiji in 1896, which in turn intensified the interventions.[67] The Buha and Buzinza principalities, both riddled with internal disputes, were conquered between 1893 and 1898. Only King Gihumbi of Buyungu, still a dissident in 1904, had to be arrested.[68] Burundi and Rwanda remained; both fell under the jurisdiction of the Ujiji district. At the time, these areas seemed accessible only via Lake Tanganyika or the Rusizi valley, despite Oskar Baumann's pioneering east-west expedition in 1892 and von Götzen's in 1894. As we saw above, the Germans were obsessed with containing the commercial and territorial ambitions of Leopold's Congo. Their attitude toward the Arabs and the Wangwana of Ujiji was therefore the reverse of what it had been toward the Baganda along Lake Victoria: the Baganda's influence was contained north of the Kagera, whereas the Arabs and the Wangwana were aided against the Congo State's agents, at least economically. The Belgians' destruction of Rumaliza's military network in the name of abolishing slavery did not end the ivory trade with the western shore of Tanganyika. In February 1895, Berlin diplomats protested to Brussels over the Congo Free State's violent acts against traders.[69] In this region, then, the former masters of ivory, caravans, and firearms (Arabs, Swahili from the coast, Wangwana from the interior, and the Banyamwezi) were reduced politically. But the colonizer rehabilitated them as auxiliaries, in the most concrete sense of the term. Members of this small Swahili-speaking world later filled the administrative, military, and commercial networks established by the German officers of the *Schutztruppe*.

The first contacts with Burundi and Rwanda in 1896 and 1897 were carried out therefore from the west and with evident anti-Congolese intention. This all took place as if the Germans saw these countries only as depositories of ivory. Indeed, it was in this spirit that Captain Ramsay founded the post of Usumbura on the northern side of the lake in 1897.[70] From then on, military operations in the two kingdoms were coordinated from this military station, which in 1901 became the headquarters of a new district separate from Ujiji. But the control of each followed quite different trajectories: paradoxically, the Rwandan monarchy, though more powerful and more centralized, very early accepted the German protectorate, whereas the Burundian royal court did not truly submit to foreign rule until seven years later.

Both external and internal factors came into play. When Captain Ramsay visited Yuhi Musinga's court in Runda, in the center of Rwanda, in March 1897, the *mwami* had just come to power through a coup d'état called *Rucunshu*, which had cost the life of his predecessor, Mibambwe Rutalindwa.[71] The chiefs related to Queen Mother Kanjogera, of the Bega clan, had driven a faction linked to the dynastic Banyiginya clan from power. After the death of the great king Rwabugiri in 1895, the country was in a state of nascent civil war, and young Musinga accepted this unexpected external aid without realizing what Ramsay's *Schutzbrief* and the flag meant.[72] This was analogous to what happened in Buganda when Mwanga was faced with Captain Lugard. Moreover, as we have seen, the Rwandan oligarchy looked for German support against Congo's Belgians, who were believed to be more dangerous since they had crushed the preceding king's army. In the beginning, Musinga's historic compromise was lived as an alliance, not as a submission. Indeed, the German presence remained distant and marginal (on the shores of Lake Kivu) until the early twentieth century. A year after Ramsay did so, his successor, Captain Bethe, visited the *mwami*'s court, but not until 1901 did an officer take up permanent residence at the Shangi post.

The most durable European settlement came from the east: Monsignor Hirth's White Fathers, based in Rusubi since 1897, decided to try their luck in this densely populated country far from Muslim influence. From 1898 on, delegations of Baganda and Basubi were sent to Musinga's court. In 1900, an expedition led by the vicar apostolic himself visited the *mwami*, with the German authorities' permission. The king offered him the site of Save, in the south, as a place to set up the first mission. Foundations proliferated in the densely populated peripheral regions until 1903: they included Zaza in Gisaka (in the east), Nyundo and Rwaza in Bugoyi and Mulera (in the northwest), and Mibirizi in Kinyaga (in the southwest). These missions, far from the Nyanza royal court, pleased both the *mwami*, who was threatened by the European presence, and the missionaries, who were more comfortable in regions where they could play the role of territorial chief, if not that of "kings without crowns." The missionaries were surrounded by mostly Bagandan armed auxiliaries, and they were

248

given immense land estates, between 100 and 200 hectares, of which they were considered both occupants and managers. They demanded corvées just like other powers, and they fed the survivors of the famine that spread during this period.[73]

The relationships between the whites and the Rwandan rulers remained ambiguous, even inconsistent, for several years. In 1901, Usumbura district's new chief, Lieutenant Werner von Grawert, captured the rebel Rukura, who had tried to restore Gisaka's independence, but his successor, Robert von Beringe, imposed a cattle fine on the king for repressive abuses in this region. In 1904, von Grawert, newly installed as the district head, energetically pacified the country's northwest, which had been disrupted by several acts of "banditry." Governor von Götzen recalled in 1903 that he "had to support the authority of Sultan Musinga before committing him to the German cause and installing [the] German administrative trusteeship."[74] Similar contradictions can be found among the missionaries. In Rwaza, the Fathers, in conflict with the region's peasants, used central authority to their advantage, while in Zaza missionaries sympathized with Gisaka's cause against the "abanayarwanda chiefs." Throughout, the first converts were marginal figures.[75] In 1906, the founding of the Kabgayi mission, near the royal court, favored a rapprochement with the aristocracy similar to that reached by the CMS in Buganda. From then on, the noose got tighter around the Rwandan government's neck, and it was forced to collaborate.

In Burundi, the situation was more confused for a long time. Old king Mwezi Gisabo (c. 1850–1908) obstinately refused all contact with the whites' world. Unlike their neighbors, he and his chiefs tolerated not a single piece of cotton clothing in their court. This might explain why, after traversing the country in 1892, Oskar Baumann believed that the monarchy no longer existed in Burundi![76] Several military expeditions took place between 1896 and 1899, notably Captain Bethe's in 1899, which destroyed the Ndago royal residence and devastated the territory of a chief who had been involved in burning the Muyaga mission. His adjunct, Lieutenant von Grawert, was later nicknamed Digidigi, an onomatopoeia that evoked machine-gun fire. The tactic devised by the Barundi warriors to fight the salvos of the Arabs' piston rifles fell short, and many deaths followed. Moreover, the Germans manipulated internal divisions. In 1903, Captain von Beringe won the support of Maconco, a son-in-law of the king who had rebelled (over the issue of a hunting dog who traveled around the country).[77] Von Beringe also won support from Kilima, an adventurer from Bushi who claimed to be the true *mwami*, the secret grandson of King Ntare Rugamba, and who had succeeded, through terror and calling on the independent spirit among the region's Hutu lineages, in carving out a territory in the country's northwest. Facing a joint attack, Mwezi was forced to flee; he later resigned himself to negotiating with the Germans in Kiganda. Two years later, in Bukeye, von Grawert, who had the same directives for both Burundi and Rwanda, officially recognized Mwezi as the country's *mwami*. The rebels were mercilessly cut down: Chief Kanugunu (leader of the northeastern Batare) and Maconco (in Usumbura) were defeated; Kilima was deported to Lake Nyasa's shores at Neu-Langenburg. For a while, the country remained in a state of disruption, especially in the south. However, in Burundi too, a significant faction within the aristocracy, led by one of the king's sons, Chief Ntarugera, chose the path of collaboration. As for the missionaries, the White Fathers' first structures, which were situated in the regions most loyal to the *mwami* (in Muyaga, Mugera, and Buhonga), now were complemented by two posts in the northwest (Kanyinya and Rugari), which became inscribed in a logic of pacification.[78]

In the end, the relative facility with which the German authorities made themselves be recognized in all these states stemmed from internal divisions within the countries, from the superiority of the Germans' automatic weapons, and from the atmosphere of catastrophe and disorder that had reigned since the late 1880s.[79] Rare were the sovereigns, like Mwezi in Burundi and Kabarega in Bunyoro, who could mobilize their populations to resist subjugation. In general, rulers quickly adopted various modes of collaboration, some of which were straightforward, while others were more ambiguous and riddled with resistance: some accepted merchants and missionaries but were cunning in the political arena (such as Kasusura); others established proper relations with the administration but interfered with the diffusion of new ideas as much as they could. The illustrative examples are Musinga, who always preferred German uniforms to the French Fathers' gandouras, and Kahigi, who, in reconstituting the "greater Kyamutwara" of his Bahinda ancestors and in opposing missionary establishments, became close to the Bukoba officers, to the point of adopting their white uniforms. Clothes were rich in meaning in this Africa in transition, a point to which we will return. What remained to be done, as in Uganda, was to put these first efforts at collaboration into operation on the institutional and socioeconomic levels.

The Far West of Deutsch-Ostafrika: The Three Residencies

Two facts prompted the Dar es Salaam administration to opt for a new protectorate model for its northwest districts (Bukoba and Usumbura, later split into Rwanda and Burundi): the manifest success of the British model of indirect rule in Uganda and the desire to avoid another popular uprising like the violent Maji Maji prophetic movement that had thrown the colony's south into a state of unrest between 1904 and 1905. These experiences informed the policies of Bernhard Dernburg, who had been appointed head of the State Secretariat of the Colonies (the *Reichskolonialamt*), which had been created in 1907, and of Baron Albrecht von Rechenberg, the governor from 1906 to 1912. Their objective was to define a more scientific method of colonization, to replace the military administration with civilian rule, to better respect indigenous political structures, and to favor local production based on peasants' interests, what was called the *Volkskultur* (in its economic sense). According to these principles, the colony's main source of wealth was its population. The Bugandan cotton industry sparked Dernburg's interest. The northwestern kingdoms, notably Rwanda, were to become a second Uganda, an effort that required adequate investments in transportation, agronomy, and health.[80]

The political precondition was a shift to a form of indirect administration. The crucial decisions had already been made under Governor von Götzen with the creation of the three residencies — Bukoba, Urundi, and Ruanda — in 1906. The first two were entrusted to officers in place, Willibald von Stuemer (who kept his position until World War I) and Werner von Grawert (who lasted until 1908), respectively. Rwanda was separated from Usumbura in 1907 and entrusted to Richard Kandt. This remarkable figure — who had been trained in psychiatry and linguistics and was a poet in his spare time, a protégé of Franz Stuhlmann and of Prussian aristocrats despite his Jewish-Polish origins, and a civilian lost in a military milieu — had been familiar with the country since 1898 (as an explorer of Lake Kivu); he ran it until 1913.[81]

Kigali, Rwanda's new headquarters as of 1908, and Bukoba incarnated two models of this German-style indirect rule, where the residents were conceived of as tutors destined slowly to transform the sovereigns into modern administrative rulers. The situation was trickier in Bukoba, given the scattered powers: von Stuemer was charged with stabilizing and hierarchizing them around Mutahangarwa of Kiziba and especially Kahigi of Kyanja. Some powers were recognized or delegated to them in matters of justice, public order, and taxation under the administration's supervision. A new class of elites, simultaneously interpreters and intermediaries between the residency and the courts, emerged, illustrated by Franzisko Lwamgira, a Kiziba notable.[82]

In Rwanda, Kandt's policy consisted of supporting and reinforcing Mwami Musinga's power, respecting the monarchy's symbols, and discouraging all subversion.[83] But the complicated "three chiefs" system led him to promote the creation of "government chiefs," responsible for law and order and for relations with the caravans and the administration.[84] However, this project, which resulted in a more direct administration, was tried only in Mutara (in the northeast). In fact, paralleling what happened in the Ugandan kingdoms, the Rwandan ruling circle divided into two parts: that of suspicion and that of collaboration. The latter, which ended up being the prevailing party, was led by the king's uncle Kabare, a major chief. Musinga manipulated both sides. The Nyanza court's shift toward collaboration was accelerated by two facts: the advancement of the White Fathers and the revolt of Ndungutse.

On several occasions, von Grawert and Kandt scolded the missionaries for their messy and sometimes brutal political interventions.[85] But starting in 1908, Father Léon Classe, a Lorraine admirer of Joseph de Maistre, became Monsignor Hirth's representative in Kabgayi.[86] This mission, established midway between Nyanza and Kigali as a third center of power that could catalyze an alliance between the other two, became the dominant pole of Rwandan politics, a position it held for more than half a century. In fact, contacts with the *mwami*'s entourage had existed from the start. A sort of palace school, the Mission of Save had opened in Nyanza in 1900 where the catechist Tobie Kibati taught a Swahili course. Musinga himself was a regular student of this course, which resulted in his being able, very early, to write and to communicate directly with the administration. Catechism was out of the question at this level. But in Kabgayi, starting between 1907 and 1910, things went further: some princes like Nshozamihigo, a son of Rwabugiri, the former king, and pages (*intore*) of good nobility frequented the mission, were instructed, and were introduced to soccer by Father Peter Schumacher.[87] Schumacher in turn adopted Tutsi aristocratic customs: he traveled with two domestic servants, one carrying food and the other tobacco for his pipe. For his part, Kabare, the major chief, drank sorghum beer from a straw in the company of Perfectus Magilirane, a Save neophyte, thus signifying, in 1907, the lifting of all discrimination toward Christians.[88] Moreover, in Rwaza in April 1910, Father Paulin Loupias paid with his life for ruling in favor of Musinga's representatives in a dispute with a local Hutu chief, Rukara, who in turn was hanged in 1912.[89]

This incident illustrates the insubordination of the country's northwest quarter, as much in relation to the *mwami* as to the Germans. Only recently conquered, the population of this region, overwhelmingly Hutu, was connected more through clan solidarities than through political ties. The region had a profound streak of independence with regard to all "foreigners," including the Tutsi chiefs from the center, the Banyenduga,who had tried to introduce new obligations like the *buletwa* corvée.[90] This regional cleavage can still be found in Rwanda's contemporary tragedies. In 1912, Musinga was confronted by another major crisis. From early in his reign, a rumor hung in the air: Rwabugiri's true heir supposedly fled with his mother in 1895, like the hidden tsarevich of Russian history. But in the north, Nyiragahumuza, a woman prophet linked to the cult of Nyabingi and to Mpororo tradition, suddenly claimed that Ndungutse, a Mututsi, was the awaited prince.[91] Rifle bullets were said to turn into water, as in the Maji Maji revolt. The entire north rose up, including Batutsi, Bahutu (with Rukara, chief of Mulera, who had been on the run in the volcanic-mountain region since 1910), and Batwa (with Chiefs Basebya and Ngurube, masters of the great Rugezi swamps). German intervention saved the day.[92]

Rwanda's ruling circle was forced to recognize the virtue of the German protectorate, but without genuine trust being established, except perhaps with Lutherans from the Bethel mission, who came to Rwanda in 1907 and lived mostly in Rubengera on Lake Kivu. On several occasions, Pastor Ernst Johanssen had spoken with Musinga on religious and cultural questions.[93]

Still, relations with the population remained problematic, given the corvées, the requisitioning of porters (sometimes by the thousands for transporting construction materials), the food deliveries to caravans (with remunerations mostly being allotted to chiefs), and abuses committed by intermediaries or those who pretended to be: interpreters, infantrymen, foremen (*nyampara*) for construction sites and missions, and Bahaya hawkers.[94]

In Burundi, relations between Europeans and their auxiliaries, on the one hand, and between Europeans and the population, on the other, were even poorer. After Mwezi Gisabo's death in 1908, it was impossible to make use of as coherent a central power as Rwanda's. Young king Mutaga Mbikije, torn between the tutelage of the queen mother, Ririkumutima, and that of his elder brother Ntarugera, was assassinated in 1915 and replaced by a young child, Mwambutsa Bangiricenge, who reigned until 1966. A new residency was established in Gitega, in the center of the country, in 1912. But the five successive officeholders, all soldiers, relied on

255

the support of loyalist chiefs — Bezi from the center as well as Batare from the east and south — while practically recognizing the autonomy of dissident chiefs, including Batare in the northeast and Kilima (who had returned from exile in 1911) in the northwest. Finally, the Lake Tanganyika littoral and the Rusizi plain, ravaged by trypanosomiasis since 1905, were removed from the *mwami*'s authority and brought under Usumbura's direct control as well as the direct control of military doctors from the eight camps afflicted by the sleeping sickness.[95]

The ups and downs of indirect rule in Rwanda and Burundi largely resulted from a misunderstanding. The German administration conceived of the state as centralized, a conceptualization through which it evaluated the efficacy of monarchical control. But, as we have seen, the monarchy was founded on a religious type of support in which effective powers were divided among aristocratic networks, which themselves were frequently divided, among lineages, and among regional authorities on the peripheries, all of which was older than the *mwami*'s control. In November 1905, Captain von Grawert, then head of the two countries, wrote:

> The ideal is: unqualified recognition of the authority of the sultans from us, whether through taxes or other means, in a way that will seem to them as little a burden as possible; this will link their interests with ours.[96]

By 1914, the goal was far from having been met, but the process that later triumphed under the Belgians had already been set in motion — namely, pyramidal feudalization, somewhat similar to the Anglo-Norman model, with "Tutsi lords" and colonialists at the top and the missionary church's religious backing, which replaced that of the ancient cults. From this point of view, Rwanda already served as a model. From the beginning of the European takeover, Christianity was at the center of the political debate in the Great Lakes region.

The change, in the three residencies, also happened through monetization. The year 1905 marked a turning point, with the monetary reform that put into circulation a rupee (worth 1.33 marks), divided into 100 hellers, and with the ordinance on the "hut tax." This tax was imposed, with the help of chiefs, only in 1914 in Rwanda and Burundi, at the rate of 1 rupee per enclosure. In Bukoba, where this tax yielded more than 100,000 rupees in 1906, a poll tax was introduced at 3 rupees per adult male. But slowly the small copper coins spread and even came to define "money": *amahera,* which is derived from *Heller,* is the word for money in the local languages. People began earning money as some wages were paid in cash in the European centers and, mostly, as profits were earned in commerce.[97]

The heaviest trade, almost totally replacing that in ivory, involved cow and goat hides; since the early part of the century, these hides had been transported to Mombasa, via Lake Victoria and the railroad. Exports from the port of Bukoba (which were nealy 100 percent skins) were thirty times greater in 1907 than in 1903. The caravan trade to the eastern coast collapsed, but the link between Bukoba and the cattle-rich mountains of Rwanda and Burundi flourished: more than twenty thousand loads of skins left Kigali each year in small caravans of a dozen or so porters, of whom half were Bahaya and half Rwandan.[98] The merchants living in small urban centers were rarely European (mostly Greek) and more often Indian (here again, the Allidina Visram firm), as well as Arab and occasionally Swahili.[99] But there were hundreds of salesmen — Bahaya, Basubi, Banyamwezi, and even Rwandan and Burundian — who were used as touts and retailers on the hills. They also distributed cotton fabric, the usage of which spread rapidly, especially in Buhaya. Usumbura was the headquarters of a sizable salt trade, which came by canoe or sailboat from Ujiji.[100] A former officer, Captain Otto Schloifer, had taken control of the Uvinza saltworks (in exchange for royalties paid to local sovereigns); in 1902, he created a monopoly company, the Central-Afrikanische Seengesellschaft, to industrialize the saltworks: the former dry-season "salt distillers" had to become porters or stevedores.[101] The 1905–1906 disturbances induced by the caravans in these countries, which were still poorly adjusted to commerce, prompted the administration to intervene to regulate access to Rwanda and Burundi, notably on behalf of Asian merchants. In fact, Dar es Salaam was divided between distrust of the merchants and recognition of their utility in fiscal matters. But soldiers and missionaries were partial to closing off the caravans' access to the countries in the name of order and morality.[102]

Different projects were drawn up to move beyond this predatory economy, which was decimating goat livestock. Bukoba's experience, coming after Uganda's with cotton, seemed convincing. The cash crop adopted here was coffee, present even before colonialism. The administration distributed this luxury crop, previously reserved for *bakama*, to peasant farms growing bananas, all under the responsibility of duly supervised sovereigns. Exports rose from 8 tons in 1904 to 500 in 1913, at a time when prices quadrupled. By 1911, 300,000 trees had been planted on peasant plots and on the *nyarubanja*, the aristocrats' reserved estates. The aristocrats were the principal actors in this expansion; they were also the primary beneficiaries, through extending their land possessions, exploiting the corvées, or collecting a tithe on peasant production.[103] The British hardly acted differently in supporting the *mailo* holders. Still, the peasants earned some profit, which allowed them to pay their taxes more easily and acquire cotton fabric. Force was certainly used, but financial motivation, induced by the export facilities created by the railroad to Mombasa, was the decisive factor. Like the Baganda, the Bahaya entered the global economy in 1905, but they were hardly its masters. Indeed, they remained marginal to the international market, because their monetary revenue covered only a small part of their needs, with the essentials coming from subsistence farming.[104]

Resident Kandt clearly envisaged the same process for Rwanda and Burundi — that is, developing arabica plantations.[105] The perennial crop required only small areas, and it had high-value returns, ones that easily covered the costs of freight. In a report drafted in 1913 that convinced Governor Heinrich Schnee, Kandt proposed forcing each taxpayer to maintain eight coffee trees. The White Fathers had been trying this at the Mibirizi mission since 1905. Like the English in Uganda, the Germans excluded both the possibility of European colonization in these populated regions and the prospect of a workforce exodus to the coast: they opted instead for making a profit from African labor on-site.[106] But this involved opening up transportation. Fascinated by the success of the Uganda Railway, the German colonial leaders were carried away by a railroad dream. The creation of a "central railway" (*Zentralbahn*), tying Dar es Salaam to Lake Tanganyika, complemented by branches to the northwest, would, according to them, not only drain eastern Congo's riches but also and especially give birth to an economy in the northwest parts of the colony.[107] The combined interests of Deutsche Bank and the Frankfurt metallurgic firm Holzmann, guaranteed by the Reich, led to a construction boom: the rail line reached Morogoro in 1907, Tabora in 1912, and Kigoma, near Ujiji, in February 1914.[108] Moreover, in March 1914, the Reichstag voted for a budget for a "Rwandan Railroad" that was to link Tabora to the southeast

Kagera elbow, but military operations in 1916 interrupted the plans. World War I forced all these projects to be aborted, at least the German ones.[109]

World War I and the Invention of Mandates

Despite the 1885 Berlin Act that in principle ensured the neutrality of Central Africa, the war did not spare the region. After several skirmishes in 1915 between the Belgians of Congo and the British of Uganda, on the one hand, and the Germans of Bukoba, Rwanda, and Burundi, on the other, a general Allied offensive took place in April 1916.[110] Two Belgian columns progressed from the north and south of Lake Kivu; several dozen German soldiers, flanked by several hundred askaris, retreated; Kigali was occupied in May, Gitega in June; the Belgians reached Tabora in September, while a British column arrived in Biharamulo.

The region was under military occupation until 1921, but the Belgians and the British quickly negotiated a partition: the Orts-Milner Convention, signed in Paris in 1919 and later ratified by the League of Nations, gave Rwanda and Burundi to the Belgians.[111] Gisaka and Bugufi (which were thought to constitute a future corridor for the Cape-to-Cairo railroad!) were amputated from Burundi's east. The former districts (*Bezirke*) of Bukoba, Ujiji, and Mwanza were integrated into the Tanganyika Territory, the heir of Deutsch-Ostafrika. Each partner received its part of the cake under a statute of the League of Nations Mandate, more precisely Mandate B. This legal creation combined the takeover with a series of commitments inherited from the Berlin Act (freedom of commerce and evangelization) and a new concept of trusteeship destined to guarantee, over an undefined period, progress and emancipation of the administered Africans. These definitions suggested a continuation of indirect rule.[112] In 1917, some residents, under the authority of a royal commissioner based in Kigoma, were placed around King Musinga of Rwanda and Mwambutsa of Burundi.

The 1914–1918 war was the whites' affair. But on several accounts, it affected the region's autochthons, and not just because of the changeover in "masters." The conflict created a retinue of suffering: brutality and pillaging by occupation troops (notably Congolese infantrymen, whose black uniforms left unhappy memories); soldier recruitments in Haya and flights from this recruitment in Uganda; massive requisitions by German troops of Burundian and Rwandan porters, some of whom were brought as far as the border with Mozambique, where General Paul von Lettow-Vorbeck's resistance ended and from where many never returned; food requisitions, commercial collapse, and food shortages, which in Rwanda turned into a real famine called *Rumanura*.[113]

In the political domain, the disarray played itself out on several levels. The prevailing disorder and the accompanying calamities sparked movements of popular revolt against the whites and their symbols (missions, fabric, and money), for example, in Mulera in Rwanda and in Kigezi in Uganda and in the prophetic sphere of the Nyabingi cult, between 1915 and 1917.[114] Similar events took place in central Burundi from May to July 1922. With the Belgian regime barely in place and with the country's principal chief, Prince Ntarugera, son of the deceased Mwezi and the kingdom's regent, having just died, peasants unhappy with taxes around Gitega and several Batare chiefs unhappy with the Bezi's hold in the northeast followed two "sorcerers" who prophesied the end of the whites, Runyota (Smoldering Ash) and Kanyarufunzo (The Little One of the Papyrus Swamp).[115]

At the same time, local leaders began scheming for ways to use the change in European masters to settle scores: in 1917 in Kinyaga, in southwest Rwanda, for example, some local elites thought they could exploit the initially bad relations between the Belgians and the royal court to get rid of their chief; in 1918, one of Musinga's nephews, the chief in Mulera, at odds with the queen mother, fled to Uganda, where the English named him chief of Bufumbira.[116] Some elites followed the retreating Germans as far as Tabora, such as Franzisko Lwamgira of Bukoba and the young Burundian prince Baranyanka, then a student in Gitega — two *évolués* indebted to those who trained them.[117] For his part, King Kahigi killed himself out of despair. But the sovereigns and their entourages generally displayed their diplomatic skills in order to gain recognition from the new authorities: the *bakama* of Buhaya flocked to Bukoba in July 1916 to meet the British *bwana mkubwa* (the big chief, in Swahili).[118] Starting in late May 1916, Musinga pleaded with the new arrivals "not to needlessly ruin his country" and declared himself ready to "obey"; then, in June 1920, during a visit by Minister of Colonies Louis Franck, he wrote to King Albert I to protest against the transfer of Gisaka to the English:

> Pity my mother, myself, and my children; we are all here in our own country, and we cry when we think how in Europe people want to divide Rwanda, my country and that of my children.[119]

When Minister Franck arrived in Burundi, he was met with the same worried and demanding deference at Prince Ntarugera's home:

> Boula Matari... I promise to assist you. I am the most important prince of the country.... I want my dignity recognized and my situation, as far as it is mine, protected.[120]

It is understandable why in 1918, when a rough draft of a referendum was drawn up, the chiefs — asked whom they would choose between the Belgians and the English — answered they would prefer whoever had the most power.

In 1924, the administrative boundaries were clarified. A campaign to return Gisaka to Rwanda, supported notably by Father Léon Classe and by Pastor Henri Anet of the Belgian Society of Protestant Missions (heirs of the Bethel missions), had succeeded in December 1923.[121] In 1924, Belgium officially accepted a mandate over what later was called the territory of Ruanda-Urundi, while the German districts were kept by the British, before being partly subdivided (Kasulu was separated from Kigoma, for example), and then regrouped into provinces in 1931 (Bukoba and Mwanza forming Lake Province).

In fact, each colonial power applied experience gained in neighboring territories — Uganda for the British and Congo for the Belgians — to its new African possessions. The administrative staff came largely from these two locations. A new wave of Baganda auxiliaries later arrived in Buhaya, Buzinza, and Buha. In August 1925, Ruanda-Urundi was attached administratively to the Belgian Congo, under the authority of a vice governor-general, with the two residents coming under his authority. The Belgian franc had replaced the rupee in 1920 (as did the shilling in Tanganyika). The repercussions of World War II were not as serious as those of World War I: certainly, the war led to requisitions for the Ethiopian front (here as in the rest of East Africa); it made Ruanda-Urundi a piece of Free Belgium (since Brussels was German and the government was in London); and it caused major shortages in 1943–1944.[122] In 1945, the transfer of the League of Nations mandate to the United Nations changed very little, though it reinforced international control, since annual reports would be completed by periodic "visiting missions."

Indirect Rule in the Northwest of British Tanganyika

In Bukoba, the British district chiefs picked up where the Germans had left off; namely, they sought *bakama* collaboration and "Gandaized" the system by subdividing each kingdom, considered a county, into *gombolola* and creating a *lukiko* in each court. Deaths and departures brought a new generation of sovereigns to power, except in Ihangiro, where Ruhinda, Nyarubamba's successor, remained. Moreover, six of the seven *bakama* were converted after 1918, four to Protestantism and two to Catholicism. Kahigi's son Alfred Kalemera ostentatiously burned the Cwezi cult's major sanctuary, tied for centuries to the Hinda dynasty. But neo-traditionalism won the day with the policies of Donald Cameron, who was governor from 1925 to 1931. The Colonial Office charged Cameron, a Creole from Antilles who was a priori skeptical of all assimilation projects, with imitating the Nigerian model—that is, with creating an indigenous administration that would be integrated into a colonial framework. The pillars of this program, sharply different from those in Buganda, with its illusion of partnership, were the tribe and the chief. All other forms of solidarity (religious, lineage, school, or professional) had to be kept in the background. The "preserved" tribal entity, with its language, customs, and chief, was to be supreme. This concept was dear to the ethnographers of the time; they thought this terminology, from the Bible and Tacitus, respected Africans more than the exotic literature, which was full of prejudices about "savages." It is interesting to trace the process of "restoration," a process that is better described as a "creation of tribes," to quote the English historian John Iliffe.[123]

In Buhaya, the strategy was to confederate the small kingdoms. None of the *bakama* stood out; the majority failed the studies they were forced to take, but joint institutions were created to supervise them: Lwamgira, already an expert in colonial collaboration, became in 1926 (through 1945) secretary of the *kiama*, the council of "chiefs" that met monthly; another clerk, Hubert Ishengoma, who had trained under the Germans, ran the "indigenous treasury." Created in 1925, this institution distributed to the *bakama* a share of the tax revenue commensurate with their diligence. Indirect rule thus became very controlling. The change was even sharper in Buzinza and Buha, where old powers were much more disrupted. In Buha, the former masters of the land, the *bateko*, were annihilated, which benefited the purely Tutsi chiefs (*batware*). However, the local aristocracies played their game well: it was estimated that in 1927 the Haya sovereigns and, in Rusubi, King Kasusura collected half the indigenous tax revenue and that the *mukama* of Kyanja earned nearly 3,000 pounds per year, which was more than the *kabaka* of Buganda received. The ancient taxes had in effect been monetized, and the land encroachments, modeled on the *nyarubanja* system, continued to allow these African-style landlords to reap huge profits from their plantations.

The rush to coffee continued under the English: in 1928, half the taxpayers cultivated it. The market economy spread in the region: hawkers called *wacuruzi* numbered in the thousands. In the late 1920s, Clemens Kiiza, a former clerk from Kiziba, had trucks and opened a pulp-removing factory. In Buhaya country, and among the Chagga of Kilimanjaro, the chiefs encountered more and more resistance as education advanced, thereby producing new cadres. Here, as in Buganda, youth mobilized to receive a general education and not the missionaries' third-rate schooling — a system that had been subsidized since 1925. The administration lent support to central schools, where English was taught and Swahili was used throughout. The Tabora Secondary School, which had many Haya students, became a virtual ticket to Makerere University in the 1930s.

This new social stratum, produced by money and education, made itself felt in increasingly political ways in the 1920s. Catechists forced Wesleyan South Africans, who had tried to succeed the Bielefeld missionaries, to leave. Some youth created a martial-style movement called *bandera* (flag). Above all, the Bukoba Bahaya Union was started in 1924: educated youth became the spokesmen of rural discontent with land despoilment — by both *nyarubanja* holders and Catholic missions.[124] In 1929, they joined the Tanganyika African Association (TAA) created by their counterparts in Dar es Salaam. In 1935, Kiiza and Rugazibwa formed the Native Growers Association, a cooperative that in 1936 and 1937 began conflicting with the administration over new coffee-growing rules. Its leaders were arrested; the association was dissolved; and the king of Kiziba, William Mutakubwa, who had supported them, was deposed.

Faced with a rising social and political consciousness that transcended "tribal" boundaries, the government tried to encourage traditionalism. In part, the educated stratum let itself be trapped by this ethnic communalism, which had been cultivated by the colonizers, whose objective clearly was to create obstacles to nationalism or "Bolshevism," as it was called.[125] But, contrary to what happened in the Belgian domain, a national consciousness rooted in civil society, notably in cooperatives, increasingly asserted itself over the years. The TAA expanded its activities in the 1950s. The Bahaya were very active in it, and in 1953 grave incidents took place near Bukoba. The TAA president, the teacher Julius Nyerere, a son of a minor chief southeast of Lake Victoria, left Makerere; he went to Bukoba to advocate nonviolence, a method later adopted by the nationalist party the Tanganyika African National Union founded the following year.

Neo-Feudalism and Christian Paternalism in Ruanda-Urundi

At first the Belgian occupiers were tempted by the idea of toppling the two-kingdom political system — notably in Rwanda, where relations with Musinga were dreadful — even though Ruanda-Urundi was divided into two zones, as if for a future partition. But in 1920, Minister Franck opted to maintain indirect rule in these countries, where political organization was "strongly constructed."[126]

Pierre Ryckmans, Urundi's resident from 1920 to 1925, the future Congo governor from 1939 to 1946, and a Catholic convinced of the colonizer's educative mission, defended the system in particularly clear terms:

> The agreement between the native king and the European authorities will lead...to this final result whereby the country will be left only with chiefs willing, or resigned, to march toward progress — and thus acceptable to the occupying power — all while maintaining legitimacy and thus being acceptable to the natives. [The native kings] are the familiar decor that permits us to act behind the scenes without alarming the people.[127]

A minor until 1932, King Mwambutsa allowed this trusteeship to be carried out.[128] A regency council composed of several major chiefs was transformed into a council of the *mwami* and consulted for problems with customary rights. The young sovereign, whose education was handled by a Belgian administrator, was the subject of much disillusionment. Seemingly superficial and pleasure-seeking, a catechumen for several years without ever having been baptized — even able to marry a Christian princess — and always venerated by the population, Mwambutsa remained enigmatic until he left the country in 1965.

In Burundi (as in Rwanda), Vice Governor Charles Voisin (1930–1932) began a vast operation to reorganize the chiefdoms and subchiefdoms as a way of countering administrative dispersion and getting rid of rulers judged incapable. The vast royal estates that covered the center of the country, once run by the *mwami*'s followers of humble origin, were parceled into chiefdoms and conferred on princes. In 1923, Kilima's ancient autonomous territory in the northwest was conferred on young Baranyanka, who, thanks to his education and savoir-faire, had gained Ryckmans's confidence.[129] At the chiefdom level, the big winners were the princes, the Baganwa, notably the Bezi close to the former regent, Ntarugera, and also the Batare, in particular Baranyanka's relatives, who in the 1950s controlled territories in the northeast and the south. In Kirundi, the term *muganwa* ultimately meant "chief," the old term *mutware* being reserved for "subchief" (the word *icariho* fell into disuse). Other beneficiaries at this level, and especially at the subchiefdom level, were the Batutsi elite. The Bahutu, who occupied about a quarter of the subchief posts at the beginning of the century, watched their numbers decrease. In 1929, they still represented 20 percent of the chiefdoms, but they represented only 7 percent in 1933 and none in 1945. During these same years, the Tutsi's share rose from 23 percent to 29 percent and the Baganwa's from 57 percent to 71 percent.[130]

Moreover, the function of the so-called customary authorities completely changed. Personal ties, often complex in the past, gave way to a purely territorial dependence. Intrigues and gifts had to give precedence, according to colonial language, to responsible activity:

> To attend to crop extension, to reforestation . . . to drying of marshes, to road maintenance, to carrying out health measures, to census taking, to tax collection, and to administration of native courts.[131]

Their remuneration was proportional to their efficiency in collecting poll taxes, which were made widespread in 1931. At the hill level, aides to the subchiefs, primarily charged with applying all this, were "town criers" (*bahamagazi*) and "guides" (*barongozi*), nicknamed "barkers," whose influence made the traditional authority of the *bashingantahe* recede.[132] The Inamujandi revolt in September 1934 between Ndora and Musigati, in the northwest mountains, was testament to the popular discontent with this bureaucratization of power and its growing coercion. Supported by the region's traditional elites, the revolt was led against the Ganwa and Tutsi subchiefs, who had been appointed by Baranyanka and, since they were originally from Gitega, were perceived as foreigners from the "upside-down governor." The system as a whole was in the hands of a smaller but omnipresent staff; it was tightly controlled by the administrators of each of the country's nine territories, who were backed up by "territorial agents." This type of management was not very different from that in the provinces of the Belgian Congo.[133]

Moreover, the ideological foundations of kingship crumbled under pressure from the Catholic missions. By 1916, hardly 7,000 had been baptized. In 1935, the number of baptized totaled 176,000, and sixteen missions had been founded since 1922 under the leadership of Julien Gorju, a Breton White Father who had come from Uganda. By 1940, 365,000 had been baptized; by 1955, more than 1 million; and by 1970, almost 2 million (equaling two-thirds of the population).[134] Even if, in this case, "Clovis [that is, Mwambutsa] had not preceded the Franks," to quote a missionary's 1930 expression, two-thirds of chiefs and half the subchiefs had been baptized by 1933, which religious journals like *Grands Lacs* called the "Holy Spirit's tornado."[135] The missions, which at first were perceived as worrisome places — dens for the marginal where youth risked being lost — became poles of "civilization" in a rural setting, like medieval abbeys. Their big brick buildings stood on high hills, ones intentionally chosen for their dominance over the landscape.[136] These high places, where thousands of devotees flocked every Sunday, replaced the sacred woods and competed with the ancient royal courts. It was now the pagans' turn to be denied access to pitchers of beer drunk collectively by straw.[137]

In a stroke of genius in 1927, Father Pio Canonica, an Italian, earned the trust of one of the young king's tutors, his uncle Nduwumwe, who had been appointed organizer of the annual *muganuro* festival, which was to take place not far from the Bukeye mission, which had recently and deliberately been founded near a royal capital.[138] In 1928, he won permission to purify the ritual of its "immoral" elements; in 1929, the ceremonies were rushed through; and in 1930, they were withdrawn. All this was replaced by a seed blessing at Christmas: public prayers substituted for the national festival! Ritualists were baptized or expelled and dispossessed of their estates, and the cult objects were seized or hidden. In 1936, a White Father in Bukeye could write:

> The mission was built in the shadow of the sacred woods [consecrated] to the spirits of the deceased king [Mutaga, who had died there in 1915], and it is from there that the Christ-King shines forth over the region today.[139]

Parallel changes occurred in Rwanda, with variations stemming from the particularities of that country and of its European leaders, notably the religious ones. From 1925 to 1926, Resident Georges Mortehan decided to homogenize the "customary" administrative system by removing the three-chief system. From then on, there would be only two levels, that of chief (*shefu* in Kinyarwanda) and that of subchief (*sushefu*). The royal estates and the ritual *bami* enclaves disappeared, as did the lineage powers in the north. As in Burundi, reform, accelerated under Governor Voisin, drastically reduced the Bahutu presence in the ruling group, to the benefit of what, in the 1950s, was called the "Tutsi monopoly," in particular those of the major families from the Bega and Banyiginya clans.[140] In 1959, out of 45 chiefs and 559 subchiefs, 43 and 549, respectively, were Batutsi.

In addition, these authorities' functions were bureaucratized, and the subchiefs and "barkers" on the hills took on a decisive role, all to the detriment of the *mwami*'s real power. Catharine Newbury observed this change in Kinyaga:

> Enclaves, formerly used by the king to ensure that men loyal to him kept an eye on political activities in the frontier region, existed no longer.... The result was a diminution of central control in the region and an augmentation of power for the provincial chiefs.[141]

On the other hand, the suppression of the army chiefs and, starting in 1930, the progressive reduction of the *bikingi* (which often were transformed into subchiefdoms) and the limiting of the *buletwa* corvée, which had spread to the entire country in 1924, to one day per week led the Tutsi aristocracy to exploit the institution of the pastoral clientage relationship, or *buhake*, as much as they could. This institution tended to spread, as an indispensable means of social protection, and to harden: after 1925, notes Jean-Népomucène Nkurikiyimfura, many (Batutsi and Bahutu) possessors of cattle "ceded their heads of cattle to their neighbors who helped them grow necessary food and cash crops, to afforest, etc."[142] All this was done in the name of "restoring" customary law, whose jurisprudence was ensured by "native courts." Hence, the statutes decreed by the *mwami*'s council in 1941 legitimized the so-called *bugaragu* contract, with the approval of the residency, which claimed:

271

Ubugaragu ... is the main cement of native society. ... It would be the worst of errors to, in the name of hypothetical social justice, weaken this foundation, which has already proved itself and which is perfectly adapted to the mentality of the country.[143]

In substituting for *muheto* (enlistment in an army), *buhake* carried obligations so similar to those of the *buletwa* corvées that it was difficult to tell them apart. In being diffused in this colonial context, the clientage relationship became less elitist and more coercive. One must recognize, wrote Monsignor Classe in 1930, that "the people's burdens, especially in certain provinces, are heavier than in the past."[144] But the ruling circle encountered no opposition from the Europeans, who had a priori seen this contract as a "pastoral serfdom" that for centuries had been part of a "feudalism of Tutsi conquerors"; they had been persuaded to respect its authenticity. This is a new example of what must be called the feudalization of society. In Rwanda, as in Burundi, these reforms and this general hardening of social relations aroused prophetic-style revolts between 1927 and 1930 against Tutsi chiefs deemed responsible for these new constraints, notably in the north and east.[145]

The role of the Catholic Church was key. The number of baptized reached 100,000 in 1933, 300,000 in 1940, 500,000 in 1955, and 700,000 in 1960. The Holy Spirit's tornado had also blown here. Conversions of Tutsi chiefs began in 1917 and accelerated in 1928; at the end of 1934, 90 percent were Catholic, while only 10 percent of the population was Catholic.[146] The administration in Catholic Belgium, as in the Congo, evidently played a role:

This mutual sympathy [between administrators and missionaries] did not escape the natives, who were fine observers. They told themselves that even if there was nothing to humanly gain by becoming Christians, there was nothing to lose either.[147]

As in Burundi and a half century earlier in Buganda, the movement in Rwanda came from the upper echelons of society. A convert of this period told Claudine Vidal:

> You went to see your patron, who told you that at such and such
> a place there was a catechist: "If you do not start learning catechism,
> I will take everything from you, destroy your house, and chase you
> from the hill!" You should know that coercion existed back then.
> So as for me, Mashiro, I told myself: "Am I going to be chased out
> because of my ancestors!" I said to my wife: "Either I learn, or the
> chief will chase me away!"[148]

The missionary Catholic Church of Rwanda took a particularly militant turn under the leadership of the vicar apostolic Léon Classe,
whose role during the German period we have seen.[149] Consulted
by the Belgian authorities when they arrived in the country and
regularly thereafter by Resident Mortehan, Classe, who operated
from Kabgayi until his death in 1945, made no secret of his views:
a medieval-style Rwanda should be constructed, with its Tutsi
aristocracy made to rule, its Hutu peasantry made to work, and its
Church made to shed light over the lot, all while working hand in
hand with civilian authorities. Rwanda would be a "Christian kingdom," of the kind Monsignor Lavigerie had once dreamed and the
Jesuits in the early seventeenth century had once imagined. This
fundamentalist atmosphere echoed that of some South American
dictatorships in the nineteenth century, as when Ecuador's ultra-
Catholic president Gabriel García Moreno dedicated the country
to the Sacred Heart. One need only read Monsignor Classe's episcopal instructions or his official texts to see this clearly:

> The question is whether the ruling elite will be for us or against us;
> whether the important places in native society will be in Catholic or

273

in non-Catholic hands; whether the Church will have through education and its formation of youth the preponderant influence in Rwanda.[150]

Administratively attaching Ruanda-Urundi to the Belgian Congo in 1925 allowed a system of educational covenants, set forth in 1906, to spread. Under the impetus of Edmond de Jonghe, director of education in the Ministry of Colonies and a fervent Catholic, Protestants were systematically marginalized. The elite chosen to carry out the clerical project were the Tutsi youth, who were defined in quasi-racial terms:

> We have in the Tutsi youth an incomparable element for progress.... Avid to learn, desirous of becoming acquainted with all that comes from Europe, wanting to imitate Europeans, enterprising, realising well enough that traditional customs have lost their raison d'être, but nonetheless preserving the political sense of the old-timers and their race's adroitness in the management of men, this youth is a force for the good and for the economic future of the country. If one asks Bahutu if they prefer to be ruled by commoners or by nobles, there is no doubt in their response; their preference goes to the Batutsi, and for good reason. Born chiefs, these latter have a sense of command.[151]

A serious obstacle to establishing a Christian kingdom remained: King Musinga, who always tried to skirt the whites' demands. In 1925, his close relations, symbols of the spirit of resistance, were dismissed, notably Bandora, the diviner, and *mwiru* Gashamura, head of the annual *muganura* ritual who was removed along with his Burundian counterpart. The White Fathers relentlessly accused Musinga of being nostalgic for paganism (or at best for German Protestantism). Monsignor Classe delivered the death-blow with an article published in Belgium in 1930 titled "Un

Triste Sire" (A pathetic specimen).[152] Scarcely a year later, Vice
Governor Voisin and the bishop had the *mwami* deposed for his
"opposition to progress." Relegated to Kamembe, in Congo, Musinga was replaced by his son Rudahihgwa, who was baptized in
1943 with three first names: Charles (like Lavigerie, Voisin, and
the Belgian royal prince), Léon (like Classe), and Pierre (like
Governor-General Ryckmans).

Thirty years later, an old Christian man commented: "The
pope, king of the Christians, and our own king, king of the converts and others, reached an agreement. The *imandwa* [spirits of
kubandwa] no longer stood a chance." In 1946, Rwanda was dedicated to the Christ-King; it had found its Constantine.[153] As for
the elites, at the start of their education they had to resign themselves to being docile and being grateful to the colonial state and
the Church that paternally took care of them. As Governor Eugène
Jungers reminded students of Astrida's Groupe Scolaire in 1940:

> Stay modest. The exit diploma you will receive is not proof of com-
> petence. It only constitutes proof that you are capable of becoming
> competent auxiliaries.[154]

A Moral Economy? Coffee and Migrant Labor

The opening to trade, barely begun under the Germans, got going
little by little in the 1920s. Routes for the first carriage roads (in
1923 between Usumbura and Kitega and in 1932 between Usumbura and Astrida, in southern Rwanda), which inaugurated one of
the densest road networks in Africa (more than 6,000 kilometers
in 1938), were built by thousands performing corvées; 10- and
20-centime Congolese coins (*makuta* and *masenge*, respectively)
were introduced; and in every chiefdom, commercial centers with
permanent shops were created.[155] But for a long time (practically
until the 1980s) money remained marginal to family economies,

and the installation of large, modern machinery at the Port of Usumbura, capital of Ruanda-Urundi, was not undertaken until the Ten Year Plan of 1951.[156]

But the first and lasting obsession of the mandate administration was to ensure stability in food production, which was upset during periodical regional famines. The famine called *Gakwege* (Wire, an evocative image) in 1928–1929 had a negative effect internationally; the Germans in particular denounced the consequences of chronic bad management by Leopold II's heirs. In response, the Belgians introduced in 1926 and in 1931 obligatory food farming: each family had to maintain 1,500 square meters, of which 500 were to be given over to cassava.[157] In 1927, drainage and farming of swamps, until then filled with reeds and papyrus and reserved as dry-season pastures, also became obligatory. New plants, like the potato, and new varieties, notably of maize, were distributed by the agronomic centers tied to the National Institute for Agronomic Studies of Congo.

The territory also had to be made financially profitable, given the failure of several plantation attempts following the crisis in the 1930s. Cotton, introduced in this period on the Imbo plains in Burundi, became important only in the 1950s, paralleling the planned resettlement of this region, which had been devastated by sleeping sickness earlier in the century.[158]

In the 1930s, the main economic program consisted in extending the German project of growing coffee, with arabica having already been tried in Gitega, through a system of obligatory peasant plantations. The administration had to fend off criticisms from two sources: on the one hand, from the League of Nations and the International Bureau of Labor, both of which were hostile to all forms of forced labor, and, on the other hand, from Kivu settlers, who resented competition from African cultivators' "cheap" labor. In emphasizing both the need for cost-price calculation and the peasants' interests, for whom the new system was said to be a stable source of income, the crisis took precedence over these objections. Paternalism also played its part: the new farming system was demanding and thus would serve as a source of education. The rural version of indirect rule could be the education of modern smallholders. A balance between morality and financial stability had been found.

The key actors in this important innovation were Vice Governors Voisin and Jungers (between 1930 and 1947), as well as Edmond Leplae, the all-powerful director of agriculture in the Ministry of Colonies (from 1910 to 1933) and an admirer of the Dutch system of obligatory farming in Java.[159] Coffee plants were distributed in five campaigns between 1931 and 1938, during which one to four million small shrubs were planted each year. By 1937, more than 50 percent of the taxpayers had become involved (100 percent in Ngozi, the northern Burundian territory most propitious for this crop). Parcels of sixty coffee trees encroached on banana gardens in lands well fertilized with manure and on grassland areas, including the Rwandan *bikingi*.[160] Maintaining tree nurseries, transporting young plants in baskets, planting in properly spaced rows, mulching with banana leaves, and combating parasites all amounted to significant new obligations and became the basis of additional workweeks, especially for men (women were occupied with foodstuffs). Surveillance of these tasks was carried out by all that Ruanda-Urundi could count as management: Belgian administrators; chiefs and subchiefs; auxiliaries to these latter; "coffee monitors," who acted as agronomic police officers; and missionaries, who were invited, as Monsignor Gorju wrote, to "preach coffee."[161] Besides having economic benefits, this was supposed to steer the natives away their laziness and from the bad habits they had acquired in Protestant Uganda when they immigrated there:

You must preach coffee everywhere, even and especially in the pul-
pit.... Far less useful things are certainly said there. Make these poor
people understand their interest; tell them that Baranyanka sold his coffee on the spot for 6.50 francs per kg; make them understand their own
interest; tell them that in two or three years, if they do well, life conditions here will be such that only lunatics will still leave for Uganda.[162]

After an interruption between 1938 and 1946, planting resumed:
each farmer was supposed to have about one hundred shrubs.
Beginning with 11 tons in 1930, Ruanda-Urundi's total production reached 10,000 tons of parchment coffee in 1942 and 50,000
tons in 1959. The Office of Industrial Crops of Ruanda-Urundi
was set up in 1946 to grade the quality of exports, which increasingly were sent to America.

Profits from coffee varied over time according to production
and world prices; they declined regularly between 1934 and 1945
but rose again through 1958. Profits also varied considerably between regions (those in the east being the most disadvantaged). A
large part of the profits did not go to the peasants: the state was
the major beneficiary, if only because at least half the peasant revenues went toward the poll tax. Asian, Greek, and local merchants
controlled harvest sales, which entailed the cheating and one-
sided contracts one would expect in a society ill used to money
dealings. Some chiefs became rich as well; Pierre Baranyanka, for
example, was considered a coffee king on a par with the Europeans.[163] But the situation the Belgians created was appreciably
different from what happened with coffee in Buhaya, cotton in
Buganda, and cocoa in the British Gold Coast. In the Belgian territories, the engine driving the cash-crop boom was not profit but a
combination of coercion, tax, intimidation, and corporal punishment, given that the *chicotte* (whip) was applied until at least the
1940s. Leplae put it this way in 1931:

278

> Must one have confidence in the natives? Our fine words and good
> intentions would not be enough to replace our physical presence. Our
> gamble is to make coffee a popular crop.... The supervision we are
> advocating will only bear fruit once we learn how to make the native
> understand that where will is absent, legal obligation will suffice.[164]

Over the years, annual returns of money from coffee, which constituted a fourth harvest (complementing the two growing seasons and the harvest of the drained marshes), could go toward
buying cotton products or building a permanent house covered
in corrugated iron. But this turning point only really came in
the 1950s. At first the young found themselves another way to
gain precious liquidity: repeated seasonal migration, sometimes
long-lasting, to the richer neighboring colonies, notably Uganda,
where, it was said, one went to "buy shillings."[165] This phenomenon took place over forty years: it started in the 1920s along the
familiar hawking routes in the east; it became more pronounced
after the 1928–1929 famine; the apogee was between 1933 and
1950, with about 100,000 migrants per year entering Uganda;
and it eventually stabilized in the 1950s — though the new border
constraints that followed independence quickly interrupted the
process. Many became established in their country of exile. In
1959, they totaled about 500,000 in Uganda (of whom 70 percent
were Rwandans), especially in Buganda, where they represented
more than a quarter of the population in the southern half of the
country.[166] They totaled 160,000 in Tanganyika, notably on the
coastal sisal plantations; the country was nicknamed *Manamba*
(the "number country," because they were numbered there).
Within the framework of the Banyarwanda Immigration Mission
organized in 1937, tens of thousands were in Congo, either in the
Katanga mines or on the plantations in northern Kivu.

For the most part, then, this was inter-rural migration: the

spontaneous departure of peasants for the homes of other peasants, planters of Baganda cotton, for whom they were agricultural
workers. At first this departure was conceived of as short-lived; in
Kirundi, it was called *kurobera*, "to disappear for a moment." But
after several trips (up to ten), many chose exile and brought along
a spouse from their country.[167] They initially formed a genuine
rural proletariat, but some became farmers who held a parcel
like the Baganda *bakopi*. Those who returned to Ruanda-Urundi
brought back new banana varieties, crates of clothes (cotton loincloths, pants, and shirts), and, in the 1950s, radio sets. They
"came back chic," as that era's songs put it, "like small chiefs," and
one imagined a world much brighter than the miserable order
that reigned on the hills of Rwanda and Burundi. One pictured
countrysides filled with permanent homes, busy streets, well-
dressed people, air of a different kind of freedom — in short,
everything modernity signified. One also envisioned a different
kind of individualism, which is exactly what the missionaries
feared when, in the 1930s and 1940s, they deplored the fact that
at least half the young people in their parishes had left for English
territory.

The motivation to leave was clear. These young people were
fleeing the system's coercion, notably the corvées, which in 1930
totaled two months a year per able-bodied male, and the whip,
which awaited the recalcitrant and the tardy. From this point
of view, Ruanda-Urundi — where "customary" prestations were
introduced only between 1935 and 1938 for taxes and in 1949 for
public works and where the whites' corvée, called "general interest," lasted until the 1950s and whip punishment until 1951 — was
ten to thirty years behind the British protectorate.[168] But these
young people were even more motivated by the quest for money,
which would pay a tax on their family, pay a dowry, or buy modern goods. Significantly, the most affected regions were in the

east, where the possibilities for earning money were the fewest; the movement slowed down in the 1950s, when other resources developed (notably coffee); and the administration's auxiliaries, the chiefs, and the missions were not affected. In addition, contrary to what the Belgian authorities explained to the anthropologist Audrey Richards in 1956, Bahutu and Batutsi of modest means participated in the movement in equal proportions.[169]

With this wave of economic migrations, the ancient westward movement that slowly whittled away land — a movement somewhat brought to a standstill by colonial borders — had now been reversed in the eastward quest for money. For its part, contemporary politics would stifle this social movement and produce a novel form of mobility, that of refugees from "ethnic" conflicts.

The Racial Registering of Society: The Hutu-Tutsi Antagonism

We have seen how the cultural cleavage between agriculturists and cattle keepers in the Great Lakes was a function of the region's ancient human settlement and complex economic and social structuring. We also have seen the importance of the monarchies' political evolution, notably in the west and especially since the eighteenth century. In addition, we have seen how aristocracies crystallized — in particular in Rwanda and Nkore, with their respective Tutsi and Hima groups — which in turn led to the introduction of a superior pastoral identity that cut across ancient clan cleavages, which previously were more salient. For the last century — that is, since the first contact with Europeans and their growing hold over the region's societies, the Tutsi-Hutu antagonism, in Rwanda and Burundi, gained practical priority and intellectual primacy. From this perspective, to ask what happened during colonization is not to deny how old this cleavage is. Rather, we must try to understand why this cleavage has become so obsessive to the point of eclipsing every other problem and being almost the only aspect of this region familiar to the Western media in the late twentieth century.[170]

Racial labeling, distinguishing "Hamito-Semites" or "Nilo-Hamites" and "Bantu Negroes," is present from the beginning of the conquest.[171] It even preexisted conquest, given the construction of a reverse "Hamitic" model by French and German philologists and ethnologists since the middle of the century: under this model, blacks, universally victims of "the curse of Ham," were distinct from a group of Africans who were classified as a superior race and said to have arrived on a civilizing invasion from Asia.[172] The Africanist study of races, exemplified in C.G. Seligman's *Races of Africa*, was strongly influenced by a cliché that opposed two half-biological, half-aesthetic types: the Batutsi, who were described as tall and fine, versus the Bahutu, who were small, had squat noses and thick lips, and were considered to typify the "Negro as such."[173] We have seen the official anthropometric refinements in the 1950s. Colonial circles, whose prejudices were reflected in the pages of missionary writings, relentlessly presented the Batutsi as "black Europeans" "having something of the Aryan type and something of the Semitic type."[174] But the colonized also, at least the first educated generation, were convinced by what I have called "scientific ethnicism." Did not the Astrida graduates' newspaper publish in 1948, in the aftermath of World War II, these extraordinary words of a teacher from the Groupe Scolaire?

> Of the Caucasian race, as well as the Semitic and the Indo-European, the Hamitic people at base have nothing in common with Negroes.... Especially in Ruanda-Urundi, the Eastern Hamites showed what they were made of. Physically, these races are superb: despite the inevitable race mixings that are a result of prolonged contact with Negroes, the preponderance of the Caucasian type has remained

deeply marked among the Batutsi.... Their elevated height — rarely less than 1.8 meters — ... the fineness of their traits, and their intelligent expression all contribute to their being worthy of the title that the explorers gave them: aristocratic Negroes.[175]

One dares not think about the impression that this Gobineauian discourse made on the establishment's Hutu graduates! The racial scheme was complemented with psychological traits, forming what one might call "missionary characterology": the "Jews of Africa" versus the "Negro braves with a heavy soul"; an "infiltration of whites," characterized as "daring," into the environment of the "apathetic Bantu"; an irruption of "bronzed herdsmen of the Caucasian type" confronted by the Muhutu, that is, by "the most common type of black, brachycephalic and prognathous, with agronomic taste and aptitudes, sociable and jovial, [using] agglutinative language"; a conquest of "fierce herdsmen" over the blacks "with thick lips and squashed noses, but so good, so simple, so loyal." In short, Oriental masters versus Aunt Jemima Negroes.[176]

We have seen the issues at stake in the historical reconstructions that, since Speke, turned the region into a second Ethiopia by transforming mythical heroes (Bacwezi in Uganda, Gihanga and Kigwa in Rwanda, Ntare in Burundi, and so on) into standard-bearers of a great "Hamitic" invasion, described as if one had the archives of these conquerors' military headquarters, to cite the humorous image of an English critic of the Aryan myth.[177] Indeed, starting with the hypothesis of a Galla conquest, endlessly repeated, all of Ethiopia and pharaonic Egypt were summoned for this ascent to the sources of the Nile: for Father Albert Pagès, the Hamites were Monophysite Christians who had forgotten their religion during their exodus; for Governor Ryckmans, the Batutsi recalled Ramses II and Sesostris.[178] The human landscape did tend to resemble Abyssinia, what with its enclosures, its systematic distribution of white-cotton clothes, and the pharaonic-style built-up hairdos, à la Queen Nefertiti, of the aristocratic women. The role of the good Fathers and Sisters in this country's neo-traditional clothing civilization would require a study unto itself.

This primordial conquest was supposed to have established a "feudal" system in which the Batutsi were the lords and the Bahutu the serfs. We have seen the problems with projecting a European medieval model. A central figure in this parallel was the "pastoral service" contract (*buhake* or *bugabire*), the cornerstone of the "premise of inequality," as the anthropologist Jacques Maquet authoritatively called it in 1954. In fact, the comparison referred more to personal ties than to a lordly regime, had more of a political than a social impact, and, in the last instance, was hung on the hypothesis of Tutsi conquest — the key to the whole explanation based on an analogy with Norman England, as witnessed by Walter Scott. Commissioner Harry Johnston later promoted this parallel in Uganda. In Rwanda and Burundi, as we have noted, the Franks (with the baptism of Clovis) flowed more quickly to the missionaries' pens: this is reminiscent of a well-known scheme in nineteenth-century French historiography (that done by Augustin Thierry and others), according to which the ancestral and quasi-racial conflict between the Franks and the Gauls accounted for all social history in France until 1789. In reality, the feudal system projected onto this African context referred to a definition first offered in the eighteenth century by Henri de Boulainvilliers: "A political system in which the monarchy was controlled by the nobility, the descendants of Frankish conquerors."[179]

But the policy of indirect rule consisted, as we have observed, in "restoring" a pyramid of powers in which local leaders (supervised by the administration) were given the main responsibilities, to the detriment of the *mwami*'s ancient authority. The members of this aristocracy-under-surveillance were selected according to their great natural ability, with an eye toward purifying elements of the "inferior" race. Pierre Ryckmans in Burundi was no different from Léon Classe in Rwanda on these matters:

> The Batutsi were destined to rule, their mere demeanor lends them considerable prestige over the inferior races that surround them.... There is nothing surprising about the fact that the less shrewd, simpler, more spontaneous, and more confiding Bahutu braves let themselves be enslaved.[180]

In fact, an equation was established between Tutsi and "chief" (in its general meaning) to the point where ordinary Batutsi who lived on the hills (who constituted at least 90 percent of all Batutsi) were invisible. In 1916, Father Classe explained to the new Belgian authorities that the Batutsi of Rwanda hardly totaled more than twenty thousand, and until the 1950s observers remained persuaded that Tutsi constituted only 5 percent of the population. Not until the 1956 demographic survey, as we have seen, was it discovered that they were 13 to 18 percent of the population (depending on the region) and that they could not all be reduced to a privileged "leisure class."[181] But the amalgam had been made: colonial-style feudalization was thus accompanied by a racialization of society. The princely Baganwa group in Burundi was assimilated to the Batutsi, and the word *muganwa* came to mean "chief." But in the two countries, noble qualities were attributed to an entire "race" — what was later called, after independence, the Tutsi ethnic group.

Schools were the main vector in the reformulation of the Hutu-Tutsi cleavage. Right up to independence, instruction remained practically confined to primary school. The reluctance of the Belgian regime to educate elites "prematurely" was well known. The only secondary establishments (before some creations

in the late 1950s) were Nyakibanda seminary in Rwanda, Mugera
seminary in Burundi, and the Groupe Scolaire, founded in Astrida
in 1932 to train auxiliary officers (including medical, veterinary,
agronomic, and administrative assistants) for the mandated territory and run by the Brothers of the Charity of Ghent. Recruitment statistics at this institution speak volumes: Rwandan Tutsi
were three to four times more numerous than Hutu until 1958;
for Burundian students, the same statistics apply beginning in
1948. Rwanda had paved the way for discrimination, since, starting in 1928, primary schools were segregated: "The Batutsi
school must rank above the Bahutu one," with different programs
and separate campuses, insisted Monsignor Classe in 1924–1925.[182]

On the eve of independence, the "social" question in Rwanda and
Burundi was less an agrarian one and more one of elites. Though
not the first to do so, Claudine Vidal called these elites, in a
somewhat caricaturing way, "the fourth ethnic group."[183] Since
the 1950s, members of this group had been the most demanding
because they had experienced the most frustration. In a general
sense, the group consisted of an educated micro bourgeoisie, of
youth won over by individualism and the spirit of initiative, and of
rural folk attracted by nonagricultural occupations. This diverse
world was stifled under Belgium's bureaucratic-clerical style of
trusteeship mixed with neo-feudalism. The civilian and religious
authorities preferred the ideal peasant — submissive, attached to
his piece of land, and present during corvées and at Mass — and,
above all, the aristocrat of noble birth — authoritarian when it
came to his own people and attentive to the whites' injunctions —
to the catechists, instructors, builders, traders, artisans, and migrants with their new experiences.[184] Modernization aimed at the
economy but not at society. In 1920, Minister Franck recalled this
golden rule of colonialism:

The Negroes need to be introduced to economic development alone.... There should be no question of affecting the very foundation of the political institutions on the pretext of inequality.[185]

As we have seen, the educated elites were taught to be modest and restrained. To monitor its elite flocks, the Church developed circles of *évolués*, Catholic action groups, and newspapers.[186]

As was the case throughout Africa, this social "order" was fundamentally conceived as "tribal": the African's normal status was that of the "native" governed by an "ethnographer state," attentive to customs and to "traditional" divisions. Governor Cameron was the same way in Tanganyika. Was this order all that far from totalitarianism? Was not Hannah Arendt right to think that European fascisms got their start during the colonial experience? In any case, authorities like Monsignor Classe also obsessed over fighting the Communist threat in Africa, a "peril" evoked even more in the 1950s.[187]

Intrinsically tied to a racist vision of society, this "moral" framework presented a challenge for the new generation, born under colonialism and educated in its schools. This generation might have united against this stifling social-racial order. Some episodes provided a glimpse of this possibility — for example, the rebellious movement that developed in the Nyakibanda seminary in 1951–1952 in which students "closed ranks as Banyarwanda against the mission."[188] But in Rwanda, the "ethnic" cleavage proved too strong. It was stoked by the claims of Tutsi intellectuals, themselves spurred by apparent proximity to power, and by the frustrations of Hutu intellectuals, themselves encouraged by their European mentors. The turning point in the 1950s was decisive: Were not the lesser elite ready to respond to modernization's true challenge? Was it possible not to believe in the ethnic idolatry that had been omnipresent for thirty years in Ruanda-

Urundi? The fact is that these countries found themselves trapped in alleged tradition, remodeled according to what colonial science declared to be immemorial.

Under the Germans, the social-racial order was woven into the decor, but under the Belgians it was in the foreground. Comparison with neighbors in the British sphere makes one pause: in these zones, the "Hamitic" obsession was marginalized. This can undoubtedly be explained by greater openness, in the form of multiple contracts, diverse religious faiths, more intense trade, respect for Swahili culture, and a more structured heritage from the German period; all this produced a confrontation between two educated generations. There, youth were more open to the wider world, and for intellectuals in particular Makerere College in the 1950s became a gateway to the University of London; by contrast, the Astrida boarding school seemed light-years away.

The Kivu Societies and the Congolese Model

This survey of changes induced by the colonial regime will end with Kivu — that is, the mosaic of principalities that existed in the late nineteenth century west of the lake of the same name. At the beginning of the century, the eleven small kingdoms of the Bafuliro, the Bashi, and the Bahavu found themselves in Leopold's Congo, which became Belgian in 1908: first in his Eastern Province, then in Costermansville Province and Kivu Province, which was created in 1933.[189] This area was thus cut off from its commercial and cultural partners to the east and was the outermost part of a new political domain that reached as far as the Atlantic, which, for this region, meant being attached to its bordering great forest.

Before World War I, the Belgian experience amounted to military rule over local powers and troop deployments on the German border.[190] The majority of sovereigns were supposed to have submitted between 1910 and 1916. But resistance manifested itself around the forest, in Burhinyi, Luhwinja, and, in the south, Kaziba until 1934. After 1920, Minister Franck inaugurated a strategy of regrouping them into "sectors" combining several "chiefdoms." Attempts at Bushi "reunification" were made, first between 1927 and 1930 to the benefit of Rugemaninzi, Kabare's *mwami*, and then between 1937 and 1944 to the benefit of Ngwe-she. In the same way, in 1921 Ijwi was subjected to the mainland Havu sovereign in Kalehe, but this island required military occu-pation, which lasted until 1929; instability persisted there until the 1940s.

Finally, the administration decided to run each ancient prin-cipality autonomously. Far from facilitating the establishment of foreign control, this political parcelization, combined with the in-fluence of local religious authorities (the *bajinji*) and with natural conditions (the regions were cut through by steep hills), favored resistance. At any rate, foreign influences on this region's people since the 1880s have been catastrophic: Zanzibari traders, police mutinies and warring Europeans, with the usual retinue of pillag-ing and violence, and the Belgian colonial regime, points to which we will return. The White Fathers established missions in the region in the early part of the century, as did Protestants from the Norwegian Free Mission.[191]

Beginning in 1928, white settlers arrived in the region to occupy lands under the auspices of the Kivu National Commit-tee.[192] This was the only case of creating Kenyan-style "White Highlands" in the Great Lakes region. In the 1950s, Kivu was de-scribed as a paradise for Europeans; some even saw it as a refuge from a Cold War that threatened to become hot. In the 1930s, Rwandan immigrants had been living by the thousands in areas northwest of the lake.[193] Wedged between corvées, obligatory crops, the whip, a cash tax established in 1914, attempts at being regrouped into villages in the 1940s, massive land despoilment, and forced employment on coffee or quinine plantations, the populations and their authorities were tempted to withdraw. The biography of Mwami Rugemaninzi is significant: a catechumen, highly regarded by the missionaries, quite Westernized in his manners and in his accession in 1926, he rebelled against the settlers, who had maltreated his subjects between 1932 and 1933; he was deposed in 1936, then worked as a chauffeur in Kinshasa; he returned to his home in 1959. Modernity and resistance to colonization were not mutually exclusive, which undoubtedly explains the hostility of the ideologues of colonization toward the "uprooted."[194] In the same way, Mwami Mafundwe of Ngweshe (1922–1937) was described both as a friend of the Fathers (he sent his sons to their school) and as an instigator of a workers' strike on a plantation; similarly, the Havu authorities were seen as wavering between resistance and inertia in the context of indirect rule. From its wars against the Rwandan monarchy to its opposition to the Mobutu regime a century later, the Kivu region was reluctant to accept any foreign domination.

CHAPTER FIVE

Regained Independence and the

Obsession with Genocide

Except for in Tanzania, the accession, or rather return, to independence in these countries has initiated a period of unprecedented violence. These wrenching episodes are not over, and they raise the specter of state collapse. The colonial powers certainly negotiated borders before the Organization of African Unity ratified them. But — and this is a rarity on the continent — the borders pertain to ancient political zones that were real potential nations, comparable to European states in the early nineteenth century. It is also true that colonization established a managerial class, but it stifled dynamics and froze an entire history into an applied ethnography strongly influenced by racial prejudice. The elites of the second half of the twentieth century received a poisoned chalice when they took control of their countries' destinies.

Uganda: A Republic and Its Kingdoms
Just after World War II, a protest movement emerged in the kingdom of Buganda. This movement expressed social discontent with the Asian monopoly on cotton and coffee processing as well as political malaise with a half century of absolute power exercised by an oligarchy that had formed an alliance with the colonizer. Ignatius Musazi, the best-known leader of the violent events in

1945 and 1949, was the spokesman of both the always-active *bataka* party and the Uganda Farmers Union. After being repressed, these groups founded in 1952 the first party that had nationalist aspirations for the entire protectorate. Inspired by the Indian model, this party was called the Uganda National Congress.

The period seemed propitious for this awakening.[1] The philosophy of indirect rule, which had spawned both administrative structures and colonial anthropology, had been exhausted. The war and its consequences led the United Kingdom to envisage for Africa what a century earlier it had experienced with Canada, namely, gradual emancipation based on a self-government model. Its defeats to Japan in the Far East and American intervention sounded the death knell for British imperial power: in 1947, India obtained independence. Labour Party members first floated the idea of a colonial "New Deal"; the central proponents were Fabian Society sympathizers, one of whose leaders became the secretary of the Colonial Office. But the Conservatives' return to power in 1952 did not prevent events from accelerating: the Mau Mau movement in Kenya, the Suez crisis, Ghanaian independence, and, in 1960, Harold Macmillan's stand for the "winds of change." In this context, Uganda, with its economic dynamism, its modernization, and its elites, seemed well positioned to become one of the first black dominions.

But the process got out of hand because of the protectorate's heterogeneity, including its heterogeneous political structures, and, in particular, Buganda's special position. The rulers of Buganda, London's privileged partners, reckoned that they had the right either to their own, separate independence or to recognition that they controlled the entire Ugandan population. With only 16 percent of the total population, the kingdom accounted for 52 percent of Uganda's gross national product, 54 percent of those in secondary school, and the majority of students at Makerere. If a compromise was found, rendering independence possible, it was because "tribal" cleavages (if the Baganda can be qualified as a tribe) were crosscut by religious cleavages, notably the Catholic-Protestant conflict that divided Ganda society itself.

During a public crisis in 1953, the English made the Bugandan monarchy central to the political debate. A new governor, Andrew Cohen, attempted to democratize the representative institutions by introducing African delegates into the protectorate's Legislative Council (Legco), and by making provisions for elections to the Bugandan *lukiko*. At the same time, there was talk again in London of restructuring all of eastern Africa into one "closer union." Pressed by his traditionalist entourage, Kabaka Mutesa II demanded guarantees for his kingdom and that management of it be switched immediately to the Foreign Office from the Colonial Office. He refused to continue to collaborate with Governor Cohen's program, and he was immediately deported to England. Universally, public opinion, including that outside Buganda, rallied behind the deposed sovereign. Ignatius Musazi fled to Sudan, and his Uganda National Congress Party showed its solidarity with the *kabaka*. Finally, the colonial power had to cede: it signed a new Buganda Agreement, which integrated a few of the promised reforms. This agreement also made Mutesa's success concrete, and he returned triumphantly to Kampala in October 1955.

But the Bugandan ruling class did not know how to manage this political victory. The conservative Anglican establishment, attached more than ever to its privileges, missed a double opportunity: on the one hand, the country was on the verge of a nationalist struggle that could have united or quasi-united the Ugandan people; on the other hand, the kingdom's politics could have been democratically reconfigured in a way that integrated Catholics, who constituted a majority of the population. Instead, the *kabaka*'s entourage, not having learned from history, stoked local nationalist

293

passions by neutralizing all internal opposition. This sectarianism was manifest in the choice of a new *katikiro*: the extremist Protestant leader Michael Kintu was favored over Matayo Mugwanya, the grandson of the Catholic leader at the beginning of the century. Mugwanya was even blocked from his allotted seat in the expanded Legco. This kind of attitude led to a decisive split in the Ugandan political class. In 1956, with the support of the German Christian Democrats, a Ugandan Catholic party, the Democratic Party (DP), was created; Mugwanya was the first to lead it, followed by Benedicto Kiwanuka.[2] Subsequently, Buganda's hostility in principle to federal institutions and to national parties broke up the Congress. In 1958, Milton Obote, the Legco representative from Lango, a Nilotic region in the north, protested in these terms:

> If the [colonial] government tries to develop this country on a unitary basis, how can it, in God's name, develop at the same time another state within the state?[3]

In 1959, Obote formed the Uganda People's Congress (UPC), whose center of gravity was outside Buganda.

The change to "self-government" in 1961 and then to independence in 1962 was carried out in a climate of recantations, an often-ridiculous prelude to the dramas that followed. The government of Mengo (the site of the royal palace) not only refused to participate in the Constitutional Commission but also boycotted the 1961 general elections and sabotaged voter-registration lists. Only 3 to 4 percent of the electorate defied intimidation from the local royalist machine. Since those who did vote were DP partisans, this party won nineteen out of twenty-one seats, which gave it a total of forty-three in the new legislative entity versus thirty-five for the UPC, even though the UPC received the majority of votes in the country. The prime minister of autonomous Uganda was thus Benedicto Kiwanuka, a Catholic Muganda.

Stupefied by this result, even though it was a product of its own intrigues, the Mengo Protestant establishment did a U-turn and negotiated with the UPC to force the Catholics out of power. An alliance was formed, one founded on a surprising bargain: Buganda agreed to rejoin the federal process of moving to independence, but it kept the right to elect its own National Assembly delegates through an indirect vote.[4] In March 1962, the London Conference ratified a shaky constitution, whereby the Ugandan state would include five federated kingdoms and the sovereign of the only truly autonomous one among them, Buganda, would become the first federal president in 1963. At the same time, the DP was practically outlawed in Uganda, and an official party was created whose name summarized its agenda: Kabaka Yekka (KY), "The King Alone." In the general elections the following April, the KY won sixty-five seats out of sixty-eight in Buganda, and the UPC was the majority for Uganda as a whole. Independence was proclaimed on October 9, 1962, with Milton Obote as prime minister.

Throughout, politics centered on regional concerns and was affected by denominational rivalry. In Bunyoro, the UPC dominated because of anti-Ganda resentment stemming from the "lost counties" issue. Supported by the Mubende Bunyoro Committee, Mukama Tito Winyi had personally distributed petitions in the 1940s and 1950s. The British proposed that some of this territory — which was home to the kingdom's holy sites — be returned to Bunyoro, but the Baganda responded that only a deluge would force them out of their country.[5] Not until 1965, under Obote and after a referendum, was a solution favorable to Bunyoro found, despite Mutesa's refusal to sign.

In Ankole, another key case, the UPC had the support of

Protestants and the majority of Bairu. In reaction, the Bahima, even the Protestants among them, allied with the Catholic Bairu to produce a DP majority. Thus, a half century after colonial conquest, the Hima-Iru rivalry powerfully intervened in the political arena. Under colonial rule, a neo-feudal structure was set up around the Hima monarchy. This evoked the Rwandan case, but with a crucial difference: the counterbalance of religious competition, which allowed this country to avoid going down the same racist path as some of the former Belgian colonies. Nonetheless, the socio-ethnic cleavage existed in Ugandan politics until the 1990s.

Uganda thus attained independence in an atmosphere much more regionalist than nationalist and under a party's leadership that, given the rivalries amid the ancient southern kingdoms, allowed northern Nilotic-culture groups to take political and especially military control.[6] It would be the revenge of a different geo-cultural universe — one that stretched across all of southern Sudan — on the formerly dominating Bantu-speaking states. The UPC won an absolute majority in 1964, and Obote reinforced his control over the army, a formerly scorned body, of which a majority were northerners. In February 1966, the Constitution was suspended, and Obote was proclaimed president. The following May, the *kabaka*'s residence was attacked, and Mutesa was forced into exile in England, where he died in 1969; the royal palace was transformed into a barracks.[7] The other monarchies were also abolished. As for Buganda, it was under a state of emergency until January 1971, the date of a coup d'état organized by the chief of staff, Idi Amin.[8] In the beginning, the new dictator earned some support from the Baganda by bringing back the king's remains in April 1971.

At this point, Uganda entered a fifteen-year period of chaos and extreme violence: expulsion of Asians in August 1972, Islamic excesses, executions, tortures and massacres, and economic collapse, all with the complicity of Western powers.[9] The fall of the Amin regime in 1979, precipitated by a Tanzanian military intervention (Tanzania's president, Julius Nyerere, considered the "socialist" Obote his friend), did not improve matters. Two Baganda, the professor Yusufu Lule and the politician Godfrey Binaisa, were successively named head of a provisional government. Then Obote, returning from Tanzania, won by rigging elections in December 1980.[10]

The country entered into five years of civil war: the army, still dominated by Nilotes, fought a guerrilla war led by Yoweri Museveni. Museveni, originally from Ankole (from one of ancient Mpororo's minor Hima lineages), an anti-imperialist, and a sympathizer of Mozambique's FRELIMO party, had been a political refugee in Tanzania for years.[11] In 1979, he was minister of defense; later dismissed by Obote, he formed an alliance with Lule to create the National Resistance Movement (NRM) in 1981. In so doing, he created a united front between Baganda and people from the west, all Bantu-speaking, against the new pro-north dictatorship. In the southern part of the country (notably in the Luwero region north of Kampala), the regime launched bloody reprisal attacks that left 100,000 dead. The height of atrocities was in July 1985, when the brothers Okello, two generals from the Acholi ethnic group (and thus Nilotic), replaced Obote with a military council; this had the stupefying backing of the DP Christian Democrats.[12] Nonetheless, until its end, the regime was supported by almost the entire international community, led by experts from the International Monetary Fund and the World Bank. In a way, these two institutions have become the region's new diviners and initiates, equivalent to those who once anointed the reigning monarchs.[13]

This civil war paved the way for the region's future. First, it revealed in all its horror the extremes to which "tribalism" could go, even in a country reputed to be "modernized." The piles of skulls in Luwero foreshadowed Rwanda's mass graves.[14] For years in Uganda, the war discredited multipartyism, which had been known only as a vector of regional conflicts, in a country that deserved more from its elites. The new regime installed by President Museveni after taking Kampala by the National Resistance Army (NRA), the armed wing of the NRM, in 1986 combined freedom of expression, economic liberalism, and a strong central government. His "no-party democracy" has not excluded "resistance councils" elected locally or general elections pitting NRM candidates against those from the former UPC and DP. Adopted in 1995 after a countrywide survey, the new constitution began not with a ritual evocation of the Declaration of Human Rights but with mention of the country's terrible experiences. Quite pragmatically, the Constitution recognized the moral authority of "cultural leaders." This amounted to an opportunity to restore the monarchies, which in fact had taken place in 1993 with the return of Buganda's kingship and Kabaka Ronald Mutebi himself. The honor of the ancient rituals was restored.[15] "Restoration fever" also swept over other ancient kingdoms and even regions without monarchical traditions, despite initial popular resistance. In the west, the ancient Bacwezi heroes again inspired veneration at the Ntusi site, even in the presence of public officials.[16] President Museveni's ability to combine state rigor and respect for difference explains his success in the 1996 presidential elections. In that contest, Museveni defeated the DP leader, Paul Ssemogerere (allied with the UPC), even in the Bugandan Catholic fiefs, where the logic of ethnicity (and religion), dear to many journalists, should have guaranteed the latter's success.[17]

Moreover, the Ugandan civil war had regional repercussions

and served as a prelude to the general conflagration in the 1990s. Museveni ultimately imposed his will on each of his neighbors: he was feared by the Kenyan and Zairian dictators (Daniel arap Moi and Marshal Mobutu); he irritated the Tanzanian president, Julius Nyerere, whose protégé was discredited; and he worried Rwanda's Juvénal Habyarimana, who symbolized the ethnicism that the Ugandan leader despised. Rwanda was most directly affected by its large northern neighbor's crises. Indeed, Rwandan refugees in Uganda totaled about 300,000 in the 1980s.[18] But Obote's regime, challenged by the NRA undergrounds, made this Tutsi community its scapegoat. The Tutsi were categorized with all the Banyarwanda autochthons from Kigezi and with Ankole's Bahima, Museveni's so-called brothers. The police were controlled by a mafia of Bairu politicians from Ankole (the so-called Bushenyi group), led by Minister Rwakasisi; this group was all too happy to plunder the cattle of these vulnerable populations. In December 1982, UPC militias looted the refugee camps and forced forty thousand to flee, notably to Rwanda, where they were left to rot in camps on the border. It was then that these young Rwandan exiles joined the NRA en masse. In 1986, Rwandans made up about 20 percent of the NRA's recruits.[19] They actively participated in the seizure of Kampala before becoming the Rwandan Patriotic Front's strike force in 1990.

Rwanda: An Exceptional "Social Revolution"

As we have seen, the prejudices and disputes linked to the Hutu-Tutsi cleavage took root among the first modern Rwandan elites in the 1950s. But Rwandan society overall was more nuanced. An inquiry in an ordinary rural setting during that period revealed that average family revenues for Bahutu and Batutsi were almost the same.[20] In fact, the ethnic obsession took hold in the small stratum of educated elites, notably those who graduated from

299

Astrida or from the seminary. Up against the Tutsi elite, with its clerical wing and its support from customary leaders, a Hutu counter-elite — of teachers, priests, catechists, and medical and agronomic auxiliaries, whose influence could be relayed by artisans, traders, and truckers — crystallized. The former group's access to printing presses and the latter group's access to transportation were ultimately useful. This entire world, which had extracted itself from the rural masses, included only several thousand people, but their role as "cultural intermediaries" proved decisive.

Until the 1950s, politics was dominated by traditional conservatism. Clientage and neighborhood relationships continued to maintain the mix of reciprocity and the sense of hierarchy that had characterized ancient society, though this was not true in the northern and western peripheral regions, where the Batutsi often struck locals as foreigners sent by the central government.[21] The composition of the customary administration's "councils," which were created in 1952, is revealing. Originally formed from electoral colleges selected by the subchiefs, the subchiefdom councils in 1956 were elected by popular vote. The Batutsi, then about 17 percent of the population, won 33 percent of the seats. But at the higher echelons, an indirect vote influenced by the ruling authorities — a vote responsible for the composition of the chiefdom councils and the High Council of Rwanda — was far more favorable to the Batutsi.[22] At the same time, Mwami Mutara, whose nationalist orientations became clear, tried to popularize the regime, in the image of his Bugandan counterpart, by abolishing the *buhake* contract in 1954; he even abolished the obligatory crop system in 1958.[23] Vice Governor Jean-Paul Harroy then distributed 300,000 tracts, letting it be known that this decision came from the Belgian administration, even though it had actually been taken by the High Council.[24] In February 1957, the High Council, which was mainly composed of major chiefs, drafted a Statement of Views that called for accelerated emancipation for Rwanda and equality of African and European officers.

The Hutu counter-elite quickly distanced itself from the aristocracy's nationalist orientation and emphasized, as a prerequisite, ending "Tutsi feudalism," even if that meant delaying independence. In March 1957, nine Hutu intellectuals, all from the seminary and aided by the White Fathers, circulated a "note on the social aspect of the indigenous racial problem." Called the "Manifesto of the Bahutu," this note denounced the "Tutsi monopoly" over access to education and leadership positions. It thus linked an egalitarian demand — elite promotion — with the old racial discourse inherited from colonialism: all Batutsi were denounced as beneficiaries of "Hamitic domination"; doctors were called on to settle cases of "crossbreeding"; and maintaining the practice of including ethnicity on identity cards was demanded. Ethnic excesses soon followed: in May 1958, a group of Tutsi notables from the Nyanza court published documents purporting to make historical claims, in which they denied all fraternity with the Hutu and attributed to the Tutsi alone the founding of the Rwandan state.[25]

The Catholic Church delivered the decisive nudge in the right direction. A new generation of missionaries, inspired by the ideals of Christian democracy, intimately supported Hutu populism.[26] Here, the Flemish found another arena in which to pursue their fight against the Francophones. André Perraudin, the Swiss bishop of Kabgayi since 1955, compared peasants' complaints in Rwanda to those of peasants in his native Valais vis-à-vis the bourgeoisie of Sion. Nine years after the 1950 jubilee, which had linked evangelical success to the Tutsi aristocrats, who were thought to have brought their country toward Christ, the 1959 Lenten pastoral clearly expressed the Church's change in policy: it claimed that "in our Ruanda... [there are] several neatly characterized races" and that "social inequalities are in large part tied to racial differences." The Hutu former seminarians called themselves "rural *évolués*" and thus benefited from the support of the Belgian Christian Workers Movement and the parish structures (Legion of Mary, associations of educators and printers, the services of the Kabgayi Bursarship, and the advice of fathers like Arthur Dejemeppe).

Their leader, Grégoire Kayibanda, had a significant career. He was a primary-school teacher and a close companion of Monsignor Perraudin; he was invited to the Christian Workers Youth meetings in Belgium. In 1954, he became editor in chief of *Kinyamateka*, which would spread the good "social" word to tens of thousands of readers; later he became a member of the board of directors of the Catholic cooperative network TRAFIPRO (Travail, Fidélité, Progrès [Work, Loyalty, Progress]), a food cooperative based on the Swiss model that was created in 1956.[27] To defend politically "the humble folk" or "the mass" (that is, the Hutu) against the abuses of the "feudals" (understood to be Tutsi), Kayibanda founded the Muhutu Social Movement in 1957, which became the Party of the Movement of Emancipation of the Bahutu (PARMEHUTU) in October 1959. In 1958, a Hutu merchant from the south, Joseph Gitera Habyarimana, created the Association for the Social Promotion of the Mass (APROSOMA) with the same objective.[28]

This effervescence coincided with the wave of independence movements that swept across the Third World and in particular across Africa in the mid-1950s. In January 1959, riots broke out in Léopoldville. Brussels, which had not envisaged Congo's independence for another thirty years, conceded it immediately (in June 1960). In Ruanda-Urundi, a parliamentary study group carried out an investigation in April and May 1959. An official declaration on November 26 set in motion a process of internal autonomy for

Rwanda and Burundi, separate from Congo. The declaration also led to the integration of two administrative networks: the chiefdoms would become territorial entities, subdivided into communes, which would group together subchiefdoms. Intermediate institutions were put in place in December, in preparation for communal and legislative elections. In 1960 and 1961, there was a race against time between the United Nations, anxious to ensure a democratic passage to independence, and Belgium, which wanted to establish autonomous authorities that would do its bidding. Belgian policy was formed on the ground, but in a context where Congolese affairs (and those of Katanga) played a huge role, arousing fear and hope among the colonized and the colonizers of the territory under trusteeship.[29]

In fact, the Hutu militants supported prolonging this; to them, the "poorly prepared mass" did not yet seem ripe for universal suffrage. Events accelerated in July 1959 after the sudden death of King Mutara, which was later considered imperialism's first crime in the region. Immediately, without consulting the Belgians, the most traditionalist group at the court enthroned a successor, Kigeri V Nadahindurwa, another of Musinga's sons. In August, the Rwandan National Union (UNAR) was founded, and it demanded immediate independence. However, not all the Tutsi chiefs supported this move. The following month, some reformist elements created the Rwandan Democratic Rally (RADER) and formed an alliance with Hutu parties. Ethnic antagonism had not yet invaded people's consciences. The tone rose in the autumn of 1959: a series of reciprocal provocations spawned a jacquerie, which PARMEHUTU directed, in the north and in the center of the country.[30] Thousands of huts were burned and several hundred Batutsi were killed; the north was practically "purified"; and Hutu leaders were assassinated in retaliation. Belgian paratroopers subsequently headed for Congo, and Colonel Guy Logiest, an admirer of apartheid, was named Special Resident.[31] Under the shadow of a military regime, the country was "de-UNARized" (that is, purified of UNAR), an operation that involved dismissing half the chiefs and three hundred out of five hundred subchiefs and replacing them with Hutu chiefs and burgomasters. In this context of ethnic consciousness-raising by forceps, communal elections in June 1960 delivered an overwhelming majority to PARMEHUTU. An autonomous Belgian-Rwandan government, presided over by Kayibanda, was formed. The United Nations let it happen. Kayibanda, counseled by the Belgian Social Christians and supported by Logiest, organized a coup d'état: in Gitarama on January 28, 1961, commune representatives declared the birth of a republic. The *mwami* fled to Léopoldville, and legislative elections in September 1961 ratified the regime change — all to the benefit of PARMEHUTU and Kayibanda, who in July 1962 became president of the republic before the proclamation of independence was even made.[32] It was the triumph of a "revolution under trusteeship" or an "assisted" one, to quote Governor Harroy's terms.

However, PARMEHUTU's racist orientation was obvious. Even RADER and APROSOMA denounced it in 1960, though in vain. PARMEHUTU claimed to "restore the country to its owners" and invited the Batutsi to "return to Abyssinia" if they were unhappy:

> Ruanda is the country of Bahutu (Bantu) and of all those, white and black, Tutsi, European, or of other provenance, who abandon feudo-colonialist ambitions.[33]

The introduction of *demokarasi* in Rwanda, so vaunted in Europe on both the left and the right, thus was quite particular.[34] It was conceived of as the power of the "humble folk" or the "majority

people." But at the same time, it was conceived of as the legitimate revenge of the "autochthons," the Bahutu, on the 17 percent
Batutsi population, who were treated as a foreign minority.[35]
Comparisons with the French Revolution have often been made,
including by the actors themselves, but this would be 1789 without the night of August 4. Indeed, far from abolishing "orders"
(here, the *amoko*), the Rwandan revolution reinforced and treated
the "Hamites" as second-class citizens, as if the French Third
Estate had considered itself *ad aeternum* as proprietor of a popular "Gaul" identity and had kept the descendants of nobles in
a ghetto of "conquering Francs."[36] The racial order of the 1930s
was thus maintained, with a simple permutation in values, to the
benefit of the majority group.

Darlings of the colonizer, the Batutsi overnight became Rwandans who were just tolerated in their country. Moreover, nearly
150,000 Batutsi, or about a third, were forced to flee to adjoining
countries. New waves in 1964 and 1973 followed, and in the late
1980s Batutsi refugees totaled about 700,000 divided among Burundi, Uganda, Zaire, and Tanzania.[37] This diaspora represented
black Africa's first refugees, and yet their kind remained stifled
for thirty years, as if they all were members of the "feudal clique"
described in Kigali's propaganda. In fact, the Batutsi became scape-
goats for every bad memory of the past, including colonial oppression, memories that were continually and vindictively recalled.
Every time a Hutu regime encountered a problem, the Tutsi in the
country were a priori considered suspect. They thus were obliged
to remain discreet about their lot. For a generation, all harassment
by the local authorities toward them was treated as an understandable and spontaneous manifestation of popular resentment,
and not a single murder was punished.[38] Thus decolonization was
accompanied here by a nation being torn apart.

The 1959–1961 "social revolution" is the key event in Rwanda, one that shaped the country's politics for the next three decades.[39] On Christmas 1963, Belgian soldiers stopped an attack led by several hundred refugees from Burundi just south of Kigali. This attack became the regime's pretext for reuniting PARME-HUTU, which had been weakened by internal rivalry. In 1964, the regime organized a manhunt of Batutsi, who had been collectively demonized: in the name of the frightened Bahutu's "popular self-defense" and "collective furor," burgomasters and prefects — backed by ministers dispatched to the provinces — organized massacres that left more than ten thousand dead. Then the Batutsi were denounced as a "fifth column" of "cockroaches" (inyenzi) who had infiltrated the country. Leading Tutsi figures in UNAR and RADER who had stayed in Rwanda were executed; in 1966, PARMEHUTU became the single party. With the Catholic hierarchy's blessing, the government minimized the killings, which Bertrand Russell denounced at the time as "the most horrible and systematic massacre since the extermination of the Jews by the Nazis."[40] How can this event not be seen as a portentous forerunner of the 1994 genocide, especially since we know that Kayibanda had warned the refugees in March 1964 that if they attacked Kigali, chaos would ensue, as would "the total and summary end of the Tutsi race"?[41]

Ten years later, there were new persecutions. This time, the events emanated from the secondary schools, the university, and even certain ecclesiastical circles. "Public Salvation Committees" denounced "Tutsi surpluses" in schools and in the administration; the committees drew up lists of people to expel, including those employed in hospitals and private enterprises. Bahutu suspected of being closely connected to Batutsi were treated as "hybrids" or "those who switched ethnic groups." The crisis left hundreds of victims dead in the center of the country. In fact, this episode occurred during a tense political period. Two "regionalist" factions — the Gitarama group (in reference to the president's prefecture) and the northern group (from Ruhengeri and Gisenyi) — were squaring off, while whether Kayibanda would fulfill another five-year term remained an open question.

Both camps may have organized this deliberate awakening of ethnic passions. PARMEHUTU had just published a type of catechism that stated, "Tutsi domination is the origin of all the evil the Hutu have suffered since the beginning of time. It is comparable to a termite mound teeming with every cruelty known to man."[42] A soldier from Ruhengeri, Alexis Kanyarengwe, ran the Secret Service, which was implicated in the movement. In this stifling atmosphere, where racial historiography had become official, elites obsessed with getting ahead resorted to Rwanda's founding discourse — the "Rwandan ideology." But, as in 1959, the cancer of ethnicism, for the most part affected only the top layer of society. Indeed, the army seemed to offer a solution: its head, General Juvénal Habyarimana, toppled Kayibanda in 1973.

The second republic established by this coup d'état shifted the government's center of gravity from the center to the north, "from Nduga to Rukiga," or, more exactly, from Gitarama to Gisenyi, from which the new president hailed.[43] After five years of military transition, the government "civilianized," as the Belgian jurist Filip Reyntjens wrote.[44] The 1978 Constitution established a presidential system, and the population was controlled by a new party, the National Revolutionary Movement for Development (MRND). For fifteen years, Rwanda seemed an uneventful country, where the only issues were ones of "development," as indicated by the the name of the new party and of the National Assembly, the National Development Council.

This "peasant order" was supported by three bases: foreign assistance, the Catholic Church, and quotidian ethnicism. Public and private aid flocked to this "country of a thousand volunteers," which was showcased as a model of "integrated rural develop- ment" and where practically every commune had its own "pro- ject." A small hard-working, honest, moral, God-fearing, and stable country — that was the tirelessly diffused image:

> Its main leaders' great moderation, their choice of democracy, and their political engagement with Christianity have profoundly influ- enced the new Rwanda.[45]

The Church worked hand in hand with the state, as it had during colonial rule. The Church represented an essential conduit to "foreign friends," notably those in the Flanders and Rhineland Christian Democratic sphere of influence. The parish network and Sunday Mass complemented the party's cells and the weekly "communitarian works" (called *umuganda*) and "cultural activi- ties" (that is, propaganda). Besides the official organs, the only press was Catholic: *Kinyamateka*, a daily, and *Dialogue*, a journal created in 1968 to exercise a moral and cultural authority over the elites. Vincent Nsengiyumva, the archbishop of Kigali from 1976 to 1994, for years was a member of the MRND's Central Commit- tee.[46] The presidential couple itself displayed a piety that was mar- veled at, for example, by those in the court of Baudouin, the king of the Belgians. Moreover, between 1981 and 1983, schoolgirls in Kibeho, in Gikongoro prefecture, "dialogued" with the Virgin Mary in public and in the media's presence.[47] This moral-order regime irresistibly evoked that of Antonio Salazar in Portugal.

These "Christian and democratic" values were accompanied by an eclipse, even a repression, of cultural references to ancient Rwanda, universally considered "feudal." True, oral literature, dance, and music — all of which were exceptionally rich — had been marginally broached at the academic, museum, and folkloric levels. But these arts were either purged from or censured in the popular sphere because, like it or not, kingship was at the heart of a so-called traditional religious and political culture. A Zairian-style musical "atmosphere" invaded the country. Its history was reduced to a racial schema; all that preceded 1959 was thrown into the dustbin of the "ancient regime," a little like so-called Gothic buildings being exposed to vandalism in post-revolutionary France. The new Rwanda declared its national past "Tutsi" and thus despicable.[48] Not until the 1970s did a new generation of historians start to focus on the country's heritage of sacred woods and oral traditions.

Refusing the past increasingly went hand in hand with political blindness about the future. Rwanda was heavily modernized in the 1980s: money, business, and individualism occupied a growing place in society, for better and for worse. The contradiction between the official pro-rural discourse and these social realities became more and more manifest. To remedy the situation, the regime resorted to colonial-era social engineering. An "equilibrium" was sought by maintaining so-called traditional cleavages: "democracy" was not to improve, since power was already in the hands of the "majority people" whose interests would be ensured through quotas, which supposedly would avoid social "disparities." In principle, this meant Batutsi could occupy only 9 percent of positions in schools and jobs. The system also extended ethnic consciousness to new generations. Indeed, a generation after the birth of the Hutu republic, the virulence of its founding principles was always on the verge of bringing about an explosion.

Burundi: The Trap of Hutu-Tutsi Ethnicism

The Rwandan ideology of ethno-racial democracy became a beacon or a foil for the entire region. Obsession with this ideology rivaled that of the Hamitic myth — from which it was born —

under colonialism. In 1965, Burundi entered a spiral of violence, one induced by this logic. However, even after the Belgian trusteeship, Burundi's society and politics remained appreciably different from those of its northern cousin. One might even wonder if Burundi's fate would have been radically different if the country had not been falsely twinned to Rwanda under colonialism. Indeed, it remains an open question what Burundi's fate would have been if it had been managed separately when the region was divided among Germany, England, and Belgium.

However, the accession to independence unfolded in a particular, new political context, even if Burundi followed the same institutional process as Rwanda.[49] The High Council, created as in Rwanda during the 1952 reforms and dominated by the princely (Ganwa) group, became the harbinger of a centuries-old nation. In 1956, on the fortieth anniversary of his reign, Mwambutsa restored (with some adjustments) the royal festival of *muganuro*, which took place annually until 1964. Mwambutsa subsequently protested against establishing Usumbura as an "extra-customary center," detached from the rest of the country.[50] In 1959, he called for Burundi's self-determination, before that of Congo. But a fault line quickly appeared in the Burundian aristocracy: Jean-Baptiste Ntidendereza, son of Baranyanka, a major chief, and several others indicated that they wanted friendly relations with the Belgians, and they publicly expressed fears that independence would plunge the country into medieval backwardness.

This division was played out when political parties were created in preparation for domestic autonomy.[51] The first initiative came from the king's eldest son, Louis Rwagasore. After studying at Astrida and in Belgium, he had founded a cooperative, based on a Tanganyikan model, that was designed to help free peasants from Greek and Pakistani traders. In 1958, he met in Muramvya, the royal capital, with chiefs and Burundian priests to found a nationalist movement, the Party of National Unity and Progress (UPRONA). On the basis of a program calling for both independence and social reforms, this party rapidly became popular among every social group, whether Hutu, Tutsi, Muslim, or Christian. Governor Harroy tried in vain to outlaw Rwagasore from all political activity, because he was heir apparent. The administration then favored the formation of a rival party, the Christian Democratic Party, led by Jean-Baptiste Ntidendereza and Joseph Birori (both sons of Baranyanka), whose agenda included delaying independence. The People's Party, largely inspired by the Rwandan model, was also created early in 1960.[52] By the summer of 1961, twenty-five parties had appeared, but they federated into three cartels: a nationalist and royalist bloc centered on UPRONA, the Common Front centered on the Christian Democratic Party, and the Union of Popular Parties centered on the People's Party. The main conflict, the one that separated UPRONA and the Common Front, in no way corresponded to the Hutu-Tutsi antagonism, which was practically absent from the Burundian political scene at this time. Rather, it centered on a rivalry between two princely factions, the Bezi and the Batare.[53] The majority of UPRONA's Central Committee members were Bahutu, among whom Rwagasore's principal aide, Paul Mirerekano, was the agronomic assistant.

Domestic politics was very tense between 1960 and 1962, but it did not lead to massacres, as it did in Rwanda. UPRONA, like UNAR, was accused of Communist sympathies because of its ties with Patrice Lumumba's Congolese Nationalist Movement and Julius Nyerere's Tanganyika African National Union. But the Burundian clergy, supported by the bishops of Gitega and Usumbura (Antoine Grauls and Michel Ntuyahaga), brought this demonization to a standstill.[54] The December 1960 communal elections handed a majority to the Common Front, and the following January, Joseph Cimpaye formed an autonomous government that

311

excluded UPRONA. But UN-supervised legislative elections in September 1961 delivered an overwhelming majority to UPRONA (fifty-eight out of sixty-four seats). "We won the Rwandan elections, but we lost them in Burundi," commented Governor Harroy. Rwagasore formed his government. But it was an ephemeral triumph: he was assassinated a month later by a Greek, a henchman of the Baranyanka clan.[55] Independence was proclaimed (as in Rwanda) on July 1, 1962, in an atmosphere of mourning.

From then on, the political class splintered into factions: the Astridians (graduates of Astrida's Groupe Scolaire) against the seminarians (graduates of the Mugera seminary); there were intrigues between the rival princely lines around King Mwambutsa, who claimed to be above parties; in Parliament, so-called Casablanca and Monrovia groups crystallized, as a function of their supposedly different positions on international politics — the former pursued "neutral progressivism" whereas the latter was in the "pro-Western" camp; and, finally, there were the personal quarrels and gaffes that inevitably seem to accompany the management of a state that must be built with paltry sums.[56]

The Rwandan syndrome rapidly infiltrated the Burundian ruling class: to the Tutsi, the spectacle of tens of thousands of Rwandan refugees inspired distrust toward the Bahutu; and to the Hutu, the prospect of having absolute power seemed a very tempting option in the wake of Kigali's "social revolution." But if relations between the two protagonists were different, the socioethnic antagonism, defined as structural, slowly crystallized into an obsessive fear: of a solution founded on a binary majority-minority relationship that would entail evicting one group or the other from the political arena. The political scientist René Lemarchand has described this process as a "self-fulfilling prophecy":

> By giving the Burundi situation a false definition to begin with, these Hutu politicians evoked a new behavior, both among themselves and the Tutsi, which made their originally false imputations true.[57]

The dramatization of this cleavage, with its all-or-nothing stakes, has been carried out through systematic mass violence. Elsewhere I have emphasized the Sorelian tone that inspires this strategy of "ethnic consciousness-raising" and its related tactics of incitement. In this political battle, an entire population is transformed into a "human shield." Each "camp" can find itself alternately in the position of torturer and victim, which renders purely humanitarian assessments particularly complex.[58] From the hills of Rwanda in November 1959 to the forests of Zaire in early 1997, the political-military exploitation of populations has been the same.

Thus Burundi has experimented with this model.[59] Every political incident between 1962 and 1964 has been invested with an ethnic interpretation, including the murder of three Christian trade unionists by extreme nationalists, the ousting of Paul Mirerekano from the presidency of UPRONA in favor of another, better-connected Hutu politician (Joseph Bamina), and the quarrels between the Casablanca and Monrovia groups. This spiral of ethnicization has been accelerated by external intervention: nearby Congo was a focal point for the Cold War; Burundi was a base for Chinese aid to the Kivu-based Lumumbist rebels; Rwanda was a base of operations for the Central Intelligence Agency.[60] Each camp has instrumentalized the ethnicism it found in the two countries: the "nonalignment" group were mainly Tutsi nationalists (Rwandan refugees of the former UNAR and leaders of the Casablanca group like Albin Nyamoya); by contrast, the Hutu leader Mirerekano went into exile in Rwanda, where he was approached by the Western "services."[61] In both Burundi and Rwanda, the missionaries have denounced "feudal Communists."

In 1964, the situation intensified: the year opened with the Rwandan killings and ended with Belgian paratroopers descending on Stanleyville and General Mobutu's troops reconquering Kivu. Mwami Mwambutsa's aura remained intact among the peasants, though he squandered some in the loose life he led in Bujumbura and Europe. Mwambutsa tried to juggle different leanings in naming his cousin André Muhirwa prime minister in 1961; this was followed in 1963 by his appointing the Hutu economist Pierre Ngendandumwe to the same position; then the Tutsi Astridian Albin Nyamoya was named prime minister in 1964, followed in January 1965 by Ngendandumwe, who was assassinated later that year, prompting Mwambutsa to govern by decree. The following May, highly ethnicized elections gave UPRONA a majority, but two-thirds of the members of Parliament were Hutu, and they were conscious of their power. The king subsequently named a prince from his lineage, old chief Léopold Biha, as prime minister — to the great displeasure of the Hutu leader, Gervais Nyangoma, who, with the complicity of the state secretary of the gendarmerie, Antoine Serukwavu, and some officers, organized a coup d'état on October 18, 1965. The king fled to Congo, then to Switzerland, where he died in 1977. In the following days, the crisis was prolonged by massacres of Tutsi peasants in Muramvya Province perpetrated by groups of youth in Deputy Mirerekano's service. At that point, the Batutsi of Burundi realized that Rwanda's fate had been reserved for them: this was a decisive split. Under the leadership of State Secretary of Defense Michel Micombero, a young captain freshly graduated from the Royal Military Academy in Brussels, the army took the rebellion in hand. The reprisals, notably against the Hutu political class, were merciless.[62]

From then on, a bloc formed among the Tutsi, who became determined to control the government and army and to carry out strictly law-and-order anti-Hutu policies. In line with this, the monarchy was abolished in two stages: first, the king's son Prince Charles Ndizeye, who had been enthroned under the name Ntare V in July 1960, was proclaimed head of state; then, the following November, a military coup d'état established the first republic under the presidency of Colonel Micombero.[63] The motives and actors in this transition were numerous: students whose leader, Gilles Bimazubute, had returned from Belgium; officers led by Albert Shibura, a graduate of the Saint-Cyr military academy; young graduates from European universities who had been promised they could run the ministries and were very hostile to the Ganwa group; and intrigues involving Jean Ntiruhwama, a graduate of the Mugera seminary, a former collaborator with the Gitega bishop, and a former minister who wanted to emulate Kayibanda by empowering the Hima subgroup, to which he belonged (as did Micombero). But the faction with an increasingly decisive role in running the new republic was defined by its home region: the Bururi group, which came from the south of the country.[64] This poor region, with few educational opportunities, had been the source of many soldiers. Arthémon Simbananiye embodied the country's new politics of revenge, which played itself out at both the regional and the ethnic level. A former seminarian who held a basic legal degree from Paris, Simbananiye was soon heading up the Burundian justice system. A Hutu official, Martin Ndayahoze, who was minister of information in 1968, has described the nasty climate at the top:

> There were some insatiable leaders who, to satisfy their shameful
> ambitions, turned ethnic division into a political strategy. As such,
> if they were Tutsi, they denounced a Hutu peril that had to be
> countered, complete with a need for supporting conspiracies; if they
> were Hutu, they disclosed a "Tutsi apartheid" that had to be fought

315

against. And that set in motion a diabolical scene in which emotion took precedence over reason.[65]

The obsession with "law and order" first took the form of political-judicial eliminations: some Hutu military and civilian leaders were assassinated in 1969, followed by liberal Tutsi politicians (qualified as royalists) in 1971. Soon after came what the Burundians call the "scourge" (*ikiza*) of 1972: a Hutu rebellion, organized by leaders exiled in East Africa, began in the south in late April; several thousand Batutsi were massacred. The repression that followed (in May and June) became a huge countrywide manhunt: it was a genuine genocide of Hutu elites. The crisis left at least 150,000 dead; double that amount became refugees in Rwanda and Tanzania, and the army and the administration were massively purified.[66]

The trap shut on Burundi: after the 1965 and 1972 crises, the break between Hutu and Tutsi became as acute as in Rwanda. It was founded on an omnipresent fear. "What is it to be Hutu or Tutsi? It is being neither Bantu or Hamite nor serf or master! It is to remember who killed one of your close relations fifteen years ago or to wonder who will kill your child in ten years, each time with a different answer," I wrote in 1989.[67]

The Micombero regime, dominated by the Simbananiye mafia, lasted for four more years.[68] A military coup d'état brought another officer from Bururi to power in 1976: Colonel Jean-Baptiste Bagaza, who essentially kept the same group in power without profoundly widening ethnic and regional representation. Bagaza also staked much on economic development, which had been remarkable for ten years, as a way of overshadowing the Hutu-Tutsi question, and he dodged the political dimension. Starting in 1983, the regime became embroiled in a quarrel with the Catholic Church, which exploited the Hutu opposition, which abroad was primarily represented by PALIPEHUTU (Party for the Liberation of the Hutu People); the regime fell in 1987 after another coup d'état. The following year, the new head of the country, Major Pierre Buyoya, also from the south, was faced with a Hutu rebellion in the northeast, in the communes of Ntega and Marangara; this new conflict started a series of reforms, to which we will return below.[69]

In Rwanda and Burundi in the late 1980s, two clichés seemed inescapable: "democracy" of the Hutu "majority people" in Kigali, and "national unity" with a strong Tutsi law-and-order connotation in Bujumbura.[70] However, the societies had changed; the two countries had more roads and more graduates. And the fall of the Berlin Wall in 1989 suddenly laid bare the shameful Leninism of the one-party systems in Africa. Official discourses had worn thin. But the "ethnic" virus — with the scent of pseudo eternity that colonial reshaping, modern politics, and the international media had attributed to the Hutu-Tutsi antagonism — was more virulent than ever. This challenge for democratization ultimately proved as serious north as it was south of the Kanyaru, despite the good intentions of the region's experts, who saw in this border river the same Manichaean demarcation that Pascal saw in the Pyrenees.

The Crisis of the 1990s: An African Racism at Work
Since the late 1980s, the region has been in a tempest, and no one knows for sure what ravages will be left behind. The tragedies in Burundi, Rwanda, and eastern Congo are political. But they have also been characterized by atrocious bloodbaths and foreign interventions that have made the Great Lakes of Africa front-page news around the world. The end of apartheid in South Africa created a huge wellspring of hope on the continent, but this bright spot has been tarnished by the contemporaneous resurgence of

317

the twentieth century's bleakest years, this time on the Dark Continent. This further fueled what has been called "Afro-pessimism"
— even if, unfortunately, as Alfred Grosser put it, "a massacre of
Africans is not felt in the same way as a massacre of Europeans."
Grosser added:

> Would we find it wise if an African considered slaughter in Europe a
> normal product of a civilization that produced Auschwitz and had
> already produced Verdun?[71]

Faced with the many commentators who consider these equatorial
massacres normal, explicable as a function of ethnography, "tribal
atavisms," demographic density, and past heritages, historians are
obliged to recall that "men resemble their times more than they
do their fathers," as Marc Bloch said.[72] Indeed, historians must put
contemporary events in a broader perspective, one that includes
the long history of mastering the environment, political structuring, and managing contacts with foreigners. It is fundamental that
we understand the specific nature of present circumstances. The
synthesis presented here will give the reader access to perspectives
that allow, I think, one to be reflective about this contemporary
situation. But how can we not feel the helplessness of every actor
who has faced the chaos unleashed on this millennial civilization
and has had to deal with this unprecedented ripping apart, which
threatens the existence of these ancient states and the survival of
entire populations? For better or worse, the literature inspired by
this crisis is already immense: more than a hundred books, as well
as hundreds of articles and Internet sites, have been produced since
1994. I, too, have tried to contribute to the analysis of the tragedies
Rwandans, Burundians, and the Congolese have experienced over
the last ten years. It is impossible in the few remaining pages to
review these events in detail; however, it is imperative to try to

show the continuities and ruptures in this "immediate" history, to quote the Congo specialist Benoît Verhaegen.[73]

The region's established order began to change in 1986, the year Museveni's partisans arrived in Kampala and ended Uganda's bloody civil war. Mobutu's regime in Zaire and Habyarimana's in Rwanda immediately understood Museveni to be an atypical leader — one who was preoccupied with restoring the rule of law — and dangerous competition. But elsewhere change was even more dramatic.

First, Burundi: On August 15, 1988, bands of Hutu peasants massacred Tutsi families in two rural communes along the border with Rwanda.[74] As the PALIPEHUTU cadres — the organizers of this affair — recommended in their tracts, one had to "surpass the Tutsi" and "do the work" necessary to neutralize the "project of Hutu extermination." President Buyoya was accused of planning this project, and he was compared to his "cousin" Micombero, the leader of the 1972 killings. As foreseen, the scenario of military provocation and repression played itself out. Thousands perished, more than fifty thousand Bahutu fled to Rwanda, and the international community denounced Bujumbura's Tutsi regime. Nonetheless, the regime's leaders quickly looked for a non-law-and-order way out of the crisis. In an attempt to escape the political-ethnic problem, they formed a government, directed by a Muhutu, Adrien Sibomana, that was composed of equal numbers of each of the two major "ethnic groups." A charter of unity condemning all "discrimination and exclusion" was drafted by a mixed commission and adopted by referendum in 1991. In 1992, a democratic constitution, which included provisions for multiple parties, was introduced. Finally, a general amnesty was offered, and efforts to return refugees were intensified. In a May 1990 speech, President Buyoya summarized the new philosophy:

319

Burundi is not exclusively a country of Bahutu where the Batutsi are only guests. It is no longer a country of Batutsi where the Bahutu are only second-class citizens.[75]

The June 1993 elections made Melchior Ndadaye head of state. The candidate for the Front for Democracy in Burundi (FRODEBU), Ndadaye became the first civilian and elected president of the Burundian republic. This election, complemented by FRODEBU's success in legislative elections, was perceived on all sides as Hutu revenge.[76] But the new president affirmed his desire to eradicate the "ethnic sickness," and he formed a government that was a third Tutsi and presided over by a technocrat close to UPRONA, Sylvie Kinigi. Despite evident tensions on both sides, the country seemed to be moving beyond its tragic destiny.[77]

In Rwanda, change also began in violence.[78] The deterioration of the economic and political situation in 1989 led many Belgian observers to speak of an "endgame atmosphere" and of the "shattered mirror" of an exemplary model of cooperation.[79] On October 1, 1990, several thousand Rwandan soldiers from the Ugandan NRA attacked in the northeast. These guerrillas, the armed wing of the Rwandan Patriotic Front (RPF), called themselves *inkotanyi*, "fighters."[80] The RPF, which emerged from its clandestine status in Kampala in 1987, defined itself as being at odds with UNAR's monarchist tradition: its program called for a reconstruction of the Rwandan state on a national basis and the return, by whatever means, of Tutsi refugees to their country of origin. This idea was backed by the Rwandan diaspora during its Washington Congress in 1988. Moreover, the RPF benefited from the participation of several Hutu leaders who were disgusted by the corruption and nepotism in the Habyarimana regime. These leaders included Colonel Alexis Kanyarengwe and Pasteur Bizimungu, the former director of the state electricity company. A clash with the regime seemed imminent.

But the October offensive was rapidly crushed by the Rwandan Armed Forces, who were supported by French, Belgian, and Zairian contingents. The *inkotanyi* leader, Fred Rwigyema, was killed during the first few days of the conflict. Kigali's resistance was surprising: in addition to external support, a resurgence of virulent ethnicism and the president's cunning contributed to its success. Habyarimana knew how to get foreign support, and he never hesitated to use ethnicist propaganda against the "feudal Tutsi" and to use provocation: after a fake attack on Kigali on the night of October 4, Habyarimana had about eight thousand suspects arrested and crammed into Kigali's prisons and stadiums.[81] But the RPF rallied exiled youth from Burundi, Zaire, and elsewhere as well as partisans in Rwanda, who reinforced the first units that came from Uganda. The growing problems with integration that Tutsi refugees encountered in most of these countries help explain their enthusiasm for joining the RPF, but the cultural and political nationalism cultivated over a generation in the diaspora also played a role. A new leader, Paul Kagame, traveled to the front near the volcanic region and developed a guerrilla war in the north, with Uganda's discreet complicity.[82] In January 1991, the RPF raided Ruhengeri and liberated all the political prisoners there.

After that, from 1991 to 1993, two logics were locked in a race against time in Rwanda: on the one hand, negotiation and democratization; on the other, war and ethnicist mobilization. The Habyarimana regime in fact pursued both strategies for three years with the unfailing military support of two French governments, both under President François Mitterrand.[83] Defending the status quo in France's Francophone "backyard," now threatened by an Anglophone irruption (this was the new Fashoda), seemed to work with the democratic opening recommended at a June 1990 conference in La Baule. Moreover, from the start, Habyarimana let it be understood that political disorder would inevitably lead to "interethnic" violence, and he presented himself both as a bastion against possible outbursts and as the legitimate representative of the "majority people." These arguments persuaded the Flemish Social Christians, who dominated the Christian Democratic International based in Brussels, as well as a number of French socialists who believed they had discovered an African 1789 to protect.[84]

However, the situation on the ground was appreciably different. In fact, there was not a single spontaneous reprisal against the Batutsi. Every time violence broke out between 1990 and 1993, it had been organized by the authorities and adapted to the political context of the day. At the same time, internal opposition against the faction in power grew stronger and stronger. The grip on power of this group — a northern clan led by the First Lady's family, which was called the *akazu*, the presidential "little home" — was denounced by elites from the center and the south, who were either nostalgic for the Kayibanda period or open to a more modern social life in which one moved beyond the Tutsi problem.

Confronted with difficult economic conditions, civil war in the north, a new Hutu opposition ready to ally itself with the rebels, and international pressure, the regime slowly made concessions: the freedoms of the press and of association were restored, and constitutional reform legalizing a multiparty system was introduced in June 1991. Several parties emerged or reappeared, including the Republican Democratic Movement, or MDR, the heir of PARMEHUTU, notably based in the prefecture of Gitarama; the Social Democratic Party, which was powerful in the university town of Butare; and the Liberal Party, which welcomed many Batutsi. The former single party rebaptized itself the

National Revolutionary Movement for Development and Democracy, or MRNDD. Powerful demonstrations in Kigali ended in April 1992 with the formation of a coalition government presided over by the MDR leader Dismas Nsengiyaremye. From then on, the political life of the country — and this is what Habyarimana's foreign friends refused to see — played itself out in three domains: the Habyarimana sphere of influence, the internal Hutu opposition, and the RPF's armed opposition. The last two groups met in Uganda and Europe, and then negotiations between the government and the RPF were held in Arusha, Tanzania. The negotiations led to a cease-fire in July 1992, to political accords in January 1993, and to a military compromise in July 1993.

But, running parallel to all this, ethnic extremism was being mobilized. Starting in May 1990, before the RPF attack, an obscure bus conductor from Gisenyi, Hassan Ngeze, supported by power networks behind the scenes, launched a bimonthly periodical called *Kangura* (The awakening) that, under the cover of freedom of the press, launched hate-filled campaigns against the *inyenzi*, the Tutsi "cockroaches," and their Hutu "accomplices" (*ibyitso*). The magazine became famous in December 1990 for publishing an "appeal to Hutu consciousness" containing the "Hutu Ten Commandments," a gospel of hate banishing all relations, whether business or sexual, between the two "ethnic groups":

> The Batutsi are bloodthirsty.... They use two weapons against the Bahutu, money and women.... The Bahutu must stop pitying the Batutsi.... The Hutu ideology must be taught to every Muhutu at all levels.[85]

This ideology was not new to Rwandans. They had known it since the late 1950s, and it had been maintained during weekly "animation" meetings. In December 1993, *Kangura* published, on its cover, a portrait of Kayibanda next to a huge machete, an evocation of the massive power of the "people." From this point forward, Hutu ethnicist propaganda was systematically carried to its extreme: the conflict between ethnic groups was continually described as an inevitable and racial fact — and one that was a priority. Practically, this meant absolute rejection of the other, even its elimination, and it meant legitimizing violence in its cruelest forms, since every kind of "self-defense" against a nonhuman "enemy" is justified. One must read *Kangura* to understand:

> Rediscover your ethnicity.... You are an important ethnic group in the larger Bantu grouping. The nation is artificial, but ethnicity is natural. (1992)

> A cockroach cannot give birth to a butterfly. It's true. A cockroach gives birth to another cockroach. If someone were to contest this, it would not be me. The history of Rwanda clearly shows that a Tutsi is always the same, that he has never changed. The malice, the wickedness are what we have known in the history of our country. (March 1993)

> The war we lead is against Batutsi who attack Bahutu. To win this war both in the public domain and on the battlefield, some should go one way and the others another way.... But to continue to mix things that do not mix together will lead us to nothing. (March 1991)

> The Tutsi found us in Rwanda; they oppressed us; and we put up with this. But now that we have left serfdom and they want to reinstall the morning *chicotte*, I think that no Hutu will be able to support this. The war Gahutu leads is just. It is a battle for the republic. (May 1991)

All history is reduced to this conflict: in essence, this perspective is akin to Gobineau's or even the Nazis'.[86] In fact, many indicators attest to a projection of anti-Semitic leitmotifs, here transmuted into anti-Hamitism. Had not the missionaries treated the Batutsi as "Semito-Hamites" for a century? Recourse to this ideology is an eminently modern phenomenon, not a simple resurgence of "tribal conflicts." The propaganda is even distributed outside Rwanda, mainly in Burundi, in a so-called international version of *Kangura*. Other, more official organs reproduced this discourse, beginning with the MRND party's *Murwanashyaka* (The militant), which denounced all confusion and all compromise between Hutu and Tutsi:

> Certain realities cannot be escaped, even through dissimulation, as, for example, when one changes one's ethnic group. When you are discovered, you are ashamed and your brothers won't hesitate to treat you like a dog.... You might belong to an ethnic group on your official documents, but from which vein will you draw the blood of this ethnic group that you claim to be yours? (April 1991)

> The enemy is among us. Some traitorous parties consider *inkotanyi* brothers. (1992)

Racist hate was folded into public opinion in this way and was physically staged during pogroms organized by burgomasters close to the president's party.[87] These pogroms occurred each time negotiations were held or a political opening seemed inevitable: early in 1991, after the RPF's raid on Ruhengeri, the Tutsi clan of Bagogwe was exterminated; in March 1992, just after the opposition entered the government, there were massacres in Bugesera (in the southeast); and in August 1992, while progress was being made in Arusha, there were killings in Kibuye (in the west), which continued in the north until January 1993.[88] The bloodbaths were primarily perpetrated by the *interahamwe* (those who act together), a militia of the MRND created in 1992; in February 1993, these atrocities provoked brief hostile reprisals by the RPF, which in turn prompted about a million people who had been displaced in the north to flee toward Kigali.

The increasingly tense climate in the country was reflected in the political arena. In November 1992, Habyarimana criticized the first Arusha documents as scraps of paper. Several days later, a top leader of his party, Léon Mugesera, a university professor, prophesied that Batutsi bodies (including those of children) would take a river-borne "express voyage" to their native Abyssinia. The preceding September, high-ranking military officials had distributed an explicit note on the "internal enemy." Still, the president managed to position himself as the apparent referee. He did this in two ways: first, by creating in March 1992 the extremist Coalition for the Defense of the Republic (CDR), which was led by top functionaries affiliated with the *akazu*; and, second, by dividing the Hutu opposition at its core by promoting, between the summer of 1992 and the summer of 1993, an ethnicist current called Hutu Power, which included Donat Murego, Froduald Karamira, and Jean Kambanda.[89] These three leaders held top positions in the MDR; their diversified regional origins (Ruhengeri, Gitarama, and Butare) were supposed to symbolize a Hutu "sacred union" and an end to the quarrel between "Banyenduga and Bakiga."[90] In February 1993, the war's reprise evidently accelerated this division, which gravely weakened the Faustin Twagiramungu, the future prime minister of the transition institutions, as designated by the Arusha Accords, and Agathe Uwilingiyimana, a courageous woman who succeeded Nsengiyaremye in June 1993 at the head of the coalition government.[91] However, the following August, when the Arusha Accords were signed, hope seemed reborn in Kigali and Bujumbura.

In both countries, managing the changes and reconciliation quickly revealed how difficult the process would be. The extremists in Rwanda were not about to disarm, despite the arrival of the United Nations Mission to Rwanda (UNAMIR) Blue Helmets in Kigali in November 1993. President Habyarimana was the only one to pledge allegiance to the new institutions, but then did much to block the establishment of Parliament and the transition government.[92] His followers spoke as if the war would resume soon. In February, the leader of the Social Democratic Party, Félicien Gatabazi, a symbol of the new Rwanda, was assassinated. In response, CDR leader Martin Bucyana was lynched in Butare. Violence proliferated in the capital. In January, *Kangura* prophesied an imminent final struggle during which "the masses" would make blood flow. A new private radio station, Radiotélévision Libre des Mille Collines (RTLM), founded and financed by an elite close to the *akazu* and technically supported by Radio Rwanda, combined entertaining music, notably Zairian, with "hot news" delivered with virulent commentary: an "interactive" style, happy, even humorous, that conditioned the Hutu public to the most venomous kind of extremist thinking. *Kangura* printed ten thousand copies, a sizable amount, but RTLM reached hundreds of thousands of listeners.[93]

But the event that triggered the ultra-Hutu reaction in Rwanda occurred in Burundi. On October 20, 1993, an armored battalion attacked the presidential palace, benefiting from either the complicity or the passivity of the rest of the army. The putsch took the lives of the elected president, Melchior Ndadaye, some of his close collaborators, and the vice president of the National Assembly, Gilles Bimazubute. With the state decapitated, the rest of the government found refuge in the French embassy, except for two ministers who tried to create a "free government" in Kigali with Habyarimana's blessing.[94] Everyone waited in vain for foreign intervention. Two days later, the most compromised putschists fled to Zaire and Uganda, and the top military brass affirmed their loyalty to Prime Minister Sylvie Kinigi.

In reaction and in parallel, on October 21 massacres of Tutsi families (they were attacked in their homes or in places they had gathered, such as schools, hospitals, and local government offices) were carried out, most often under the control of FRODEBU local authorities, in the northern half of the country. Tens of thousands were killed. Some Bahutu in UPRONA also were killed, in reprisal attacks for the president's death. The government said nothing, and Rwandan radio stations broadcast messages of encouragement for this "resistance." During a second round, military units intervened, blocking off roads, saving surrounded Batutsi, attacking bands armed with machetes, and then proceeding to commit reprisal attacks against Bahutu. This crisis left 100,000 dead, according to the Red Cross. Some foreign journalists described "this unbearable horror" and were indignant at this confusion between defending democracy and lynching poor people.[95]

In neighboring Rwanda, the counterexample of this catastrophe proved disastrous. The Hutu distrusted the RPF, which they perceived as close to the majority-Tutsi Burundian army. At the same time, the international community's incapacity to defend both the rule of law and a population threatened with genocide reinforced the extremists in their most radical projects.[96] Some, moreover, had participated in the killings in northern Burundi, in collaboration with PALIPEHUTU-supervised Burundian refugees who were still in camps in southern Rwanda. Cross-border ethnic solidarities were from then on forged openly, making these killings a portent of what happened in Rwanda six months later.

In Burundi, national reconstruction seemed hopeless: each political-ethnic camp held to its positions, and cohabitation between Hutu and Tutsi appeared impossible.[97] Around 200,000 "displaced" Tutsi (and some displaced Hutu UPRONA members) found themselves in makeshift camps near administrative centers or military bases, while thousands of Hutu peasants "dispersed," in fear of the army, and hid in the bush. In Bujumbura in early 1994, residential districts became segregated: in the north, Kamenge became a fortressed camp of Hutu militias; the majority of other parties in the city were slowly eliminated by bands of young Batutsi when the capital was shut down. However, in December 1993, institutions were slowly reestablished through a government holed up in a hotel on the shores of Lake Tanganyika: the former minister of foreign affairs Sylvestre Ntibantunganya became president of the National Assembly, and in January 1994 the assembly elected the former minister of agriculture Cyprien Ntaryamira as president of the republic. This was the result of a governmental compromise negotiated between FRODEBU and UPRONA under the auspices of the United Nations secretary general's representative Ahmedou Ould Abdallah, a Mauritanian diplomat.[98] A new government was formed and headed up by a moderate Tutsi from the north of the country, Anatole Kanyenkiko.

Rwanda soon picked up the thread of violence. On the night of April 6, a plane returning President Habyarimana and his counterpart Ntaryamira from Dar es Salaam was shot down at Kigali airport. The origin of the attack is still not clear, given the lack of a true investigation of the Rwandans, Belgians, and French who were there at the time. One must be content with guesses on which camp would have benefited the most from Habyarimana's disappearance and with belated — and often suspect — revelations. Both the logistics of the attack (two missiles were fired from a hill controlled by the presidential guard) and the information collected by Belgian intelligence services and high UN officials on the ground since early 1994 seem to implicate the extremist Hutu faction that seized power in the days after the assassination. On April 7, a military committee took control and quickly fell into the clutches of a retired officer and member of the *akazu*, Colonel Théoneste Bagosora. On April 8, a government composed exclusively of hard-liners from the MRND, the CDR, and the Hutu Power wing of the ex-opposition was formed with Théodore Sindikubwabo as interim president and Jean Kambanda as prime minister. Starting on the afternoon of April 7, the RPF quarters in Kigali, where a small battalion was stationed in accordance with the Arusha Accords, were bombarded. The following day, Major Kagame launched his troops stationed in the north of the country. They advanced toward Kigali on April 11, and the next day the "government" moved its headquarters to Gitarama. The war eventually ended on July 18 with the arrival of the RPF in Gisenyi on the Zairian border. But on April 7, ten Belgian Blue Helmets had been killed, which led to the rapid retreat of the contingent sent by Brussels; UNAMIR's numbers were cut to a minimum — a decision taken by the Security Council, where a representative of Rwanda's putschist government sat. From April 9 to 12, the French intervened in Kigali to evacuate Europeans. The *akazu*'s upper crust was also taken to safety then, but the embassy's Tutsi employees were left to their sad fate.[99]

On the evening of April 6, the genocide began.[100] The presidential guard set up roadblocks on Kigali's main arteries; the *interahamwe* retrieved hidden weapons; and in the morning, groups of militias and soldiers, equipped with lists, started massacring Batutsi families and those Bahutu judged "accomplices"; the first to be attacked were the leaders of democratic groups (notably Prime Minister Agathe Uwilingiyimana). Simultaneously, killings began in neighboring prefectures; then militia roadblocks cropped up throughout the country; and the manhunt was launched, based on supposed Tutsi features and on identity papers. Reluctant local authorities were eliminated; by mid-April, tens of thousands of victims had been killed in each prefecture, and nearly all the burgomasters and prefects had been won over to the cause. On April 19, "President" Sindikubwabo went in person to lobby the prefect of Butare (who was assassinated just afterward) and preached the necessity of the "work" (understood to be killings) in each southern region, which until then had been spared; he did so by evoking "civilian self-defense."[101]

This was genocide, not an anarchic effect of "popular anger" provoked by the death of the "father of the nation" or by an "interethnic quarrel" — arguments that the interim government used with some success.[102] These massacres stemmed from a deliberate choice by a modern elite, and they convey the Rwandan state's capacity to manage and mobilize the population. The organizers included high-ranking military officers; leaders of political groups that subscribed to the logic of Hutu Power; senior administrative officials, who organized not only the gathering of victims in stadiums, churches, and schools, which turned into slaughterhouse after slaughterhouse, but also the redistribution of the victims' goods and the preparation of mass graves; and gendarmes, who flushed the human game by threatening it with guns, thereby facilitating the work of militias equipped with machetes.[103] This decentralized machinery also included diplomats charged with justifying the killings inside the UN; bishops who affirmed their support for the "interim government" or refused to answer appeals for aid from terrorized schoolchildren; religious officials who called for "security" meetings, organized regroupments but gradually skimmed off some victims for the militias, and slowed down the evacuation of those in danger; academics who drafted disinformation; doctors who rushed to purify their hospital; teachers who worried about "order" in their schools; and journalists who denounced the "cockroaches" and rejoiced at their death on RTLM's airwaves:

These people are the Antichrist; they are a race of very bad people. I do not know how God will aid us in exterminating them.... But continue to exterminate them so that our grandchildren will no longer hear of *inkotanyi*.... Come, dear friends, let's celebrate! [And the announcer sings:] The *inkotanyi* have been exterminated. Come, dear friends, let us celebrate, God is just![104]

These well-dressed assassins let the peasants dirty their hands, but they were behind the front lines coordinating events. In this atmosphere, several thousand militiamen initially did the work, but they little by little recruited the masses to man the patrols and the barriers and to join in mobs, in which people covered themselves with banana leaves, around slaughter sites. The killers participated in communal tasks, in "work" (*akazi*) that, if not finished at night, was completed the next morning. They exterminated "cockroaches" and "rats," and they "swept dry banana leaves before burning them." Even the French troops in Operation Turquoise fell into the trap in June 1994. During the last campaigns of the fight against the pseudo infiltrators in Bisesero, near Kibuye, the troops intervened too late or let the executioners — those who had welcomed them with French flags — do what they wanted.

The objective of the genocide ("genocide" has been integrated into Kinyarwanda through the verb *gutsembatsemba*, "to exterminate") was achieved on two accounts. First, about 800,000 persons were killed (the victims were mainly Tutsi but also included some liberal Hutus) — in other words, three-quarters of the resident Tutsi population in Rwanda, which is half the total population of Rwandan Batutsi, were exterminated. This is clear in the photographs of thousands of bodies laid out near the parishes of

Ngarama, Nyamata, and in so many other places we have seen in the media. Second, thousands of young without a future were transformed into killers; they were caught up in war hysteria, and the desire to do a good job, and in the hysteria of licit pillage, encouraged sadism, and calculated cruelty.[105]

Interrogations into the origins of this horror are as complex as those for the Shoah. Functionalism or intentionalism ... Demographic pressure as well as lack of land and employment has been invoked. In fact, the bulk of the executioners were futureless youth who had been recruited into the militias.[106] But the Hutu bourgeoisie also played a part during the massacres. Indeed, since Tutsi houses were razed and replaced by banana plants, can one really speak of a "social" riot? Ethnicism was an affair of the elite before it became one of the rural masses, even if its referents are part of Rwandan culture. Danielle de Lame's remarkable sociological investigation, before the crisis, on a hill in western Rwanda demonstrates the crucial role of the "fourth ethnic group," that of the local petite bourgeoisie, in a confusion between ethnic and social grievances:

> In a context of poverty and of a harsh, sometimes desperate struggle for access to modernity, ethnicism furnished an easy outlet for resentment born from common poverty or incomplete resignation. It hides the fundamental inequalities between the peasantry among the three traditional ethnic groups and the "fourth ethnic group," which itself was partly built with assets from the colonial era.[107]

The context of civil war equally played a part, in particular in the way it affected the northern populations: many militia members came from displaced-persons camps. But since, for everyone, "war" took the form of massacring one's neighbors' families, including children, women, and the elderly, while the RPF progressed, how can one not recall the way Nazi Germany "supplied" Auschwitz with matériel and men when such mobilization would have been more useful on the different fronts of the world conflict? The crux of genocide, here as elsewhere, is first and foremost racism, that of Hutu "true citizens" against Tutsi "cockroaches." But why does this racism have such a hold in Rwanda and Burundi while analogous socio-anthropological heritages exist in all the neighboring countries? Even if some say this is a cliché, one must reflect on the specificity of Ruanda-Urundi's colonial experience, in particular the closed-off, secluded environment in which the first generation of modern elites was raised. In Uganda, Tanganyika, and even Congo, different populations were brought into close contact; Catholicism and Protestantism competed; economic activity favored the formation of genuine petites bourgeoisies, which were autonomous from the administration and the missions; and multifaceted associational experiences abounded. As we have seen, the Belgian moral order of denominational paternalism curbed every form of mobility, urbanization, modern association, criticism, and imagination, and the independent states more or less reproduced this situation.[108] Throughout, the colonial order was a combination of uprooting, with regard to ancient references, and restriction, with regard to modern references that were supposed to accompany European civilization. The malaise caused by this ambiguous situation was particularly deep in Rwanda and Burundi. By contrast, the Ugandan and Tanzanian elites, among others, redefined themselves through syntheses that emerged through the meeting of two cultures. In Rwanda and Burundi, the most powerful theme connecting the past and the present was ethnic. This theme in turn was trotted out again and again and applied as the alpha and omega of one's quest for identity, to the point of becoming obsessive. This mental confinement is, I believe, key to the social pathology that produced the genocide. Unlike the genocide of Jews in Germany, Rwanda's genocide was carried out in broad daylight and with a good conscience of sorts.[109] It was a simple "war" founded on "respectable racism," so much so that even the Virgin Mary was asked to bless it in May 1994 during an "appearance" on the radio.[110] Has this tragedy been transformed into a farce by cynical propagandists — as suggested by the brightly colored uniforms worn by the *interahamwe* on festival days — or does it resonate in deep waters, ones that have more to do with psychoanalysis than with the "mystery of evil"?[111]

The survivors and the executioners, especially after the return of every category of exile between 1994 and 1996 (including the Tutsi diaspora and the Hutu refugees), had to live together. Rwandans searched in vain for a historical precedent that could help them manage so deep a tear and reconstruct their nation. Maybe France, just after the Wars of Religion, could have been proposed.[112] In addition to getting a devastated country, with tens of thousands of maimed, widows, and orphans, the new government in Kigali inherited this moral obstacle when it was installed on July 19, 1994. The "government of national unity" that was supposed to conform to the Arusha Accords, absent the MRND, had Pasteur Bizimungu, a Muhutu member of the RPF, as president of the republic and Faustin Twagiramungu, a survivor of the MDR, as prime minister. The majority of ministers were Hutu, but the vice president, Paul Kagame, appeared to be the regime's strongman in his role as head of the Rwandan Patriotic Army, which grew out of the RPF.

The new regime's contradictions were evident. It pretended to incarnate the Rwandan nation, but it inspired great distrust among the majority of Bahutu, more than 1.5 million of whom had fled to Zaire and, in smaller numbers, to Tanzania and Burundi.[113] The regime offered social progress, but in the beginning it did not have the means to implement this goal, because the former government left by destroying and pillaging everything and because Rwanda's usual partners (excepting the United States, the Netherlands, and Germany) refused to have anything to do with the new regime.[114] It made justice a priority; in three years, 100,000 suspects were in prison, but the regime had neither the means nor the staff to judge them within reasonable waiting periods.[115] However, trials started in 1996 on the basis of a genocide law that distinguished several charge categories and allowed penalties to be reduced by admission of guilt.[116] Hundreds of hearings have been held, and ten thousand detainees were liberated in May 1998. But in the same year, twenty-eight of those with death sentences were shot, including the Hutu Power leader Froduald Karamira, prompting protests from abroad. Distrust was mutual between Kigali and the international community, which Kigali found to be as unreliable after as it was during the genocide.

In fact, the blockage owed much to the reluctance of Western countries and humanitarian organizations to engage in a fight against the ideology of genocide. This was the case for different reasons: indifference, skepticism about the role of ideologies in Africa, difficulty in breaking ties with former friends (and the Habyarimana regime had many of them), a refusal to recognize errors, and an ease with offering moralizing advice against hate and in favor of pardon. The most common discourse remains that of "reconciliation."[117] And as early as July 1994, some organizations based in the refugee camps in Zaire recuperated this discourse to justify their militant practice of denial, which equated the authors of the genocide with the RPF:

> Interethnic massacres had devastating effects.... The Kambanda government organized a pacification campaign.... The efficacy of

these actions remained limited.... The RPF was obstinate in not recognizing the government in place, which amounted to refusing all
compromise with it.[118]

After working in Gitarama beside the "interim" government,
some leaders of Rwandan NGOs effectively put in place networks
structured around Goma and Bukavu. Much aid was put toward
propaganda and training activities, which allowed them to present
themselves as refugee representatives with a clear political agenda.
Between October 1994 and April 1995, in Bukavu and Mugunga
camp (North Kivu), they helped construct the Rally for Democracy and the Return of Refugees, which benefited from the active
support of both the Christian Democratic International (essentially the Flemish Christian People's Party) and the former top
military brass of the Rwandan Armed Forces. The latter, who
entered Zaire with their arms, trained in the Kivu camps, notably
in Mugunga and Panzi (South Kivu). The arguments of these
groups, who claimed to offer a third way, were simple: the genocide was only one aspect of the "war's" massacres; the RPF killed
many (a point that is not inaccurate), so many as to qualify as
another genocide, one that had been kept secret.[119] This "double
genocide" was inscribed in the centuries-old conflict between
Hutu and Tutsi, and it was even suggested that the 1994 episode was
a media fabrication that stemmed from Tutsi deceit. From then
on, the only remaining issues were reciprocal pardons and negotiation between Kigali's Tutsi government and representatives of
Hutu refugees. If these things did not happen, revenge would be
inevitable. In fact, the masses living in the camps were under the
control of the former armed forces and the militias, who taxed at
the rate of at least 10 percent of all international aid. At the end of
1994, about twenty humanitarian organizations protested, and
Médecins sans Frontières (Doctors Without Borders) pulled out.

337

Too late. With the complicity of the Mobutu regime, whose tarnished image was being repolished during these events, notably by France, the camps remained only several kilometers away from the Rwandan border, a position that facilitated raids against survivors and witnesses of genocide in the west of the country.[120]

All this happened as if, in Europe in particular, one wanted to compel Kigali to negotiate with these forces on the basis of a general amnesty and a compromise founded on ethnic dualism. In "balancing" responsibility for 1994, the revisionist ideology effectively aimed at making both camps — Hutu and Tutsi — culpable, a strategy that excused everyone, beginning with the promoters of the genocide. Said another way, here again, the Hutu community in exile was morally taken hostage and used as a "human shield" instead of being freed from the political responsibility that belonged to very specific groups among them. This reproduced the logic of ethnic totalitarianism that had dominated the history of a generation.

This context allows one to understand the deterioration of the situation in Rwanda starting in 1995. The government was manifestly torn between two tendencies. On one side, it was rebuilding the rule of law (for example, the justice system); it refused ethnicism; it reintegrated thousands of former soldiers of the Rwandan Armed Forces, including important officers; it organized debates on reconciliation and "solidarity camps" to encourage the reintegrated functionaries to move beyond racism; it fixed rules of restitution for when Hutu proprietors returned from exile to find their homes and lands occupied by Batutsi; and it launched a house-building campaign (because about 150,000 homes had been destroyed).[121] But on the other side, the government was sensitive to the demands and worries of survivors and especially the Batutsi from the diaspora, who returned en masse (more than 600,000) starting in the summer of 1994. Its recent guerrilla-war past as well as the vigilance necessary in the face of events in Zaire led to an obsession with policing that often transformed all Bahutu into potential suspects and therefore into second-class citizens.

The regime's law-and-order priority got going in two ways. Internally, in April 1995, the government brutally closed camps for displaced persons (notably Kibeho's); these camps were holdovers from the former Turquoise Zone that the French army had created in the west of the country between June and August 1994.[122] After this, Prime Minister Twagiramungu was removed and replaced by Pierre-Célestin Rwigema, who was a member of the MDR), in August 1995; this was followed by the departure of other Hutu officials. All this coincided with the growing grip of the police and the army (both of which were dominated by officers from Uganda, the RPF's first cadres) and with, over time, the abuses and corruption that stem from this kind of situation, as Kigali's press made clear. Externally, starting in 1996, Rwanda began its headlong pursuit of military adventures, which ultimately engulfed all of Central Africa.

During this period, Burundi got bogged down in an impasse born of a dormant civil war. However, the country got over the dangerous hurdle of April 1994 without incident. Cyprien Ntaryamira, dead in Kigali, was replaced by the president of the National Assembly, Sylvestre Ntibantunganya, and the following September the government spelled out a power-sharing agreement among FRODEBU, UPRONA, and a series of small parties, which, in general, were more radical and demanded their part of the cake.[123]

But violence followed: ethnic apartheid reigned in Bujumbura, where the militias laid down the law and the last "mixed" neighborhoods (notably the Muslim suburb of Buyenzi) were "purified" in March 1995. In June 1994, a wing of FRODEBU, led by

339

Interior Minister Léonard Nyangoma (a former rival of Melchior Ndadaye's in FRODEBU and renowned for his virulence), split off and created the National Council for the Defense of Democracy, whose armed wing, the FDD, allied with other extremist rebel groups (PALIPEHUTU in the north and FROLINA in the south). Without access to a rear base in Rwanda, these underground rebels regrouped in South Kivu, from where their radio station, *Voice of Democracy*, broadcast and they did their best to control the regional gold traffic.[124] The forest zone of Kibira, on the crest north of Bujumbura, became their principal regional hideout; from here they controlled the Imbo plains and tried to isolate the capital by carrying out murderous attacks on the roads. Internally, at the ethnic level, the country became a leopard skin of sorts, with "displaced" Batutsi and "regrouped" or repatriated Bahutu (those who fled Rwanda), not to mention the camps for Rwandan Hutu refugees, which were controlled by militias, as were the ones in Zaire.[125] Deadly attacks were carried out against some displaced-persons camps between December 1995 and July 1996, killing hundreds on each occasion. The peasants, caught between a rock and a hard place, were sometimes induced to participate, whether they liked it or not, in rebel actions in which they served as "human shields" and were sometimes seized during the Tutsi-dominated army's reprisal attacks. Since 1995, some observers have spoken of a "genocide in dribs and drabs" or one "in the making" in Burundi, without specifying who is against whom. In reality, the country is torn at its heart: the army and the police follow differing orders, while some leaders reside in Bujumbura and others on the Zairian border or even in Uvira. In March 1996, the states in the region, supported by the European Union, conferred to Julius Nyerere — the former Tanzanian president who was considered "Africa's wise man" because of his former solidarity with the liberation movements of southern Africa

— the role of mediator.[126] Nyerere, who put Burundi more or less in the same category as South Africa, badly judged the complexity of "democratization" in this country, which is surprising after what had just happened in Rwanda. He contemplated a joint Ugandan-Tanzanian military intervention, which seemed about to be implemented with Western backing in June 1996.

But on July 26 — several days after displaced persons were massacred in Bugendana, an event that brought Tutsi exasperation to its height and demonstrated the government's powerlessness — former president Buyoya retook power with the army's support. He was immediately subjected to an embargo by the region's countries; the sanctions remained in place until January 1999. Surprisingly, Burundi withstood these pressures, but at the cost of extraordinary impoverishment and the rise of a parallel, even mafia-style economy. Burundi's policy had two parts: military reinforcements and population regroupments over several months in the zones affected by the rebellion; and gradual development of a partnership with FRODEBU — indicated in 1998 by the creation of two vice presidents, one Muhutu and one Mututsi — as well as participation in negotiations held in Arusha and chaired by Nyerere.

The fragmentation of the Burundian political arena was manifest throughout: factions accumulated in Arusha, while FRODEBU and UPRONA split between moderates and radicals. The international hope for peace predicated on an agreement between the extremist parties seemed illusory,[127] because the "partnership" was so fragile. In fact, Burundi has been trapped for a long time between two extremist camps whose actors refuse to recognize their historical errors: on the one hand is the Tutsi conglomerate, which has always controlled the army and succeeded in limiting the extent of legal actions brought against the leaders of the October 1993 putsch to the prosecution of several underlings; on the other hand is the Hutu conglomerate, which is nostalgic for the 1960s Rwandan model and refuses to admit that this genocidal project has produced an impasse in the country. Because the violence and the interests at play have crystallized so-called ethnic solidarities, the fatigue and clear-sightedness of many Burundians barely see the light of day in the political arena.

Neighboring Rwanda has been caught in the same type of contradiction. But the sympathy created by an internationally recognized genocide makes the country more comprehensible. However, as we have seen, this capital has been squandered in its headlong, Israeli-style law-and-order and militaristic pursuits. Since late 1996, Kivu has been the center of these actions. The explosive situation created by the Hutu refugee camps was coupled with Kivu's own problems. As we have seen, the region's ancient political parcelization has not hindered its ability to resist foreign incursions. Still, land and political disputes between communities — born out of ancient Havu, Shi, and Fuliro kingdoms and decentralized political structures, like the Banande and Bahunde in the north, the Babembe and Barega in the south — proliferated during decolonization.[128] Moreover, the colonial borders had cut collectivities in two and facilitated migrations.

Migrations occurred especially among those groups of Rwandan culture who in the 1960s represented half of North Kivu's population and about a fifth of South Kivu's.[129] Among these, of course, were Tutsi who began arriving in 1959 as well as descendants of immigrant workers from the 1930s; they also included Kinyarwanda speakers present in this region from a time before Congo's border was created, notably in the Goma and Rutshuru regions, the Itombwe massif, and Bembe country above Uvira. These people, who in the 1970s were called Banyarwanda in the north and Banyamulenge in the south, were the offspring of subjects of Rwanda's ancient monarchy, as well as migrants who had fled quarrels related to the Nyiginya dynasty's conquests in the eighteenth century.[130] Upon independence, citizenship was granted only to natives of Congolese territory, and in 1972 it was extended to all Rwandan immigrants; but in 1981, it again was restricted to populations living in the Belgian Congo in 1908. After these recantations by Mobutu's dictatorship, events were sparked off by electoral defeats related to democratization: the Kinyarwanda speakers were excluded from delegations to the 1991 National Conference, and a 1995 resolution by the transition Parliament established in Kinshasa rescinded Zairian nationality from all Rwandophones.[131] Local politicians readily tried their hand at xenophobia and ethnic communitarianism in order to become regional leaders — a rift in Kivu's civil society that had to please the Mobutu crowd. Until 1993, the hostility of those who claimed to be "autochthons" with regard to the Banyarwanda "non-natives" was applied to Bahutu and Batutsi alike. Rwandan-born cleavages and fantasies progressively infiltrated the region: in the 1970s, one of Mobutu's most influential advisers, the Rwandan Tutsi Barthélemy Bisengimana, acquired huge tracts of land on Ijwi Island; in the 1980s, an agricultural cooperative in North Kivu, MAGRIVI, gave voice to the Habyarimana regime's arguments against the Tutsi cattle keepers; and in 1994, the exodus of about a million Rwandan Hutu led to the construction of a front between them and Zairian Hutu to create a veritable Hutu-land in North Kivu by way of massacres that, in 1995–1996, covered the Masisi region in blood and drove 400,000 Tutsi refugees toward Rwanda, supposedly their country. The same fate befell South Kivu's Banyamulenge in July 1996.

Then the surprise came: a blitz operation, led by Tutsi rebels and supported by the Rwandan and Ugandan armies, swept away the refugee camps in South and North Kivu in September–October

1996. In November, 700,000 refugees reentered Rwanda over several days. Soldiers and militias — those who did not reenter disguised as peaceful civilians — continued the war in the Zairian forest and brought the remaining refugees along with them. The hardiest reached the Central African Republic and Brazzaville, but about 200,000 went missing: dead from exhaustion, scattered here and there, but also massacred by the rebels. The massacres captured the most attention because, once again, observers wanted to see them as a "second genocide," counterbalancing 1994's — all the more so since every attempt to conduct an international investigation was sabotaged.

The other side of this war concerned Zaire itself. The rebels included Zairians nostalgic for the Lumumba era, beginning with Laurent-Désiré Kabila, the spokesman of the Alliance of Democratic Forces for the Liberation of Congo, which was formed in Lemera, north of Uvira, in October 1996. Kabila, who was derided for the various kinds of trafficking in which he had engaged, had been an underground supporter of every anti-Mobutist venture over the previous thirty years. This time he leaned on this Kivu rebellion and on Rwandan plans to bring down a regime that had seemed ineradicable. Kinshasa was taken in May 1997, and Zaire again became the "Democratic Congo." But relations between Kabila, who had become president, and his allies rapidly deteriorated. He tried to extricate himself from the situation by leaning on South Africa and especially Angola. The problem of Banyamulenge nationality remained unresolved. Moreover, insecurity reigned in northwestern Rwanda, where militiamen, using Kivu as a rear base, massacred genocide survivors, Batutsi refugees from Masisi, and Bahutu who collaborated with the new regime. The violence took on the intensity of a war in 1998, and the Rwandan Patriotic Army proceeded, as in Burundi, to regroup the population. Little by little, peace returned, but Kivu's neutralization remained more of a priority than ever for Kigali. This in part explains the conflict that broke out in Congo during the summer of 1998: a rebellion began again in Kivu with the support of Rwanda and Uganda. But this time the region's two godfathers were isolated, and they squared off against Angola and Zimbabwe. Even the Congolese Banyarwanda wondered if they were pawns in a larger political plan that only worsened their lot.[132]

Sticking to the discussion of the Great Lakes region, I should note a major political failure after the genocide, namely, the continuation and expansion of the ideology that inspired it. Hatred of the Tutsi, perceived as invaders, has taken over Congo. A race hunt (of which even Malians were victims) occurred in Kinshasa in August 1998, and some Congolese intellectuals started calling the victims "vermin." Each regime in "middle Africa" likened the Tutsi to its own adversaries: for Denis Sassou-Nguesso in Brazzaville, they were equivalent to the "feudal" Bakongo; for Robert Mugabe in Harare, they were brothers of the Ndebele of Zulu ancestry, and so forth. The region's press, in Congo, Zimbabwe, Tanzania, and even Uganda, revisited the theme of a "Hima empire," which had been introduced in the 1960s during Kivu's political quarrels, then reintroduced in the 1980s by the Habyarimana regime, amplified by *Kangura*'s racist campaigns starting in November 1990, and repeated by the French under the variant "black Khmers." These complex situations and the often-contradictory politics are synthesized from a crazy conspiracy theory, which itself is worthy of the *Protocols of the Elders of Zion* in the early twentieth century.[133] Still, fantasy took its course and inspired political-racist alliances, in which the main issue became defending the "Bantu people." In particular, rebels from different countries are networking, including the Rwandan *interahamwe*, the Burundian FDD and PALIPEHUTU, and Ugandan rebels. Everywhere the conflict is pitched as a holy war of "Bantu"

345

against Tutsi infiltrators, who are invited to "return to Ethiopia." This war of massacres is perpetrated in the midst of whistles, drums, and hymns (in western Burundi in 1996, in northwest Rwanda in 1998, and so on). Though its birthplace was the inter-lacustrine zone, this racial ideology, omnipresent in Africanist scholarship during the first half of the century, is today being reconstructed as a contemporary African political ideology.

CONCLUSION

The Fragments of History

After this voyage over nearly three millennia in the Great Lakes region of eastern Africa, we can see why the contemporary crisis is difficult to understand. It is no longer possible to entertain a caricaturized ethnographic notion of tribal atavisms or a simplistic notion of colonizers who destroyed an idyllic setting. But two major areas of interrogation remain open: the first relates to the continuities and ruptures in this history and the second to the future of this ancient African civilization, which today seems threatened with implosion.

A Political Culture's Legacy or Its End?

The history of these African societies, as well as the geography of the countries, underlines their originality and their undeniable specificity. This impression stems less from a claim to homogeneity than from a feeling of overwhelming complexity.

The region's human settlement, its agricultural and pastoral practices, and its dialects reflect a long period of development in a part of Africa where human movements and various influences crossed. These mountainous high plateaus between the lakes, before being presented to the world as bastions of inaccessibility, were a veritable crossroads of the Congolese forest, the Upper

347

Nile, and the East African plateaus; the Bantu linguistic family discussed in detail here and the Nilotic and Cushitic groups still found on the region's northern edges and in its east; cut plant crops and cereal agriculture; banana cider and sorghum beer; land clearing and pastoral transhumance; and the life of lakes and marshes (fishing, hunting, saltworks, and pottery) and that of the agro-pastoral highlands. This meeting was the fruit of an infinite number of displacements and land erosions, contacts and imitations, inventions and common adoptions. The region is blessed with good climate, is rich with diverse soils and plants, and has prospered thanks to some strong basic techniques: the association of cattle keeping and agriculture; the diffusion of the banana a millennium ago; and the mastery of iron metallurgy two millennia ago.

These diverse activities and interests came together more closely than in other African regions with more extensive economies. In these other societies, fishermen, cattle keepers, cereal farmers, and blacksmiths both were spatially separate and belonged to well-delineated castes.[1] Spatial integration in the Great Lakes, and the clashes it engendered, demanded both cultural and political responses. The social world of what ethnographers called the "interlacustrine" civilization was constructed against this diverse background. The commonalities are in fact quite real: similar clan structures, except in Buganda; a categorical cleavage between cattle keepers, agriculturists, and hunters (except, again, in Buganda) with regional variations, social layering, clan intersections, and a marginal but decisive political role; refined oral literature covering every activity; a common universe of origin myths, with its pantheon, its repetitive sequences from one country to another, and its symbols; cults called Cwezi or Bandwa in which everyone could participate, free from disturbing ancestors; sacred woods and their "guardians," the kingdoms' sites of memory whose influence might overshadow that of sovereigns and cross borders; and, transcending everything, the idea of kingship, which expressed itself in the drum's intoxicating language, the reassuring belief in the terrestrial authority of a benefactor spirit, the absolute respect for a power exercised behind the high walls of dynastic capitals (those of the Hinda, Bito, Nyiginya, Ganwa, and so on), and the capacity of the reigning sovereign's representatives to mobilize men's shields, spears, and bows and collect specialized prestations and services from every subject. Monarchies and kingdoms, institutions and territories were constructed over at least three centuries around an idea that was the unwritten constitution of these societies: the need for a central authority, which in turn became a fact of culture, if not of collective psychology.

But harmony and unanimity were not the result: discontents, injustices, revolts, disorders, violence, succession battles, splits, and wars all were real, and, here as elsewhere, the rules were given to excesses, violations, dysfunctions, and ruptures. The authority emanating from the king (*mwami, mukama, mugabe, kabaka*) also gave rise to debates, advice, and arbitrations where linguistic cleverness, intrigue, and bids for influence had free rein, even if there were common references and a complicity of sorts, even in dissidence. Any one dictum could always be opposed to another; a drum can be beaten to different rhythms. These societies were profoundly political, and that may be their most lasting heritage.

At this level, one can see aristocracies emerge, ones that nowhere stem from a social premise or a divine decision. Rather, the aristocracies depended on proximity to the sovereign, achieved in particular by matrimonial alliances and personal connections, which are the nerve center of money-less economies. Indeed, influence resided in trust born out of personal relationships, in oaths, and in resource availability, which allowed one to forge relations that went far beyond the hill or banana garden where one lived.

349

The most important distinction for politics can be found between the lacustrine horizon and the more mountainous domain.
Toward Lake Victoria, and especially in Buganda, the canoe (for
fishing, commerce, and war), coupled with the banana, which
greatly freed up men's time, offered possibilities for expansion and
influence. One finds this situation, but without the same political
consequences, among the salt workers near Lakes Edward, George,
and Albert and among the residents of Lake Tanganyika (from
Bujiji to the Burundian Imbo). By contrast, on the mountains,
wealth and power resided in cattle — a source of food and manure
and the basis for every contract and for the collective imagination.
The possession of large herds became a tool for social ascent and
power, thus benefiting the best-off Tutsi and Hima pastoralists.
This tendency toward crystallizing ranks and "status," which a priori privileged the pastoralists, occurred primarily in the eighteenth
century and ran parallel to the centralization of the western high-
land monarchies. Even if wealth and power are found in extra-agri-
cultural activities, agriculture remained present in patrimony and
in nearly every family's practices (except among some restricted
groups). In addition, the dry plateaus stretching from Lake Albert
to the Malagarasi waned in favor of the most fertile regions, where,
in the east, bushy banana trees could grow and, in the west, residents could have two annual harvests, especially after the diffusion
of the American maize-bean crop combination. Kingdoms such as
Nkore, Rwanda, and Burundi carved out (especially the last two) a
territorial power, because they controlled complementary ecological zones and their agro-pastoral systems were well integrated.
Generally speaking, at this time, nowhere could the social dialectic
be reduced to a Hutu-Tutsi or Hima-Iru cleavage.

The limits of these dynamics became clear in the nineteenth century. Success seemed increasingly tied to expansion into new

areas — whether through raiding, colonizing, or annexing — in particular toward the west. From this point of view, the region's two "heavies" were Buganda and Rwanda. But the irruption of the whites blocked all this in the name of colonial peace and of respect for borders demarcated between 1885 and 1919. The complexity of local societies was such that there were still many ways to pursue different strategies. More or less throughout, parties of collaboration and of resistance took shape, either adapting to or reacting against a foreign presence that was weak in number but technologically superior, militarily unbeatable, and able to bring a much larger horizon under its control.

At first blush, European rule in this African region was not original. The colonizer, whether English, German, or Belgian, set out to win over and use the powers that it considered the most effective, such as the monarchies in Buganda, Rwanda, and Burundi. At the same time, it consolidated them, notably when it came to territorial control. In some cases, it provided a wider foundation to the more modest principalities, for example, Kahigi's "greater Kyamutwara" under the Germans, Ankole under the English, and, to an extent, Bushi under the Belgians. The colonizer thus sought out privileged allies to befriend in the different aristocracies in the royal courts: the Baganwa in Burundi, the Bahinda in Buhaya country and Ankole, the Bega chiefs and the Banyiginya in Rwanda, the Baluzi in Bushi, and so on.

Running parallel — and this is original — the colonial administrations introduced new forms of production destined for export (notably coffee and cotton); they diffused money, the privileged means of taxation; and they opened schools, mainly through Protestant or Catholic missionary societies. Thus the Europeans introduced new logics of profit, money, instruction, technical expertise, and mobility — in short, new logics of individual advancement, which in principle was a break with the ancient lineage networks.

But this region underwent a unique form of acculturation. Its own past was picked up and intensively invested in clichés forged by the anthropology of the late nineteenth century, even before these societies were truly understood. Political hierarchies and social differentiations were assimilated into a schema opposing "true Negroes" to "false Negroes," to "Semito-Hamites" lost "in the heart of darkness" that was Central Africa. The whites wanted to find in the chiefs with whom they aligned themselves lost brothers or at least descendants of pharaohs or Prester John. For a century, this racial schema was so ensconced in the literature on this region — reflecting an obsessive conviction — that any challenge to it was considered bizarre. This classificatory and intrinsically inegalitarian vision gave the illusion of scientifically interpreting hierarchies and of making references to filiation-based identity understandable, while transmuting these African realities into quasi-biological categories with all the authority of a conqueror who knows everything. A veritable scientific ethnicism — or, to put it more crudely, racism — took hold in the heart of these societies. The first generations of Western-educated elites were trained in this perspective, and they were motivated by it. This was especially true in Ruanda-Urundi, where, in the first half of the twentieth century, the terms "Hutu" and "Tutsi" became the alpha and omega of all social engineering. Among the educated youth, who regained control of their countries' destinies in the 1960s, the arrogance of some matched the frustration of others. Consciousness of one's own "ethnic" identity congealed and became legitimized in this way (for example, Baganda against Banyoro or Banyankole and Bantu against Nilotes in Uganda, Bahima against Bairu in Ankole, and especially Tutsi Hamites against Hutu Bantu in the Belgian zone). A fracture crystallized around these identities that extended far beyond exotic decor. Mental structures can be as concrete as economic ones. In the same way, a fundamental contradiction shaped "modernity": new values opened up space for personal aspirations, but these hopes were dashed because of an official policy that locked people in a racial and supposedly traditional framework.

Another observation, which is valid even today, should be made on the conditions of external contact in this isolated region. For decades, external contact was limited to a small number of administrators, missionaries, technicians, and military officers; there were a few dozen foreigners in the beginning and a few hundred on the eve of decolonization. On the far-flung margins of colonial empire, except perhaps in Uganda, strong personalities were the exception. Moreover, in general, the views of the administrators closest to realities on the ground or the most open did not prevail. Rather, in this small world, the views that carried the day were expressed in reports that based their understanding of this "cultural zone" on both ethnological literature and the apparent successes of indirect rule.[2] As for the native "culturalintermediaries," who were trained in the "disciplinary and theological" context that characterized the colonial model (authority and truth always came from the white man), their interest lay in adapting their dialogue to the conquerors' worldviews.[3] They exercised liberty in the interstices of the colonial order by ruse and detour, which was later described by experts in human psychology as typically Bantu or typically Tutsi.[4] The colonized and the colonizers had their strategies and agendas, but the logic of their actions and interests converged over the long run.

Toward Implosion of a Historic Zone or Toward Its Reconstruction?

This dialogue, steeped in misunderstandings, did not end with independence. The new ruling bureaucrats of the south were always in search of "development" aid. For this reason, they often had to deal with officials who, on the basis of brief trips of assessment, reportage, official visit, or humanitarian action, fell back on reports that contained the racial bible discussed above.[5] On the ground, the break in the 1960s was only relative. Cultural, economic, and political dependence did not magically disappear. Guarantees of a scientific nature and truth always came from foreign sources, though this could arouse angry responses or be contested in private.

This being the case, the "paradigm of the yoke," as Jean-François Bayart has written, can be another way of reducing the responsibility of the members of the ruling African strata to a handy abstraction: Beijing, the CIA, the Elysée, or the Christian Democratic International can be used as alibis.[6] During and after colonization, initiatives by elites — whether old, new, or those who were never totally elite — were vital. From this point of view, some actors noted the failure of a generation that did not know how to construct or reconstruct real nations from ancient and modern heritages. Whether their discourse was conservative or revolutionary, the rulers of different republics established during the mid-1960s seemed content with confiscating the state machines left by the colonizers. Moreover, the "revolutionary," "democratic," "national," or "progressive" platforms were full of doublespeak, given the gulf that separated politics in the capitals and life in rural areas, even though the rural areas produced the majority of wealth and were the stakes in every conflict, much to their great unhappiness. Except in Tanzania, this history ended in millions of deaths between the mid-1960s and the close of the century. Never had the region known such terrible tragedy. Never, as in 1994 in Rwanda, had a government planned the extermination of an entire population.

The generation catapulted to the top of the former kingdoms thus squandered the opportunity offered by independence. In its own way, this generation largely reproduced deadly ethnographic divisions. Its leaders were persuaded that ethnic calculations would re-create the categorical logic of the ancient kingdoms at their apogee. The historical investigations carried out during the last few decades in Burundi (in which I participated) revealed a dramatic sociological gulf: on the one hand, peasants were lucid to the cleavages, games, and conflicts of the past, but they were also intimately convinced, and not without nostalgia, of the ancient existence of their nation; on the other hand, the ruling circles in the cities were haunted by a passion — which some admitted and others covered up — about the supremacy and the survival of their ethnic group, a priority in national life, with the realized and imagined practices of exclusion.

Ethnic fundamentalism is justified in three ways: first, through a loyalty to a tradition that is described as inescapable, and has (colonial) texts to support it, a new mythology of "good-to-think," as Claude Lévi-Strauss would have said, one that began with what I have called "legitimized fratricides";[7] second, through the ease of mobilizing masses for elections and violent acts by appealing to their heritage and playing on strong sentiments, such as hate and especially fear; and, third, through the effective realization of ethnicist "prophecies" by a spiral of alternating massacres and a rule of blood that inevitably radicalizes consciousness. A generation after independence, two-thirds of the population, all of whom were born since independence and have grown up with an oral culture that is less and less that of their grandparents and more and more that of radios (we have seen the role an RTLM can play), is convinced of the eternity of the struggles in which they were raised. The ethnicism opposing a Muganda to a Nilote, a Tutsi to a Hutu, a Munyarwanda to a Kivu "autochthon" has become second nature.

355

We have seen the result. The region is threatened with implosion; its ruptures are contagious. The contemporary situation leaves open two possible trajectories. On the one hand, the human, economic, and political chaos might lead to state disintegration and to permanent "warlords," more or less controlled by external regional powers or by a massive international intervention (which is improbable). On the other hand, positive factors might take root. In the new governments in Kampala, Kigali, and Bujumbura, movements have tried to structure civil societies (human-rights associations, mutual-aid associations, intellectual and/or religious groups), and small groups have resisted the racist trend — both of which give hope for new initiatives. Many Kivu citizens believe their future will be decided not in Kinshasa, Kigali, or Brussels but at home. Rwanda has learned how to fare on its own in the face of the most extreme kinds of danger. Burundi has shown that it can fend off a regional embargo. Uganda has shown that it can move beyond a civil war that seemed endless. The region's historical challenge is to escape the ghettos that "Africanist" discourse has signaled are the continent's destiny and redefine itself in contemporary Africa. But this passage to a new regional life can only happen one country at a time. It clearly involves a concerted and broad-based reconstruction that would consist of population flows, economic growth, security, environmental management, and real democratic practice. The institutional forms this will take are waiting to be invented, and they might cut across current borders without necessarily redrawing them. Europe was not made in a day. But in this region of Africa, union is urgent.

A final observation concerns the writing of history. A newsweekly recently reported a Greek's words concerning Turks: "We like the same food, the same music.... If only our two peoples could like each other like brothers, we would burn our history books."[8] Each individual will think of analogous situations. The

Great Lakes region is not unique. But nowhere is amnesia the solution. Not long ago, the need for accurate history mobilized German and French historians. Today UNESCO is taking this kind of initiative in the region. The challenge is enormous because at the heart of the melee the leaders on each side would rather see their antagonistic vision of history, based on age-old grievances, made authentic. But the historian's skill is not in bargaining. It is in reflecting on long-term processes and past ruptures and challenging fixed memories. Africa also needs this pedagogical shift.

Notes

1. Mainly English, French, and German, but also Italian, Dutch, Swahili, Luganda, Kinyarwanda, and so on.

2. See the works of David Newbury, Michèle Wagner, Jan Vansina, Gérard Prunier, Henri Médard (especially his recent "Croissance et crises de la royauté du Buganda au XIXe siècle," Ph.D. thesis, Paris I, 2001), David Schoenbrun, Luc de Heusch, Iris Berger, Jim Freedman, and Jean-Pierre Chrétien. However, it should be noted that the White Fathers had paved the way for this crossing of political-linguistic borders in the late nineteenth century, through their internationalism and their presence in the region's different countries. The watertightness of regional borders worsened after World War I, and independence remedied nothing in this respect. Examples of regional meetings include one in Bujumbura in 1979 (the proceedings of which were published in 1981 as *La Civilisation ancienne des peuples des Grands Lacs*) and one in Bukavu in 1982 (the proceedings of which, unfortunately, were not published because of deficiencies in the Zairian running of the meeting). The "linguistic" cleavage sometimes continues today in ridiculous ways: see, for example, the bibliographies in Mahmood Mamdani (cited below) and in Robertshaw and Taylor, "Climate Change and the Rise of Political Complexity in Western Uganda," neither of which includes French works that are directly related to the subject at hand.

3. Without forgetting the publications of Luc de Heusch, Iris Berger, Emile

359

Mworoha, Peter Schmidt, David Schoenbrun, Jean-Pierre Chrétien, and recently Markus Boller (see the bibliography).

4. Until the works of Chubaka Bishikwabo and David Newbury.

5. For example, the PALIPEHUTU ideology developed in Tanzania's camps in the 1980s; see Malkki, *Purity and Exile*; for an ultra-Tutsi ideology, see Jean Bwejeri, "Mémorandum de Havila: Adresse à son excellence le président Nelson Mandela," Brussels, Jan. 25, 2000, where the Tutsi are presented as Falasha from the White Nile. In both cases, the biblical idea of the "chosen people" is recuperated.

6. White, *Metahistory*; White, *The Content of the Form*.

7. Vansina, *Le Rwanda ancien*; Mamdani, *When Victims Become Killers*.

8. Vansina, *Rwanda ancien*, pp. 33, 177, 245, and 178.

9. Not without contradicting the assertion here and there of a primordialism of "three biologically different populations."

10. Mamdani, *When Victims Become Killers*, p. 38.

11. Mamdani distinguishes, artificially in this case, racism from ethnicism.

12. Except in the illusions of "collective memory," which would lead us to another discussion.

INTRODUCTION: WRITING HISTORY IN AFRICA

1. Milley, *Afrique des Grands Lacs*, p. 5.

2. The film was based on a British novel by H. Rider Haggard, *King Solomon's Mines*, in which the author adventured along the banks of the Zambezi. Another, more recent novel was written in the same vein; see Perugia, *Derniers Rois mages*.

3. These terms were used in international media stories about the 1988 crisis in Burundi.

4. McCullum, *Angels Have Left Us*. This expression — "Was God in Rwanda?" — is found in the French-translation title: *Dieu, était-il au Rwanda? La Faillite des églises* (Paris: L'Harmattan, 1996). — TRANS.

5. An excellent synthesis of recent research on the history of Africa is furnished by Iliffe, *Africans: History of a Continent*. Still, the Africanist terrain

remains encumbered by the classic ethnographic image of the continent's past as a series of wars between chiefs, migrations, and tribal dispersions. An important example in the series Que je-sais? is Stamm, *Histoire de l'Afrique précoloniale.*

6. For more details, see Chrétien, "Afrique des Grands Lacs existe-t-elle?"

7. Burton, *Lake Regions of Central Africa.* Note that the 1862 translation into French used the expression "Great Lakes" in its title. See Richard Burton, *Voyages aux Grands Lacs de l'Afrique orientale,* trans. H. Loreau (Paris: Hachette). — TRANS.

8. The toponymy of the lakes has undergone several episodes. Lake Victoria was called Nyanza by the Swahili merchants who ventured from the eastern coast; lakeside communities named Lakes Albert, Edward, and George Rwitanzige or Rwicanzige (meaning "locust killer"), Rweru (a term that refers to a luminous surface), and Masyoro, respectively. Dictators Mobutu and Idi Amin wanted to lend their names to the first two lakes — an initiative that did not last long. The British royal family of the nineteenth century has had more longevity.... In these pages, I will use the denominations listed in current atlases, while being conscious of their Eurocentric dimension.

9. For example, Czekanowski, *Ethnographie.*

10. See Chilver, "Feudalism in the Interlacustrine Kingdoms"; Hertefelt, Trouwborst, and Scherer, *Anciens Royaumes*; and Maquet, "Institutionalisation féodale."

11. See, for example, Centre de Civilisation Burundaise, *Civilisation ancienne des peuples des Grands Lacs.*

12. Gourou, *Afrique*; Gourou, *Densité de la population du Ruanda-Urundi*; Morgan, *East Africa*; Raison, *Afrique des Hautes Terres*; and Chrétien, ed., *Histoire rurale.*

13. Hertefelt, Trouwborst, and Scherer, *Anciens Royaumes*, p. 4.

14. Maquet, *Système des relations sociales*; his translation into English, *Premise of Inequality in Ruanda,* reinforced the grip this book had on the marketplace of ideas concerning this region of Africa. Fallers, *Bantu Bureaucracy*; Fallers, *King's Men*; Oberg, "Kingdom of Ankole in Uganda"; Georges Balandier, *Anthropologie politique* (Paris: Presses Universitaires de France, 1967) [English translation: Balandier, *Political Anthropology* — TRANS.]; Maquet, "Institutionalisation

féodale"; Vidal, "Economie de la société féodale rwandaise"; Maquet, *Power and Society in Africa*. The importance of a historical orientation notably influenced the later work of Claudine Vidal on Rwanda.

15. For examples of this type of racial interpretation, see Seligman's book *Races of Africa*, republished until 1966. See p. 96: "The civilizations of Africa are the civilizations of the Hamites." See also the anthropologist Erny, *Rwanda 1994*, p. 36: "In Europe, racial theory is a domain rife with something akin to intellectual terrorism. If in biological terms ... the racial factor seems to have little importance, the same is not evidently true for social questions"; see also the historian Lugan, *Histoire du Rwanda*, p. 27: "In Africa as in everywhere else in the world, 'race' comes before ethnicity. It predates ethnicity too."

16. For definitions of the spear and the cow civilization, see Herskovits, "Cattle Complex in East Africa"; he strongly influenced Maquet's *Civilizations of Black Africa*, notably pp. 113–32. For German diffusionist ethnology, see Ankermann, "Kulturkreise und Kulturschichten in Afrika"; and Stuhlmann, *Handwerk und Industrie in Ostafrika*; also see Chrétien, "Ethnologie et économie." Stuhlmann, a naturalist and a high civil-service officer in East Africa who finished his career as director of the German Colonial Institute, wrote: "With regard to every feature of civilization in Africa, we will always have to ask ourselves if it did not just come from the exterior, that is to say from Asia" (p. 77). For an example of the Weberian approach, see the work of the anthropologist John Beattie on the Bunyoro kingdom in Uganda; Beattie's research was conducted between 1951 and 1955 and synthesized in *Nyoro State*. For examples of the Marxist debates, see Botte, "Processus de Formation"; and Vidal, "De la Contradiction sauvage." For a structuralist approach, see Heusch, *Rois nés d'un coeur de vache*; also see Vansina's critique "Is Elegance Proof?"

17. Rotberg (ed.), *Africa and Its Explorers*. For lists of explorations in East Africa, see Langlands, "Early Travelers in Uganda," and Roberts, "Bibliography of Primary Sources for Tanzania, 1799–1899." The expression "armchair geographers" was used in Cooley, *Inner Africa Laid Open*.

18. Oliver, *Missionary Factor in East Africa*; Renault, *Afrique centrale*.

19. Catalogs for the sources can be found in Matthews and Wainwright,

Guide to Manuscripts and Documents in the British Isles Relating to Africa; Harlow and Chilver (eds.), *History of East Africa*, vol. 2, pp. 701–705; Grieken-Taverniers, *Colonisation belge en Afrique centrale*; Franz and Geissler, *Deutsch-Ostafrika-Archiv*; and Lamey, *Archives des Pères Blancs, Maison Généralice*.

20. For a Belgian example, see Deslaurier, "Du nouveau pour l'histoire politique."

21. In addition to the bibliographies in UNESCO's *General History of Africa* and *Cambridge History of Africa*, see Chrétien (ed.), *Histoire rurale*; Mworoha, *Peuples et rois*; Iliffe, *Modern History of Tanganyika*; Prunier and Calas (eds.), *Ouganda contemporain*; Mworoha et al. (eds.), *Histoire du Burundi*; Rodegem, *Documentation bibliographique sur le Burundi*; Hertefelt and Lame, *Société, culture et histoire du Rwanda*; Vellat et al. (eds.), *Bibliographie historique du Zaïre à l'époque coloniale (1880–1960)*; and Bishikwabo and Newbury, "Recent Historical Research in the Area of Lake Kivu."

22. Coupland, *East Africa and Its Invaders*, p. 14; Vansina, *Oral Tradition: A Study in Historical Methodology*; Vansina, *Oral Tradition as History*; and Perrot, ed., *Sources orales de l'histoire de l'Afrique*.

23. The confrontation between oral narratives, taking the form of traditions, and written accounts reveals the surprising exactitude of many facts, the precision of the original information on local politics, and the backward-looking interpretation of unpublished events — a source of another problem. See Chrétien, *Burundi, l'histoire retrouvée*, pp. 107–19; and Chrétien, "Passage de l'expédition d'Oscar Baumann."

24. Burundian peasants distinguish clearly between *imigani*, "legends, dicta, imaginary stories," and *amakuru*, "news, information."

25. Vansina, *Oral Tradition as History*, p. 31: "Most situations and trends in tradition seem to be summaries of events generalized." See also Chrétien, "Mwami Ntare dans l'histoire du Burundi."

26. Cohen, "Survey of Interlacustrine Chronology." On the uncertainty of the lists, see Henige, *Chronology of Oral Tradition*. On Rwanda, see Nkurikiyimfura, "Révision d'une chronologie"; and David Newbury, "Trick Cyclists?"

27. Gray, "Eclipse Maps," and Gray, "Annular Eclipse Maps"; Webster (ed.),

Chronology, Migration, and Drought in Interlacustrine Africa; Chrétien and Bahenduzi, "Ntare Rushatsi."

28. Chrétien, "Confronting the Unequal Exchange Between the Oral and the Written"; Chrétien, "Traditionnistes lettrés du Burundi à l'école des bibliothèques missionaires (1940–1960)."

29. *Evolué* is a term used in Belgian territories to refer to educated elites. — TRANS. For a discussion of the term and its implications, see Young and Turner, *Rise and Decline of the Zairian State*, pp. 111–14.

30. Vidal, *Sociologie des passions*, pp. 45–61.

31. The *biru* was the Rwandan king's council of advisers, who were custodians of the royal codes. — TRANS.

32. Lacger, *Ruanda*.

33. Chrétien, "Du Hirsute au Hamite"; Chrétien, "Nouvelles Hypothèses sur les origines du Burundi." This is how the "known" dynastic list passed suddenly from two cycles of four kings to four cycles and how the number IV was attached to the name of the era's king — Mwambutsa. The Burundians did not want to be demeaned by their Rwandan brother-enemies, with whom they had been aligned for more than twenty reigns!

34. Detienne, *Creation of Mythology*, p. 81.

35. Twaddle, "On Ganda Historiography"; see also Smith, "Personnages de légende."

36. Chrétien, "Arbres et les rois."

37. Peter R. Schmidt, *Historical Archaeology*.

38. Sutton, "Antecedents of the Interlacustrine Kingdoms"; Chrétien, "Empire des Bacwezi."

39. On the mythologies inspired by the massive walls of southern Africa, see Summers, *Zimbabwe: A Rhodesian Mystery*.

40. Chrétien, "Refus et les perspectives d'une 'Histoire rurale' en Afrique des Grands Lacs"; Vellut, "Pour une Histoire sociale de l'Afrique centrale."

41. On the resurgence of Cwezi mythology in Uganda, see, for example, the story in the June 21, 1994, issue of the semiofficial *New Vision*; this came in the context of a movement to restore monarchies in the country. The cartogra-

phy of Rwanda was inspired by the abbot Kagame and published by La Coopération Française; see Prioul and Sirven (eds.), *Atlas du Rwanda*, map 12. In Burundi
in October 1993 and in Rwanda between April and June 1994, Hutu militias
killed Tutsi to send them back to Egypt (Misri); in November 1992, a Rwandan
professor prophetically knew that Tutsi corpses would be returned to Ethiopia
via the rivers that feed the Nile!

42. Malkki, *Purity and Exile*. See also Chrétien, *Le Défi de l'ethnisme*, notably
the section "L'Immatriculation ethnique, vocation de l'africanisme interlacustre?" pp. 11–28.

43. See Mbembe, *Afriques indocile*.

44. Malkki, *Purity and Exile*, p. 104. On this debate in historiography, see
Schoenbrun, "Past Whose Time Has Come"; and Carbone, "Etnie, storiografia e
storia del Burundi e del Rwanda contemporanei."

45. Bloch, *Feudal Society*, pp. 90–92. See Chrétien and Triaud (eds.), *Histoire d'Afrique*.

46. Vidal-Naquet, "Atlantide et les nations."

47. Anonymous, *Essai d'histoire*.

CHAPTER ONE: AN ANCIENT HUMAN SETTLEMENT AND ITS ENIGMAS

1. Regarding "Bantu migrations," see the observations of Vansina, "New
Linguistic Evidence and the 'Bantu Expansion,'" p. 191.

2. Chrétien, "Alibi ethnique dans les politiques africaines," and Chrétien,
"Ethnies et ethnisme."

3. For a recent synthesis, see Schoenbrun, "Contours of Vegetation Change
and Human Agency in Eastern Africa's Great Lakes Region, ca. 2000 B.C.
to ca. A.D. 1000." Also see Roche et al., "Evolution du paléoenvironnement
quatenaire au Rwanda et au Burundi"; Bonnefille and Riollet, "Histoire
forestière du Burundi d'apres l'étude des tourbières"; Livingstone, "Environmental Changes in the Nile Headwaters"; and Vincens, "Paléoenvironnements
du bassin Nord-Tanganyika (Zaïre, Burundi, Tanzanie) au cours des 13 derniers
mille ans.

4. Sutton, "Aquatic Civilization of Middle Africa."

5. Chrétien, "Peuples et leur histoire avant la colonisation"; Mworoha et al. (eds.), *Histoire du Burundi*, pp. 102–103 and 187–88 (maps).

6. Coupez et al., "Classification d'un échantillon de langues bantoues d'après la lexicostatistique," p. 152, and Guthrie, *Classification of the Bantu Languages*. The demarcation between Zones D and E strangely coincides with the boundary between the Francophone and Anglophone colonial territories!

7. The radicals designating languages are preceded by a prefix: *ru-* (or *lu-*), *ki-* (or *gi-*), or *ma-*. The names of the corresponding countries are generally preceded by the prefix Bu- (Buganda, Burundi, Buzinza, Bushi) with the exceptions of Rwanda and Nkore.

8. Chrétien, "Bantous."

9. Bleek, *Über den Ursprung der Sprache*, p. xxii.

10. Meinhof, *Gründzuge einer vergleichenden Grammatik der Bantusprachen*.

11. Seligman, *Races of Africa*, p. 164.

12. Among the partisans of this theory are the erudite French colonial Maurice Delafosse and the missionary-historians of Rwanda, including Pagès, *Au Ruanda*, pp. 11–13, and Lacger, *Ruanda*, p. 49.

13. This approach can still be found in Van Bulck, "Les Langues bantoues," pp. 847–48.

14. Johnston, "Survey of the Ethnography of Africa," p. 413. The same theories can be found in Stuhlmann, *Handwerk und Industrie in Ostafrika*.

15. See the example of an American observer who was in the region from 1919 to 1920: Shantz, "Agricultural Regions of Africa," p. 347. For many years, the same prejudice prevented seeing the walls of Zimbabwe, in the heart of Bantu-speaking country, as other than the work of Phoenicians or Sabaeans.

16. Vansina, "Bantu in the Crystal Ball, I," and Vansina, "Bantu in the Crystal Ball, II."

17. The north-south circulation network can be found in Johnston's cartography in Chrétien, "Bantous," p. 54. Johnston, *Comparative Study of the Bantu and Semi-Bantu Languages*.

18. Radiocarbon measurements provide a new source of dating, but one that, for the time being, has a margin of error between roughly two hundred and four hundred years.

19. Greenberg, *Studies in African Linguistic Classification*, and Murdock, *Africa: Its Peoples and Their Culture History*.

20. Hiernaux and Maquet, *Cultures préhistoriques*, p. 102; Posnansky "Pottery Types from Archaeological Sites in East Africa." On these questions, see Mworoha's bibliography and his synthesis in Mworoha et al. (eds.), *Histoire du Burundi*, pp. 92–100.

21. Guthrie, *Comparative Bantu*, and Guthrie, "Some Developments in the Prehistory of the Bantu Languages."

22. Oliver, "Problem of the Bantu Expansion."

23. Hiernaux, "Bantu Expansion."

24. See Greenberg, "Linguistic Evidence Regarding Bantu Origins"; Ehret, "Bantu Origins and History"; and Heine, "Zur genetischen Gliederung der Bantu-Sprachen." Also see syntheses in Dalby (ed.), *Language and History in Africa*, and Bouquiaux (ed.), *Expansion bantoue*.

25. Posnansky, "Bantu Genesis — Archaeological Reflections"; Soper, "General Review of the Early Iron Age of the Southern Half of Africa."

26. Maret and Nsuka, "History of Bantu Metallurgy."

27. Oliver and Fagan, "Emergence of Bantu Africa."

28. Phillipson, *Later Prehistory of Eastern and Southern Africa*.

29. Ki-Zerbo, *Histoire de l'Afrique noire*, p. 91.

30. Schmidt, *Historical Archaeology*.

31. Grunderbeek, Roche, and Doutrelepont, "Age du fer"; Vignati, "*Du Fourneau à la fosse*." For a review, see Chrétien, "Ages du fer dans la région des Grands Lacs," and Claudette Vanacker, in Mworoha et al. (eds.), *Histoire du Burundi*, chap. 3 and 4.

32. Célis and Nzikobanyanka, *Métallurgie traditionnelle du Burundi*; Célis, "Métallurgie traditionnelle au Burundi, au Rwanda et au Buha"; and Chrétien, "Production du fer."

33. Noten, *Histoire archéologique du Rwanda*, p. 29; Posnansky, "Terminol-

ogy in the Early Iron Age of Eastern Africa with Particular Reference to the Dimple-Based Wares of Lolui Island, Uganda."

34. Soper, "Early Iron Age Pottery Types from East Africa"; Noten, "Early Iron Age in the Interlacustrine Region."

35. Desmedt, "Poteries anciennes décorées à la roulette dans la région des grands lacs." An analogous scheme for "A" pottery (Urewe) and "B" pottery (roulettes) was identified in Rwanda and Burundi. See Hiernaux and Maquet, *Cultures préhistoriques*. Several years ago, a propagandist for the Rwandan Hutu republic deduced from this evidence of a Nilotic invasion that destroyed another Bantu Zimbabwe in the lakes region. See Paternostre de la Mairieu, *Rwanda: Son Effort de Développement*, p. 24.

36. Sutton, *Archaeology of the Western Highlands of Kenya*, p. 152.

37. Sutton, "Antecedents of the Interlacustrine Kingdom."

38. Twaddle, "Towards an Early History of the East African Interior."

39. Sassoon, "Kings, Cattle, and Blacksmiths"; Mturi, "Ancient Civilisation of the Peoples of the Great Lakes."

40. Vansina, "New Linguistic Evidence and the 'Bantu Expansion.'"

41. *Ibid.*, pp. 191–92.

42. The discourse on the Ionians and the Dorians of ancient Greece has for years been taken literally. According to the "Celtic migrations" theory, a civilization would have been transported from Danubian Europe to the banks of the English Channel and the Mediterranean. See Sergent, "Penser — et mal penser — les Indo-Européens (note critique)"; Renfrew, *Archaeology and Language*. The "waves" model, which the linguist Johannes Schmidt introduced in 1872, in *Verwantschaftsverhaltnisse der indogermanischen Sprachen*, has more recently been developed with regards to Europe by Colin Renfrew; see Renfrew, *Archaeology and Language*, pp. 105–111.

43. This can also be seen by juxtaposing vegetal essences taken from several phytogeographic landscapes.

44. Clark, "Spread of Food Production in Sub-Saharan Africa"; Harlan, de Wet, and Stemler (eds.), *Origins of African Plant Domestication*; Harlan, *Crops & Man*; Gwynne, "Origin and Spread of Some Domestic Food Plants of Eastern

Africa"; Vansina, "Esquisse historique de l'agriculture en milieu forestier (Afrique équatoriale)"; Chrétien (ed.), *Histoire rurale*.

45. Some examples include, for Uganda, Emin Pascha, *Tagebücher von Emin Pascha*; and Johnston, *Uganda Protectorate*. For examples of the area west of Lake Victoria, see Grant, "Summary of Observations on the Geography, Climate, and Natural History of the Lake Region of Equatorial Africa"; Richter, "Einige weitere ethnographische Notizen über den Bezirk Bukoba" and "Notizen über Lebensweise, Zeitrechnung, Industrie und Handwerk der Bewohnwer des Bezirks Bukoba." For Rwandan examples, see Czekanowski, *Ethnographie*; and Pagès, "Flore domestique du Rwanda." For Burundi, see Meyer, *Barundi*. Inventories can be found in Heremans and Bart, "Agriculture et paysages rwandais à travers les sources missionaires (1900–1950)"; and Chrétien, "Agronomie, consommation, et travail."

46. Formerly called *Coleus dazo*, identified more exactly as *Plectranthus esculentus* or *Solenostemon rotundifolius*.

47. The first observers sometimes defined the coffee tree as arabica and sometimes as robusta. See Jervis, "History of *Robusta* Coffee in Bukoba." It is identified with precision in Pernès et al., *Gestion des ressources génétiques des plantes*, vol. 1. These grains were gnawed on or sucked, either as stimulants or during certain social rituals.

48. Schoenbrun, "Early history in Eastern Africa's Great Lakes Region." Synthesized by the author in Schoenbrun, "We Are What We Eat," and in Schoenbrun, *Green Place, Good Place*.

49. A linguistic table is in Prunier and Calas (eds.), *Ouganda contemporaine*, p. 22. A map is in Chrétien, "Afrique noire, histoire précoloniale. I. L'Afrique orientale," p. 108. The central Sudanic group is the distant ancestor of the Lugbara of northwest Uganda; the proto-Nilotic group is the ancestor of the Lwo, the Karamojong, the Kalenjin, and other groups in the outermost regions of contemporary Uganda, Kenya, and Tanzania; and the southern Cushitic group is the distant ancestor of the Iraqw in the Tanzanian Rift.

50. Schoenbrun, "We Are What We Eat," p. 26. His reasoning is based on the comparative study of specialized vocabularies and their position (regarding

innovations or loanwords) in the chronology of the respective languages. See also Ehret, "Agricultural History in Central and Southern Africa, c. 1000 B.C. to A.D. 500."

51. Chrétien, "Anciens Haricots."

52. *Musa sapientium* type AAA, a very original group, corresponding to the *-toke* radical in all the languages of the region. McMaster, "Speculations on the Coming of the Banana to Uganda." On linguistics and agriculture, see De Langhe et al., "Plantain in the Early Bantu World"; and Philippson and Bahuchet, "Cultivated Crops and Bantu Migrations in Central and Eastern Africa."

53. Schoenbrun, "Cattle Herds and Banana Gardens."

54. Kottak, "Ecological Variables in the Origin and Evolution of African States."

55. Chrétien, "Années de l'éleusine, du sorgho et du haricot"; Chrétien, *Burundi, l'histoire retrouvée*, pp. 79–103; and Chrétien, "Anciens Haricots."

56. Rodegem, *Sagesse kirundi*; Dion, *Devinettes du Rwanda*; and Chrétien, "Agronomie, consommation et travail," pp. 149–53.

57. Chrétien, "Agronomie, consommation et travail," pp. 157–60. Vansina made an analogous observation with regard to Central Africa.

58. Sutton, "East Africa Before the Seventh Century"; Denbow, "New Look at the Later Prehistory of the Kalahari." See the synthesis in Nkurikiyimfura, *Gros Bétail et la société rwandaise*, pp. 21–32.

59. A. Gautier in Noten, *Histoire archéologique du Rwanda*, pp. 104–20; Grunderbeek, Roche, and Doutrelepont, "Age du fer."

60. Epstein, *Origin of the Domestic Animals of Africa.*

61. Schoenbrun, "We Are What We Eat"; Ehret, "Cattle-Keeping and Milking in Eastern and Southern African History"; Wrigley, "Cattle and Language Between the Lakes."

62. Schoenbrun, "Cattle Herds and Banana Gardens."

63. Andrew Reid, "Role of Cattle in the Later Iron Age Communities of Southern Africa."

64. Sutton, "Antecedents of the Interlacustrine Kingdoms."

65. *Ibid.*; Steinhart, "Herders and Farmers"; Sutton, "Irrigation and Soil

Conservation in African Agricultural History" (for another example of an ancient ecological crisis in East Africa).

66. The relationship between sorghum and cattle has been durable; see Chrétien, "Sorgho dans l'agriculture, la culture et l'histoire du Burundi."

67. Speke, *Journal of the Discovery of the Source of the Nile*, p. 203.

68. Götzen, *Durch Afrika von Ost nach West*, pp. 180, 187, 188, and 190–91.

69. Burgt, *Dictionnaire Français-Kirundi*, p. 75; Césard, "Muhaya," *Anthropos* 30 (1935), p. 94; Sasserath, *Le Ruanda-Urundi*, pp. 27–28; *Point*, Sept. 4, 1988; *Economist*, Aug. 27, 1988.

70. Czekanowski, *Ethnographie*, p. 49; Gille, "Notes sur l'organisation des Barundi," p. 75; Posnansky, "Kingship, Archaeology, and Historical Myth," p. 6.

71. See the photo in Johnston, *Uganda Protectorate*, vol. 1, p. 249.

72. Hiernaux, *Caractères physiques des populations du Ruanda et de l'Urundi*.

73. Deschamps et al., *Histoire générale de l'Afrique noire, de Madagascar, et des Archipels*, vol. 1, p. 65.

74. See the synthesis of Lainé, "Génétique des Populations," notably ch. 3 on "La Géopolitique des polymorphismes africains."   •

75. Hubinont, Hiernaux, and Massart-Guiot, "Blood Groups of the ABO, MN, and CDE-cde Systems in the Native Populations of Ruanda-Urundi Territories"; Hiernaux, "Données génétiques sur six populations de la République du Congo"; Hiernaux, "Début de l'âge des métaux dans la région des Grands Lacs"; Hiernaux, *Découvertes récentes sur l'origine de l'homme*, p. 32.

76. Ssebabi and Nzaro, "Distribution of ABO and Rh(D) Phenotypes in Uganda."

77. Cavalli-Sforza, *Great Human Diasporas*.

78. Hiernaux, *People of Africa*; Langaney, *Hommes*, pp. 159–84.

79. Lainé, "Génétique des populations." A study carried out in Bujumbura in the beginning of the 1980s set out to show the relationship between Burundian and Rwandan Tutsi in contrast to that between Burundian Hutu and Zairian "Bantu." The population was sampled mostly from cities and was based a priori on the historical pertinence of the Bantu/Hamite scheme, as per Hiernaux in 1954. See Le Gall, Le Gall, Godin, and Serre, "Study of Genetic Markers of the

Blood in Four Central African Population Groups." Observations can also be made about studies that investigate the presence or lack of a lactic enzyme, which might be a quasi racial marker.

80. Chrétien, "Mythes et stratégies," pp. 305–307; Mworoha, *Peuples et rois*, pp. 66–67; and Beattie, *Nyoro State*, pp. 36–37. The radical -*hanga* also refers to a superior divine being.

81. From now on, when broaching these societies' internal dynamics, we also will respect language, in particular the use of prefixes. See p. 19. We therefore will speak of a Muhima, several Bahima, Kahima (the little Hima), and so on.

82. See Vansina, *Légende du passé*, p. 113.

83. Elam, *Social and Sexual Roles of Hima Women*.

84. Some examples come from southern Ethiopia and from the Incas of South America.

85. Maquet, *Système des relations sociales*. See Heusch, *Rwanda et la civilisation interlacustre*, pp. 364–74.

86. Desmarais, "Rwanda des anthropologues."

87. Hertefelt, Trouwborst, and Scherer, *Anciens Royaumes*, notably pp. 17, 23, 120–21, 178, and 184.

88. Anacleti and Nagala, "Cattle Complex in the Ancient West Lake Kingdoms," p. 158.

89. Cochet, "Burundi: Quelques Questions."

90. Karugire, *History of the Kingdom of Nkore*, pp. 41 and 66. On the possible conjunction of exchange logics and a domination process, also see Chrétien, "Echanges et hiérarchies," and Chrétien, "Agronomie, consommation et travail," pp. 157–70.

91. For the Marxist perspective, see Botte, "Agriculteurs/éleveurs et domination du groupe pastoral." Vidal, "Rwanda des anthropologues et le fétichisme de la vache"; Vidal, "Economie de la société féodale rwandaise." Note that, in the first work, Vidal attributed the "fetishism of the cow" to anthropologists like Maquet more than to Rwandan society. Czekanowski, *Ethnographie*, pp. 261–63. Chrétien, "Les Identités Hutu et Tutsi: Perspectives historiques et manipulations politiques," in Chrétien (ed.), *Burundi, l'histoire retrouvée*, pp. 316–19.

92. Catharine Newbury, "Ethnicity in Rwanda."

93. Ndikuriyo, "Contrats de bétail."

94. Johnston, *Uganda Protectorate*, vol. 2, pp. 600–602; Rehse, *Kiziba, Land und Leute*, pp. 105–110.

95. Ntezimana, "Histoire, culture et conscience nationale," esp. pp. 488–89.

CHAPTER TWO: THE EMERGENCE OF KINGSHIP: POWER AND RELIGION

1. Stanley, *Through the Dark Continent*, vol. 1, pp. 393–94.

2. Kandt, *Caput Nili*, vol. 2, pp. 12–15. The text also was published in Mworoha, *Peuples et rois*, pp. 311–12. Note that on this day Kandt had not seen the king himself, but rather a double, who, for safety reasons, was presented to foreign visitors, particularly those who were a priori judged to be evil.

3. The word "clan" is of Scottish origin and was adopted by Anglo-Saxon anthropologists at the end of the 1860s.

4. Sundkler, *Bara Bukoba*, p. 15.

5. Mworoha, *Peuples et rois*, pp. 30–46. On an analogous situation in western Uganda, see Buchanan, "Perceptions of Ethnic Interactions in the East African Interior."

6. See the biography of Bireme, who lost his father but had been welcomed in the royal court after having recited his clan genealogy: Mworoha, *Peuples et rois*, pp. 175–77.

7. For Burundi, see Rodegem, *Onomastique rundi*, pp. 77–95; for Bunyoro and Buhaya, see Cory and Hartnoll, *Customary Law of the Haya Tribe, Tanganyika Territory*, pp. 263–84; for the Buhavu, see David Newbury, *Kings and Clans*; and for northern Buha, see Van Sambeek, *Croyances et coutumes des Baha*, vol. 2, pp. 26–30.

8. Nsimbi, "Clan System in Buganda"; Fallers, *King's Men*, pp. 71–92. The names of clan subdivisions literally mean in Luganda: home rocks, ficus trees, and descent lines.

9. Beattie, *Nyoro State*, pp. 249–56; Roscoe, *Bakitara or Banyoro*, pp. 14–18.

10. Hertefelt, *Clans du Rwanda ancien*; Karugire, *History of the Kingdom of Nkore*, pp. 71–78.

11. For the Rwandan example, see Nyagahene, "Histoire et peuplement."

12. Buchanan, "Kitara Complex."

13. Delmas, *Généalogies de la noblesse (les Batutsi) du Ruanda*; and Pagès, *Au Ruanda*.

14. Nyagahene, "Histoire et Peuplement," recalls that the term *ubwoko* was used to designate "ethnic groups" only after the 1950s and after the politicization of this entity. Other sources suggest a link between this semantic evolution and making ethnic groups official on identity cards starting in the 1930s.

15. Géraud, "Settlement of the Bakiga"; Hertefelt, *Clans du Rwanda ancien*, p. 6; Mworoha, *Peuples et rois*, pp. 35–38; and David Newbury, *Kings and Clans*, pp. 120–25.

16. Jervis, "History of *Robusta* Coffee in Bukoba," p. 56.

17. Cited in Mworoha, *Peuples et rois*, p. 37.

18. David Newbury, "Clans of Rwanda."

19. Complete tables are in Mworoha, *Peuples et rois*, pp. 44–45.

20. Beattie, *Nyoro State*, p. 167.

21. Karugire, *History of the Kingdom of Nkore*, p. 71.

22. Fallers, *King's Men*, pp. 88–89.

23. Nahimana, "Principautés Hutu du Rwanda septentrional"; Nahimana, *Rwanda* (a thesis on the Bushiru).

24. Chrétien, "Roi, religion, lignages en Afrique orientale précoloniale."

25. Were, "Western Bantu Peoples from A.D. 1300 to 1800"; Oliver, "Afrique orientale," pp. 434–36; and Fage, *Atlas of African History*, pp. 21–22.

26. Wrigley, "Some Thoughts on the Bacwezi"; Wrigley, "Story of Rukidi."

27. Chrétien, "Empire des Bacwezi."

28. Fisher, *Twilight Tales of the Black Baganda*; Roscoe, *Bakitara or Banyoro*, pp. 323–27; Gorju, *Entre le Victoria, l'Albert et l'Edouard*, pp. 38–55; Nicolet, "Essai historique."

29. Rehse, *Kiziba, Land und Leute*, pp. 37–39; Césard, "Comment les Bahaya interprètent leurs origines."

30. Lanning, "Masaka Hill."

31. Roscoe, *Bakitara or Banyoro*, p. 87.

32. Cory and Hartnoll, *Customary Laws*, p. 272.

33. Welbourn, "Some Aspects of Kiganda Religion"; Zuure, *Croyances et pratiques religieuses des Barundi*; Van Sambeek, *Croyances et coutumes des Baha*, vol. 2, pp. 49–53.

34. Kiwanuka, *History of Buganda*, pp. 35–43.

35. Berger, "Deities, Dynasties, and Oral Traditions."

36. Webster and Herring, "Labongo."

37. "Kingdom of Kitara" is an ancient toponym located near the south of this area that was taken up again in the twentieth century to characterize the Bunyoro under the Bacwezi.

38. Wrigley, "Story of Rukidi"; Nicolet, "Essai historique," pp. 194–222; Mworoha, *Peuples et rois*, pp. 76–77.

39. K.W. (Tito Winyi, king of Bunyoro), "Kings of Bunyoro-Kitara"; Nyakatura, *Anatomy of an African Kingdom*, pp. 26–27. Already in Johnston, *Uganda Protectorate*, p. 595.

40. Besides recognizing the symbolism of base colors, one should know that the first Europeans seen by these Africans were perceived not as whites but as "reds."

41. Speke, *Journal of the Discovery of the Source of the Nile*, pp. 246–49. The Galla are more precisely the Oromo of Ethiopia, the term "Galla" being only a sobriquet.

42. Baker, *Albert N'yanza*, pp. 107 and 187–88.

43. Speke, *Journal of the Discovery of the Source of the Nile*, pp. 246 and 248.

44. Emin Pascha, "Zur Ethnologie des Albert-Sees," pp. 351–55; Stuhlmann, *Mit Emin Pascha ins Herz von Afrika*, pp. 651 and 713–15.

45. Johnston, *Uganda Protectorate*, vol. 2, pp. 594–96 and 600–602. He apparently was reusing ideas dear to Protestant missionaries; Czekanowski, *Ethnographie*, p. 55; Gorju, *Entre le Victoria, l'Albert et l'Edouard*, p. 50; Fisher, *Twilight Tales of the Black Baganda*, pp. 39–40; Nicolet, *Mucondozi*, pp. 1–2.

46. Nyakatura, *Anatomy of an African Kingdom*, pp. 17 and 27.

47. On the history of archaeological excavations and their interpretations, see Chrétien, "Empire des Bacwezi," pp. 1345–50; on the contemporary status

of the question, see Sutton, "Antecedents of the Interlacustrine Kingdoms," and linguistic map on p. 481 below.

48. Oliver, "East African Interior," p. 632. Also see Oliver, "Question About the Bachwezi"; and Oliver, "Interior c. 1500–1840."

49. The second theory was already that of the German naturalist Franz Stuhlmann in *Mit Emin Pascha ins Herz von Afrika*. This theory was taken up again by authors who saw in the Cwezi religion the manifestation of a culture that preceded the Hima conquest and was in opposition to it; see Berger, "Kubandwa Religious Complex."

50. Sutton, "Antecedents of the Interlacustrine Kingdoms," p. 58.

51. Roscoe, *Banyankole*, p. 24; Chrétien, *Burundi, l'histoire retrouvée*, p. 356.

52. Nicolet, "Régions qui se détachèrent du Kitara et devinrent des royaumes indépendants"; Jean-Baptiste Lapioche, "Notes sur le Buhaya"; Mors, "Geschichte der Bahaya," pp. 13–21; Thiel, "Buzinza unter der Dynastie der Bahinda"; Rehse, *Kiziba, Land und Leute*, pp. 285–88; *District Book of Bukoba*, pp. 19–21. For syntheses, see Heusch, *Rwanda et la civilisation interlacustre*, pp. 29–35; Mworoha, *Peuples et rois*, pp. 83–87; Berger, "Kubandwa Religious Complex," pp. 49–54.

53. Césard, "Histoires des rois du Kyamtwara d'après l'ensemble des traditions des familles régnantes," pp. 533–45.

54. Chrétien, "Empire des Bacwezi," p. 1362. Even in Burundi the White Fathers tried to prove that Ruhinda was the dynastic ancestor.

55. Kakaira, *Histoire d'Uzinza*, Mwanza; cited in Mworoha, *Peuples et rois*, p. 74.

56. Crazzolara, *Lwoo*. 3 vols. Besides several written statements by missionaries and English administrators in Bukoba, Luc de Heusch's work (*Le Rwanda et la civilisation interlacustre*) primarily develops this hypothesis. As far as it is based on a linguistic misunderstanding, this hypothesis is not far from Speke's theory of the "Wawitu": the Bayango's *nkende* monkey totem was supposed to have been repulsed by the Bahinda's *tumbili* monkey totem. The problem is that these are the same animal, but one that is designated differently in the region's language (Ruhaya) and in Swahili, the lingua franca that the administrative auxiliaries used in colonial inquiries.

57. On the Buganda myths and their interpretations, see Ray, *Myth, Ritual, and Kingship in Buganda*, pp. 54–103.

58. Cohen, *Historical Tradition of Busoga, Mukama, and Kintu.*

59. Chrétien, "Mythes et stratégies," pp. 281–320. See also Vansina, *Evolution du royaume Rwanda des origines à 1900*, pp. 42–48; Smith, "Forge de l'intelligence."

60. Rennie, "Precolonial Kingdom of Rwanda" (see the map).

61. Vansina, *Légende du passé*, pp. 55–117. Chrétien, "Du Hirsute au Hamite"; Chrétien, "Variantes dans les sources orales"; Chrétien, "Nouvelles Hypothèses sur les origines du Burundi." See also Chrétien, *Burundi, l'histoire retrouvée*, pp. 33–43 and 343–77.

62. Gorju, *Face au royaume hamite du Ruanda, le royaume frère de l'Urundi.* The title itself is quite revealing.

63. Chrétien, "Buha à la fin du XIXe siècle."

64. David Newbury, *Kings and Clans*; Bishikwabo, "Origine des chefferies de l'ouest de la Rusizi"; Bishikwabo, "Histoire d'un état Shi"; Bishikwabo and Newbury, "Recent Historical Research in the Area of Lake Kivu"; Depelchin, "From Precapitalism to Imperialism," which is useful, despite the jargon in the title.

65. Sigwalt, "Early History of Bushi."

66. Nahimana, *Rwanda*, pp. 115–27; Willis, "Kinyonyi and Kateizi."

67. The Burundian hero Kiranga is an example. See Smith, "Personnages de légende."

68. Moeller de Laddersous, *Grandes Lignes des migrations des Bantous de la province orientale au Congo belge.*

69. Mworoha, *Peuples et rois*, pp. 103–105.

70. Heusch, *Essais sur le symbolisme de l'inceste royal en Afrique.*

71. David Newbury, *Kings and Clans*, p. 164.

72. Chrétien, "Le *Mwami* Ntare: Le Héros fondateur d'une protonation," in *Burundi, l'histoire retrouvée*, pp. 56–57; Nizigiyimana, "Contes d'ogres (*ibisizimwe*)."

73. Willis, "Kinyonyi and Kateizi."

74. Mworoha, *Peuples et rois*, pp. 282–91; Chrétien and Mworoha, "Tombeaux des *bami* du Burundi"; Amélie Gahama, *Reine mère et ses prêtres au Burundi*; Coupez and Hertefelt, *Royauté sacrée de l'ancien Rwanda*, pp. 203–219; Chrétien, "Le Buha à la fin du XIXe siècle," pp. 18–19; Bishikwabo, "Histoire d'un état Shi," pp. 219–26; Ingham, "Amagasani of the Abakama of Bunyoro"; Oliver, "Royal Tombs of Buganda."

75. Mworoha, *Peuples et rois*, pp. 265–81; Pascal Ndayishinguje, *Intronisation d'un mwami*; Coupez and Hertefelt, *Royauté sacrée de l'ancien Rwanda*, pp. 221–79; Bishikwabo, ""Histoire d'un état Shi," pp. 219–26; and Mors, "Geschichte der Bahaya."

76. Report of Major von Langenn, resident of Urundi, to the governor of East Africa, Jan. 4, 1916; cited in Ndayishinguje, *Intronisation d'un mwami*, pp. 53–56.

77. Cowries are small shells that came from the Indian Ocean and brought magic before taking on monetary value in the nineteenth century.

78. Evans-Pritchard, *Divine Kingship of the Shilluk of the Nilotic Sudan*, p. 27.

79. A Burundian hymn was recorded by Zacharie Ntibakivayo and transcribed in *Culture et société: Revue civilisation burundaise* 2 (1979), pp. 92–97.

80. Ndoricimpa and Guillet, *Tambours du Burundi*, captioned photographs.

81. Jean-Baptiste Lapioche, "Buhaya et son histoire."

82. Ray, *Myth, Ritual, and Kingship in Buganda*, pp. 74–103.

83. Bahenduzi, "Rituel du muganuro"; Bahenduzi, "Kirwa"; Chrétien, "Années de l'éleusine, du sorgho et du haricot"; Chrétien, "Sorgho dans l'agriculture, la culture et l'histoire du Burundi."

84. David Newbury, "What Role Has Kingship?"

85. Mworoha, *Peuples et rois*, pp. 253–64; David Newbury, *Kings and Clans*, pp. 200–226; Bishikwabo, "Histoire d'un état Shi," pp. 235–38.

86. Chrétien, "Années de l'éleusine, du sorgo et du haricot," repr. in Chrétien, *Burundi, l'histoire retrouvée*, pp. 79–103.

87. David Newbury, *Kings and Clans*, pp. 56–58.

88. A dimension that is found in other places too; see Kantorowicz, *King's Two Bodies*.

89. Mworoha, *Peuples et rois*, pp. 128–30 and 150–62; Mworoha, "Cour du roi Mwezi Gisabo." See also the papers of Georges Smets's investigations, collected by Albert Trouwborst (University of Nimègue).

90. One finds equivalents in the other royal courts: in Rwanda there also was a sacred monkey; in Buhaya there was a jester (a *mushegu*) who woke the king with the sound of a flute, and so on.

91. See the map in Mworoha et al. (eds.), *Histoire du Burundi*, p. 215.

92. Chrétien, "Religion des Grands Lacs"; Zuure, *Croyances et pratiques religieuses des Barundi*, pp. 5–6 (the preface by Monsignor Gorju).

93. Arnoux, "Culte de la société secrète des Imandwa au Ruanda"; Struck, "Bermerkungen über die 'Mbandwa' des Zwischenseengebiets"; Vix, "Beitrag zur Ethnologie des Zwischenseengebietes von deutsch Ostafrika."

94. On Buha, see Grant, "Uha in Tanganyika Territory," pp. 420–21.

95. Vidal, "Anthropologie et histoire." For an opposing point of view, see Heusch, "Mythe et société féodale," and Heusch, *Rwanda et la civilisation interlacustre.*

96. Freedman, *Nyabingi.*

97. On the misunderstanding, see Chrétien, "Roi, religion, lignages en Afrique orientale précoloniale," repr. in Chrétien, *Burundi, l'histoire retrouvée*, pp. 59–78. For examples of the "contest" interpretation, see Berger, *Religion and Resistance* (which came out of Berger, *Kubandwa Religious Complex*); Berger, "Deities, Dynasties, and Oral Traditions"; Berger, "Rebels or Status-Seekers?" On Dionysus, see Detienne, *Dionysos Slain*; and Vidal-Naquet, "Bêtes, hommes et dieux chez les Grecs."

98. Kenny, "Mutesa's Crime."

99. Biebuyck, *Lega Culture*; Bishikwabo, "Notes sur l'origine de l'institution du bwami et fondements du pouvoir politique au Kivu oriental."

100. David Newbury, *Kings and Clans*, pp. 331–32.

CHAPTER THREE: THE FORMATION OF MONARCHICAL STATES

1. See the tables on pp. 473–76, which are drawn from existing research; the lists are questionable before 1700.

2. Gray, "Eclipse Maps," and Gray, "Annular Eclipse Maps"; Sykes, "Eclipse at Biharwe."

3. See Herodotus, *The Histories* (New York: Penguin Books, 1996), vol. 3, para. 122. Kagame, *Notion de génération appliquée à la généalogie dynastique et à l'histoire du Rwanda*. For the comparative studies, see Cohen, "Survey of Interlacustrine Chronology"; in *Evolution du royaume Rwanda des origines à 1900*, however, Vansina proposed twenty-four years; see also Henige, "Reflections on Early Interlacustrine Chronology." Kagame, *Inganji karinga*; see also Smith, "Forge de l'intelligence"; in contrast to Delmas, *Généalogies de la noblesse (les Batutsi) de Ruanda*.

4. On the two Ntares, see Chrétien, *Burundi, l'histoire retrouvée*, p. 52. On the distinction between the dynastic list and a genealogy, see Person, "Tradition orale et chronologie." On the difficulties of identification, see David Newbury, "Trick Cyclists?"; and especially Nkurikiyimfura's remarkable analysis in "Révision d'une chronologie." On Rushatsi, see Chrétien and Bahenduzi, "Ntare Rushatsi," pp. 38–55.

5. For the Sumerian expression, see André Parrot, "Sumer," *Encyclopaedia universalis*, vol. 15, p. 543 (tablet WB 62). For accounts of the disturbances, see Webster, "Noi! Noi!," and Herring, "Hydrology and Chronology"; also see my comments on methodology in the introduction, and Robertshaw and Taylor, "Climate Change and the Rise of Political Complexity in Western Uganda."

6. Chrétien, "Années de l'éleusine, du sorgho et du haricot"; see also Cochet, "Burundi: Quelques Questions."

7. Sassoon, "Kings, Cattle, and Blacksmiths."

8. Chrétien, "Sorgho dans l'agriculture, la culture et l'histoire du Burundi."

9. There are descriptions of these groups in several exploration narratives from the second half of the nineteenth century. Their original dialects have been identified; see Dahl, "Termini technici der Rinderzucht treibenden Watusi in Deutsch-Ostafrika."

10. An earlier migration that is the origin of Rwandaphone Congolese in South Kivu and has been labeled the "Banyamulenge" in recent years. See Mutambo, *Banyamulenge*.

11. Steinhart, "Herders and Farmers"; Edward Steinhart, "Food Production in Pre-colonial Ankole," paper presented at the International Congress of Anthropology, Amsterdam, 1981.

12. Rwabukumba and Mudandagizi, "Formes historiques de la dépendance personnelle dans l'état rwandais," p. 10. This article appeared in a special issue on the "problem of statist domination in Rwanda," edited by Claudine Vidal.

13. The hypothesis merits more systematic development than that done by its author. See Vidal, "Enquêtes sur l'histoire et l'au-delà," Vidal, "Désinformation en histoire," p. 18, in which the start of "sedentarization" is fixed to 1725. (*Dialogue*, in which this second article appeared, is a Belgian-Rwandan Catholic journal of militant popularization.) See also the commentary of Moniot, "Nouvelles Recherches sur l'histoire sociale du Rwanda," p. 341 (the land clearing was dated to the turn of the eighteenth and nineteenth centuries).

14. Cochet, "Burundi: Quelques Questions"; Joseph Gahama and Thibon (eds.), *Régions orientales du Burundi*.

15. Trouwborst, "Kinship and Geographical Mobility in Burundi (East Central Africa)."

16. See the maps on pp. 482–83, which more or less represent the situation in the region from the early eighteenth century to the late nineteenth century. The main sources for this are Czekanowski, *Ethnographie*, and Posnansky, "Towards an Historical Geography of Uganda"; also see maps by Chrétien in Mworoha et al. (eds.), *Histoire du Burundi*, p. 118, and in Ogot (ed.), *General History of Africa*, p. 816.

17. Kagame, *Abrégé de l'ethno-histoire du Rwanda*, vol. 1, pp. 71–78; Mors, "Geschichte der Bahaya," pp. 25–110; Karugire, *History of the Kingdom of Nkore*, pp. 158–60.

18. Dunbar, *History of Bunyoro-Kitara*; Beattie, *Nyoro State*; Nyakatura, *Anatomy of an African Kingdom*.

19. Ingham, *Kingdom of Toro in Uganda*.

20. Freedman, *Nyabingi*.

21. Karugire, *History of the Kingdom of Nkore*; Katate and Kamugungunu, *Abagabe b'Ankole*.

22. Mors, "Geschichte der Bahaya"; Ford and Hall, "History of Karagwe (Bukoba District)"; Katoke, *Karagwe Kingdom.*

23. Vansina, *Évolution du royaume Rwanda des origines à 1900*, p. 51.

24. Arianoff, *Histoire des Bagesera, souverains du Gisaka.*

25. Kagame, *Abrégé de l'ethno-histoire du Rwanda*, vol. 1, pp. 81–82, 105–106, 111–13; Vansina, *Évolution du royaume Rwanda des origines à 1900*, pp. 84–86; Hertefelt, *Clans du Rwanda ancien*, pp. 31–45; Chrétien, "Nouvelles Hypothèses sur les origines du Burundi," pp. 21–26; Nkurikiyimfura, *Gros Bétail et la société rwandaise*, pp. 141–54.

26. Chrétien, "Buha à la fin du XIXe siècle."

27. On the ancientness and precolonial activity of these saltworks, which are still in operation today, see Sutton and Roberts, "Uvinza and Its Salt Industry," and Chrétien, *Burundi l'histoire retrouvée*, pp. 163–87.

28. Mors, "Geschichte der Bahaya," pp. 83–84; Thiel, "Buzinza unter der Dynastie der Bahinda," Betbeder, "Kingdom of Buzinza."

29. Rusubi is not to be confused with the small kingdom of Bushubi, with its mixed population. Bushubi was coveted by its various neighbors, which undoubtedly is how it could survive until colonization.

30. Mors, "Geschichte der Bahaya"; Rehse, *Kiziba, Land und Leute*; Richter, "Bezirk Bukoba"; Césard, "Muhaya"; *District Book of Bukoba*; Cory, *History of the Bukoba District*; Peter Schmidt, *Historical Archaeology.*

31. Maruku is too small to have a place on the map on p. 483.

32. Wrigley, *Kingship and State*; Richard Reid, "Reign of *Kabaka* Nakibinge."

33. Kagwa, *Kings of Buganda*; Kiwanuka, *History of Buganda*; Karugire, *Political History of Uganda*, pp. 34–40; Chrétien, "Peuples et leur histoire avant colonisation," pp. 41–42.

34. Hartwig, *Art of Survival in East Africa*. In fact, its Silanga dynasty had come from Ihangiro in the seventeenth century.

35. Kottak, "Ecological Variables in the Origin and Evolution of African States."

36. Lacger, *Ruanda*; Kagame, *Abrégé de l'ethno-histoire du Rwanda*, vol. 1; Kagame, *Abrégé de l'histoire du Rwanda de 1853 à 1972*, vol. 2; Coupez and

Kamanzi, *Récits historiques Rwanda*; Vansina, *Evolution du royaume Rwanda des origines à 1900*; Heremans, *Introduction à l'histoire du Rwanda*.

37. It is unclear from the tradition whether Nsibura was the king of the Bahavu or the Bashi.

38. David Newbury, "Trick Cyclists?"

39. Coupez and Hertefelt, *Royauté sacrée de l'ancien Rwanda*, pp. 478–79.

40. Rennie, "Precolonial Kingdom of Rwanda," pp. 11–53 (see the maps on pages 476–84).

41. The royal tomb of Rutare that the archaeologist van Noten excavated in 1969 contained a body, deposed there around 1931 and dated to the first third of the seventeenth century. The identification of Cyirima Rujugira is thus not apparent, contrary to what van Noten suggested. See Noten, *Tombes*. See the accounts rendered in Jean-Pierre Chrétien, book review, *Revue française d'histoire d'outre-mer* 223 (1974), pp. 327–28, and Vidal, "Rêve et réalité en ethnohistoire."

42. Kagame, *Milices du Rwanda précolonial*; and Kagame, *Histoire des armées-bovines de l'ancien Rwanda*.

43. David Newbury, "Trick Cyclists?" p. 210; Nkurikiyimfura, *Gros Bétail et la société rwandaise*, pp. 52–60.

44. David Newbury, "Bunyabungo"; Schumacher, *Physische und soziale Umwelt der Kivu-Pygmäen (Twiden)*, pp. 17–18.

45. Mworoha et al. (eds.), *Histoire du Burundi*, pp. 105–163 and pp. 207–253.

46. Circumstances that Roger Botte structurally established; see Botte, "Guerre interne au Burundi."

47. Bishikwabo and Newbury, "Recent Historical Research in the Area of Lake Kivu"; Depelchin, "From Precapitalism to Imperialism," pp. 43–52 and 100–106; Bishikwabo, "Origine des chefferies de l'ouest de Rusizi"; Bishikwabo, "Bushi au XIXe siècle"; Bishikwabo, "Histoire d'un état Shi"; David Newbury, *Kings and Clans*, see the map on p. 148.

48. Mworoha, *Peuples et rois*, pp. 239–40.

49. Contrary to what is suggested in Coquery-Vidrovitch, *Histoire des villes d'Afrique noire*, pp. 85–90.

50. J.M. Van der Burgt, *Diaire de la mission de Kanyinga*, November 16, 1904, White Fathers Archives, Rome.

51. Diary of Rubaga, July 24, 1885, White Fathers Archives, Rome.

52. Mworoha, *Peuples et rois*, pp. 117–32 (Burundi), 211–14 (Bunyoro), 217–20 (Buhaya), 224 (Rwanda), 237–40 (Buganda); Mworoha, "Cour du roi Mwezi Gisabo"; Nsanze, *Domaine royal au Burundi, Mbuye*; Lugan, "Nyanza"; Mors, "Geschichte der Bahaya," pp. 133–49; Gutkind, *Royal Capital of Buganda*; Kiwanuka, *History of Buganda* (see the sketch of Mutesa's palace in Nabulagala, pp. 160–61); and Bishikwabo, "Histoire d'un état Shi," pp. 251–66.

53. Mworoha, *Peuples et rois*, pp. 122 and 224.

54. Acquier, *Burundi*. Note that this is part of the Traditional Architecture series.

55. Here we should not neglect colonialism's impact, which occasionally interfered with the description of so-called traditional situations. For an example in Burundi, see Botte, "De quoi vivait l'état?," which was founded essentially on data furnished by administrative inquiries between 1927 and 1929.

56. Wilson and Felkin, *Uganda and the Egyptian Soudan*, vol. 1, p. 193; Von Nordeck zu Rabenau, "Usumbura," Archives Africaines, Fonds Allemands, microfilm 160, Brussels, March 11, 1905; Ménard, "Barundi (moeurs et coutumes)," p. 117; Burgt, "Diary of Saint-Antoine."

57. Vidal, "Présentation," and Vidal, "Économie de la société féodale rwandaise."

58. Vidal, "Rwanda des anthropologues et le fétichisme de la vache"; Rodney, *How Europe Underdeveloped Africa*, pp. 139–40 (at the time, this revolutionary intellectual from Guyana was a professor in Dar es Salaam); Beattie, "Bunyoro: An African Feudality?"

59. Smets, "Institutions féodales de l'Urundi." Also see Trouwborst, "Ethnographie du Burundi pendant l'occupation belge." Trouwborst, an anthropologist at Nimègue University, made Smets's papers accessible.

60. Goody, "Feudalism in Africa?"; Steinhart, "Vassal and Fief in Three Lacustrine Kingdoms"; Chrétien, "Vocabulaire et concepts."

61. Chrétien, "Echanges et hiérarchies" (this article was published in a

special issue of *Annales E.S.C.* on "anthropological history" and "the notion of reciprocity").

62. Tardits, ed., *Princes & serviteurs du royaume.*

63. Mworoha, *Peuples et rois*, pp. 132–50 and 213–51.

64. Beattie, *Nyoro State*, pp. 119–25; Steinhart, "From 'Empire' to State."

65. Mukasa, "Rule of the Kings of Buganda."

66. On the notion of bureaucratic-style spatial homogenization, see Pourtier, "Nommer l'espace." More generally, see Trouwborst, "Base territoriale de l'état du Burundi ancien."

67. Fuchs, "Urundi und Ruanda" (based on a report of August 1906 by Resident Richard Kandt). On Kinyaga, see Catharine Newbury, *Cohesion of Oppression.*

68. Leakey, "Historical Note"; Bishikwabo, "Histoire d'un état Shi," pp. 264–86.

69. The term designating this appointment, *kwatirwa*, is the same as that which designates initiation of a medium of the cult of *kubandwa*. On this institution, see Delacauw, "Féodalité ou démocratie en Urundi," and Laely, *Autorität und Staat in Burundi*, pp. 141–76.

70. On Nkore, see Steinhart, "Ankole," pp. 142–44. On Buganda, see Kiwanuka, *History of Buganda*, pp. 111–26, and Fallers, *King's Men.*

71. Steinhart, "Vassal and Fief in Three Lacustrine Kingdoms," pp. 613–14. For the comparison to kingdoms of the late Middle Ages, see Werner, *Naissance de la noblesse.*

72. Mors, "Geschichte der Bahaya," pp. 136–37.

73. Mworoha, "Redevances et prestations"; Nsanze, *Domaine royal au Burundi, Mbuye*; Nsanze, "Bases économiques des pouvoirs au Burundi de 1875 à 1920"; Botte, "De quoi vivait l'état?"; Chrétien, "Agronomie, consommation et travail." Many equivalent statements have been made with regard to the kingdom Kaziba in Bushi; see Bishikwabo, "Histoire d'un état Shi," pp. 278–89.

74. Catharine Newbury, *Cohesion of Oppression.*

75. Rwabukumba and Mudandagizi, "Formes historiques de la dépendance personnelle dans l'état rwandais," pp. 21–22; Vidal, "Economie de la société féodale rwandaise," p. 59; and Mworoha, *Peuples et rois*, pp. 232–33. In a recent

work, Vansina proposes an etymology associated with the word *kuleta*, which refers to the flow of milk into a cow's udders. This image for an agricultural corvée and recourse to this intransitive verb's passive form render this interpretation not very convincing. When asked the same question in 1979 (at an international colloquium held in Bujumbura on the "ancient civilization of the people of the Great Lakes"), Alexis Kagame could only respond by proffering the name of an aspiring prince named Kanyabuletwa!

76. On this often-broached theme, see the extensive bibliography in Chrétien (ed.), *Histoire rurale*, pp. 155–62 (with an introduction by Charles de Lespinay). For a precise study on Rwanda, see Reisdorff, "Enquêtes foncières au Ruanda."

77. On Burundi, see Chrétien, "Agronomie, consommation et travail," pp. 157–70; and Kayondi, "Murunga, colline du Burundi."

78. Botte, "Processus de formation"; Vidal, "Economie de la société féodale rwandaise"; Reining, "Haya Land Tenure."

79. Gravel, *Remera*. On Burundi, see Nsanze, *Domaine royal au Burundi, Mbuye* and Nsanze, "Bases économiques des pouvoirs au Burundi de 1875 à 1920."

80. Vidal "Economie de la société féodale rwandaise," p. 55; Mworoha, "Redevances et prestations," p. 765.

81. Czekanowski, *Ethnographie*, p. 263.

82. Maquet, *Système des relations sociales*; Lacger, *Ruanda*, pp. 116–17; Nkurikiyimfura, *Gros Bétail et la société rwandaise*, p. 126.

83. Elam, *Social and Sexual Roles of Hima Women*; Nkurikiyimfura, *Gros Bétail et la société rwandaise*, pp. 102–118; Morris, *Heroic Recitations of the Bahima of Ankole*; Coupez and Kamanzi, *Littérature de cour au Rwanda*; Rodegem, *Anthologie rundi*, pp. 39–61; Ndimurukundo, "Ages et les espaces de l'enfance dans le Burundi Traditionnel." For a very instructive work that demonstrates this aestheticism, see Maquet, *Ruanda: Essai photographique*. Also see Vidal, "Rwanda des anthropologues et le fétichisme de la vache."

84. On southern Buha and Bushi, see Mbwiliza, "Hoe and the Stick"; and Bishikwabo, "Histoire d'un état Shi," pp. 270–77. On Burundi, see Mworoha et al. (eds.), *Histoire du Burundi*, pp. 125–63. On Uganda and Rwanda, see Stein-

hart, "Kingdoms of the March"; and Nkurikiyimfura, *Gros Bétail et la société rwandaise*, pp. 58–99 and pp. 124–140.

85. Nkurikiyimfura was a victim, along with his family, of the 1994 genocide.

86. Reining, "Haya Land Tenure." See also Meschi, "Evolution des structures foncières au Rwanda."

87. For a Burundian example, see the use of *biturire* for *amarari*. Trouwborst, "Organisation politique en tant que système d'échanges au Burundi."

88. Catharine Newbury, "Ethnicity in Rwanda," p. 21. See also Catharine Newbury, "Deux Lignages au Kinyaga," p. 37 and (1988).

89. Marcel Mauss, "Essai sur le don: Forme et raison de l'echange dans les sociétés archaïques," in *Sociologie et anthropologie* (Paris: PUF, 1966).

90. Mworoha, *Peuples et rois*, pp. 186–92; Ndikuriyo, "Contrats de bétail"; Trouwborst, "Quelques Aspects symbolique des échanges de bière au Burundi (Afrique centrale)"; Tawney, "Ugabire."

91. Meyer, *Barundi*, p. 96.

92. Vidal, "Economie de la société féodale rwandaise," pp. 56–62. Gravel, *Remera*, pp. 53–54. For a description of starving Batutsi, see Buhonga's diary, Archives of the White Fathers, Rome, Oct. 24, 1904. On the Nkore situation, see Steinhart, "Herders and Farmers," p. 142, and Steinhart, "Ankole," p. 145.

93. The majority of Bagogwe were victims of pogroms in 1991. On the primacy of clan membership in Rwanda, see Nyagahene, "Histoire et peuplement." See Chrétien, "Hutu et Tutsi au Rwanda et au Burundi," p. 141.

94. Desmarais, "Rwanda des anthropologues."

95. Cohen, "Food Production and Food Exchange in the Precolonial Lakes Plateau Region"; Cohen, "Peoples and States of the Great Lakes Region"; Cohen, "East Africa 1870–1905"; Tosh, "The Northern Lacustrine Region"; Roberts, "Nyamwezi Trade"; and Chrétien, "Peuples et leur histoire avant la colonisation," pp. 46–49 (see the map).

96. Chrétien et al., "Technologie et économie du sel végétal dans l'ancien Burundi." The locative prefix *U-* has taken root in Buvinza because of Swahili

being spoken there for the last century (such as "Uganda" instead of "Buganda" or, of late, "Urundi" instead of "Burundi").

97. Chrétien, *Burundi, l'histoire retrouvée*, pp. 163–87; Lugan and Mutombo, "Sel dans le Rwanda ancien"; Kabanda, "Technologie et économie du sel dans la région des Grands Lacs d'Afrique de l'est (1850–1920)"; Kamuhangire, "Precolonial History of Salt"; Kamuhangire, "Pre-colonial Economic and Social History of East Africa."

98. Célis and Nzikobanyanka, *Métallurgie traditionnelle au Burundi*; Chrétien, "Production du fer," pp. 311–25; and Kandt, "Gewerbe in Ruanda."

99. David Newbury, "Lake Kivu Regional Trade in the Nineteenth Century"; Chrétien, "Buha à la fin du XIXe siècle," pp. 19–24; Mworoha et al. (eds.), *Histoire du Burundi*, pp. 170–71 (see the map).

100. Bishikwabo, "Histoire d'un état Shi," pp. 181–92; Lugan, "Echanges et routes commerciales au Rwanda, 1880–1914"; Lugan, "Reseaux commerciaux au Rwanda dans le dernier quart du XIXe siècle"; Lugan and Nyagahene, "Activités commerciales du Sud-Kivu au XIXe siècle à travers l'exemple de Kinyaga (Rwanda)" (see the maps); Uzoigwe, "Precolonial Markets in Bunyoro-Kitara"; Kenny, "Precolonial Trade in Eastern Lake Victoria."

101. Later *icambu* was replaced by the Swahili word *isoko* (derived from the Arab word *souk*). Even *iguliro*, proposed by Lugan, seems to be a neologism forged from the radical *ku-gura*, "to exchange."

102. Roberts, "Sub-imperialism of the Baganda"; David Newbury, "Campagnes de Rwabugiri."

103. Chrétien, "Banyamwezi au gré de la conjoncture."

104. Wrigley, "Buganda: An Outline Economic History."

105. Götzen, *Durch Afrika von Ost nach West*, pp. 137–38.

106. The White Fathers from the missions of Zaza (in Gisaka), Katoke (in Rusubi), and Ushirombo (in northwestern Nyamwezi country) observed this traffic between 1894 and 1905. On this subject, a Rwandan historian has written a remarkable master's thesis: Mujawimana, "Commerce des esclaves au Rwanda."

107. Maquet, *Premise of Inequality in Ruanda*. How much this work succeeds

is as ambiguous as the famous *Bantu Philosophy* published by Father Tempels in 1949.

Chapter Four: Colonial Trusteeships and Reconstructions of Tradition

1. Rotberg, ed., *Africa and Its Explorers*; Hugon, *Afrique des explorateurs*.

2. See Chapter I, pp. XXXX (56–57) (regarding theories on Tutsi and Hima settlement), and Chapter II, pp. XXXX (85–87) (regarding racial reinterpretations of the Cwezi mythology).

3. Chrétien, "Passage de l'expédition d'Oscar Baumann"; Kandt, *Caput Nili*, vol. 1. For the discovery of Lake Kivu, see Götzen, *Durch Afrika von Ost nach West*.

4. Dunbar, *History of Bunyoro-Kitara*, pp. 51–80; Kiwanuka, *History of Buganda*, pp. 154–91. Also see the bibliography in Langlands, "Early Travelers in Uganda."

5. Bleuchot, "Soudan au XIXe siècle."

6. Schnitzer, a doctor of Silesian ancestry who lived in the Ottoman Empire, left behind notebooks rich with descriptions of Uganda's nineteenth-century landscapes and societies; see *Tagebücher von Emin Pascha*.

7. Sheriff, *Slaves, Spices, and Ivory in Zanzibar*.

8. Oliver, *Missionary Factor in East Africa*.

9. Renault, *Cardinal Lavigerie*; and Renault, *Afrique Centrale*.

10. Letter to Maret, dean of the faculty of theology in Paris, Oct. 1869.

11. The missionaries became known as White Fathers because of their gandouras — an Arabic word for tunic — which they had adopted as North African "indigenous" clothing when in mission there. These gandouras later made these missionaries seem to be related to Arabs in Central Africa!

12. The White Fathers kept their society informed through correspondence; through a journal, or diary, kept on the mission; and through internal periodicals (*Chroniques trimestrielles, Rapports annuels*) and journals like *Missions d'Afrique* (edited in Algiers) and other outlets published in Belgium, Germany, and elsewhere.

13. Tourigny, *So Abundant a Harvest*; Médard, "Succès du christianisme en Ouganda (1875–1962)."

14. Peel, "Conversion and Tradition in Two African Societies."

15. Henri Médard, "La Naissance et le déclin des partis politico-religieux en Ouganda (1887–1996)," in Hervé Maupeu and Christian Delmet (eds.), *Religions et politique en Afrique de l'Est* (Paris, forthcoming).

16. Renault, "Réflexion historique sur des martyrs africains."

17. See Wright, *Buganda in the Heroic Age*.

18. Wolf, *Missionary to Tanganyika, 1877–1888*.

19. See Renault, *Afrique centrale*. Three thousand "buybacks" took place between 1879 and 1891 in this region.

20. See the maps and statistics published by Heremans, *Education dans les missions des Pères Blancs en Afrique centrale, 1879–1914*, pp. 456–60.

21. Chrétien, "Conversions et crise de légitimité politique"; Linden, *Church and Revolution in Rwanda*, pp. 29–49.

22. There are many dossiers in the German, Belgian, and British Foreign Affairs archives that pertain to this issue. I have tried to summarize the main points here. See also Louis, *Ruanda-Urundi*.

23. Directed by the American John Huston and released in 1951, a year after *King Solomon's Mines*, another film that inspired dreams about the Great Lakes region.

24. In principle, only Bufumbira, a Kinyarwandan-speaking region north of the Virunga volcanic mountains, was awarded to the English. This was done under the name "Mfumbiro massif," as indicated by Stanley.

25. Marissal, "Mohammed ben Khalfan."

26. Kjekshus, *Ecology Control and Economic Development in East African History*; Chrétien, "Démographie et écologie en Afrique orientale à la fin du XIXe siècle."

27. *Gambiense* trypanosomiases was diffused by the *palpalis* tsetse fly from West Africa, while *rhodesiense* trypanosomiases, the vector of which is the *morsitans* tsetse fly, was spread from southern Africa. See Ford, *Role of the Trypanosomiases in African Ecology*; Chrétien, *Burundi, l'histoire retrouvée*, pp. 121–61; Langlands, *The Sleeping Sickness Epidemic in Uganda, 1900–1920*.

28. The word *Gakwege* comes from *kwegeka*, "to stretch iron," "to wire-draw," which may have indicated a famine that transformed people into match-sticks or that forced them to sell their iron bracelets. Lugan, "Famines et disettes au Rwanda"; Kavakure, "Famines et disettes au Burundi"; David Newbury, "'Rwakayihura' Famine of 1928–1929"; Feltz and Bidou, "Famine manori au Burundi, 1943–1944."

29. Thibon, "Siècle de croissance démographique au Burundi (1850–1950)"; Thibon, "Crise démographique et mise en dépendance au Burundi et dans la région des Grands Lacs, 1880–1910"; Kuczynski, *Demographic Survey of the British Colonial Empire*, vol. 2; Hartwig, "Demographic Considerations in East Africa During the Nineteenth Century"; Boller, *Kaffee, Kinder, Kolonialismus*; Doyle, "Environmental History of the Kingdom of Bunyoro in Western Uganda, from c. 1860 to 1940."

30. At first, the salaries were in the form of a commission on the direct taxes collected in their jurisdiction.

31. See the text in Low, *Mind of Buganda*, pp. 39–40.

32. On this period of transition, see Ingham, *History of East Africa*; Low, "Uganda: The Establishment of the Protectorate, 1894–1919"; Low, *Buganda in Modern History*; Karugire, *Political History of Uganda*, pp. 49–122; Low and Pratt, *Buganda and British Overrule, 1900–1955*; West, *Land Policy in Buganda*; Chrétien, "Vocabulaire et concepts"; and *Diaries of Lord Lugard*.

33. The Swahili *U-* prefix replaced the Luganda *Bu-* prefix.

34. On western Uganda in the early twentieth century, see Steinhart, *Conflict and Collaboration*.

35. We saw in Chapter II how John Nyakatura, a Western-educated notable, put Cwezi traditions to the service of this nationalism. The writings multiplied (including under the pen of King Tito Winyi in the 1930s) on these mythical heroes, a process that ran parallel to the demand for the "lost counties."

36. Karugire, *Political History of Uganda*, pp. 116–21; Lwanga-Lunyiigo, "Ere coloniale," pp. 73–75.

37. Influenced, Steinhart suggested, by the dramatic sense these concepts took on during World War II.

38. On this binary game, also observable in nineteenth-century West African political formations, such as those in Ashanti and Dahomey, see Barth, "Segmentary Opposition and the Theory of Games."

39. Tuma, "African Chiefs and Church Work in Busoga Province of Uganda, 1900–1940 — Part I," and Tuma, "African Chiefs and Church Work in Busoga Province of Uganda, 1900–1940 — Part II."

40. Steinhart, *Conflict and Collaboration*, p. 213.

41. King's College is near the sacred hill of Naggalabi.

42. See Lwanga-Lunyiigo, "Ere coloniale," pp. 76–81; Ehrlich, "Ugandan Economy"; Pratt, "Administration and Politics in Uganda"; and Roberts, "East Africa."

43. British East Africa, which extended to a territory northeast of Lake Victoria and which initially was integrated with the Uganda protectorate, became the Kenya colony in 1920.

44. A stretch from Jinja (in Busoga) to Lake Kyoga was built in 1912 for the transportation of cotton.

45. As part of a development plan launched in 1947 and concretized between 1955 and 1960.

46. A train could carry the freight equivalent to what fifteen to twenty thousand porters could carry.

47. In 1902, one could travel from London to Entebbe in twenty-four days; previously the journey took three and a half months. See Meyer, *Eisenbahnen im tropischen Afrika*, pp. 140–52.

48. The Indian rupee, used at first, was replaced by the shilling in 1922.

49. In 1911, there were more than 2,000 Indians in the protectorate, as opposed to 642 Europeans; the respective statistics in 1941 were 18,381 and 2,186. See Prunier, *Ouganda et la question indienne (1896–1972)*, and Ramchandani, *Ugandan Asians*. Many Indians had worked on railroad sites, but they did not all stay in Africa.

50. Narandas Rajaram, already well established in the cotton sector in Bombay in the late nineteenth century, arrived in Uganda in 1916.

51. Bell was governor from 1905 to 1910. A bushel weighed 181 kilograms.

For the proportions for various countries, see O'Connor, *Economic Geography of East Africa*, p. 83. Forty percent of these exports went to Bombay.

52. "Black Man's Country" was Hesketh Bell's own expression. The hut tax created in 1900 was replaced by a poll tax in 1907.

53. The Catholics (the White Fathers and Mill Hill Fathers) were more cautious than the Protestants in promoting Africans: in 1914, there were only two Ugandan Catholic priests versus thirty-three Anglican priests. But the first black bishop in contemporary Africa came from Buganda when Monsignor Kiwanuka (a product of the White Fathers) was named to Masaka in 1939.

54. A pessimist vision, antinomic to all assimilationist and egalitarian ideals, developed in a period when the condition of blacks in the United States was, as one wrote, at "its nadir."

55. Reforms that had already been introduced in Toro and Busoga.

56. Taylor, *Growth of the Church in Buganda*, p. 125.

57. Karugire, *Political History of Uganda*, pp. 123–43.

58. Pratt, "Administration and Politics in Uganda," p. 519.

59. These migrant workers were called *bapakasi* or "porters," both of which had a strong pejorative connotation, indicating a carrier or a laborer.

60. Prunier, "Evolution des critères de définition ethnique en Ouganda."

61. Some men of the same caliber as the soldiers of the Indian Army were used by the English at the beginning of their expansion in East Africa. In Africa, one also found the "Germany of the Ruhr" and that of the *Gold of the Rhine*. See Gann and Duignan, *Rulers of German Africa*, and Müller, *Deutschland, Zanzibar, Ostafrika*. Also see Langheld's memoirs, *Zwanzig Jahre in deutschen Kolonien*; Langheld was chief of the Bukoba and Mwanza stations in the 1890s.

62. One also finds here civilians like Oskar Baumann; see Chrétien, "Passage de l'expédition d'Oscar Baumann."

63. The former elephant-hunting troops of Banyamwezi had become bands of mercenaries, equipped with firearms, who were called the *ruga ruga*.

64. The enlargement of Kahigi's kingdom was notably at Kyamutwara's expense: its sovereign, Mukotani (from the Bankango clan), at first friendly, had a change in attitude. Once he rebelled, his country was plundered, and he fled to

Uganda in 1895. He was replaced by his brother Muntu. *Obersultan* translates as "supreme sultan." "Sultan" is derived from the Swahili word *sultani*, which, according to the Coast interpreters, referred to all African chiefs. On the German conquest of this region, see Stuhlmann, *Mit Emin Pascha ins Herz von Afrika*; Langheld, *Zwanzig Jahre in deutschen Kolonien*; many articles in *Mitteilungen von Forschungsreisenden und Gelehrten aus den deutschen Schutzgebieten (M.D.S.)*; the histories of different kingdoms discussed in Chapter III; and Austen, *Northwest Tanzania Under German and British Rule*, pp. 29–49.

65. Götzen, *Durch Afrika von Ost nach West*, pp. 136–40 (see Chapter III, p. 198). This *Schutzbrief* was shown at the national museum in Dar es Salaam.

66. The Ngoni groups, present in the region since the 1850s, also were forced to leave in 1891.

67. At first, they were led from the station of Tabora.

68. Chrétien, "Buha à la fin du XIXe siècle," and Chrétien, "Arbres et les rois."

69. In January 1895, the hanging of the Irish trader Charles Stokes (married to a Nyamwezi princess and friend of the Germans) by a Belgian officer who had arrested him west of Lake Edward caused a major splash. Three months earlier, a Congolese raid had been led against Rumonge, a Swahili commercial post in southern Burundi.

70. The expected profit in ivory, even after accounting for price differences between the Great Lakes and the Coast as well as the transport costs, was about 200 percent. The name Usumbura came from the local, Swahilized pronunciation (*Uzumbura*) of *Bujumbura*, the name again used after independence.

71. Ramsay, "Über seine Expeditionen nach Ruanda und dem Rukwasee."

72. Musinga himself was not present at the time. For several years, a double of sorts was charged with receiving the Europeans.

73. Ian Linden has called the Bagandan armed auxiliaries "*askari*-catechists." In 1900, the missionaries were allotted 700 hectares in Save and Zaza, part of which they returned following a request from the administration; but subsequent foundations were as well endowed as the first ones. See also Mbonimana and Ntezimana, "Pères Blancs et missionaires de Bethel"; Linden, *Church and Revolution in Rwanda*, pp. 29–72; and Des Forges, "Kings Without Crowns."

74. Honke, "Pour l'empereur et le roi."

75. Among whom one also found Batutsi, contrary to what is often written.

76. Chrétien, "Passage de l'expédition d'Oscar Baumann"; Baumann, *Durch Massailand zur Nilquelle*, pp. 80 and 223.

77. Chrétien, "Le Cycle de l'histoire de Maconco (1899–1905): Naissance d'un conte et résistance morale," in Chrétien, *Burundi, l'histoire retrouvée*, pp. 107–119.

78. Kiganda and Bukeye are two important hills on the royal estate, in central Burundi (Muramvya province). On Rwanda and Burundi under the Germans, see Ryckmans, *Page d'histoire coloniale*; Louis, *Ruanda-Urundi*; and Chrétien and Mworoha, "Mwezi Gisabo et le maintien d'une fragile indépendance au Burundi."

79. The Africans' firearms (there were about sixteen hundred old rifles in Buhaya in 1890) were outmatched technically.

80. Iliffe, "Effects of the Maji Maji Rebellion of 1905–1906 on German Occupation Policy in East Africa." At first, the colonies came under a department in the Ministry of Foreign Affairs. In 1907, traveling on the Uganda Railroad with members of the Reichstag, Dernberg went as far as Bukoba. In general, see Iliffe, *Tanganyika Under German Rule, 1905–1912*.

81. He came from the Kantorowicz family of Poznan. See Bindseil, *Ruanda und Deutschland seit den Tagen Richard Kandts*.

82. Austen, *Northwest Tanzania Under German and British Rule*, pp. 84–91.

83. Kabagema, *Ruanda unter deutscher Kolonialherrschaft*.

84. See Chapter III, p. 175.

85. For example, Father Alphonse Brard, Save's founder, ran the parish like a military post and departed in 1906.

86. Father Classe was nicknamed the "marquis" by his more "rustic" compatriots, notably those from Burundi placed under his jurisdiction in 1912, when Rwanda and Burundi were grouped, for about a dozen years, as part of the Kivu apostolic vicariate under the theoretical leadership of Monsignor Hirth. See Mbonimana and Ntezimana, "Pères Blancs et missionaires de Bethel," pp. 135–36. Also see the hagiography by Overschelde, *Audacieux pacifique*.

87. Schumacher was one of the very rare German Fathers, the author of several ethnographic works, and the head of Kabgayi in 1912.

88. Linden, *Church and Revolution in Rwanda*, pp. 73–122; Mbonimana, "Instauration d'un royaume chrétien au Rwanda."

89. Chrétien, "Mission, pouvoir colonial et pouvoir africain."

90. "Banyenduga" means "the people of Nduga," in other words, those from the region where the royal capitals were located. On the *buletwa*, see Chapter III, p. 180.

91. On the cult of Nyabingi and Mpororo tradition, see Chapters II and III, pp. 135 and 149.

92. Chrétien, "Révolte de Ndungutse (1912)"; Des Forges, "'Drum Is Greater Than the Shout.'"

93. A missionary society founded in 1886 for German East Africa, the Bethel mission had created five posts in Rwanda by 1914; see Johanssen, *Ruanda*; and Honke, "Eglise évangélique." The conversations between Johanssen and Musinga, held in 1908 and 1909, worried many White Fathers. They also revealed the depth of misunderstanding between Europeans and Rwandans on the subjects of God and government; see Kabagema, *Ruanda unter deutscher Kolonialherrschaft*, pp. 257–61.

94. Kabagema, *Ruanda unter deutscher Kolonialherrschaft*, pp. 137–42, cites Muhutu Rubasha, coordinator of the corvées at the post of Ruhengeri and feared by all, even the Tutsi chiefs, as a particularly abusive intermediary. Nyampara is a Nyamwezi term referring to caravan leaders, but here it assumed a larger meaning.

95. The loyalist chiefs were princes who were part of Mwezi Gisabo's line and their cousins who were part of Ntare Rugamba's (see Chapter II, pp. 163–64). Some Protestant missionaries of the Society of Neukirchen even became established in the northwest in 1911. On Lake Tanganyika and the Rusizi plain, see Chrétien, "Colonisation allemande" (see map 12 with commentary); Chrétien, "La Crise écologique de la Plaine du Lac Tanganyika entre 1890 et 1916," in Chrétien, *Burundi, l'histoire retrouvée*, pp. 121–62. Lake Victoria's shores, at the residency of Bukoba, were also affected by this epidemic.

96. Chrétien, "Vocabulaire et Concepts," p. 52. English-language translation found in Lemarchand, *Rwanda and Burundi*, p. 49.

97. On this new economy, see Boller, *Kaffee, Kinder, Kolonialismus*; Kabagema, *Ruanda unter deutscher Kolonialherrschaft*, pp. 143–51. The figures are reported in various annual reports produced by the residencies of Urundi and Ruanda from 1906 to 1913 (in the Brussels-based African Archives, German collection).

98. Some loads were nearly 30 kilograms.

99. In Bukoba, the Hamburg-based company O'Swald, represented in Zanzibar since the mid-nineteenth century, was the main coffee exporter. The Greeks mostly came from the Ottoman Empire. They arrived on Lake Tanganyika with the Germans when Usumbura was founded. Let us note, finally, that in 1913 there were only seventy-one Europeans in Burundi and ninety-six in Rwanda, of whom half were religious figures and a third military ones.

100. A lone small steamship had been launched on the lake.

101. Chrétien, "Le Commerce du sel de l'Uvinza au XIXe siècle: De la cueillette au monopole capitaliste," in Chrétien, *Burundi, l'histoire retrouvée*; Schloifer, *Bana Uleia*.

102. Chrétien, "Fermeture du Burundi et du Rwanda aux commerçants de l'exterieur (1905–1906)."

103. On the *nyarubanja*, see Chapter III, p. 187. Among the major producers of coffee were *bakama* Mutahangarwa of Kiziba and Kahigi of Kyanja.

104. Boller, *Kaffee, Kinder, Kolonialismus*, pp. 118–67.

105. A variety selected in Insulinde, then at the Amani Station in the eastern part of the colony.

106. The abundance of *Elaeis* palm trees on Tanganyika's shores also had attracted attention, but sleeping sickness killed this activity.

107. Chrétien, "'Désenclavement' de la région des Grands Lacs dans les projets economiques allemands au début du XXe siècle."

108. Holzmann had earlier built the *Bagdadbahn*.

109. The Belgians later seized the rails of the Rwandan Railroad in the name of "reparations," but the "central" line is still used for Burundian cargo,

even after the construction of an asphalt road that links Bujumbura to Mombasa via Rwanda and Uganda.

110. An ambush near the lake around Bukoba cost the life of the German resident Schimmer in Burundi.

111. As in 1890, the possibility of annexing Rwanda to Uganda was put forward during the 1919 negotiations; after 1994, when the part-Anglophone Rwandan Patriotic Front won, this idea again became fashionable in some Francophone circles obsessed by the phantom of Fashoda.

112. Louis, *Great Britain and Germany's Lost Colonies, 1914–1919*; Joseph Gahama, *Burundi sous administration belge*, pp. 37–47 (primary texts on pp. 410–15); Lugard, *Dual Mandate in British Tropical Africa*.

113. Lugan, "Causes et effets de la famine 'Rumanura' au Rwanda, 1916–1918."

114. For a discussion of the *Bicubirenga* (The Clouds Pass By) movement against the Rwaza mission, see Linden, *Church and Revolution in Rwanda*, p. 123; and for a discussion of the *Ntokibiri* (Two Fingers) movement against the English, see Brazier, "Incident at Nyakishenyi, 1917."

115. Joseph Gahama, "Révolte de Runyota-Kanyarufunzo au Burundi, 1922"; Joseph Gahama, *Burundi sous administration belge*, pp. 383–88 (N.B.: the two "sorcerers" are not a single person, contrary to what was believed for a long time).

116. Catharine Newbury, *Cohesion of Oppression*, pp. 129–30. On Rwanda during this transition period, see Rumiya, *Rwanda sous le régime du mandat belge*, pp. 25–129 (for a discussion of this incident, see pp. 48–49).

117. Both quickly came back. Baranyanka later became a great friend to the Belgians and was nicknamed by his subjects Musemyi — a Kirundi neologism based on the Swahili verb stem *-sema*, meaning "to talk," signifying that he spoke in a foreign language, that is, he spoke for the whites.

118. On the Bukoba region under British administration, see Austen, *Northwest Tanzania Under German and British Rule*, pp. 120–29 and 133–38.

119. Rumiya, *Rwanda sous le régime du mandat belge*, pp. 29 and 112.

120. "Boula Matari" (The Crusher of Rocks, in Lingala) was the title formerly applied to Stanley; the term also referred to the Belgian Congo state. Franck, *Congo belge*, vol. 1, p. 289.

121. The Burundian Bugufi remained in Tanganyika, under the name Buhangaza. In 1946 and 1948, Mwami Mwambutsa attempted in vain, before the United Nations, to win restitution.

122. Académie Royale des Sciences d'Outre-Mer, *Congo belge durant la Second Guerre mondiale.*

123. On Tanganyika during this period, see Iliffe's fundamental work *Modern History of Tanganyika*, pp. 318–41.

124. On this, see the memoirs of the Anglican bishop Bengt Sundkler, *Bara Bukoba.* A reply of sorts to *bandera* later was tried with the development of scouting, which became international in 1920. Its founder, Robert Baden-Powell, had an attachment with Anglophone Africa (from the Boer War to his death in Nyeri, Kenya, in 1941). Several of the educated youth were of Kizibian princely ancestry, such as Herbert Rugazibwa and Ludviko Kazoya.

125. For an example, see Chrétien, "Banyamwezi au gré de la conjoncture," pp. 191–93.

126. Cited in Linden, *Church and Revolution in Rwanda*, p. 136.

127. Ministère des Colonies, *Rapport sur l'administration belge*, p. 63. See also Ryckmans, *Dominer pour servir*, pp. 153–68, and his biography by Vanderlinden, *Pierre Ryckmans, 1891–1959.*

128. On the Belgian period in Burundi, see Joseph Gahama, *Burundi sous administration belge*; Chrétien, "Féodalité ou féodalisation sous le mandat belge," in Chrétien, *Burundi, L'histoire retrouvée*, pp. 189–217.

129. Kilima, a former rebel, died around 1920, and his family was deported to Congo. Baranyanka was baptized with the first name Pierre, that of his godfather in more than just name.

130. Maps on the distribution of chiefdoms in 1929, 1933, 1937, and 1945 can be found in Joseph Gahama, *Burundi sous administration belge*, pp. 105–108; for 1954, when the Baganwa were 74 percent, see Chrétien, *Burundi, l'histoire retrouvée*, p. 197.

131. Ministère des Colonies, *Rapport sur l'administration belge, 1933*, p. 75. See Chrétien, "Vocabulaire et concepts," p. 54.

132. See Chapter III, pp. 175–76. On the deterioration under financial and

political pressure of the *mushingantahe* function in the twentieth century, see Laely, *Autorität und Staat in Burundi*, pp. 327–32.

133. Chrétien, "Révolte au Burundi en 1934"; repr. in Chrétien, *Burundi, l'histoire retrouvée*, pp. 219–74. The administrative map was stabilized in 1943, and this became the basis for provinces in independent Burundi until the 1980s. See Stengers, *Congo, mythes et réalités*; Jewsiewicki, "Belgian Africa."

134. Chrétien, "Eglise et état au Burundi"; Mvuyekure, "Approche historique des conversions au catholicisme au Burundi (1922–1962)." The Protestants were as marginalized here as they were in the other Belgian territories. As for the Muslims, essentially thousands of Swahili on the lake's shores, who had been relatively respected by the Germans, they received the opprobrium reserved for the "Arabized," the sons of slavers. The term referring to the *évolués, basirimu* (plural of *musirimu* — a Kirundi derivation on the word for Muslim, *Munyeslamu*), kept a trace of their influence at the beginning of the century.

135. Published in Namur, *Grands Lacs* was the forerunner of *Vivant Univers*. See, notably, the March 1936 and February 1949 special editions.

136. Chrétien, *Burundi, l'histoire retrouvée*, pp. 347–71; Bahimanga, "Mission dans l'est du Burundi." In 1959, there were about sixty parishes of this kind in Burundi and about fifty in Rwanda.

137. A photo taken at Corpus Christi in front of the Rushubi mission in Burundi shows, as in Poland during the 1980s, the triumphalist aspect of these crowds; see Delacroix (ed.), *Histoire universelle des missions*, vol. 3, pp. 54–55. This type of denying access is termed *kunena*, a certain sign of reprobation and discrimination.

138. See Chapter II, pp. 128–29. On the suppression of this festival, see Bahenduzi, "Rituel du muganuro," pp. 301–394; and Joseph Gahama, "Disparition du muganuro." On the placement of these missions, see Joseph Gahama, "Hauts Lieux d'inscription des traditions et de la modernité au Burundi."

139. Monnens, "Grands Heures de l'Afrique," p. 274.

140. On these reforms, see Rutembesa, "Réorganisation administrative et ses conséquences au Rwanda entre 1926 et 1931." Batutsi from the Bega and

Banyigina clans controlled more than half the chiefdoms and subchiefdoms in 1948.

141. Catharine Newbury, *Cohesion of Oppression*, p. 63.

142. Nkurikiyimfura, *Gros Bétail et la société rwandaise*, p. 244.

143. Declaration of 1938, cited in Reyntjens, *Pouvoir et droit au Rwanda*, p. 201.

144. On the evolution of "the clientage relationship," see Catharine Newbury, *Cohesion of Oppression*, pp. 131–40; Nkurikiyimfura, *Gros Bétail et la société rwandaise*, pp. 234–44; Vidal, "Economie de la société féodale rwandaise"; and Vidal, "Situations ethniques au Rwanda," pp. 182–83. Classe, "Pour moderniser le Ruanda," p. 7.

145. Des Forges, "Defeat Is the Only Bad News," pp. 337–42; Mbonimana, "Christianisation indirecte," pp. 129–31.

146. Among the converted chiefs, one of former King Rwabugiri's sons and one of Chief Kabare's sons are notable.

147. Markovitz, *Cross and Sword*. The citation is extracted from *Grands Lacs*, Feb. 1947, p. 130. See Chrétien, "Eglise, pouvoir et culture," pp. 33–35. The 1916 Belgian victory has sometimes been described as providential: it was a "Catholic and Latin victory," wrote the French historian Canon Louis de Lacger in *Ruanda*, p. 463. One is also reminded of the baptism of the Saxons under Charlemagne....

148. Vidal, "De la Religion subie au modernisme refusé," p. 80.

149. Rutayisire, *Christianisation du Rwanda (1900–1945)*; Mbonimana, "Instauration d'un royaume chrétien au Rwanda"; and Linden, *Church and Revolution in Rwanda*, pp. 152–219.

150. Pastoral letter, July 16, 1927, cited in Linden, *Church and Revolution in Rwanda*, p. 162.

151. Letter to Resident Mortehan, Sept. 21, 1927, cited in Linden, *Church and Revolution in Rwanda*, p. 161, and Lacger, *Ruanda*, pp. 523–24. (The English translation of the first two sentences is taken from Linden. — TRANS.)

152. *Essor colonial et maritime*, Dec. 11, 1930, p. 9.

153. For the quotation, see the testimony of Rwakarenga, in Vidal, "De la

Religion subie au modernisme refusé," p. 81. On Rwanda's dedication to the Christ-King, see *Grands Lacs*, 1950, special issue on the fiftieth anniversary of evangelization.

154. Extracted from *Servir*, Astrida 1 (1940), pp. 8–10. See below on this institution.

155. During Belgian rule, "Gitega" was spelled "Kitega." Astrida, what is today Butare, was once conceived of as a future capital of Ruanda-Urundi.

156. Ministère des Colonies, *Plan décennal pour le développement économique et social du Ruanda-Urundi*. See also Harroy, *Burundi, 1955–1962*, pp. 113–80. For the 1920s–1930s in Burundi, see Joseph Gahama, *Burundi sous administration belge*, pp. 145–213. Also see the statistics in the annual reports submitted to the League of Nations and then to the United Nations: Ministère des Colonies, *Rapport sur l'administration belge*.

157. Lands that peasants called *bipimo*, which is derived from the Swahili verb *kupima*, "to measure."

158. On these "peasantries," see Joseph Gahama, "Innovation agricole grandiose."

159. Hatungimana, "La Caféiculture au Burundi"; the main points discussed here stem from this excellent study. Leplae, *Plantations de café au Congo belge*.

160. Nkurikiyimfura, *Gros Bétail et la société rwandaise*, pp. 226–27.

161. In 1930, the chiefs and subchiefs were obligated to plant 1,000 and 250 coffee trees, respectively.

162. Circular of August 1, 1933. Note that the missions themselves were plantations of many hectares.

163. The merchants were designated, as in Buhaya, by the Swahili term *wacuruzi*; there also were usurious contracts in the form of advance sales of future harvests. For citations from 1948–1949 see Sasserath, *Ruanda-Urundi*, p. 74, and Joseph Gahama, *Burundi sous administration belge*, p. 185.

164. "Culture du café par les indigènes du Ruanda-Urundi," African Archives, Brussels, cited in Hatungimana, "Caféiculture au Burundi," p. 198.

165. Chrétien, in collaboration with Mworoha, "Migrations du XXe siècle en Afrique orientale" (including many maps and graphs); Chrétien, "Des Séden-

taires devenues migrants: Les Départs des burundais et des rwandais vers l'Ouganda (1920–1960)," in Chrétien, *Burundi, l'histoire retrouvée*, pp. 275–310; Chrétien, "*Kurobera*, l'émigration en Ouganda et en 'Manamba' dans la première moitié du XXe siècle," pp. 427–36; Richards, *Economic Development and Tribal Change*. See the map on p. 484.

166. In light of the depopulation in Buganda from sleeping sickness at the start of the century as well as the significant labor needs for cotton.

167. In this case, the notion is better conveyed by the verb *kwambuka*, "to cross the river."

168. See above, p. 241. On the corvées under Belgian rule, see Chrétien, "Agronomie, consommation et travail," pp. 171–75. The Swahili term *akazi*, or "work," was first reserved for this type of task: a social experience as positive as that of slavery for the people of Antilles!

169. On Burundi, see Mworoha's inquiry in the northwest, cited in Chrétien with Mworoha, "Migrations du XXe siècle en Afrique orientales," pp. 659–60; on eastern Rwanda, see Gravel's monograph, *Remera*, pp. 107–117.

170. Chrétien, *Défi de l'ethnicisme*, pp. 11–28.

171. See the explorers' and missionaries' citations in Chapter I, pp. 70–73. Let me add that the White Fathers were persuaded in 1879 that they had found in Uganda "Ham's tomb" (an interpretation of Kintu's sacred woods); see Chrétien, "Deux Visages de Cham," p. 195.

172. See the many references in Chrétien, "Deux Visages de Cham"; Chrétien, "Hutu et Tutsi au Rwanda et au Burundi"; and Chrétien, "Les Identités Hutu et Tutsi: Perspectives historiques et manipulations politiques," in Chrétien, *Burundi, l'histoire retrouvée*, pp. 313–34.

173. Against all evidence, one added the former's light tint versus the latter's black tint.

174. The extracts cited in this section are staggered between 1902 and 1939 and were written by several missionaries (Classe, Gorju, Ménard, Pagès, and de Lacger). They are reprinted at greater length in Chrétien, "Hutu et Tutsi au Rwanda et au Burundi," pp. 136–39, and Chrétien, *Eglise, pouvoir et culture*, p. 43.

175. Piron, "Migrations hamitiques."

176. The term "missionary characterology" is from Vidal, "Situations eth-niques au Rwanda," p. 176. According to de Lacger, author of the image of "bronzed herdsmen," the term "Hamite" came from an Arab word meaning "reddish brown." In general, see Aminade, *Aux Sources du Nil*, cited in Mvuye-kure, "Idéologie missionaire et classifications ethniques en Afrique centrale," pp. 323–24. See, in the same vein, Sasserath, *Ruanda-Urundi* (see the citation, Chap-ter I, p. 72, and also the commentaries on the reporting at the time in Luc de Heusch's film, *La République devenue folle* (Brussels, 1995). As I noted in the introduction, these fantasies remain vivid.

177. Poliakov, *Aryan Myth.* On the ethnicist manipulation of the origin myths, done with the complicity of interested "informers," see Chrétien, "Nou-velles Hypothèses sur les origines du Burundi," pp. 12–15; Chrétien, "Mythes et stratégies," pp. 299–315; and Servaes, "Etude ethnographique du Rwanda," p. 106.

178. A fantasy popularized in Europe in 1950 by the film *King Solomon's Mines.*

179. Furet, "Feudal System," p. 684. On this score in Rwanda and Burundi, see Chrétien, "Deux Visages de Cham," p. 196; and especially Franche, "Généa-logie du génocide Rwandais." Also see Chrétien, "Vocabulaire et concepts."

180. Ryckmans, *Dominer pour servir*, p. 26.

181. Neesen, "Aspects de l'économie démographique du Ruanda-Urundi." A "dominant caste" of 3 percent of the population, the interim resident, Wint-gens, wrote in 1914; cited in Honke, "Pour l'empereur et le roi," p. 125.

182. Chrétien, *Burundi, l'histoire retrouvée*, pp. 324–26 (with graphs); Mbonimana, "Christianisation indirecte," pp. 138–45.

183. Vidal, *Sociologie des passions*, p. 28.

184. See the biography of "the jewel of the mission of Sabi," Siméon Rutare, in Vidal, "De la Religion subie au modernisme refusé," pp. 74–78, and that of the head builder of Muyaga, Joseph Burashahu, in Chrétien, *Burundi, l'histoire retrouvée*, pp. 367–69.

185. Cited in Linden, *Church and Revolution in Rwanda*, p. 136.

186. In Rwanda, the Catholic newspaper *Kinyamateka* was started in 1933; in Burundi, *Rusiziramarembe* goes back to 1940.

187. On the "ethnographer state," see Chauveau and Dozon, "Au Coeur des ethnies ivoiriennes...l'état." An irony of history is that Franck was close to the socialists and that Cameron was named by a labor minister. Arendt, *Origins of Totalitarianism*; an analysis along these lines can be found in Jewsiewicki, "African Peasants and Totalitarian Colonial Society in the Belgian Congo, 1917–1960." "To remove the Mututsi caste...would lead the country to a heinously anti-European Communism," *Essor colonial et maritime*, Dec. 4, 1930, cited in Lacger, *Ruanda*, p. 524.

188. Linden, *Church and Revolution in Rwanda*, p. 229. Unfortunately, the author, rather won over to the ethnic vision of some White Fathers who witnessed this period, holds a reductive view of this nationalism. Let's note that most intellectuals at the time were clerks in the medieval sense of the term: they were more Rwandan abbots than European priests. The first black bishop was consecrated there in 1952, thirteen years after one was consecrated in Uganda, in the person of Aloïs Bigirumwami, a descendant of the royal family of ancient Gisaka.

189. On the Bashi, see Bishikwabo, "Histoire d'un état Shi," pp. 328–486; and Bishikwabo, "Deux Chefs du Bushi sous le régime colonial"; on the Bahavu, see David Newbury and Catharine Newbury, "King and Chief on Ijwi Island, Zaire."

190. On this period, see the brilliant synthesis of Ndaywel è Nziem, *Histoire du Congo*, pp. 309–423.

191. In Ruanda-Urundi, one finds Danes and Swedes.

192. In 1939, there were nearly two thousand in the single district of Kivu (the region of Costermansville, the future Bukavu), and in 1928, 5,000 hectares were alienated in the Kabare chiefdom.

193. They totaled nearly thirty thousand in the early 1950s.

194. This was the logic that guided Father Placide Tempels when he published, in Léopoldville in 1945, right after an *évolué* revolt in Katanga, his *Philosophie bantoue*, inspired by St. Thomas, Lucien Lévy-Bruhl, and Alexis Carrel, to remind the Congolese of their "traditional" thought, in theory

observed among the Baluba of Kasai. See Chrétien, "Bantous," pp. 64–65, and Eboussi, "Bantou problématique."

CHAPTER FIVE: REGAINED INDEPENDENCE AND THE OBSESSION WITH GENOCIDE

1. On Ugandan decolonization, see Prunier, "'Roi-gentleman et le président terroriste'"; Karugire, *Political History of Uganda*, pp. 144–98; Welbourn, *Religion and Politics in Uganda, 1952–1962*; and Henri Médard, "La Naissance et le déclin des partis politico-religieux en Ouganda (1887–1996)," in Hervé Maupeu and Christian Delmet (eds.), *Religions et politique en Afrique de l'Est* (Paris, forthcoming). See also Pirouet, *Historical Dictionary of Uganda*.

2. The creation of this party also took place in the context of the Cold War: Catholic Action and the White Fathers denounced the Communist sympathies of the Congress Party. See Gertzel, "Kingdoms, Districts, and the Unitary State," p. 87.

3. Cited in Prunier, "'Roi-gentleman et le président terroriste,'" p. 249.

4. The Bugandan *lukiko* chose the federal representatives.

5. Notable among the holy places was the Cwezi site of Mubende. See Chapter IV, p. 230.

6. On the period from 1962 to today, see Prunier and Calas (eds.), *Ouganda contemporain*, pp. 89–154.

7. Edward Frederick Mutesa, nicknamed King Freddy, ended his life in destitution despite his popularity in Buganda.

8. A member of the Kakwa Nilote ethnic group, this colonial infantryman was renowned for his repression of the Mau Mau and later for handling Obote's dirty work.

9. At the time, Asians controlled three-quarters of the industrial and commercial enterprises. The executions included the murder of the Anglican archbishop Jani Luwum in 1977. Even progressive intellectuals, impressed by Idi Amin's "anti-imperialist" clowning around, judged him a genius, without ever having asked for a single Ugandan's opinion. See, for instance, Chesneaux, *Pasts and Future*, pp. 43–44.

10. The Catholic-inspired DP should have won these elections, not the UPC.

11. FRELIMO is a Portuguese acronym for the Mozambican Liberation Front.

12. Note that the two ruffian soldiers in power were Catholic.

13. The same was true for the dictatorships in Rwanda and Burundi in the 1980s, but in a context then that was certainly less grotesque than that in Uganda. To the outsider, Obote, in his three-piece suits, appeared as "the IMF's obedient student."

14. As did the kind of graffiti left by the killers: "A good Muganda is a dead one," a phrase that has more of a Western inspiration than a local one. See the photographs in Kasozi, *Social Origins of Violence in Uganda, 1964–1985*, p. xvii.

15. Prunier, "Lieux de la mémoire royale au Buganda."

16. See articles in the semiofficial daily *New Vision*, April, 7, 1999, and July 14, 1999.

17. One might compare this case, where the political dynamic was able to subvert or transcend ethnic gravity, with that of the 1994 elections in South Africa, where Nelson Mandela's African National Congress was successful, even in Zulu country, when facing his rival's Inkatha Freedom Party.

18. See below for the motives for their departure.

19. Prunier, "Elements pour une histoire du Front Patriotique Rwandais."

20. Leurquin, *Niveau de vie des populations rurales du Ruanda-Urundi*, p. 250; the statistics were 4,249 and 4,439 francs, respectively.

21. Chrétien, "Echanges et hiérarchies."

22. Maquet and Hertefelt, *Elections en société féodale*. See also Catharine Newbury, *Cohesion of Oppression*, pp. 180–206.

23. After the English made him stand down, Mutesa II went to Nyanza in 1957 for the twenty-fifth anniversary of Mutara's rule.

24. Harroy, *Rwanda*, p. 241. Harroy became governor in 1955. An irony of history: this Freemason carried out policies that the Church wanted.

25. On the manipulation of traditions, see Chrétien, "Mythes et stratégies," pp. 309–315. These documents can be found in two collections: Nkundabagenzi,

Rwanda politique, 1958–1960, "Décolonisation et indépendance du Rwanda et du Burundi." [For an English translation of the "Manifesto of the Bahutu," see United Nations, *United Nations Visiting Mission to Trust Territories in East Africa, 1957,* pp. 39–42. — TRANS.] On the decolonization of Rwanda, see Lemarchand, *Rwanda and Burundi,* pp. 93–196; and Chrétien, "'Révolution assistée' au Rwanda," pp. 233–38.

26. Bragard, "Vers l'Indépendance du Ruanda-Urundi": the social doctrine of the Church turned on "the physical distinction... between the Bantu race and Hamite cattle keepers."

27. The circulation of *Kinyamateka* reached twenty-five thousand in 1955.

28. Not to be confused with the future president Juvénal Habyarimana.

29. Patrice Lumumba's rise to power in Léopoldville in July 1960, followed by his assassination in January 1961, had the repercussions that one can imagine in very Christian Ruanda-Urundi: obsessive fear about Communism in Ruanda, nationalist passion in Urundi.

30. Hubert, *Toussaint rwandaise et sa répression;* Willame, "*Muyaga* ou la 'révolution' rwandaise revisitée."

31. Logiest, *Mission au Rwanda.*

32. Gitarama is in the center of the country, not far from Kabgayi. A referendum that accompanied the elections delivered the final blow to the monarchy. Indeed, the referendum was nicknamed *Kamarampaka,* "that which definitively decides." Kigeri subsequently left for Uganda, then Beijing and New York.

33. Declaration of the Central Committee of PARMEHUTU in May 1960. See Chrétien, "Crise politique rwandaise," pp. 124–26.

34. The word "democracy" is transcribed in Kinyarwanda as such.

35. In his memoir, Governor Harroy (*Rwanda,* pp. 506–507) claimed that the "great mass of victims were the simple Tutsi... who deserved to be spared." But "that was the price to pay," he concluded.

36. In the hypothesis where the ideology of races, in the style of Boulain-villiers, would have prevailed in revolutionary France over class consciousness.

37. The statistics are much debated, for political reasons, but also because many exiles left without being counted by the United Nations High Commis-

sioner for Refugees and were found in the adjoining populations, among whom some (in Uganda's Kigezi and in Kivu) spoke Kinyarwanda. See Guichaoua, *Le Problème des réfugiés rwandais*; and Prunier, *Rwanda Crisis*, pp. 61–74.

38. The limited success of some (notably in business and in the Church), tolerated by the government, overshadowed the actual daily lives of the majority of Batutsi. Today, several authors still retrospectively judge the quotas to be satisfactory, but they are unaware of what the realities on the hills were.

39. Chrétien, "Ethnicité et politique."

40. *Monde*, Feb. 6, 1964.

41. Segal, *Massacre in Rwanda*; Heusch, "Massacres collectifs au Rwanda?"; Willame, *Aux Sources de la hécatombe rwandaise*, pp. 64–90. The quote comes from Kayibanda's March 11, 1964 speech "Adresse aux rwandais émigrés ou réfugiés à l'etranger,'" cited in S. Sebasoni, *Les origines du Rwanda* (Paris: L'Harmattan, 2000), pp. 146–47.

42. *Ingingo z'ingenzi mu mateka y'uRwanda* (Fundamental principles of the history of Rwanda), July 1972, on the tenth anniversary of independence.

43. Chrétien, "Crise politique rwandaise," pp. 126–32.

44. Reyntjens, "Nouvelle Constitution rwandaise du 20 décembre 1978"; Reyntjens, "Deuxième République rwandaise." The author was one of three jurists on a restricted commission that had been charged by Habyarimana with drafting a pilot study for this constitution. According to Article 7 of the document, every Rwandan citizen was a "militant" of the single party.

45. Paternostre de la Mairieu, *A la Source du Nil*, p. 31. The author was a longtime adviser to President Kayibanda, a fact that the "new" regime buried.

46. John Paul II caused him to withdraw his membership in 1990.

47. Maindron, *Des Apparitions à Kibeho*. Besides the various kinds of manipulation that accompanied this phenomenon, some of the recorded "messages" conveyed the malaise and the anxiety latent in this society, ones that lay behind its apparent "equilibrium."

48. Rare were the Rwandan intellectuals who emulated Jules Michelet or Marc Bloch in being able to respect the coronation of Reims as much as the seizure of the Bastille. Two examples were the historians Emmanuel Ntezimana

(cited in Chapter I) and Cyprien Rugamba, who was killed in 1994. See "Préa-lables à l'interprétation de la tradition orale," in Centre de Civilisation Burun-daise, *La Civilisation ancienne des peuples des Grands Lacs*, pp. 331–48. As for the remarkably erudite Alexis Kagame, unfortunately trapped by Hamitic ideology, we saw in the introduction the ambiguity of his situation in republican Rwanda.

49. Joseph Gahama, "Options d'une indépendance sous tutelle au Rwanda et au Burundi"; Joseph Gahama, "Partis politiques et la recherche de l'indépen-dance au Burundi"; Deslaurier, "Vie politique à la veille de l'indépendance"; Deslaurier, "Du nouveau pour l'histoire politique"; Ghislain, "Souvenirs de la territoriale au Burundi."

50. Bahenduzi, "Rituel du muganuro," pp. 395–416. Only the suburbs called Camp Belge (the Belgian camp) and Quartier Swahili (the Swahili district) fell under the status of extra-customary centers, starting in 1941.

51. Lechat, *Burundi politique*.

52. The party was supported by a leader of the European community of colonial settlers, Albert Maus, a former Scheutist Father who became a follower of the sun cult of the pharaoh Akhenaton [*sic*].

53. With some nuances: some Batare princes were with Rwagasore (such as Chief Muhirwa, who came from a lineage from the northeast), and some Bezi princes were in the Common Front (such as Chief Bigayimpunzi, a close cousin of the king).

54. The Catholic journal *Ndongozi* was very close to the nationalists.

55. The People's Party, which claimed to represent the Bahutu, received less than 8 percent of the votes in 1960 and less than 1 percent in 1961. The Hutu ethnicist politicians of the 1990s are rewriting history when they claim either that their "ethnic group" had been "tricked" by Rwagasore or that UPRONA had initially been a "Hutu party" (since it won a majority) and then changed camps. For the quotation, see Harroy, *Burundi, 1955–1962*. The two Christian Democratic Party leaders were hanged after independence. The Burundian nationalists saw Rwagasore as a hero and the Belgians' third victim, after Mutara and Lumumba.

56. Lemarchand, *Rwanda and Burundi*, pp. 343–401. The names Casablanca

and Monrovia pertain to the cities where relatively antagonistic groups of the newly independent African states met; this was before the Organization of African Unity was created in 1963.

57. Lemarchand, *Rwanda and Burundi*, p. 344. This Franco-American expert, very critical in 1970 of ambiguities in the Rwandan ideology, then evolved toward a position close to Hutu ethnic fundamentalism; see Lemarchand, "Burundian Glaasnost or Falsification of History?" The article was published in *Burundi Newsletter*, a periodical of the PALIPEHUTU party, and Lemarchand, *Burundi: Ethnocide as Discourse and Practice* (Cambridge: Cambridge University Press, 1994).

58. Chrétien, "Ethnicité et violence: La Conscientisation par la peur," in Chrétien, *Défi de l'ethnisme*, pp. 29–46. One is here entering the domain of "immediate history," where rumors abound. There are still many secrets about how the strategies leading to each of the violent crises in this region were elaborated. However, it is difficult not to see the importance of cynical calculations by politicians convinced that "the majority" would win in the end just because of numbers and no matter the price: a barbarous calculation, but also a very modern one.

59. On the Burundi crises since 1965, see Chrétien, "La Tragédie Hutu-Tutsi: Une Dette de sens contemporaine," in Chrétien, *Burundi, l'histoire retrouvée*, pp. 415–92; Chrétien, "Burundi: L'Autodestruction assistée d'une nation," in Chrétien, *Défi de l'ethnisme*, pp. 145–98; and Chrétien, "Ethnicité et politique."

60. On the Congolese rebellions between 1963 and 1965, also called Mulelist, where both anti-Castro and "Guevarist" Cubans also intervened, see Weiss and Verhaegen (eds.), *Rébellions dans l'est du Zaïre, 1964–1967*. In Peking, Chou En-lai then inspired an active "pro–Third World" politics. Gaston Soumialot, member of the National Council of Liberation, briefly lived in Bujumbura. It was then that Che Guevara met Laurent-Désiré Kabila in southern Uvira.

61. Note here also that the cleavage is not automatic: Pierre Ngendandumwe (Hutu) is "Casablancan," whereas Thaddée Siryuyumunsi (Tutsi) is "Monrovian"; see Manirakiza, *Fin de la monarchie burundaise, 1962–1966*. See Lemarchand, "The C.I.A. in Africa."

62. The total number of victims of both the massacres and repression in Muramvya Province is between twenty-five hundred and five thousand. Eighty key Hutu figures were shot, including UPRONA's president, Joseph Bamina.

63. UPRONA became the single party until 1992.

64. The "Bururi group" can be compared to the "northern" faction in Habyarimana's regime in Rwanda.

65. A statement circulated in November 1968 (personal archives).

66. Malkki, *Purity and Exile*. On this occasion, the former king Ntare V, who had returned to Burundi in obscure circumstances, was assassinated in Gitega.

67. I have closely followed the evolution of Burundi since 1964. See Chrétien, Guichaoua, and Le Jeune, *Crise d'août 1988 au Burundi*, pp. 39–57.

68. Hutu leaders in exile asserted there was a "Simbananiye plan" to equalize Burundi's ethnic groups, a rumor that brought with it the hate that one can imagine.

69. The three successive military presidents came from the same commune (Rutovu) in the province of Bururi and belonged to two clans from the Hima subgroup, a fact that inspired the cliché of a "Hima government" in the press, even though the majority of Batutsi from the south (and members of the "Bururi group") are not Hima.

70. Chrétien, "La Démocratisation face aux intégrismes ethniques au Rwanda et au Burundi," in Chrétien, *Burundi, l'histoire retrouvée*, pp. 481–92, earlier published in Guichaoua (ed.), *Enjeux nationaux et dynamiques régionales dans l'Afrique des Grands Lacs*, pp. 31–58.

71. Grosser, *Crime et la mémoire*, p. 20.

72. Bloch, *The Historian's Craft*, p. 35.

73. Chrétien, *Défi de l'ethnisme*. Also see the syntheses of Colette Braeckman, a journalist with the Belgian newspaper *Le Soir*: *Terreurs africaines* and *Enjeu congolais*. Also see Reyntjens, *Afrique des Grands Lacs en crise*; and Guichaoua (ed.), *Crises politiques au Burundi et au Rwanda (1993–1994)*, which has a very useful collection of articles and appendices. Verhaegen, *Introduction à l'histoire immédiate*.

74. Chrétien, Guichaoua, and Le Jeune, *La Crise d'août 1988 au Burundi*, pp.

91–152 (dossiers of eyewitness accounts that were recorded with Tutsi and Hutu peasants in two communes in September 1988).

75. Chrétien, *Défi de l'ethnisme*, p. 164.

76. FRODEBU respectively obtained two-thirds and three-quarters of the votes in these two successive elections.

77. Chrétien, "Tournant historique au Burundi et au Rwanda," *Marchés tropicaux et méditerranéens* (1993), pp. 2420–22; repr. in Chrétien, *Défi de l'ethnisme*, pp. 47–54.

78. Prunier, *Rwanda Crisis*; Chrétien, "Crise politique rwandaise"; *Défi de l'ethnisme*, notably "Rwanda, la résistible maturation du génocide."

79. *Libre belgique*, Oct. 31, 1989, by Marie-France Cros, who later incisively denounced "the respectable racism" reigning in Rwanda. Willame, "Panne rwandaise." Note that the prices of coffee collapsed after 1986 and that external debt had risen by more than 200 percent since 1970.

80. See above, p. 299, on the motives of many young Rwandans who rallied to Museveni's NRA, starting in 1982. *Inkotanyi* also was the name of Mwami Rwabugiri's army that fought south of Lake Kivu in the late nineteenth century — which led defenders of the Habyarimana regime to denounce the RPF as a "monarchist" and "feudal" movement.

81. Nonetheless, this provoked hostility in the Belgian public and the retreat of the Toussaint's Belgian contingent, despite the sympathies at King Baudouin's court and in Social Christian circles.

82. Kagame was a childhood friend of Rwigyema's and, like him, one of Museveni's first fellow guerrilla fighters.

83. The French military units (in Operation Noroît and those on temporary assignment) included several hundred men; they were not withdrawn until December 1993.

84. Saur, *Influences parallèles*. (The author was a leader of the Francophone Social Christian Party.) Franche, *Rwanda*; Gouteux, *Génocide secret d'état*.

85. Chrétien, Dupaquier, Kabanda, and Ngarambe, *Rwanda*; Chrétien, "'Presse libre' et propagande raciste au Rwanda." Several MRND intellectuals in Belgium seemingly concocted this "appeal."

86. Chrétien, "'Nazisme tropical' au Rwanda?"

87. See Fédération Internationale des Droits de l'Homme and other organizations, *Commission Internationale d'Enquête*. The documents published by Rwandan human-rights associations and opposition parties in 1992–1993 were also very explicit on this point.

88. The Bagogwe, cattle keepers in the northern part of the country, had never played a role in politics and were therefore killed on a strictly racist basis; see Chapter III, p. 189. The massacres of Bugesera were sparked by an announcement on national radio of a faked document "revealing" a plan to assassinate all key Hutu figures.

89. Respectively, a former ideologue of PARMEHUTU, a businessman turned powerful orator of Hutu Power, and a manager of the "Popular Banks." On the evolution of the MDR, see Bertrand, *Rwanda, le piège de l'histoire*.

90. This logic of making "ethnic solidarity" a priority (a so-called third way between *akazu* and the RPF) was clearly supported by the Christian Democratic International in Brussels and by the Elysée in Paris. On these points, see Saur, *Influences parallèles*, pp. 57–95, and Prunier, *Rwanda Crisis*, pp. 178–79.

91. Twagiramungu was Kayibanda's son-in-law; kinship still mattered under the republic! Education minister in the preceding government, Uwilingiyimana had dared to attack the quota system in the schools; as a result, she was beaten up by militias and dragged through the mud by caricatures in the extremist press.

92. Notably in demanding the integration of the CDR in the peace accords.

93. One of the station's promoters was the historian Ferdinand Nahimana, a relative of the president; he had been the director of official radio when it sadly became famous for diffusing the false news that unleashed the massacres in Bugesera (March 1992). For works by this university professor, see Chapter II, p. 374 (note 23). In addition to playing Zairian music, the station aired songs by Simon Bikindi on Rwandan history, notably "Bene Sebahinzi" (The sons of the Land Clearer), revisited here to mobilize the "Hutu people." The number of listeners is based on an estimate of about one radio per ten inhabitants during that period. See Chrétien, Dupaquier, Kabanda, and Ngarambe, *Rwanda*, and Chrétien, "Rwanda: La Médiatisation d'un génocide."

94. In general, see Reyntjens, *Rwanda*, pp. 93–115. Bimazubute was one of the rare Batutsi in FRODEBU, an original person who had been a student leader in the 1960s and a minister when Micombero was in power. The health minister, Jean Minani, one of the two who tried to create a free government, had been presented by the Christian Democratic International as Ndadaye's heir.

95. See Chrétien, "Burundi: Pogromes sur les collines" (based on a personal collection of eyewitness accounts and many unpublished documents).

96. The international community's incapacity was evident, despite the multiplicity of Western initiatives, both private and public, that accompanied democratization in this country since 1989.

97. Chrétien, "Burundi: The Obsession with Genocide." See also Chrétien, *Défi de l'ethnicisme*, pp. 183–98.

98. Ould Abdallah, *Diplomatie Pyromane.*

99. A regional conference was held in Dar es Salaam to advance the implementation of the Arusha Accords. The presence of the Burundian president on this plane was improvised at the last minute. Some French military units providing assistance were still on the ground and were the first to observe the plane's wreckage. To aggravate everything, a former gendarme who was close to the Elysée and to the Habyarimana clan, Captain Paul Barril, made pseudo revelations the following May, which operated as a smoke screen. On this debate, see Reyntjens, *Rwanda*, pp. 21–50; Prunier, *Rwanda Crisis*, pp. 213–29; and Assemblée Nationale, *Rapport de la Mission parlementaire d'information sur le Rwanda.* In January 1994, the UNAMIR commander, Canadian general Roméo Dallaire, sent a telegram to the United Nations Secretariat in which he described preparations for genocide that had been revealed by a renegade; see also Sénat de Belgique, *Rapport de la Commission d'enquête parlementaire concernant les événements du Rwanda.* Former director in the Ministry of Defense, Bagosora had announced when the Arusha negotiations were taking place that he was going to "prepare for the Apocalypse." Kambanda's supporters labeled the government "saviors" (*batabazi*). Paris stayed in contact with Kambanda's government until July 1994, and it even received his minister of foreign affairs, Jérôme Bicamumpaka, on April 27. See Verschave, *Complicité de génocide?*; and Chrétien, "Responsabilités politiques du génocide."

100. This genocide already has an abundant bibliography: Braeckman, *Rwanda, histoire d'un génocide*; Prunier, *Rwanda Crisis*, pp. 229–80; Willame, *Aux Sources de la hécatombe rwandaise*; Vidal (ed.), *Politiques de la haine*; Verdier, Decaux, and Chrétien (eds.), *Rwanda*; Brauman, *Devant le mal*; Destexhe, *Rwanda and Genocide in the Twentieth Century*; Bührer, *Rwanda*; Mukagasana, *Mort ne veut pas de moi*; Blam, "Témoignage à Kibuye." Two synthetic works are particularly noteworthy, given the richness of eyewitness accounts and the analytic precision therein: African Rights, *Rwanda: Death, Despair, and Defiance*; and Des Forges, *Leave None to Tell the Story*. An exhaustive, though already dated, bibliography can be found in Chrétien, "Interprétations du génocide de 1994 dans l'histoire contemporaine du Rwanda."

101. Structured since 1993 under Bagosora's impetus, as was attested in his date book that was discovered during investigations by Human Rights Watch.

102. This was the dominant framework used by the Western media during the three months.

103. Besides receiving arms deliveries during the height of the genocide, the state bought 600,000 machetes between January 1993 and March 1994 under the cover of purchasing agricultural equipment; these purchases were financed with credits accorded by the World Bank and other foreign donors, which today remain on the Rwanda government's debt accounts.

104. The bishop of Gikongoro in Kibeho apparently refused to help schoolchildren; see African Rights, *Rwanda: Death, Despair, and Defiance*, pp. 299–315. The investigation led by Alison Des Forges provided proof of the systematic development by Butare intellectuals of false propaganda, consisting, by "mirror effect," in attributing to "the enemy" what was being prepared for it. For an account of how doctors responded, see Blam, "Témoignage à Kibuye." For the quotation, see RTLM, Kantano Habimana, July 2, 1994.

105. People were cut beginning with their extremities; babies were killed in front of their mothers; Hutu husbands were required to kill their Tutsi wives, and so on. I am abridging the details of these atrocities, which themselves are quite repetitive. But this does not signal support for the idea that the historian's objectivity must mean indifference to extreme events and to the trampling of

416

values. The sterilized evocation of massacres is simplistic, unless one subscribes to the famous "omelet of history" theory. The anthropological study of the conduct of killers involves not turning away and not just being a "sociologist" of their frustrations. See Vidal, "Génocide des rwandais Tutsi"; also see Corbin, *Village of Cannibals*.

106. On the demographic rise, the lack of hope for social advancement, and the risks for scapegoating inherent in frustrated expectations, see Guichaoua, *Ordre paysan des Hautes Terres centrales du Burundi et du Rwanda*; Cochet, *Burundi: La Paysannerie dans la tourmente*; and Imbs, Bart, and Bart, "Rwanda."

107. Lame, *Colline entre mille*, p. 74.

108. Even in 1987, Father Guy Theunis, the intellectual leader of the journal *Dialogue*, rejected criticism in favor of "confirmation through symbols" — in other words, systematic emphasis on all that was positive in the situation; see Theunis, "Philosophie pour *Dialogue*."

109. Despite the work of Goldhagen in *Hitler's Willing Executioners*, which suggests that German society was predisposed to the persecution of the Jews.

110. The journalist Dominique Makeli recorded a supposed "dialogue" between the Virgin and the clairvoyant Valentine Nyiramukiza.

111. A pious expression, used, for example, by Monsignor Etchegaray on his return from a visit to Rwanda carried out in the name of the pope. Some missionaries blamed the genocide on Satan; see the citation in Chrétien, *Défi de l'ethnicisme*, pp. 236–37.

112. This comparison prompted Michel Rocard, the former French prime minister, to write a preface to a new edition of the Edict of Nantes, just after a trip to Rwanda that was coincident with the fourth centenary of this founding text; see Rocard, *Edit de Nantes et l'art de la paix*, pp. 7–97.

113. See the estimates on the number of refugees in Guichaoua, "Mobilité forcée dans la région des Grands Lacs."

114. I was in Kigali in the autumn of 1994, and it was easy to see that the smallest Western NGO was better equipped than the devastated public services.

115. The International Criminal Tribunal for Rwanda, created by the United Nations, was located in Arusha in 1995, and by the summer of 1999 it

had sentenced five of the thirty high-ranking culprits whom the tribunal slowly succeeded in having arrested throughout Africa.

116. Based on the American plea-bargaining model.

117. One had to wait three years in Belgium before a parliamentary commission looked into the events of 1994, four years in France, five years for the Organization of African Unity, and the same for the United Nations Secretariat. In 1998, the American president Bill Clinton, on a short trip to Kigali airport, expressed his country's regrets for its reprehensible indifference at the Security Council in April–May 1994. Reconciliation is a theme dear to international organizations when dealing with African conflicts, even the most unjustifiable and the most heinous, as in Sierra Leone in 1999.

118. Collective of Goma NGOs (supported by Belgian and French NGOs), July 26, 1994. Many other examples and references can be found in Chrétien, *Défi de l'ethnicisme*, pp. 199–388 (the section titled "La Négation dans tous ses états").

119. The debate on the statistics (the margin would go from 10,000 to 100,000 between April 1994 and late 1995) and on the causes: Was it vengeance or a desire to terrorize? The question was obscured by the inadequacy of the data, which were often anonymous, indirect, or hampered by the prejudices of their authors and the media that gave them play. The massive recruitment of the genocide's killers was also an explanation: the members of the RPF underground were confronted by piles of bodies of their kin, which prompted them to see every Muhutu as a machete wielder. Moral evaluation is here particularly delicate, and efforts to draw equivalents misplaced: does one think of the militarily useless bombardments of Hamburg and Dresden at the end of World War II? On this subject, see Prunier, *Rwanda Crisis*, pp. 358–62, and especially Des Forges, *Leave None to Tell the Story*, pp. 701–35.

120. International aid was estimated at a million dollars per day in 1996. Médecins sans Frontières, *Deadlock in the Rwandan Refugee Crisis*; African Rights, *Rwanda: Assassinated Proof*.

121. Reclaiming property was a nagging issue in this country, where family ownership had been recognized for a long time and space was scarce.

122. This "humanitarian intervention," done in the name of the United Nations, probably aimed to create a sort of provisionary partition of the country, and it bailed out many leaders of the genocide. The majority of displaced-persons camps in this "secure humanitarian zone" had been closed without much difficulty in 1995. But when Kibeho was closed, some provocation by former militias, who were numerous there, was followed by the killing of several thousand (according to the eyewitness account collected from a former UN observer).

123. Chrétien, *Défi de l'ethnicisme*, pp. 186–98; Braeckman, *Terreurs africaines*, pp. 127–201; Braeckman, *Enjeu congolais*, pp. 191–202; and the reports by the Brussels-based International Crisis Group since 1998. See Ntibantunganya's memoirs, *Guerre "ethno"-civile s'installe, 1993–1996*. In March 1995, Anatole Kanyenkiko was replaced at the head of the government by Antoine Nduwayo, a man from the south who was best regarded in the most hard-line Tutsi circles.

124. From the Congolese rebellions of the 1960s to those of the 1990s, the gold of this region has remained essential to war. Its export also had a (not clear) political-economic stake in Burundi in the wake of President Ndadaye's assassination.

125. The considerable Rwandan Tutsi diaspora has regained control of its country since the summer of 1994.

126. He is nicknamed *mwalimu*, the "schoolteacher," in his country.

127. Based on the peace model in Mozambique, which forgot that this country was not torn apart by the same type of racism.

128. On the region's ability to resist foreign incursions, see Chapter III, pp. 164–65, and Chapter IV, pp. 288–90. On land and political disputes, see Young, *Politics in the Congo*, pp. 302–305 and 533–71.

129. On this question, see Lacoste (ed.), *Géopolitique d'une Afrique médiane*, notably Pourtier, "Congo-Zaïre-Congo," and Prunier, "Crise du Kivu et ses conséquences dans la région des Grands Lacs." Also see Willame, *Banyarwanda et Banyamulenge*; and Chajmowiecz, "Kivu."

130. The word "Banyamulenge" comes from the name of the Mulenge hill, above Uvira, that was supposed to be the first settlement of these cattle keepers

of Rwandan origin. On these earlier migrations, see Chapter II, pp. 146–47 and pp. 161–62, and Chapter IV, p. 28.

131. In this instance, a resolution prepared by the vice president, Anzuluni Bembe, a politician from Uvira who was very hostile toward the Banyamulenge.

132. Kabila was a Muluba from North Katanga. On the regime he wanted to depose, see Willame, *Automne d'un despotism*. The strange ins and outs of this regime would bring us too far afield for the subject of this book. Zaire is the so-called authentic name of Congo-Kinshasa since 1971, based on the name given to the Congo River by the Portuguese in the fifteenth century (in fact, the name of the river in Kikongo is *nzadi*). Uganda was worried about the support that two rebel movements obtained in Congo. The first was the messianic and terrorist movement called the Lord's Resistance, which had ravaged northern Uganda; the second was the Allied Democratic Forces, which had ravaged the west. The latter organization brought under one tent Muslim fundamentalists, traditional dissidents from the Konjo ethnic group (see Chapter III, p. 186, and Rwanda *interahamwe*. On the situation in Congo, see Braeckman, *Enjeu congolais*. Burundi itself also took the opportunity to quash the FDD undergrounds based near Uvira: they withdrew to Kigoma, in Tanzania.

133. The "black Khmers" theme is repeated in the book of a doctor and former minister, Debré, *Retour de mwami*. A good example of contradictory politics is furnished by Museveni's hostility toward Buyoya, even though they both come from Hima groups in their respective countries, Uganda and Burundi, and even though their politics correspond on many other concerns.

Conclusion: The Fragments of History

1. For an example in the western parts of Sahelian Africa, see Gallais, *Hommes du Sahel*.

2. Some examples of this ethnological literature include Ray's *Myth, Ritual, and Kingship in Buganda*, which shows the feedback between James Frazer's theories and Reverend John Roscoe's investigations; Czekanowski's work in German on Rwanda fell into oblivion in favor of feudal theorizing that culminated in Maquet's synthesis; and the best historical research on Burundi in the 1930s, that

of the Belgian historian Smets, was stifled by the popularity of the White Fathers' interpretation, led by Monsignor Gorju.

3. Mbembe, *Afriques indociles.*

4. See Ruytinx, *Morale bantou*, pp. 20–22 and 39–44; and Rodegem, "Fonction hyperphatique du langage."

5 The "historical notes" that introduce the memoranda of visiting Western heads of state, economic and international social assessments, and humanitarian NGO reports are worthy of a study, but one whose conclusions would undoubtedly be distressing. This does not mean, of course, that different types of "cooperation" have not benefited from quality interactions, but what was their impact?

6. See Bayart, *State in Africa.*

7. In *Esprit*, Dec. 1976, and repr. in Chrétien, *Burundi, l'histoire retrouvée*, pp. 433–45. Claude Lévi-Strauss's formulation comes from *Le Totémisme aujourd'hui* (Paris: PUF, 1962), p. 128, in reference to natural species preferred by a group not as "good to eat" but as "good to think." For a discussion of mythical thought, see also Lévi-Strauss's considerations on "intellectual bricolage" in *La Pensée Sauvage* (Paris: Plon, 1962), pp. 26–27.

8. *Courrier international*, Sept. 16, 1999, p. 29.

Bibliography

General works

Ageron, Charles-Robert and Marc Michel (eds.), *L'Ere des décolonisations: Sélection de textes du colloque "Décolonisations comparées," Aix-en-Provence, 30 Septembre – 3 Octobre 1993* (Paris: Karthala, 1995).

Amselle, Jean-Loup and Elikia M'Bokolo (eds.), *Au Coeur de l'ethnie: Ethnie, tribalisme, et état en Afrique* (Paris: La Découverte/Poche, 1985).

Ankermann, Bernard, "Kulturkreise und Kulturschichten in Afrika," *Zeitschrift für Ethnologie* (1905).

Arendt, Hannah, *The Origins of Totalitarianism* (New York: Harcourt, Brace, & Co., 1951).

Balandier, Georges, *Political Anthropology*, trans. A.M. Sheridan Smith (London: Allen Lane, 1970).

Barth, Frederick, "Segmentary Opposition and the Theory of Games: A Study of Pathan Organization," *Journal of the Royal Anthropological Institute of Great Britain and Ireland* 89.1 (1959).

Bayart, Jean-François, *The State in Africa: The Politics of the Belly* (London: Longman, 1993).

Bleek, Wilhelm, *Über den Ursprung der Sprache* (Weimar: H. Boehlau, 1868).

Bleuchot, Hervé H., "Le Soudan au XIXe siècle," in Marc Lavergne (ed.), *Le Soudan contemporain: De l'invasion turco-égyptienne à la rébellion africaine (1821–1989)* (Paris: Karthala, 1989).

Bloch, Marc, *Feudal Society*, trans. L.A. Manyon (Chicago: University of Chicago Press, 1961).

——, *The Historians Craft*, trans. Peter Putnam (New York: Alfred Knopf, 1962).

Bouquiaux, Luc (ed.), *L'Expansion bantoue* (Paris: SELAF, 1980).

Braeckman, Colette, *L'Enjeu congolais: L'Afrique centrale après Mobutu* (Paris: Fayard, 1999).

Cavalli-Sforza, Francesco, *The Great Human Diasporas: The History of Diversity and Evolution*, trans. Sarah Thorne (Reading, MA: Addison-Wesley, 1995).

Chastanet, Monique (ed.), *Plantes et paysages d'Afrique: Une Histoire à explorer* (Paris: Karthala, 1998).

Chauveau, Jean-Pierre and Jean-Pierre Dozon, "Au Coeur des ethnies ivoiriennes … l'état," in Emmanuel Terray (ed.), *L'état contemporain en Afrique* (Paris: L'Harmattan, 1987).

Chesneaux, Jean, *Pasts and Futures: or, What Is History For?*, trans. Schofield Coryell (London: Thames and Hudson, 1978).

Chrétien, Jean-Pierre, "Afrique noire, histoire précoloniale. I. L'Afrique orientale," in *Encyclopaedia universalis*, supp. 1 (Paris, 1980).

——, "L'Alibi ethnique dans les politiques africaines," *Esprit* 55–56 (July 1981).

——, "Les Bantous, de la philologie allemande à l'authenticité africaine: Un Mythe racial contemporain," *Vingtième siècle* 8 (1985).

——, "Les Deux Visages de Cham," in Pierre Guiral and Emile Témime (eds.), *L'Idée de race dans la pensée politique française contemporaine* (Paris: Editions du Centre National de la Recherche Scientifique, 1977).

——, "Ethnies et ethnisme," in *Larousse annuel 95* (Paris: Larousse, 1995).

—— (ed.), *L'Invention religieuse en Afrique: Histoire et religion en Afrique noire* (Paris: Karthala, 1993).

Chrétien, Jean-Pierre and Gérard Prunier (eds.), *Les Ethnies ont une histoire* (Paris: Karthala, 1989).

Chrétien, Jean-Pierre and Jean-Louis Triaud (eds.), *Histoire d'Afrique: Les Enjeux de mémoire* (Paris: Karthala, 1999).

Clark, J. Desmond, "The Spread of Food Production in Sub-Saharan Africa," *Journal of African History* 3.2 (1962).

Coquery-Vidrovitch, Catherine, *Histoire des villes d'Afrique noire: Des Origines à la colonisation* (Paris: Albin Michel, 1993).

Corbin, Alain, *The Village of Cannibals: Rage and Murder in France, 1870*, trans. Arthur Goldhammer (Cambridge, MA: Harvard University Press, 1992).

Coupez, André et al., "Classification d'un échantillon de langues bantoues d'après la lexicostatistique," in *Africana Linguistica*, vol. 6 (Tervuren: Musée Royal de l'Afrique Centrale, 1975).

Coupland, Reginald, *East Africa and Its Invaders: From the Earliest Times to the Death of Seyyid Said in 1856* (Oxford: Clarendon Press, 1938).

Dalby, David (ed.), *Language and History in Africa: A Volume of Collected Papers Presented to the London Seminar on Language and History in Africa (Held at the School of Oriental and African Studies, 1967–69)* (New York: Africana Publishing Corporation, 1970).

Delacroix, S. (ed.), *Histoire universelle des missions* (Paris: Grund, 1957), vol. 3.

De Langhe, E. et al., "Plantain in the Early Bantu World," *Azania* 29–30 (1996).

Denbow, J., "A New Look at the Later Prehistory of the Kalahari," *Journal of African History* 27.1 (1986).

Département d'histoire de l'Université du Burundi, *Histoire sociale de l'Afrique de l'Est (XIXe–XXe siècle): Actes du colloque de Bujumbura, 17–24 Octobre 1989* (Paris: Karthala, 1991).

Deschamps, Hubert et al., *Histoire générale de l'Afrique noire, de Madagascar, et des Archipels*, 2 vols. (Paris: Presses Universitaires de France, 1970).

Detienne, Marcel, *The Creation of Mythology*, trans. Margaret Cook (Chicago: University of Chicago Press, 1986).

———, *Dionysos Slain*, trans. Mireille Muellner and Leonard Muellner (Baltimore: Johns Hopkins University Press, 1979).

Eboussi, Fabien, "Le Bantou problématique," *Présence africaine* 66 (1986).

Ehret, Christopher, "Agricultural History in Central and Southern Africa, c. 1000 B.C. to A.D. 500," *Transafrican Journal of History* 2.1 (1974).

———, "Bantu Origins and History: Critique and Interpretation," *Transafrican Journal of History* 2.1 (1972).

———, "Cattle-Keeping and Milking in Eastern and Southern African History: The Linguistic Evidence," *Journal of African History* 4.1 (1967).

Epstein, Hellmut, *The Origin of the Domestic Animals of Africa*, 2 vols. (New York: Africana Publishing Corporation, 1971).

Evans-Pritchard, Edward, *The Divine Kingship of the Shilluk of the Nilotic Sudan* (Cambridge, UK: Cambridge University Press, 1948).

Fage, J.D., *An Atlas of African History* (London: E. Arnold, 1968).

Ford, John, *The Role of the Trypanosomiases in African Ecology: A Study of the Tsetse Fly Problem* (Oxford: Clarendon Press, 1971).

Fortes, Meyers and Edward Evans-Pritchard (eds.), *African Political Systems* (London: Oxford University Press, 1958).

Franz, E.G. and P. Geissler, *Das Deutsch-Ostafrika-Archiv. Guide to the German Records. Inventar der Abteilung "German Records" im Nationalarchiv der Vereinigten Republik Tansania, Dar-es-Salaam* (Marburg: Archivschule Marburg, 1973).

Furet, François, "Feudal System," in François Furet and Mona Ozouf (eds.), *A Critical Dictionary of the French Revolution*, trans. Arthur Goldhammer (Cambridge, MA: Harvard University Press, 1989).

Gallais, Jean, *Hommes du Sahel: Espaces-temps et pouvoirs: Le Delta intérieur du Niger, 1960–1980* (Paris: Flammarion, 1984).

Gann, Lewis and Peter Duignan, *The Rulers of German Africa, 1884–1914* (Stanford, CA: Stanford University Press, 1977).

Goldhagen, Daniel, *Hitler's Willing Executioners: Ordinary Germans and the Holocaust* (New York: Random House, 1996).

Goody, Jack, "Feudalism in Africa?" *Journal of African History* 4.1 (1963).

Gourou, Pierre, *L'Afrique* (Paris: Hachette, 1970).

Gray, Richard, "Annular Eclipse Maps," *Journal of African History* 9.1 (1968).

———, "Eclipse Maps," *Journal of African History* 6.3 (1965).

Gray, Richard and David Birmingham (eds.), *Pre-colonial African Trade: Essays on Trade in Central and Eastern Africa Before 1900* (London: Oxford University Press, 1970).

Greenberg, Joseph, "Linguistic Evidence Regarding Bantu Origins," *Journal of African History* 13.2 (1972).

———, *Studies in African Linguistic Classification* (New Haven, CT: Compass Publishing Co., 1955).

Grieken-Taverniers, Madeleine van, *La Colonisation belge en Afrique centrale: Guide des archives africaines du ministère des affaires étrangères, 1885–1962* (Brussels: Ministère des Affaires Etrangères, du Commerce Extérieur et de la Coopération au Développement, 1981).

Grosser, Alfred, *Le Crime et la mémoire* (Paris: Flammarion, 1989).

Guthrie, Malcolm, *The Classification of the Bantu Languages* (London: Oxford University Press, 1948), republished in 1967.

———, *Comparative Bantu: An Introduction to the Comparative Linguistics and Prehistory of the Bantu Languages*, 4 vols. (Farnborough, UK: Gregg, 1967–1971).

———, "Some Developments in the Prehistory of the Bantu Languages," *Journal of African History* 3.2 (1962).

Gwynne, M.D., "The Origin and Spread of Some Domestic Food Plants of Eastern Africa," in Neville Chittick and Robert I. Rotberg (eds.), *East Africa and the Orient: Cultural Syntheses in Pre-colonial Times* (New York: Africana Publishing Corporation, 1975).

Harlan, Jack R., *Crops & Man* (Madison, WI: American Society of Agronomy, 1975).

Harlan, Jack R., Jan M.J. de Wet, and Ann B.L. Stemler (eds.), *Origins of African Plant Domestication* (The Hague: Mouton, 1976).

Harlow, Vincent and E.M. Chilver (eds.), *History of East Africa* (Oxford: Clarendon Press, 1965), vol. 2.

Heine, Bernd, "Zur genetischen Gliederung der Bantu-Sprachen," *Afrika und Übersee* 3 (1973).

Henige, David, *The Chronology of Oral Tradition: Quest for a Chimera* (Oxford: Clarendon Press, 1974).

Herskovits, Melville, "The Cattle Complex in East Africa," *American Anthropologist* 28 (1926).

Heusch, Luc de, *Essais sur le symbolisme de l'inceste royal en Afrique* (Brussels: Université Libre, 1958).

Hiernaux, Jean, "Bantu Expansion: The Evidence from Physical Anthropology Confronted with Linguistic and Archaeological Evidence," *Journal of African History* 9.4 (1968).

————, *Découvertes récentes sur l'origine de l'homme* (Paris: Pavillon, 1968).

————, *The People of Africa* (London: Weidenfeld and Nicolson, 1974).

Iliffe, John, *Africans: History of a Continent* (Cambridge, UK: Cambridge University Press, 1995).

Ingham, Kenneth, *A History of East Africa*, 3rd ed. (London: Longmans, 1965).

Johnston, Harry, *A Comparative Study of the Bantu and Semi-Bantu Languages* (Oxford: Clarendon Press, 1919).

————, "A Survey of the Ethnography of Africa: And the Former Racial and Tribal Migrations in That Continent," *Journal of the Royal Anthropological Institute of Great Britain and Ireland* 43 (1913).

Kantorowicz, Ernst, *The King's Two Bodies: A Study in Mediaeval Political Theology* (Princeton, NJ: Princeton University Press, 1957).

Ki-Zerbo, Joseph, *Histoire de l'Afrique noire: D'Hier à demain* (Paris: Hatier, 1972).

Kuczynski, Robert R., *Demographic Survey of the British Colonial Empire* (London: Oxford University Press, 1948), vol. 2.

Lacoste, Yves, ed., *Géopolitique d'une Afrique médiane*, special issue of *Hérodote* 86/87.3–4 (1997).

Lainé, Agnès, "Génétique des populations et histoire du peuplement de l'Afrique: Essai d'historiographie et d'épistémologie," Ph.D. thesis, Paris I, 1998.

Lamey, René, *Archives des Pères Blancs, Maison Généralice* (Rome, 1970)

Langaney, André, *Les Hommes: Passé, présent, conditionnel* (Paris: A. Colin, 1988).

Lassailly-Jacob, Véronique et al. (eds.), *Déplacés et réfugiés: La Mobilité sous contrainte* (Paris: IRD Editions, 1999).

Maquet, Jacques J., *Civilizations of Black Africa*, trans. Joan Rayfield (New York: Oxford University Press, 1972).

————, *Power and Society in Africa*, trans. Jeannette Kupfermann (London: Weidenfeld and Nicolson, 1971).

Maret, Pierre de and F. Nsuka, "History of Bantu Metallurgy: Some Linguistic Aspects," *History in Africa* 4 (1977).

Matthews, Noel and Doreen M. Wainwright, *A Guide to Manuscripts and Documents in the British Isles Relating to Africa* (London: Oxford University Press, 1971).

Mbembe, Achille, *Afriques indociles: Christianisme, pouvoir et état en société postcoloniale* (Paris: Karthala, 1988).

Meinhof, Carl, *Grundzüge einer vergleichenden Grammatik der Bantusprachen* (Berlin: D. Reimer, 1906), reed. in 1948.

Monnens, J. "Les Grands Heures de l'Afrique," *Grands Lacs* (March 1936).

Morgan, W.T.W., *East Africa* (London: Longman, 1973).

Murdock, George, *Africa: Its Peoples and Their Culture History* (New York: McGraw-Hill, 1959).

O'Connor, A.M., *An Economic Geography of East Africa* (London: Bell, 1966).

Ogot, B.A. (ed.), *General History of Africa: Africa from the Sixteenth to the Eighteenth Century* (Paris: UNESCO, 1992), vol. 5.

Oliver, Roland, "L'Afrique orientale," in Hubert Deschamps (ed.), *Histoire générale de l'Afrique noire, de Madagascar, et des Archipels* (Paris: Presses Universitaires de France, 1970), vol. 1.

———, "The East African Interior," in Roland Oliver (ed.), *The Cambridge History of Africa* (Cambridge, UK: Cambridge University Press, 1977), vol. 3.

———, "The Interior c. 1500–1840," in Roland Oliver and Gervase Mathew (eds.), *History of East Africa* (Oxford: Oxford University Press, 1963), vol. 1.

———, *The Missionary Factor in East Africa* (London: Longman, 1965).

———, "The Problem of the Bantu Expansion," *Journal of African History* 7.3 (1966).

Oliver, Roland and B. Fagan, "The Emergence of Bantu Africa," in J.D. Fage (ed.), *The Cambridge History of Africa: From c. 500 B.C. to A.D. 1050* (London: Cambridge University Press, 1978), vol. 2.

Pernès, J. et al., *Gestion des ressources génétiques des plantes* (Paris: Agence de Cooperation Culturelle et Technique, 1984), vol. 1.

Perrot, Claude-Hélène, ed., *Démographie historique*, special issue of *Cahiers d'études africaines* 105/106 (1987).

————, *Sources orales de l'histoire de l'Afrique* (Paris: Editions du Centre National de la Recherche Scientifique, 1989).

Person, Yves, "Tradition orale et chronologie," *Cahiers d'études africaines* 7.3 (1962).

Phillipson, D.W., *The Later Prehistory of Eastern and Southern Africa* (New York: Africana Publishing Corporation, 1977).

Philippson, Gérard and Serge Bahuchet, "Cultivated Crops and Bantu Migrations in Central and Eastern Africa," *Azania* 29–30 (1996).

Poliakov, Leon, *The Aryan Myth: A History of Racist and Nationalist Ideas in Europe*, trans. Edmund Howard (London: Sussex University Press, 1974).

Posnansky, Merrick, "Bantu Genesis — Archaeological Reflections," *Journal of African History* 9.1 (1968).

Pourtier, Roland, "Nommer l'espace: L'Emergence de l'état territorial en Afrique noire," *L'Espace géographique* 4 (1983).

Raison, Jean-Pierre, *L'Afrique des hautes terres* (Paris: A. Colin, 1974).

Renault, François, *Afrique centrale*, vol. 1 of *Lavigerie, l'esclavage africain et l'Europe, 1868–1892* (Paris: E. de Boccard, 1971).

————, *Le Cardinal Lavigerie* (Paris: Fayard, 1992).

Renfrew, Colin, *Archaeology and Language: The Puzzle of Indo-European Origins* (London: J. Cape, 1987).

Rodney, Walter, *How Europe Underdeveloped Africa* (London: Bogle-L'Ouverture Publications, 1972).

Rotberg, Robert I., (ed.), *Africa and Its Explorers: Motives, Methods, and Impact* (Cambridge, MA: Harvard University Press, 1970).

————, *Imperialism, Colonialism, and Hunger: East and Central Africa* (Lexington, MA: Lexington Books, 1983).

Ruytinx, Jacques, *La Morale bantoue et le problème de l'éducation morale au Congo* (Brussels: Université Libre de Bruxelles, 1960).

Schmidt, Johannes, *Die Verwantschaftsverhältnisse der indogermanischen Sprachen* (Weimar: H. Böhlau, 1872).

Seligman, C.G., *Races of Africa* (London: Oxford University Press, 1930).

Sergent, B., "Penser — et mal penser — les Indo-Européens (note critique)," *Annales économies, sociétés, civilisations* 37.4 (1982).

Sheriff, Abdul, *Slaves, Spices, and Ivory in Zanzibar: Integration of an East African Commercial Empire into the World Economy, 1770–1873* (London: James Currey, 1987).

Soper, Robert, "Early Iron Age Pottery Types from East Africa: Comparative Analysis," *Azania* 6 (1971).

———, "A General Review of the Early Iron Age of the Southern Half of Africa," *Azania* 6 (1971).

Stamm, Anne, *Histoire de l'Afrique précoloniale* (Paris: Presses Universitaires de France, 1997).

Summers, Roger, *Zimbabwe: A Rhodesian Mystery* (Johannesburg: Nelson, 1963).

Sutton, John, "The Aquatic Civilization of Middle Africa," *Journal of African History* 15.4 (1974).

———, *The Archaeology of the Western Highlands of Kenya* (Nairobi: British Institute in Eastern Africa, 1973).

———, "East Africa Before the Seventh Century," in G. Mokhtar (ed.), *General History of Africa: Ancient Civilizations of Africa* (Paris: UNESCO, 1981), vol. 2.

———, "Irrigation and Soil Conservation in African Agricultural History," *Journal of African History* 25.1 (1984).

——— (ed.), *The Growth of Farming Communities in Africa from the Equator Southwards*, special issue of *Azania*, 29–30 (1996).

Tardits, Claude (ed.), *Princes & serviteurs du royaume: Cinq études de monarchies africaines* (Paris: Société d'Ethnographie, 1987).

Tempels, Placide, *Philosophie bantoue*, trans. A. Rubbens (Paris: Editions Africaines, 1949).

UNESCO, *Histoire générale de l'Afrique*, 8 vols. (Paris: UNESCO, 1980–1996).

Van Bulck, C., "Les Langues bantoues," in A. Meillet and M. Cohen (eds.), *Les Langues du monde* (Paris: Centre National de la Recherche Scientifique, 1952).

Vanderlinden, Jacques, *Pierre Ryckmans, 1891–1959: Coloniser dans l'honneur* (Brussels: De Boeck Université, 1994).

Vansina, Jan, "Bantu in the Crystal Ball, I," *History in Africa* 6 (1979).

————, "Bantu in the Crystal Ball, II," *History in Africa* 7 (1980).

————, "Esquisse historique de l'agriculture en Milieu Forestier (Afrique Équatoriale)," *Muntu* 2 (1985).

————, "New Linguistic Evidence and the 'Bantu Expansion,'" *Journal of African History* 36.2 (1995).

————, *Oral Tradition as History* (Madison: University of Wisconsin Press, 1985).

————, *Oral Tradition: A Study in Historical Methodology*, trans. H.M. Wright (Chicago: Aldine Pub. Co., 1965).

Verhaegen, Benoît, *Introduction à l'histoire immédiate, essai de méthodologie qualitative* (Gembloux: Duculot, 1974).

Vidal-Naquet, Pierre, "L'Atlantide et les nations," in Pierre Vidal-Naquet, *La Démocratie grecque vue d'ailleurs: Essais d'historiographie ancienne et moderne* (Paris: Flammarion, 1990).

————, "Bêtes, hommes et dieux chez les Grecs," in Léon Poliakov (ed.), *Hommes et bêtes: Entretiens sur le racisme: Actes du colloque tenu du 12 au 15 Mai 1973 au Centre Culturel International de Cerisy-la-Salle* (Paris: Mouton, 1975).

Werner, Karl Ferdinand, *Naissance de la noblesse: L'Essor des élites politiques en Europe* (Paris: Fayard, 1998).

White, Hayden, *The Content of the Form: Narrative Discourse and Historical Representation* (Baltimore: Johns Hopkins University Press, 1987).

————, *Metahistory: The Historical Imagination in Nineteenth-Century Europe* (Baltimore: Johns Hopkins University Press, 1987).

The Great Lakes Region

Berger, Iris, "The Kubandwa Religious Complex of Interlacustrine East Africa: An Historical Study, ca, 1500–1900," Ph.D. thesis, University of Wisconsin, 1973.

————, "Rebels or Status-Seekers? Women as Spirit Mediums in East Africa," in Nancy J. Hafkin and Edna G. Bay (eds.), *Women in Africa: Studies in Social and Economic Change* (Stanford, CA: Stanford University Press, 1976).

————, *Religion and Resistance: East African Kingdoms in the Precolonial Period* (Tervuren, Belgium: Musée Royal de l'Afrique Centrale, 1981).

Braeckman, Colette, *Terreur africaine: Burundi, Rwanda, Zaïre, les racines de la violence* (Paris: Fayard, 1996).

Burton, Richard Francis, *The Lake Regions of Central Africa: A Picture of Exploration*, 2 vols. (London: Longman, Green, Longman, and Roberts, 1860).

Centre de Civilisation Burundaise, *La Civilisation ancienne des peuples des Grands Lacs* (Paris: Karthala, 1981).

Chilver, E.M., "Feudalism in the Interlacustrine Kingdoms," in Audrey Richards (ed.), *East African Chiefs: A Study of Political Development in Some Uganda and Tanganyika Tribes* (New York: Praeger, 1960).

Chrétien, Jean-Pierre, "L'Afrique des Grands Lacs existe-t-elle?" *Revue Tiers-Monde* 27.106 (1986).

————, "Les Ages du fer dans la région des Grands Lacs," *Recherche, pédagogie, et culture* 55 (1981).

————, "Anciens Haricots et anciens tubercules dans la région des Grands Lacs," in Monique Chastanet (ed.), *Plantes et Paysages d'Afrique: Une Histoire à explorer* (Paris: Karthala, 1998).

————, "Les Années de l'éleusine, du sorgho et du haricot: écologie et idéologie," *African Economic History* 7 (1979).

————, "Confronting the Unequal Exchange Between the Oral and the Written," in Bogumil Jewsiewicki and David Newbury (eds.), *African Historiographies: What History for Which Africa?* (Beverly Hills, CA: Sage Publications, 1986).

————, "Démographie et écologie en Afrique orientale à la fin du XIXe siècle: Une Crise exceptionnelle?" *Cahiers d'études africaines* 105/106.1-2 (1987).

————, "Echanges et hiérarchies dans les royaumes des Grands Lacs de l'est africain," *Annales économies, sociétés, civilisations* 29.6 (1974).

————, "Ethnologie et économie: Les Productions de l'Afrique des Grands Lacs dans le miroir de la colonisation allemande (1890–1918)," *Journal des africanistes* 58.1 (1988).

————, "Les Refus et les perspectives d'une 'histoire rurale' en Afrique des

Grands Lacs," in Chrétien (ed.), *Histoire rurale de L'Afrique des Grands Lacs.*

———, "La Religion des Grands Lacs...," in F. Lenoir and Y. Tardan-Masquelier (eds.), *Encyclopédie des réligions* (Paris: Bayard, 1997).

———, "Roi, religion, lignages en Afrique orientale précoloniale," in Emmanuel Le Roy Ladurie (ed.), *Les Monarchies* (Paris: Presses Universitaires de France, 1986).

———, "Vocabulaire et concepts tirés de la féodalité occidentale et administration indirecte en Afrique orientale," in Daniel Nordman and Jean-Pierre Raison (eds.), *Sciences de l'homme et conquête coloniale: Constitution et usages des sciences humaines en Afrique, XIXe-XXe siècles* (Paris: Presses de l'Ecole Normale Supérieure, 1980).

——— (ed.), *Histoire rurale de L'Afrique des Grands Lacs: Guide de recherches: Bibliographie et textes* (Paris: Karthala, 1983).

Chrétien, Jean-Pierre with Emile Mworoha, "Les Migrations du XXe siècle en Afrique orientale: Le Cas de l'émigration des Banyarwanda et des Barundi vers l'Uganda," in Commission Internationale d'Histoire des Mouvements Sociaux et des Structures Sociales, *Les Migrations internationales de la fin du XVIIIe siècle à nos jours* (Paris: Editions du Centre National de la Recherche Scientifique, 1980).

Cohen, David, "East Africa 1870–1905," in Roland Oliver and George Neville Sanderson (eds.), *The Cambridge History of Africa* (London: Cambridge University Press, 1985), vol. 6.

———, "Food Production and Food Exchange in the Precolonial Lakes Plateau Region," in Robert Rotberg (ed.), *Imperialism, Colonialism, and Hunger: East and Central Africa* (Lexington, MA: Lexington Books, 1983).

———, "Peoples and States of the Great Lakes Region," in J.F. Ade Ajayi (ed.), *General History of Africa VI: Africa in the Nineteenth Century Until the 1880s* (Paris: UNESCO, 1989).

———, "A Survey of Interlacustrine Chronology," *Journal of African History* 11.2 (1970).

Cooley, William D., *Inner Africa Laid Open, in an Attempt to Trace the Chief Lines of Communication Across That Continent South of the Equator; with the Routes*

434

to the Muropue and the Cazembe, Moenemoezi and Lake Nyassa; the Journeys of the Rev. Dr. Krapf and the Rev. J. Rebmann on the Eastern Coast; and the Discoveries of Messrs. Oswell and Livingstone in the Heart of the Continent (New York: Negro Universities Press, 1852).

Crazzolara, J.P., *The Lwoo*, 3 vols. (Verona: Instituto Missioni Africane, 1950–1954).

Dahl, E., "Termini technici der Rinderzucht treibenden Watusi in Deutsch-Ostafrika," *Mitteilungen des Seminars für Orientalische Sprachen*, Berlin (1907).

Desmedt, Christiane, "Poteries anciennes décorées à la roulette dans la région des Grands Lacs," *African Archaeological Review* 9 (1991).

Grant, J.A., "Summary of Observations on the Geography, Climate, and Natural History of the Lake Region of Equatorial Africa," *Journal of the Royal Geographical Society* 42 (1872).

Guichaoua, André, "Mobilité forcée dans la région des Grands Lacs," in Véronique Lassailly-Jacob, Jean-Yves Marchal, and André Quesnel (eds.), *Déplacés et réfugiés: La Mobilité sous contrainte* (Paris: Editions de l'IRD, 1999).

———— (ed.), *L'Afrique des Grands Lacs*, special issue of *Revue Tiers-Monde* 106 (1986).

Haggard, H. Rider, *King Solomon's Mines* (London: Cassell & Company Limited, 1885).

Henige, David, "Reflections on Early Interlacustrine Chronology: An Essay in Source Criticism," *Journal of African History* 15.1 (1974).

Heremans, Roger, *L'Education dans les missions des Pères Blancs en Afrique centrale, 1879–1914: Objectifs et réalisations* (Brussels: Editions Nauwelaerts, 1983).

Herring, Ralph, "Hydrology and Chronology: The Rodah Nilometer as an Aid in Dating Interlacustrine History," in J.B. Webster (ed.), *Chronology, Migration, and Drought in Interlacustrine Africa* (London: Longman, 1979).

Heusch, Luc de, *Le Rwanda et la civilisation interlacustre* (Brussels: Université Libre de Bruxelles, 1966).

Hiernaux, Jean, "Le Début de l'âge des métaux dans la région des Grands Lacs," in Georges Mortelmans and Jacques Nenquin (eds.), *Actes du IVe congrès panafrican du prehistoire et de l'étude du quaternaire* (Tervuren: Musée Royal de l'Afrique Centrale, 1962).

Hiernaux, Jean and Emma Maquet, *Cultures préhistoriques de l'âge des métaux au Ruanda-Urundi et au Kivu (Congo belge)* (Brussels: Académie Royale des Sciences d'Outre-Mer, 1956, 1960), vols. 1 and 2.

Hugon, Anne, *L'Afrique des explorateurs: Vers les sources du Nil* (Paris: Gallimard, 1991).

Jewsiewicki, Bogumil, "Belgian Africa," in Andrew Roberts (ed.), *The Cambridge History of Africa* (Cambridge, UK: Cambridge University Press, 1986), vol. 7.

Kabanda, Marcel, "Technologie et économie du sel dans la région des Grands Lacs d'Afrique de l'est (1850–1920)," Ph.D. thesis, Paris I, 1991.

Langheld, Wilhelm, *Zwanzig Jahre in deutschen Kolonien* (Berlin: W. Weicher, 1909).

Le Gall, J.Y., M. Le Gall, Y. Godin, and J.L. Serre, "A Study of Genetic Markers of the Blood in Four Central African Population Groups," *Human Heredity* 32 (1982).

Livingstone, D.A., "Environmental Changes in the Nile Headwaters," in Martin A.J. Williams and Hugues Faure (eds.), *The Sahara and the Nile: Quaternary Environments and Prehistoric Occupation in Northern Africa* (Rotterdam: Balkema, 1980).

Maquet, Jacques J., "Institutionalisation féodale des relations de dépendance dans quatre cultures interlacustres," *Cahiers d'études africaines* 35.3 (1969).

Marissal, Jacques, "Mohammed ben Khalfan, ou la fin de la puissance arabe sur le Tanganyika," in Charles André Julien (ed.), *Les Africains* (Paris: Editions J.A., 1978), vol. 11.

Milley, Jacques. *Afrique des Grands Lacs* (Paris: Editions du Seuil, 1968).

Mturi, A.A., "Ancient Civilisation of the Peoples of the Great Lakes: The Linguistic and Archaeological Evidence: An Overview," in Centre de Civilisation Burundaise, *Civilisation ancienne des peuples des Grands Lacs.*

Mvuyekure, Augustin, "Idéologie Missionaire et Classifications Ethniques en Afrique Centrale," in Jean-Pierre Chrétien and Gérard Prunier (eds.), *Les Ethnies ont une histoire* (Paris: Karthala, 1989).

Mworoha, Emile, Peuples et rois de l'Afrique des lacs: *Le Burundi et les royaumes voisins au XIXe siècle* (Dakar: Nouvelles Editions Africaines, 1977).

Newbury, David, "Lake Kivu Regional Trade in the Nineteenth Century," *Journal des africanistes* 50.2 (1980).

Noten, Francis van, "The Early Iron Age in the Interlacustrine Region: The Diffusion of Iron Technology," *Azania* 14 (1979).

Perugia, Paul del, *Les Derniers rois mages* (Paris: Gallimard, 1970).

Roberts, Andrew, "East Africa," in Andrew Roberts (ed.), *The Cambridge History of Africa* (Cambridge, UK: Cambridge University Press, 1986), vol. 7.

Sassoon, Hamo, "Kings, Cattle, and Blacksmiths: Royal Insignia and Religious Symbolism in the Interlacustrine States," *Azania* 18 (1983).

Schloifer, Otto, *Bana Uleia; ein Lebenswerk in Afrika; aus den Tagebüchern eines alten Kolonialpioniers* (Berlin: D. Reimer, 1943).

Schoenbrun, David, "Cattle Herds and Banana Gardens: The Historical Geography of the Western Great Lakes Region, ca. A.D. 800–1500," *African Archaeological Review* 11 (1993).

———, "The Contours of Vegetation Change and Human Agency in Eastern Africa's Great Lakes Region: ca. 2000 B.C. to ca. A.D. 1000," *History in Africa* 21 (1994).

———, "Early History in Eastern Africa's Great Lakes Region: Linguistic, Ecological, and Archaeological Approaches, ca. 500 B.C. to ca. A.D. 1000," Ph.D. thesis, University of California at Los Angeles, 1990.

———, *A Green Place, a Good Place: Agrarian Change, Gender, and Social Identity in the Great Lakes Region to the 15th Century* (Portsmouth, NH: Heinemann, 1998).

———, *The Historical Reconstruction of Great Lakes Bantu Cultural Vocabulary: Etymologies and Distributions* (Cologne: Rüdiger Köppe, 1997).

———, "A Past Whose Time Has Come: Historical Context and History in Eastern Africa's Great Lakes," in V.Y. Mudimbe and Bogumil Jewsiewicki (eds.), *History Making in Africa* (Middletown, CT: Wesleyan University Press, 1993).

———, "We Are What We Eat: Ancient Agriculture Between the Great Lakes," *Journal of African History* 34.1 (1993).

Speke, John Hanning, *Journal of the Discovery of the Source of the Nile* (Edinburgh and London: William Blackwood and Sons, 1863).

Stanley, Henry M., *Through the Dark Continent; or, The Sources of the Nile Around the Great Lakes of Equatorial Africa and down the Livingstone River to the Atlantic Ocean* (New York: Harper & Brothers, 1878), vol. 1.

Tosh, John, "The Northern Lacustrine Region," in Richard Gray and David Birmingham (eds.), *Pre-colonial African Trade: Essays on Trade in Central and Eastern Africa Before 1900* (London: 1970).

Vellut, Jean-Luc, ed., *L'Afrique des Grands Lacs*, special issue of *Etudes d'histoire africaine* 7 (1975).

Vincens, A., "Paléoenvironnements du Bassin Nord-Tanganyika (Zaïre, Burundi, Tanzanie) au cours des 13 derniers mille ans: Apport de la palynologie," *Review of Palaeobotany and Palynology* 61.1–2 (1989).

Webster, J.B., "Noi! Noi! Famine as an Aid to Interlacustrine Chronology," in Webster (ed.), *Chronology, Migration, and Drought in Interlacustrine Africa*.

———— (ed.), *Chronology, Migration, and Drought in Interlacustrine Africa* (London: Longman, 1979).

Were, Gideon, "The Western Bantu Peoples from A.D. 1300 to 1800," in B.A. Ogot and J.A. Kieran (eds.), *Zamani: A Survey of East African History* (New York: Humanities Press, 1968).

Wolf, James B. (ed.), *Missionary to Tanganyika, 1877–1888: The Writings of Edward Coode Hore* (London: Frank Cass, 1970).

The Ugandan Area

Baker, Samuel, *The Albert N'yanza, Great Basin of the Nile, and Explorations of the Nile Sources* (London: Macmillan, 1866).

Beattie, John, "Bunyoro: An African Feudality?" *Journal of African History* 5.1 (1964).

————, *The Nyoro State* (Oxford: Clarendon Press, 1971).

Berger, Iris, "Deities, Dynasties, and Oral Traditions: The History and Legend of the Abacwezi," in J.C. Miller (ed.), *The African Past Speaks: Essays on Oral Tradition and History* (Folkestone, UK: Archon, 1980).

Brazier, F.S., "The Incident at Nyakishenyi, 1917," *Uganda Journal* 32.1 (1968).

Buchanan, Carole, "The Kitara Complex: The Historical Tradition of Western Uganda to the XVIth Century," Ph.D. thesis, Indiana University, 1974.

——, "Perceptions of Ethnic Interactions in the East African Interior: The Kitara Complex," *International Journal of African Historical Studies* 3 (1978).

Chrétien, Jean-Pierre, "L'Empire des Bacwezi: La Construction d'un imaginaire géopolitique," *Annales économies, sociétés, civilisations* 40.6 (1985).

——, "*Kurobera*, l'émigration en Ouganda et en 'Manamba' dans la première moitié du XXe siècle," in Joseph Gahama and Christian Thibon (eds.), *Les Régions orientales du Burundi: Une Périphérie à l'épreuve du développement* (Paris: Karthala, 1994).

——, "Les Peuples et leur histoire avant la colonisation," in Prunier and Calas (eds.), *L'Ouganda contemporain*.

Cohen, David, *The Historical Tradition of Busoga, Mukama, and Kintu* (Oxford: Clarendon Press, 1972).

Doyle, Shane D., "An Environmental History of the Kingdom of Bunyoro in Western Uganda, from c. 1860 to 1940," Ph.D. thesis, Cambridge University, 1998.

Dunbar, A.R., *A History of Bunyoro-Kitara* (Nairobi: Oxford University Press, 1968).

Ehrlich, Cyril, "The Ugandan Economy: 1903–1945," in Vincent Harlow and E.M. Chilver (eds.), *History of East Africa* (Oxford: Clarendon Press, 1965), vol. 2.

Elam, Yitzchak, *The Social and Sexual Roles of Hima Women: A Study of Nomadic Cattle Breeders in Nyabushozi County, Ankole, Uganda* (Manchester, UK: Manchester University Press, 1973).

Emin Pascha, *Die Tagebücher von Emin Pascha*, ed. Franz Stuhlmann, 4 vols. (Hamburg: G. Westermann, 1916–1927).

——, "Zur Ethnologie des Albert-Sees," *Das Ausland* 18 (1891).

Fallers, Lloyd, *Bantu Bureaucracy: A Study of Integration and Conflict in the Political Institutions of an East African People* (Cambridge, UK: East African Institute of Social Research, 1956).

439

————, *The King's Men: Leadership and Status in Buganda on the Eve of Independence* (London: Oxford University Press, 1964).

Fisher, Ruth, *Twilight Tales of the Black Baganda: The Traditional History of Bunyoro-Kitara a Former Uganda Kingdom* (1911; London: Frank E. Cass, 1970).

Géraud, Félix, "The Settlement of the Bakiga," in Donald Denoon et al. (eds.), *A History of Kigezi* (Kampala, n.d.), pp. 23–55.

Gertzel, Chetry, "Kingdoms, Districts, and the Unitary State: Uganda, 1945–1962," in D. Anthony Low and Alison Smith, *History of East Africa* (Oxford: Clarendon Press, 1976).

Gorju, Julien, *Entre le Victoria, l'Albert et l'Edouard; Ethnographie de la partie anglaise du vicariat de l'Uganda: Origines, histoire, religion, coutumes* (Rennes: Oberthür, 1920).

Gutkind, Peter, *The Royal Capital of Buganda: A Study of Internal Conflict and External Ambiguity* (The Hague: Mouton, 1963).

Ingham, Kenneth, "The Amagasani of the Abakama of Bunyoro," *Uganda Journal* 17.2 (1953).

————, *The Kingdom of Toro in Uganda* (London: Harper & Row, 1975).

Johnston, Harry, *The Uganda Protectorate: An Attempt to Give Some Description of the Physical Geography, Botany, Zoology, Anthropology, Languages, and History of the Territories Under British Protection in East Central Africa, Between the Congo Free State and the Rift Valley and Between the First Degree of South Latitude and the Fifth Degree of North Latitude*, 2 vols. (London: Hutchinson & Co., 1902).

Kagwa, Apolo, *The Kings of Buganda*, trans. S. Kiwanuka (Nairobi: East African Pub. House, 1971).

Kamuhangire, Ephraim, "The Pre-colonial Economic and Social History of East Africa, with Special Reference to South-Western Uganda Salt Lakes Region," in Bethwell Ogot (ed.), *Hadith*, Nairobi 5 (1975).

————, "The Pre-colonial History of Salt Lakes Region of South-Western Uganda, c. 1000–1900 AD," Ph.D. thesis, Makerere University, 1993.

Karugire, Samwiri, *A History of the Kingdom of Nkore in Western Uganda to 1896* (Oxford: Clarendon Press, 1971).

————, *A Political History of Uganda* (Nairobi: Heinemann Educational Books, 1980).

Kasozi, A.B.K., *The Social Origins of Violence in Uganda, 1964–1985* (Montreal: McGill-Queen's University Press, 1994).

Katate, A.G. and L. Kamugungunu, *Abagabe b'Ankole* (Kampala: Eagle Press, 1955).

Kenny, Michael, "Mutesa's Crime: Hubris and the Control of African Kings," *Comparative Studies in Society and History* 30 (1988).

————, "Precolonial Trade in Eastern Lake Victoria," *Azania* 14 (1979).

Kiwanuka, Semakula, *A History of Buganda: From the Foundation of the Kingdom to 1900* (London: Longman, 1971).

Kottak, Conrad P., "Ecological Variables in the Origin and Evolution of African States: The Buganda Example," *Comparative Studies in Society and History* 14.3 (1972).

K.W. [Winyi, Tito], "The Kings of Bunyoro-Kitara," *Uganda Journal* 3.2 (1935).

Langlands, Bryan W., "Early Travelers in Uganda," *Uganda Journal* 26.1 (1962).

————, *The Sleeping Sickness Epidemic in Uganda, 1900–1920: A Study in Historical Geography* (Kampala: Makerere University College, 1967).

Lanning, Eric, "Masaka Hill: An Ancient Center of Worship," *Uganda Journal* 18.1 (1954).

Low, D. Anthony, *Buganda in Modern History* (London: Weidenfeld & Nicolson, 1971).

————, *The Mind of Buganda: Documents of the Modern History of an African Kingdom* (London: Heinemann Educational, 1971).

————, "Uganda: The Establishment of the Protectorate, 1894–1919," in Vincent Harlow and E.M. Chilver (eds.), *History of East Africa* (Oxford: Clarendon Press, 1965), vol. 2.

Low, D. Anthony and R. Cranford Pratt, *Buganda and British Overrule, 1900–1955* (London: Oxford University Press, 1960).

Lugard, Frederick, *Diaries of Lord Lugard*, 3 vols. (London: Faber and Faber, 1959).

————, *The Dual Mandate in British Tropical Africa* (London: W. Blackwood and Sons, 1922).

441

Lwanga-Lunyiigo, Samwiri, "L'Ere coloniale (1894–1962)," in Prunier and Calas (eds.), *L'Ouganda contemporain*.

McMaster, D.N., "Speculations on the Coming of the Banana to Uganda," *Uganda Journal* 27.2 (1963).

Médard, Henri, "Le Succès du Christianisme en Ouganda (1875–1962)," in Prunier and Calas (eds.), *L'Ouganda Contemporain*.

Morris, Henry, *The Heroic Recitations of the Bahima of Ankole* (Oxford: Clarendon Press, 1964).

Mukasa, Ham, "The Rule of the Kings of Buganda," *Uganda Journal* 10.2 (1946).

Nicolet, J., "Essai historique de l'ancien royaume du Kitara de l'Uganda," *Annali del Pontificio Museo Missionario Etnologico*, The Vatican (1972).

———, *Mucondozi* (Mbarara, 1953).

———, "Régions qui se détachèrent du Kitara et devinrent des royaumes indépendants," *Annali del Pontificio Museo Missionario Etnologico*, The Vatican (1972).

Nsimbi, M.B., "The Clan System in Buganda," *Uganda Journal* 28.1 (1964).

Nyakatura, John, *The Anatomy of an African Kingdom*, trans. Teopista Muganwa (Garden City, NY: Anchor Press, 1973).

Oberg, K., "The Kingdom of Ankole in Uganda," in Meyers Fortes and Edward Evans-Pritchard (eds.), *African Political Systems* (London: Oxford University Press, 1958).

Oliver, Roland, "A Question about the Bachwezi," *Uganda Journal* 17.2 (1953).

———, "The Royal Tombs of Buganda," *Uganda Journal* 23.2 (1959).

Peel, John J., "Conversion and Tradition in Two African Societies: Ijebu and Buganda," *Past and Present* 77 (1977).

Pirouet, Marie-Louise, *Historical Dictionary of Uganda* (Metuchen, NJ: Scarecrow Press, 1995).

Posnansky, Merrick, "Kingship, Archaeology, and Historical Myth," *Uganda Journal* 30.1 (1966).

———, "Pottery Types from Archaeological Sites in East Africa," *Journal of African History* 2.2 (1961).

————, "Terminology in the Early Iron Age of Eastern Africa with Particular Reference to the Dimple-Based Wares of Lolui Island, Uganda," *Actes de VIe Congrès Panafricain de Préhistoire* (Dakar: IFAN, 1973).

————, "Towards an Historical Geography of Uganda," *East African Geographical Review* 1 (1963).

Pratt, R.C., "Administration and Politics in Uganda, 1919–1945," in Vincent Harlow and E.M. Chilver (eds.), *History of East Africa* (Oxford: Clarendon Press, 1965), vol. 2.

Prunier, Gérard, "Evolution des critères de définition ethnique en Ouganda, du XVIe siècle à la fin de l'ère coloniale," in Jean-Pierre Chrétien and Gérard Prunier (eds.), *Les Ethnies ont une histoire* (Paris: Karthala, 1989).

————, "Les Lieux de la mémoire royale au Buganda," in Jean-Pierre Chrétien and Jean-Louis Triaud (eds.), *Histoire d'Afrique: Les Enjeux de mémoire* (Paris: Karthala, 1999).

————, *L'Ouganda et la question indienne (1896–1972)* (Paris: Editions Recherche sur les Civilisations, 1990).

————, "Le 'Roi-gentleman et le président terroriste': Mythes et réalitiés de deux décolonisations comparées: L'Ouganda et le Kenya," in Charles-Robert Ageron and Marc Michel (eds.), *L'Ere des décolonisations: Sélection de textes du colloque "Décolonisations comparées," Aix-en-Provence, 30 Septembre–3 Octobre 1993* (Paris: Karthala, 1995).

Prunier, Gérard and Bernard Calas (eds.), *L'Ouganda contemporain* (Paris: Karthala, 1994).

Ramchandani, R.R., *Ugandan Asians: The End of an Enterprise: A Study of the Role of the People of Indian Origin in the Economic Development of Uganda and Their Expulsion, 1894–1972* (Bombay: United Asia Publications, 1976).

Ray, Benjamin, *Myth, Ritual, and Kingship in Buganda* (New York: Oxford University Press, 1991).

Reid, Andrew, "The Role of Cattle in the Later Iron Age Communities of Southern Africa," Ph.D. thesis, Cambridge University, 1991.

Reid, Richard, "The Reign of *Kabaka* Nakibinge: Myth or Watershed?" *History in Africa* 24 (1997).

Renault, François, "Réflexion historique sur des martyrs africains," *Revue française d'histoire d'outre-mer* 272.3 (1986).

Richards, Audrey, *Economic Development and Tribal Change: A Study of Immigrant Labour in Buganda* (Cambridge, UK: W. Heffer, 1956).

Roberts, Andrew, "The Sub-imperialism of the Baganda," *Journal of African History* 3.3 (1962).

Robertshaw, Peter and David Taylor, "Climate Change and the Rise of Political Complexity in Western Uganda," *Journal of African History* 41.1 (2000).

Roscoe, John, *The Bakitara or Banyoro: The First Part of the Report of the Mackie Ethnological Expedition to Central Africa* (Cambridge, UK: The University Press, 1923).

——, *The Banyankole: The Second Part of the Report of the Mackie Ethnological Expedition to Central Africa* (Cambridge, UK: The University Press, 1923).

Ssebabi, E.C.T. and E. Nzaro, "Distribution of ABO and Rh(D) Phenotypes in Uganda," *Vox Sanguinis*, Switzerland (1974).

Steinhart, Edward, "Ankole: Pastoral Hegemony," in Henri Claessen and Peter Skalnik (eds.), *The Early State* (The Hague: Mouton, 1978).

——, *Conflict and Collaboration: The Kingdoms of Western Uganda, 1890–1907* (Princeton, NJ: Princeton University Press, 1977).

——, "From 'Empire' to State: The Emergence of the Kingdom of Bunyoro-Kitara, c. 1350–1890," in Henri Claessen and Peter Skalnik (eds.), *The Study of the State* (The Hague: Mouton, 1981).

——, "Herders and Farmers: The Tributary Mode of Production in Western Uganda," in Donald Crummey and C.C. Stewart (eds.), *Modes of Production in Africa: The Precolonial Era* (Beverly Hills, CA: Sage Publications, 1981).

——, "The Kingdoms of the March: Speculations on Social and Political Change," in J.B. Webster (ed.), *Chronology, Migration, and Drought in Interlacustrine Africa* (London: Longman, 1979).

——, "Vassal and Fief in Three Lacustrine Kingdoms," *Cahiers d'études africaines* 28.4 (1967).

Sutton, John, "The Antecedents of the Interlacustrine Kingdoms," *Journal of African History* 34.1 (1993).

Sykes, J., "The Eclipse at Biharwe," *Uganda Journal* 23.1 (1959).

Taylor, John, *The Growth of the Church in Buganda: An Attempt at Understanding* (London: SCM Press, 1958).

Tourigny, Yves, *So Abundant a Harvest: The Catholic Church in Uganda, 1879–1979* (London: Darton, Longman and Todd, 1979).

Tuma, Tom, "African Chiefs and Church Work in Busoga Province of Uganda, 1900–1940 – Part I," *Kenya Historical Review* 4.2 (1976).

————, "African Chiefs and Church Work in Busoga Province of Uganda, 1900–1940 – Part II," *Kenya Historical Review* 5.1 (1977).

Twaddle, Michael, *Kakungulu & the Creation of Uganda, 1868–1928* (London: James Currey, 1993).

————, "On Ganda Historiography," *History in Africa* 1 (1974).

————, "Towards an Early History of the East African Interior," *History in Africa* 2 (1975).

Uzoigwe, Godfrey, "Precolonial Markets in Bunyoro-Kitara," *Comparative Studies in Society and History* 14.4 (1972).

Webster, Bertin and Ralph Herring, "Labongo," *Kenya Historical Review* 3.1 (1975).

Welbourn, Frederick, *Religion and Politics in Uganda, 1952–1962* (Nairobi: East African Publishing House, 1965).

————, "Some Aspects of Kiganda Religion," *Uganda Journal* 26.2 (1962).

West, H.W., *Land Policy in Buganda* (London: Cambridge University Press, 1972).

Willis, Justin, "Kinyonyi and Kateizi: The Contested Origins of Pastoralist Dominance in South-Western Uganda," in Jean-Pierre Chrétien and Jean-Louis Triaud (eds.), *Histoire d'Afrique: Les Enjeux de mémoire* (Paris: Karthala, 1999).

Wilson, C.T. and R.W. Felkin, *Uganda and the Egyptian Soudan* (London: S. Low, Marston, Searle & Rivington, 1882), vol. 1.

Wright, Michael, *Buganda in the Heroic Age* (Oxford: Oxford University Press, 1971).

Wrigley, Christopher, "Buganda: An Outline Economic History," *Economic History Review* 10.1 (1957).

445

————, "Cattle and Language Between the Lakes," *Sprache und Geschichte in Afrika* 8 (1987).

————, *Kingship and State: The Buganda Dynasty* (Cambridge, UK: Cambridge University Press, 1996).

————, "Some Thoughts on the Bacwezi," *Uganda Journal* 22.1 (1958).

————, "The Story of Rukidi," *Africa* 43.3 (1973).

Rwanda and Burundi

Acquier, Jean-Louis, *Le Burundi* (Marseilles: Editions Parenthèses, 1986).

African Rights, *Rwanda: Assassinated Proof* (London: African Rights, 1996).

———— (under Rakiya Omaar's direction), *Rwanda: Death, Despair, and Defiance* (London: African Rights, 1995 [1994]).

Anonymous, *Essai d'histoire* (Usumbura, c. 1958).

Arianoff, Alexandre d', *Histoire des Bagesera, souverains du Gisaka* (Brussels: Institut Royal Colonial Belge, 1952).

Arnoux, Alexandre, "Le Culte de la société secrète des Imandwa au Ruanda," parts 1–5, *Anthropos* 7 (1912) and 8 (1913).

Assemblée Nationale, *Rapport de la Mission parlementaire d'information sur le Rwanda* (Paris, 1998).

Bahenduzi, Michel, "Kirwa: Un Jalon sur l'itinéraire de l'*Isugi*," in Ndoricimpa and Guillet (eds.), *L'Arbre-mémoire*.

————, "Le Rituel du muganuro dans l'histoire du Burundi, des origines au XXe siècle," Ph.D. thesis, Paris I, 1991.

Bahimanga, Antoine, "Une Mission dans l'Est du Burundi: Saint-Joseph de Rusengo (1924–1949)," in Gahama and Thibon (eds.), *Les Régions orientales du Burundi*.

Baumann, Oskar, *Durch Massailand zur Nilquelle ; Reisen und Forschungen der Massai-Expedition des deutschen Antisklaverei-Komite in den Jahren 1891–1893* (Berlin: D. Reimer, 1894).

Bertrand, Jordane, *Rwanda, le piège de l'histoire: L'Opposition démocratique avant le génocide, 1990–1994* (Paris: Karthala, 2000).

Bindseil, Reinhart, *Ruanda und Deutschland seit den Tagen Richard Kandts* (Berlin: D. Reimer, 1988).

Blam, Wolfgang, "Témoignage à Kibuye: Le Génocide comme instrument politique 'moderne,'" trans. by and repr. in Chrétien, *Le Défi de l'ethnicisme.*

Bonnefille, Raymonde and Guy Riollet, "L'Histoire forestière du Burundi d'après l'étude des tourbières," *Cahiers d'histoire* 2 / Cahiers du C.R.A. 4 (1984).

Botte, Roger, "Agriculteurs/éleveurs et domination du groupe pastoral," in Equipe Ecologie et Anthropologie des Sociétés Pastorales, *Pastoral Production and Society: Proceedings of the International Meeting on Nomadic Pastoralism, Paris, 1–3 Dec. 1976* (Cambridge, UK: Cambridge University Press, 1979).

——, "De quoi vivait l'état?" *Cahiers d'études africaines* 87–88.3/4 (1982).

——, "La Guerre interne au Burundi," in Jean Bazin and Emmanuel Terray (eds.), *Guerres de lignages et guerres d'états en Afrique* (Paris: Editions des Archives Contemporaines, 1982).

——, "Processus de formation d'une classe sociale dans une société précapitaliste," *Cahiers d'études africaines* 56.4 (1974).

Braeckman, Colette, *Rwanda, histoire d'un génocide* (Paris: Fayard, 1994).

Bragard, Lucie, "Vers l'indépendance du Ruanda-Urundi: Les Problèmes essentials," *Dossiers de l'action sociale catholique* 8 (1959).

Brauman, Rony, *Devant le mal: Rwanda, essai sur le génocide* (Paris: Le Seuil, 1994).

Bührer, Michel, *Rwanda: Mémoire d'un génocide* (Paris: Le Cherche midi/ UNESCO, 1996).

Burgt, Johannes-Michael van der, "Diary of Saint-Antoine," White Fathers Archives, Rome, July 25, 1896.

——, *Dictionnaire Français-Kirundi* (Bois-le-Duc: Société l'illustration catholique, 1903).

Carbone, Carlo, "Etnie, storiografia e storia del Burundi e del Rwanda contemporanei," *Africa*, Rome 2 (1997).

Célis, Georges, "La Métallurgie traditionnelle au Burundi, au Rwanda et au Buha: Essai de synthèse," *Anthropos* 84 (1989).

Célis, Georges and Emmanuel Nzikobanyanka, *La Métallurgie traditionnelle du*

Burundi: Techniques et croyances (Tervuren: Musée Royal de l'Afrique Centrale, 1976).

Chrétien, Jean-Pierre, "Agronomie, consommation, et travail dans l'agriculture du Burundi du XVIIIe au XXe siècle," in Michel Cartier (ed.), *Le Travail et ses représentations* (Paris: Editions des Archives Contemporaines, 1984).

———, "Les Arbres et les rois: Sites historiques du Burundi," *Culture et société: Revue de civilisation burundaise* 1 (1978).

———, *Burundi, l'histoire retrouvée: 25 Ans de métier d'historien en Afrique* (Paris: Karthala, 1993).

———, "Burundi: The Obsession with Genocide," *Current History* 95.601 (1996).

———, "Burundi: Pogromes sur les collines," *Esprit* 203 (1994).

———, "La Colonisation allemande (1896–1916)," in Lasserre (ed.), *Atlas du Burundi*.

———, "Conversions et crise de légitimité politique: Muyaga, poste missionaire catholique et la société de l'Est dur Burundi (1896–1916), in Jean-Pierre Chrétien (ed.), *L'Invention religieuse en Afrique: Histoire et religion en Afrique noire* (Paris: Karthala, 1993).

———, "La Crise politique rwandaise," *Genève-Afrique* 30.2 (1992).

———, *Le Défi de l'ethnisme* (Paris: Karthala, 1997).

———, "Le 'Désenclavement' de la région des Grands Lacs dans les projets economiques allemands au début du XXe siècle," in Département d'histoire de l'Université du Burundi, *Histoire sociale de l'Afrique de l'Est (XIXe–XXe siècle): Actes du colloque de Bujumbura, 17–24 Octobre 1989* (Paris: Karthala, 1991).

———, "Du Hirsute au Hamite: Les Variations du cycle de Ntare Rushatsi, fondateur du royaume du Burundi," *History in Africa* 8 (1981).

———, "Eglise et état au Burundi," *Cultures et développement*, Louvain 1 (1975).

———, "Eglise, pouvoir et culture: L'Itinéraire d'une chrétienté africaine," *Quatre Fleuves* 10.2 (1979).

———, "Ethnicité et politique: Les Crises du Rwanda et du Burundi depuis l'indépendance," *Guerres mondiales et conflits contemporains* 181 (1996).

————, "La Fermeture du Burundi et du Rwanda aux commerçants de l'exterieur (1905–1906)," in Colloque, *Actes du colloque entreprises et entrepreneurs en Afrique, XIXe–XXe siècles* (Paris: L'Harmattan, 1983), vol. 2.

————, "Hutu et Tutsi au Rwanda et au Burundi," in Jean-Loup Amselle and Elikia M'Bokolo (eds.), *Au Coeur de l'ethnie: Ethnie, tribalisme, et état en Afrique* (Paris: La Découverte/Poche, 1985).

————, "Interprétations du génocide de 1994 dans l'histoire contemporaine du Rwanda," *Clio en Afrique* (June 1997), http://www.up.univ-mrs.fr/~wclio-af.

————, "Mission, pouvoir colonial et pouvoir africain: Un Exemple au Rwanda sous la colonisation allemande: Le Meurtre du Père Loupias en 1910," in Maurice Carrez et al. (eds.), *Christianisme et pouvoirs politiques: Etudes d'histoire religieuse* (Lille: Université de Lille III, 1973).

————, "Le Mwami Ntare dans l'histoire du Burundi," in Guillet and Ndayishinguje (eds.), *Légendes historiques du Burundi*.

————, "Mythes et stratégies autour des origines du Rwanda (XIXe–XXe siècles) Kigwa et Gihanga, entre le ciel, les collines et l'Ethiopie," in Jean-Pierre Chrétien and Jean-Louis Triaud (eds.), *Histoire d'Afrique: Les Enjeux de mémoire* (Paris: Karthala, 1999).

————, "Un 'Nazisme tropical' au Rwanda? Image ou logique d'un génocide," *Vingtième siècle* 48 (1995).

————, "Nouvelles Hypothèses sur les origines du Burundi; Les Traditions du nord," in Ndoricimpa and Guillet (eds.), *L'Arbre-mémoire*.

————, "Le Passage de l'expédition d'Oscar Baumann au Burundi (Septembre–Octobre 1892)," *Cahiers d'études africaines* 29.1 (1968).

————, "'Presse libre' et propagande raciste au Rwanda: Kangura et 'les 10 Commandements du Hutu,'" *Politique africaine* 42 (June 1991).

————, "La Production du fer au Burundi avant la mainmise coloniale," in Nicole Echard (ed.), *Métallurgies africaines: Nouvelles Contributions* (Paris: Société des Africanistes, 1983).

————, "Les Responsabilités politiques du génocide, vues de Bruxelles et de Paris," *Politique africaine* 73 (1999).

————, "Une Révolte au Burundi en 1934: Les Racines traditionalistes de l'hostilité à la colonisation," *Annales économies, sociétés, civilisations* 25.6 (1970).

————, "La Révolte de Ndungutse (1912): Forces traditionelles et pression coloniale au Rwanda allemand," *Revue française d'outre-mer* 4 (1972).

————, "La 'Révolution assistée' au Rwanda," in Charles-Robert Ageron and Marc Michel (eds.), *L'Ere des décolonisations: sélection de textes du colloque "Décolonisations comparées," Aix-en-Provence, 30 Septembre–3 Octobre 1993* (Paris: Karthala, 1995).

————, "Rwanda: La Médiatisation d'un génocide," in Fabrice d'Almeida (ed.), *La Question médiatique: Les enjeux historiques et sociaux de la critique des médias* (Paris: Séli Arslan, 1997).

————, "Le Sorgho dans l'agriculture, la culture et l'histoire du Burundi," *Journal des africanistes* 52.1–2 (1982).

————, "Les Traditionnistes lettrés du Burundi à l'école des bibliothèques missionaires (1940–1960)," *History in Africa* 15 (1988).

————, "Les Variantes dans les sources orales: Un Exemple dans les récits d'origine du royaume du Burundi," *Culture et société: Revue de civilisation burundaise* 4 (1981).

Chrétien, Jean-Pierre et al., "Technologie et économie du sel végétal dans l'ancien Burundi," in Centre de Civilisation Burundaise, *La Civilisation ancienne des peuples des Grands Lacs* (Paris: Karthala, 1981).

Chrétien, Jean-Pierre, André Guichaoua, and Gabriel Le Jeune, *La Crise d'Août 1988 au Burundi*, Cahiers du C.R.A. 6 (Paris: Afera-Karthala, 1989).

Chrétien, Jean-Pierre and Emile Mworoha, "Mwezi Gisabo et le maintien d'une fragile indépendance au Burundi," in Charles André Julien (ed.), *Les Africains* (Paris: Éditions J.A., 1977), vol. 2.

————, "Les Tombeaux des *bami* du Burundi: Un Aspect de la monarchie sacrée en Afrique orientale," *Cahiers d'études africaines* 37.1 (1970).

Chrétien, Jean-Pierre, Jean-François Dupaquier, Marcel Kabanda, and Joseph Ngarambe, *Rwanda: Les Médias du Génocide* (Paris: Karthala, 1995).

Chrétien, Jean-Pierre and Michel Bahenduzi, "Ntare Rushatsi est-il passé à Magamba en mars 1680 ou en août 1701?" *Culture et société: Revue de civilisation burundaise* 11 (1990).

Classe, Léon, "Pour moderniser le Ruanda: Le Problème des Batutsi," *L'Essor colonial et maritime*, Dec. 7, 1930.

Cochet, Hubert, *Burundi: La Paysannerie dans la tourmente: Eléments d'analyse sur les origines du conflit politico-ethnique* (Paris: Librarie FPH, 1996).

———, "Burundi: Quelques Questions sur l'origine et la différenciation d'un système agraire," *African Economic History* 2 (1998).

Coupez, André and Marcel d'Hertefelt, *La Royauté sacrée de l'ancien Rwanda: Texte, traduction et commentaire de son rituel* (Tervuren: Musée Royal de l'Afrique Centrale, 1964).

Coupez, André and Thomas Kamanzi, *Littérature de cour au Rwanda* (Oxford: Clarendon Press, 1970).

———, *Récits historiques Rwanda* (Tervuren: Musée Royal de l'Afrique Centrale, 1962).

Czekanowski, Jan, *Ethnographie: Zwischenseengebiet: Mpororo, Ruanda*, vol. 1 of *Forschungen im Nil-Kongo-Zwischengebiet* (Leipzig: Klinkhardt, 1917).

Debré, Bernard, *Le Retour de mwami: La Vraie Histoire des génocides rwandais* (Paris: Ramsay, 1998).

"Décolonisation et indépendance du Rwanda et du Burundi," *Chronique de politique étrangère*, Brussels, 16.4–6 (1963).

Delacauw, A., "Féodalité ou démocratie en Urundi," *Temps nouveaux d'Afrique*, Usumbura, Sept. 2, 1956.

Delmas, Léon, *Généalogies de la noblesse (les Batutsi) du Ruanda* (Kabgayi: Vicariat Apostolique du Ruanda, 1950).

Des Forges, Alison, "Defeat Is the Only Bad News: Rwanda Under Musiinga, 1896–1931," Ph.D. thesis, Yale University, 1972.

———, "'The Drum Is Greater Than the Shout': The 1912 Rebellion in Northern Rwanda," in Donald Crummey (ed.), *Banditry, Rebellion, and Social Protest in Africa* (London: James Currey, 1986).

———, "Kings Without Crowns: The White Fathers in Rwanda," in Daniel

McCall, Norman Bennett, and Jeffrey Butlers (eds.), *Eastern African History* (New York: Praeger, 1969).

————, *Leave None to Tell the Story: Genocide in Rwanda* (New York: Human Rights Watch, 1999).

Deslaurier, Christine, "Du nouveau pour l'histoire politique du Burundi à la veille de l'indépendance; La Documentation secrète de la sûreté (1958–1961)," in *Autres Sources, nouveaux regards sur l'histoire africaine* (Paris: AFERA Editions, 1998).

————, "La Vie politique à la veille de l'indépendance: Les Elections de 1960 et 1961 en territoire de Rutana," in Gahama and Thibon (eds.), *Les Régions orientales du Burundi.*

Desmarais, Jean-Claude, "Le Rwanda des anthropologues: L'Arcéologie de l'idéologie raciale," *Anthropologie et sociétés* 2.1 (1978).

Destexhe, Alain, *Rwanda and Genocide in the Twentieth Century*, trans. Alison Marschner (New York: New York University Press, 1995).

Dion, Gilles-Marius, *Devinettes du Rwanda: Ibisakuze* (Butare: Editions Universitaires du Rwanda, 1971).

Erny, Pierre, *Rwanda 1994: Clés pour comprendre le calvaire d'un peuple* (Paris: L'Harmattan, 1994).

Fédération Internationale des Droits de l'Homme and other organizations, *Commission internationale d'enquête sur les violations des droits de l'homme au Rwanda depuis le 1er Octobre 1990. Rapport Final*, Paris, March 1993.

Feltz, Gaëtan and Jean-Etienne Bidou, "La Famine manori au Burundi, 1943–1944," *Revue française d'histoire d'outre-mer* 304.3 (1994).

Franche, Dominique, "Généalogie du génocide rwandais: Hutu et Tutsi: Gaulois et Francs?" *Temps modernes* 582 (1995).

————, *Rwanda: Généalogie d'un génocide* (Paris: Mille et Une Nuits, 1997).

Freedman, Jim, *Nyabingi: The Social History of an African Divinity* (Tervuren: Musée Royal de l'Afrique Centrale, 1984).

Fuchs, Paul, "Urundi und Ruanda," Deutsch-Ostafrikanische Zeitung, Dar es Salaam, Sept. 14, 1907.

Gahama, Amélie, *La Reine mère et ses prêtres au Burundi* (Nanterre: Laboratoire d'Ethnologie et de Sociologie Comparative, 1979).

Gahama, Joseph, *Le Burundi sous administration belge: La Période du mandat, 1919-1939* (Paris: Karthala, 1983).

———, "La Disparition du muganuro," in Ndoricimpa and Guillet (eds.), *L'Arbre-mémoire*.

———, "Les Hauts Lieux d'inscription des traditions et de la modernité au Burundi," in Jean-Pierre Chrétien and Jean-Louis Triaud (eds.), *Histoire d'Afrique: Les Enjeux de mémoire* (Paris: Karthala, 1999).

———, "Une Innovation agricole grandiose: L'Exemple de l'aménagement de la plaine de la Rusizi," in La Faculté des Lettres et Sciences Humaines, *Questions sur la paysannerie au Burundi* (Bujumbura: La Faculté, 1987).

———, "Les Options d'une indépendance sous tutelle au Rwanda et au Burundi: Nationalismes ou révolutions internes," in Charles-Robert Ageron and Marc Michel (eds.), *L'Ere des décolonisations: Sélection de textes du colloque "Décolonisations comparées," Aix-en-Provence, 30 Septembre–3 Octobre 1993* (Paris: Karthala, 1995).

———, "Les Partis politiques et la recherche de l'indépendance au Burundi," in Département d'histoire de l'Université du Burundi, *Histoire sociale de l'Afrique de l'Est (XIXe–XXe siècle): Actes du colloque de Bujumbura, 17–24 Octobre 1989* (Paris: Karthala, 1991).

———, "La Révolte de Runyota-Kanyarufunzo au Burundi, 1922," *Cahiers d'histoire*, Bujumbura 3 (1985).

Gahama, Joseph and Christian Thibon, eds., *Les Régions orientales du Burundi: Une Périphérie à l'épreuve du développement* (Paris: Karthala, 1994).

Ghislain, Jean, "Souvenirs de la territoriale au Burundi: Le Brouillard sur la Kibira," *Enquêtes et documents d'histoire africaine* 11 (1992).

Gille, Albert, "Notes sur l'organisation des Barundi," *Bulletin des jurisdictions indigènes et du droit coutumier congolais* 1 (1937).

Gorju, Julien, *Face au royaume Hamite du Ruanda: Le Royaume frère de l'Urundi: Essai de reconstitution historique; moeurs pastorales; folklore* (Brussels: Vromant, 1938).

Götzen, Gustav Adolf von, *Durch Afrika von Ost nach West Resultate und Begebenheiten einer Reise von der Deutsch-Ostafrikanischen Küste bis zur Kongomündung in den Jahren 1893/94* (Berlin: D. Reimer, 1895).

Gourou, Pierre, *La Densité de la population du Ruanda-Urundi: Esquisse d'une étude géographique* (Brussels: Institut Royal Colonial Belge, 1953).

Gouteux, Jean-Paul, *Un Génocide secret d'état: La France et le Rwanda, 1990–1997* (Paris: Editions Sociales, 1998).

Gravel, Pierre, *Remera: A Community in Eastern Rwanda* (The Hague: Mouton, 1968).

Grunderbeek, Marie-Claude van, Emile Roche, and Hugues Doutrelepont, "L'Age du fer ancien au Rwanda et au Burundi: Archéologie et environnement," *Journal des africanistes* 52.1–2 (1982).

Guichaoua, André, *L'Ordre paysan des Hautes Terres centrales du Burundi et du Rwanda*, vol. 1 of *Destins paysans et politiques agraires en Afrique centrale* (Paris: L'Harmattan, 1989).

———, *Le Problème des réfugiés rwandais et des populations banyarwanda dans la région des Grands Lacs africains* (Geneva: UNHCR, 1992).

——— (ed.), *Les Crises politiques au Burundi et au Rwanda (1993–1994)* (Paris: Karthala, 1995).

———, *Enjeux nationaux et dynamiques régionales dans l'Afrique des Grands Lacs* (Lille: Université des Sciences et Technologies, 1992).

Guillet, Claude and Pascal Ndayishinguje (eds.), *Légendes historiques du Burundi: Les Multiples Visages du roi Ntáre* (Paris: Karthala, 1987).

Harroy, Jean-Paul, *Burundi, 1955–1962: Souvenirs d'un combattant d'une guerre perdue* (Brussels: Hayez, 1987).

———, *Rwanda: De la Féodalité à la démocratie, 1955–1962* (Brussels: Hayez, 1984).

Hatungimana, Alexandre, "La caféiculture au Burundi: économie et société des débuts à l'indépendance, 1920–1962," Ph.D. thesis, Paris I, 1999.

Heremans, Roger, *Introduction à l'histoire du Rwanda* (Kigali: Editions Rwandaises, 1971).

Heremans, Roger and François Bart, "Agriculture et paysages rwandais à travers les sources missionaires (1900–1950)," *Cultures et développement* 14.1 (1982).

Hertefelt, Marcel d', *Les Clans du Rwanda ancien: Eléments d'ethnosociologie et d'ethnohistoire* (Tervuren: Musée Royal de l'Afrique Centrale, 1971).

Hertefelt, Marcel d' and Danielle de Lame, *Société, culture et histoire du Rwanda: Encyclopédie bibliographique, 1863–1980/87*, 2 vols. (Tervuren: Musée Royal d'Afrique Centrale, 1987).

Hertefelt, Marcel d', Albert A. Trouwborst, and J.H. Scherer, *Les Anciens Royaumes de la zone interlacustre méridionale* (Tervuren: Musée Royal de l'Afrique Centrale, 1962).

Heusch, Luc de, "Massacres collectifs au Rwanda?" *Synthèses*, Brussels 221 (1964).

———, "Mythe et société féodale: Le Culte du Kubandwa dans le Rwanda traditionnel," *Archives de sociologie des religions* 18 (1964).

———, *Rois nés d'un coeur de vache: Mythes et rites bantous* (Paris: Gallimard, 1982).

Hiernaux, Jean, *Les Caractères physiques des populations du Ruanda et de l'Urundi* (Brussels: Institut Royal des Sciences Naturelles de Belgique, 1954).

Honke, Gudrun, "L'Eglise évangélique," in Gudrun Honke (ed.), *Au plus profond de l'Afrique: Le Rwanda et la colonisation allemande, 1885–1919* (Wuppertal: P. Hammer, 1990).

———, "Pour l'Empereur et le roi: L'Etablissement de la domination coloniale allemande," in Gudrun Honke (ed.), *Au plus profond de l'Afrique: Le Rwanda et la colonisation allemande, 1885–1919* (Wuppertal: P. Hammer, 1990).

Hubert, Jean R., *La Toussaint rwandaise et sa répression* (Brussels: Académie Royale des Sciences d'Outre-Mer, 1965).

Hubinont, P.O., Jean Hiernaux, and T. Massart-Guiot, "Blood Groups of the ABO, MN, and CDE-cde Systems in the Native Populations of Ruanda-Urundi Territories," *Annals of Eugenics* 18 (1953).

Imbs, Françoise, François Bart, and Annie Bart, "Le Rwanda: Les Données sociogéographiques," *Hérodote: Revue de géographique et de géopolitique*, Paris 72/73 (1994).

Johanssen, Ernst, *Ruanda. Kleine Anfänge, grosse Aufgaben der evangelischen Mission im Zwischenseengebiet Deutsch-Ostafrikas* (Bielefeld: Bethel, 1912).

Kabagema, Innocent, *Ruanda unter deutscher Kolonialherrschaft, 1899–1916* (Frankfurt: Lang, 1993).

Kagame, Alexis, *Un Abrégé de l'ethno-histoire du Rwanda* (Butare: Editions Uni-

455

versitaires du Rwanda, 1972), vol. 1.

———, *Un Abrégé de l'histoire du Rwanda de 1853 à 1972* (Butare: Éditions Universitaires du Rwanda, 1975), vol. 2.

———, *L'Histoire des armées-bovines de l'ancien Rwanda* (Brussels: Académie Royale des Sciences d'Outre-Mer, 1961).

———, *Inganji karinga*, 2 vols. (Kabgayi, 1959 [1943 and 1947]).

———, *Les Milices du Rwanda précolonial* (Brussels: Académie Royale des Sciences d'Outre-Mer, 1963).

———, *La Notion de génération appliquée à la généalogie dynastique et à l'histoire du Rwanda: Des Xe–XIe siècles à nos jours* (Brussels: Académie Royale des Sciences Colonials, 1959).

Kandt, Richard, *Caput Nili; Eine empfindsame Reise zu den Quellen des Nils*, 2 vols. (Berlin: D. Reimer, 1904, 1919).

———, "Gewerbe in Ruanda," *Zeitschrift für Ethnologie* (1904).

Kavakure, Laurent, "Famines et disettes au Burundi (fin du XIXe siècle–1re moitié du XXe siècle)," unpublished MS, Bujumbura, 1982.

Kayondi, Cyprien, "Murunga, colline du Burundi: Etude géographique," *Cahiers d'outre-mer* 25.98 (1972).

Lacger, Louis de, *Ruanda* (Namur, Belgium: Grands Lacs, 1939), reed. and repub. in 1961.

Laely, Thomas, *Autorität und Staat in Burundi* (Berlin: D. Reimer, 1995).

Lame, Danielle de, *Une Colline entre mille; ou, le Calme avant la tempête: Transformations et blocages du Rwanda rural* (Tervuren: Musée Royal de l'Afrique Centrale, 1996).

Lasserre, Guy, ed., *Atlas du Burundi* (Bordeaux: Association pour l'Atlas du Burundi, 1979).

Lechat, Michel, *Le Burundi politique* (Usumbura: Service de l'information du Ruanda-Urundi, 1961).

Lemarchand, René, *Burundi: Ethnocide as Discourse and Practice* (Cambridge, UK: Cambridge University Press, 1994).

———, "Burundian Glaasnost or Falsification of History?" *Burundi Newsletter*, no. 2, Svendborg, Denmark (1989).

————, "The C.I.A. in Africa: How Central? How Intelligent?" *Journal of Modern African Studies* 14.3 (1976).

————, *Rwanda and Burundi* (London: Pall Mall Press, 1970).

Leurquin, Philippe, *Le Niveau de vie des populations rurales du Ruanda-Urundi* (Louvain: Institut de Recherches Economiques et Sociales, 1960).

Linden, Ian, *Church and Revolution in Rwanda* (Manchester, UK: Manchester University Press, 1977).

Logiest, Guy, *Mission au Rwanda: Un Blanc dans la bagarre Tutsi-Hutu* (Brussels: Didier-Hatier, 1988).

Louis, William Roger, *Ruanda-Urundi, 1884–1919* (Oxford: Clarendon Press, 1963).

Lugan, Bernard, "Causes et effets de la famine 'Rumanura' au Rwanda, 1916–1918," *Canadian Journal of African Studies* 10.2 (1976).

————, "Echanges et routes commerciales au Rwanda, 1880–1914," *Africa-Tervuren* 22.2/3/4 (1976).

————, "Famines et disettes au Rwanda," *Cahiers d'outre-mer* 38.150 (1985).

————, *Histoire du Rwanda: De la préhistoire à nos jours* (Paris: Bartillat, 1997).

————, "Nyanza: Une Capitale royale du Rwanda ancien," *Africa-Tervuren* 26.4 (1980).

————, "Les Reseaux commerciaux au Rwanda dans le dernier quart du XIXe siècle," *Etudes d'histoire africaine* 9–10 (1977–1978).

Lugan, Bernard and Antoine Nyagahene, "Les Activités commerciales du Sud-Kivu au XIXe siècle à travers l'exemple de Kinyaga (Rwanda)," *Cahiers d'outre-mer* 36.141 (1983).

Lugan, Bernard and Raphaël Mutombo, "Le Sel dans le Rwanda ancien," *Cahiers d'outre-mer* 24.136 (1981).

Maindron, Gabriel, *Des Apparitions à Kibeho: Annonce de Marie au coeur de l'Afrique* (Paris: O.E.I.L., 1994).

Malkki, Liisa, *Purity and Exile: Violence, Memory, and National Cosmology Among Hutu Refugees in Tanzania* (Chicago: University of Chicago Press, 1995).

Mamdani, Mahmood, *When Victims Become Killers: Colonialism, Nativism, and the*

Genocide in Rwanda (Princeton, NJ: Princeton University Press, 2001).

Manirakiza, Marc, *La Fin de la monarchie burundaise, 1962–1966* (Brussels: Le Mât de Misaine, 1990).

Maquet, Jacques J., *The Premise of Inequality in Ruanda: A Study of Political Relations in a Central African Kingdom* (London: Oxford University Press, 1961).

————, *Ruanda: Essai photographique sur une société africaine en transition* (Brussels: Elsevier, 1957).

————, *Le Système des relations sociales dans le Ruanda ancien* (Tervuren: Musée Royal du Congo Belge, 1954).

Maquet, Jacques J. and Marcel d'Hertefelt, *Elections en société féodale: Une Etude sur l'introduction de vote populaire au Ruanda-Urundi* (Brussels: Académie Royale des Sciences Coloniales, 1959).

Mbonimana, Gamaliel, "Christianisation indirecte et cristallisation des clivages ethniques au Rwanda (1925–1931)," *Enquêtes et documents d'histoire africaine,* Louvain 3 (1978).

————, "L'Instauration d'un royaume chrétien au Rwanda (1900–1931), Ph.D. thesis, Louvain-la-Neuve, 1981."

Mbonimana, Gamaliel and Emmanuel Ntezimana, "Pères Blancs et missionaires de Bethel: L'Eglise catholique," in Gudrun Honke (ed.), *Au plus profond de l'Afrique: Le Rwanda et la colonisation allemande, 1885–1919* (Wuppertal: P. Hammer, 1990).

McCullum, Hugh, *The Angels Have Left Us: The Rwanda Tragedy and the Churches,* Risk Book Series, no. 66 (Geneva: WCC Publications, 1995).

Médecins sans Frontières, *Deadlock in the Rwandan Refugee Crisis: Virtual Standstill or Repatriation* (Paris, July 1995).

Ménard, François, "Barundi (moeurs et coutumes)," MS, White Fathers Archives, Rome, 1918.

Meschi, Lydia, "Evolution des structures foncières au Rwanda: Le Cas d'un lignage Hutu," *Cahiers d'études africaines* 53.1 (1974).

Meyer, Hans, *Die Barundi: Eine völkerkundliche Studie aus Deutsch-Ostafrika* (Leipzig: O. Spamer, 1916).

Ministère des Colonies (Belgium), *Plan décennal pour le développement économique et social du Ruanda-Urundi* (Brussels, Ministry of Colonies, 1951).

―――, *Rapport sur l'administration belge du Ruanda-Urundi pendant l'année* (Brussels, Ministry of Colonies, annually from 1921 to 1961).

Moniot, Henri, "Nouvelles Recherches sur l'histoire sociale du Rwanda," *Annales E.S.C.* 2 (1977).

Mujawimana, Eugénie, "Le Commerce des esclaves au Rwanda," unpublished MS, Ruhengeri, 1983.

Mukagasana, Yolande, *Le Mort ne veut pas de moi: Document* (Paris: Fixot, 1997).

Mvuyekure, Augustin, "Approche historique des conversions au catholicisme au Burundi (1922–1962)," Ph.D. thesis, Paris I, 1988.

Mworoha, Emile, "La Cour du roi Mwezi Gisabo (1852–1908) du Burundi à la fin du XIXe siècle," *Etudes d'histoire africaine* 7 (1975), pp. 39–58.

―――, "Redevances et prestations dans les domaines royaux du Burundi précolonial," in *Le Sol, la parole et l'écrit: Mélanges en hommage à Raymond Mauny* (Paris: L'Harmattan, 1981).

Mworoha, Emile et al. (eds.), *Histoire du Burundi:Des Origines à la fin du XIXe siècle* (Paris: Hatier, 1987).

Nahimana, Ferdinand, "Les Principautés Hutu du Rwanda septentrional," in Centre de Civilisation Burundaise, *La Civilisation ancienne des peuples des Grands Lacs* (Paris: Karthala, 1981).

―――, *Le Rwanda: Emergence d'un état* (Paris: L'Harmattan, 1993).

Ndayishinguje, Pascal, *L'Intronisation d'un mwami* (Nanterre: Laboratoire d'Ethnologie et de Sociologie Comparative, 1977).

Ndikuriyo, Adrien, "Contrats de bétail, contrats de clientèle et pouvoir politique dans le Batutsi du XIXe siècle," *Etudes d'histoire africaine* 7 (1975).

Ndimurukundo, Nicéphore, "Les Ages et les espaces de l'enfance dans le Burundi traditionnel," *Journal des africanistes* 51.1/2 (1981).

Ndoricimpa, Léonidas and Claude Guillet, *Les Tambours du Burundi* (Bujumbura: Ministère de la Jeunesse, des Sports et de la Culture, 1983).

―――― (eds.), *L'Arbre-mémoire: Traditions orales au Burundi* (Paris: Karthala, 1984).

Neesen, Victor, "Aspects de l'économie démographique du Ruanda-Urundi," *Bulletin de l'Institut de Recherches Economiques et Sociales*, Louvain, 22.5 (1956).

Newbury, Catharine, *The Cohesion of Oppression: Clientship and Ethnicity in Rwanda, 1860–1960* (New York: Columbia University Press, 1988).

———, "Deux Lignages au Kinyaga," *Cahiers d'études africaines* 53.1 (1974).

———, "Ethnicity in Rwanda: The Case of Kinyaga," *Africa* 48.1 (1978).

Newbury, David, "'Bunyabungo': The Western Rwanda Frontier, c. 1750–1850," in Igor Kopytoff (ed.), *The African Frontier: The Reproduction of African Societies* (Bloomington: Indiana University Press, 1986).

———, "Les Campagnes de Rwabugiri: Chronologie et bibliographie," *Cahiers d'études africaines* 53.1 (1974).

———, "The Clans of Rwanda: A Historical Hypothesis," in Centre de Civilisation Burundaise, *La Civilisation ancienne des peuples des Grands Lacs* (Paris: Karthala, 1981).

———, "The 'Rwakayihura' Famine of 1928–1929: A Nexus of Colonial Rule," in Département d'histoire de l'Université du Burundi, *Histoire sociale de l'Afrique de l'Est (XIXe–XXe siècle): Actes du colloque de Bujumbura, 17–24 Octobre 1989* (Paris: Karthala, 1991).

———, "Trick Cyclists? Recontextualizing Rwandan Dynastic Chronology," *History in Africa* 21 (1994).

———, "What Role Has Kingship? An Analysis of the *Umuganura* Ritual of Rwanda," *Africa-Tervuren* 4 (1981).

Nizigiyimana, Domitien, "Les Contes d'ogres (*ibisizimwe*): Contribution à l'analyse des textes narratifs de littérature orale du Burundi," Ph.D. thesis, Paris III, 1985.

Nkundabagenzi, Fidèle, *Rwanda politique, 1958–1960* (Brussels: CRISP, 1962).

Nkurikiyimfura, Jean-Népomucène, *Le Gros Bétail et la société rwandaise: évolution historique: Des XIIe–XIVe siècles à 1958* (Paris: L'Harmattan, 1994).

———, "La Révision d'une chronologie: Le Cas du royaume du Rwanda," in Claude-Hélène Perrot (ed.), *Sources orales de l'histoire de l'Afrique* (Paris: Editions du Centre National de la Recherche Scientifique, 1989).

Noten, Francis van, *Histoire archéologique du Rwanda* (Tervuren: Musée Royal de l'Afrique Centrale, 1983).

———, *Les Tombes du roi Cyirima Rujugira et de la reine mère Nyirayuhi Kanjogera: Description archéologique* (Tervuren: Musée Royal de l'Afrique Centrale, 1972).

Nsanze, Augustin, "Les Bases Économiques des Pouvoirs au Burundi de 1875 à 1920," Ph.D. thesis, Paris I, 1987.

———, *Un Domaine royal au Burundi, Mbuye: Env. 1850–1945* (Paris: Société Française d'Histoire d'Outre-Mer, 1980).

Ntezimana, Emmanuel, "Histoire, culture et conscience nationale: Le Cas du Rwanda des origines à 1900," *Etudes rwandaises* 4 (1987).

Ntibantunganya, Sylvestre, *La Guerre "ethno"-civile s'installe, 1993–1996*, vol. 2 of *Une Démocratie pour tous les Burundais* (Paris: L'Harmattan, 1999).

Nyagahene, Antoine, "Histoire et peuplement: Ethnies, clans, et lignages dans le Rwanda ancien et contemporain," Ph.D. thesis, Paris VII, 1997.

Ould Abdallah, Ahmedou, *La Diplomatie Pyromane: Entretiens avec Stephen Smith* (Paris: Calmann-Lévy, 1996).

Overschelde, Antoine van, *Un Audacieux pacifique: Monseigneur Léon Paul Classe, apôtre du Ruanda* (Namur: Grands Lacs, 1948).

Pagès, Albert, *Au Ruanda, sur les bords du Lac Kivu (Congo belge): Un Royaume hamite au centre de l'Afrique* (Brussels: Institut Royal Colonial Belge, 1933).

———, "Flore domestique du Rwanda, I. Les Plantes alimentaires," *Bulletin agricole du Congo belge* 19.1 (1928).

Paternostre de la Mairieu, Baudouin, *A la Source du Nil: Les Mille Collines du Rwanda* (Paris: Téqui, 1985).

———, *Le Rwanda: Son Effort de développement: Antecedents historiques et conquètes de la revolution rwandaise* (Brussels: A. De Boeck, 1972).

Perugia, Paul del, *Les Derniers Rois mages* (Paris: Gallimard, 1970).

Piron, M., "Les Migrations hamitiques," *Servir* 9.6 (1948).

Prioul, Christian and Pierre Sirven (eds.), *Atlas du Rwanda* (Nantes: Association pour l'Atlas des Pays de Loire, 1981).

Prunier, Gérard, "Elements pour une histoire du Front Patriotique Rwandais," *Politique africaine* 51 (October 1993).

————, *The Rwanda Crisis: History of a Genocide* (New York: Columbia University Press, 1995).

Ramsay, Hans, "Über seine Expeditionen nach Ruanda und dem Rukwasee," *Verhandlungen der Gesellschaft für Erdkunde zu Berlin* (1898).

Reisdorff, Ivan, "Enquêtes foncières au Ruanda," duplicated lecture notes, 1952.

Rennie, J.K., "The Precolonial Kingdom of Rwanda: A Reinterpretation," *Transafrican Journal of History* 2.2 (1972).

Reyntjens, Filip, *L'Afrique des Grands Lacs en crise: Rwanda, Burundi, 1988–1994* (Paris: Karthala, 1994).

————, "La Deuxième République rwandaise: Evolution, bilan et perspectives," *Afrika Focus* 3–4 (1986).

————, "La Nouvelle Constitution rwandaise du 20 Décembre 1978," *Penant* 768 (1980).*

————, *Pouvoir et droit au Rwanda: Droit public et évolution politique, 1916–1973* (Tervuren: Musée Royal de l'Afrique Centrale, 1985).

————, *Rwanda: Trois Jours qui ont fait basculer l'histoire* (Brussels: Institut Africain, 1995).

Rocard, Michel, *L'Edit de Nantes et l'art de la paix* (Biarritz: Editions Atlantica, 1997).

Roche, Emile et al., "Evolution du paléoenvironnement quatenaire au Rwanda et au Burundi," in *Actes du Xeme symposium de l'Association des Palynologues de Langue Francaise*, 1988.

Rodegem, F., *Anthologie rundi* (Paris: A. Colin, 1973).

————, *Documentation bibliographique sur le Burundi* (Bologne: EMI, 1978).

————, "La Fonction hyperphatique du langage," *Cultures et développement* 6.2 (1974).

————, *Onomastique rundi* (Bujumbura, 1965).

————, *Sagesse kirundi: Proverbs, dictions, locutions usités au Burundi* (Tervuren: Musée Royal du Congo Belge, 1961).

Rumiya, Jean, *Le Rwanda sous le régime du mandat belge (1916–1931)* (Paris: L'Harmattan, 1992).

Rutayisire, Paul, *La Christianisation du Rwanda (1900–1945): Méthode missionaire et politique selon Mgr. Léon Classe* (Freiburg: Editions Universitaires, 1987).

Rutembesa, Faustin, "La Réorganisation administrative et ses conséquences au Rwanda entre 1926 et 1931," *Cahiers d'histoire* 2 (Bujumbura) *Cahiers du C.R.A.4* (Paris) (1984).

Rwabukumba, Joseph and Vincent Mudandagizi, "Les Formes historiques de la dépendance personnelle dans l'état rwandais," *Cahiers d'études africaines* 53.1 (1974).

Ryckmans, Pierre, *Dominer pour servir* (Brussels: Universelle, 1931).

————, *Une Page d'histoire coloniale: L'Occupation allemande dans l'Urundi* (Brussels: Institut Royal Colonial Belge, 1953).

Sasserath, Jules, *Le Ruanda-Urundi: Un Etrange Royaume féodal au cour de l'Afrique* (Brussels: Germinal, 1948).

Saur, Léon, *Influences parallèles: L'Internationale Démocrate Chrétienne au Rwanda* (Brussels: Luc Pire, 1998).

Schumacher, Peter, *Die physische und soziale Umwelt der Kivu-Pygmäen* (Twiden) (Brussels: Van Campenhout, 1949).

Segal, Aaron, *Massacre in Rwanda* (London: Fabian Society, 1964).

Sénat de Belgique, *Rapport de la Commission d'enquête parlementaire concernant les événements du Rwanda*, Brussels, 1997.

Servaes, Sylvia, "L'Etude ethnographique du Rwanda," in Gudrun Honke (ed.), *Au plus profond de l'Afrique: Le Rwanda et la colonisation allemande, 1885–1919* (Wuppertal: P. Hammer, 1990).

Shantz, H.L., "Agricultural Regions of Africa," *Economic Geography* (1942).

Smets, Georges, "Les Institutions féodales de l'Urundi," *Revue de l'Université Libre de Bruxelles* 2 (1949).

Smith, Pierre, "La Forge de l'intelligence," *L'Homme* 10.2 (1970).

————, "Personnages de légende," in Centre de Civilisation Burundaise, *La Civilisation ancienne des peuples des Grands Lacs* (Paris: Karthala, 1981).

————, *Le Récit populaire au Rwanda* (Paris: A. Colin, 1975).

Theunis, Guy, "Une Philosophie pour *Dialogue*," *Dialogue* 121 (1987).

Thibon, Christian, "Crise démographique et mise en dépendance au Burundi et dans la région des Grands Lacs, 1880–1910," *Cahiers d'histoire* 2 (Bujumbura), *Cahiers du C.R.A.* 4 (Paris) (1984).

———, "Un Siècle de croissance démographique au Burundi (1850–1950), *Cahiers d'études africaines* 105/106.1–2 (1987).

Trouwborst, Albert, "La Base territoriale de l'état du Burundi ancien," *Revue de l'Université du Burundi* 1.3/4 (1973).

———, "L'Ethnographie du Burundi pendant l'occupation belge: Première Période (1916–1945): L'Oeuvre de George Smets (1881–1961)," in Centre de Civilisation Burundaise, *La Civilisation ancienne des peuples des Grands Lacs* (Paris: Karthala, 1981).

———, "Kinship and Geographical Mobility in Burundi (East Central Africa)," *International Journal of Comparative Sociology* 6.1 (1965).

———, "L'Organisation politique en tant que système d'échanges au Burundi," *Anthropologica* 3.1 (1961).

———, "Quelques Aspects symbolique des échanges de bière au Burundi (Afrique centrale)," in *Anniversary Contributions to Anthropology: Twelve Essays Published on the Occasion of the 40th Anniversary of the Leiden Ethnological Society* (Leiden: Brill, 1970).

United Nations, *United Nations Visiting Mission to Trust Territories in East Africa, 1957: Report on Ruanda-Urundi* (New York: United Nations, 1958).

Université du Burundi, *Questions sur la paysannerie au Burundi* (Bujumbura, 1987).

Vansina, Jan, *L'Evolution du royaume Rwanda des origines à 1900* (Brussels: Académie Royale des Sciences d'Outre-Mer, 1962).

———, "Is Elegance Proof? Structuralism and African History," *History in Africa* 10 (1983).

———, *La Légende du passé: Traditions orales du Burundi* (Tervuren: Musée Royal de l'Afrique Centrale, 1972).

———, *Le Rwanda ancien: Le Royaume Nyiginya* (Paris: Karthala, 2001).

Verdier, Raymond, Emmanuel Decaux, and Jean-Pierre Chrétien (eds.), *Rwanda: Un Génocide du XXe siècle* (Paris: Harmattan, 1995).

Verschave, François, *Complicité de génocide? La Politique de la France au Rwanda* (Paris: La Découverte, 1994).

Vidal, Claudine, "Anthropologie et histoire: Le Cas du Rwanda," *Cahiers internationaux de sociologie* 43 (1967).

———, "De la Contradiction sauvage," *L'Homme*, 14.3–4 (1974).

———, "De la Religion subie au modernisme refusé: 'Théophagie,' ancêstres clandestins et résistance populaire au Rwanda," *Archives de sciences sociales des religions* 38 (1974).

———, "La Désinformation en histoire: Données historiques sur les relations entre Hutu, Tutsi et Twa durant la période précoloniale," *Dialogue* 200 (1997).

———, "Économie de la société féodale rwandaise," *Cahiers d'études africaines* 53.1 (1974).

———, "Enquêtes sur l'histoire et l'au-delà: Rwanda, 1800–1970," *L'Homme* 24.3–4 (1984).

———, "Le Génocide des rwandais Tutsi: Cruaté délibérée et logiques de haines," in Françoise Héritier (ed.), *De la Violence* (Paris: O. Jacob, 1996).

———, "Présentation," *Cahiers d'études africaines* 53.1 (1974).

———, "Rêve et réalité en ethnohistoire: Note sceptique sur J. Freedman et L. de Heusch," *Cahiers d'études africaines* 100.4 (1985).

———, "Le Rwanda des anthropologues et le fétichisme de la vache," *Cahiers d'études africaines* 35.3 (1969).

———, "Situations ethniques au Rwanda," in Jean-Loup Amselle and Elikia M'Bokolo (eds.), *Au Coeur de l'ethnie: Ethnie, tribalisme, et état en Afrique* (Paris: La Découverte, 1985).

———, *Sociologie des passions: Rwanda, Côte d'Ivoire* (Paris: Karthala, 1991).

——— (ed.), "Les Politiques de la haine: Rwanda, Burundi, 1994–1995," special issue of *Temps modernes* 583 (1995).

——— (ed.), *Le Problème de la domination étatique au Rwanda: Histoire et économie*, special issue of *Cahiers d'études africaines* 53.1 (1974).

Vignati, Elizabeth, "Du Fourneau à la fosse: Changements Techniques dans la métallurgie du fer au Burundi au cours des deux derniers millénaires," Ph.D. thesis, Paris I, 1995.

Willame, Jean-Claude, *Aux Sources de la hécatombe rwandaise* (Brussels: Institut Africain-CEDAF, 1995).

———, "Le *Muyaga* ou la 'révolution' rwandaise revisitée," *Revue française d'histoire d'outre-mer* 304.3 (1994).

———, "La Panne rwandaise," *Revue Nouvelle* 12 (1990).

Zuure, Bernard, *Croyances et pratiques religieuses des Barundi* (Brussels: L'Essorial, 1929).

Kivu

Académie Royale des Sciences d'Outre-Mer, *Le Congo belge durant la second guerre mondiale* (Brussels: Académie Royale des Sciences d'Outre-Mer, 1983).

Biebuyck, Daniel, *Lega Culture: Art, Initiation, and Moral Philosophy Among a Central African People* (Berkeley: University of California Press, 1973).

Bishikwabo, Chubaka, "Le Bushi au XIXe siècle: Un Peuple, sept royaumes," *Revue française d'histoire d'outre-mer* 246–47 (1980).

———, "Deux Chefs du Bushi sous le régime colonial: Kabare et Ngweshe (1912–1960)," *Etudes d'histoire africaine* 7 (1975).

———, "Histoire d'un état Shi en Afrique des Grands Lacs: Kaziba au Zaire (c. 1850–1940)," Ph.D. thesis, Louvain-la-Neuve, 1982.

———, "Notes sur l'origine de l'institution du bwami et fondements du pouvoir politique au Kivu oriental," *Cahiers du Cedaf* 8 (1979).

———, "L'Origine des chefferies de l'ouest de la Rusizi: Bufulero, Buvira, et Burundi au XIXe–XXe siècle," *Culture et société: Revue de civilisation burundaise* 4 (1981).

Bishikwabo, Chubaka and David Newbury, "Recent Historical Research in the Area of Lake Kivu: Rwanda and Zaire," *History in Africa* 7 (1980).

Chajmowiecz, Monique, "Kivu: Les Banyamulenge enfin à l'honneur!" *Politique africaine* 64 (Dec. 1996).

Depelchin, Jacques, "From Precapitalism to Imperialism: A History of Social and Economic Formations in Eastern Zaire (Uvira Zone, c. 1800–1965)," Ph.D. thesis, Stanford University, 1974.

Franck, Louis, *Le Congo belge* (Brussels: La Renaissance du Livre, 1930), vol. 1.

Hiernaux, Jean, "Données génétiques sur six populations de la République du Congo," *Annales de la Société Belge de Médecine Tropicale* 2 (1962).

Jewsiewicki, Bogumil, "African Peasants and Totalitarian Colonial Society in the Belgian Congo, 1917–1960," in Martin Klein (ed.), *Peasants in Africa: Historical and Contemporary Perspectives* (Beverly Hills, CA: Sage Publications, 1980).

Leplae, Edmond, *Les Plantations de café au Congo belge: Leur Histoire (1881–1935), leur importance actuelle* (Brussels: Van Campenhart, 1936).

Markovitz, Marvin, *Cross and Sword: The Political Role of Christian Missions in the Belgian Congo, 1908–1960* (Stanford, CA: Hoover Institution, 1973).

Moeller de Laddersous, A., *Les Grandes Lignes des migrations des Bantous de la province orientale au congo belge* (Brussels: Académie Royale des Sciences Coloniales, 1936).

Mutambo, Joseph, *Les Banyamulenge* (Kinshasa: Imprimerie Saint-Paul, 1997).

Ndaywel è Nziem, Isidore, *Histoire du Congo: De l'Héritage ancien à la république* (Brussels: De Boeck & Larcier, 1998).

Newbury, David, *Kings and Clans: Ijwi Island and the Lake Kivu Rift, 1780–1840* (Madison: University of Wisconsin Press, 1991).

Newbury, David and Catharine Newbury, "King and Chief on Ijwi Island, Zaire," *International Journal of African Historical Studies* 15.2 (1982).

Pourtier, Roland, "Congo-Zaïre-Congo: Un Itinéraire géopolitique au coeur d'Afrique," in Yves Lacoste (ed.), *Géopolitique d'une Afrique médiane*, special issue of *Hérodote* 86/87.3–4 (1997).

Prunier, Gérard, "La Crise du Kivu et ses conséquences dans la région des Grands Lacs," in Lacoste, *Géopolitique d'une Afrique médiane*, special issue of *Hérodote* 86/87.3–4 (1997).

Sigwalt, Richard, "The Early History of Bushi: An Essay in the Historical Use of Genesis Traditions," Ph.D. thesis, University of Wisconsin, 1975.

Stengers, Jean, *Congo, mythes et réalités: 100 Ans d'histoire* (Paris: Duculot, 1989).

Vellut, Jean-Luc, *Guide de l'étudiant en histoire du Zaïre* (Kinshasa, 1974).

————, "Pour une histoire sociale de l'Afrique centrale," *Cultures et développement*, Louvain, 1 (1974).

Vellut, Jean-Luc et al. (eds.), *Bibliographie historique du Zaïre à l'époque coloniale (1880–1960): Travaux publiés en 1960–1996* (Louvain-la-Neuve: Université Catholique de Louvain; Tervuren: Musée Royal de l'Afrique Centrale, 1996).

Weiss, Herbert and Benoît Verhaegen (eds.), *Les Rébellions dans l'est du Zaïre, 1964–1967* (Brussels: Centre d'Etude et de Documentation Africaines, 1986).

Willame, Jean-Claude, *L'Automne d'un despotisme: Pouvoir, argent et obéissance dans le Zaïre des années quatre-vingt* (Paris: Karthala, 1992).

————, *Banyarwanda et Banyamulenge: Violences ethniques et gestion de l'identitaire au Kivu* (Brussels: Institut Africain-CEDAF, 1997).

Young, Crawford, *Politics in the Congo: Decolonization and Independence* (Princeton, NJ: Princeton University Press, 1965).

Young, Crawford and Thomas Turner, *The Rise and Decline of the Zairian State* (Madison: University of Wisconsin Press, 1985).

Northwestern Tanzania

Anacleti, A.O. and D.K. Nagala, "The Cattle Complex in the Ancient West Lake Kingdoms," in Centre de Civilisation Burundaise, *La Civilisation ancienne des peuples des Grands Lacs* (Paris: Karthala, 1981).

Austen, Ralph, *Northwest Tanzania Under German and British Rule: Colonial Policy and Tribal Politics, 1889–1939* (New Haven, CT: Yale University Press, 1968).

Betbeder, Paul, "The Kingdom of Buzinza," *Cahiers d'histoire mondiale* 13.4 (1971).

Boller, Markus, *Kaffee, Kinder, Kolonialismus: Wirtschafts- und Bevölkerungsentwicklung in Buhaya (Tansania) in der deutschen Kolonialzeit* (Munster: Lit, 1994).

Césard, Edmond, "Comment les Bahaya interprètent leurs origines," *Anthropos* 22.3–4 (1927).

————, "Histoires des rois du Kyamtwara d'après l'ensemble des traditions des familles régnantes," *Anthropos* 26 (1931).

————, "Le Muhaya," *Anthropos* 30 (1935), 31 (1936), 32 (1937).

Chrétien, Jean-Pierre, "Les Banyamwezi au gré de la conjoncture (XIXe–XXe siècles): Des 'Monts de la lune' aux faubourgs de Dar es Salaam," in Jean-Pierre Chrétien and Gérard Prunier (eds.), *Les Ethnies ont une histoire* (Paris: Karthala, 1989).

————, "Le Buha à la fin du XIXe siècle: Un Peuple, six royaumes," *Etudes d'histoire africaine* 7 (1975).

Cory, Hans, *History of the Bukoba District* (Mwanza, Tanzania: Lake Printing Works, n.d., c. 1960).

Cory, Hans and M.M. Hartnoll, *Customary Law of the Haya Tribe, Tanganyika Territory* (London: Humphries & Co., 1945).

District Book of Bukoba (London: School of Oriental and African Studies Ar - chives, n.d.).

Ford, J. and R. de Z. Hall, "The History of Karagwe (Bukoba District)," *Tanganyika Notes and Records* 24 (1947).

Grant, C.H.B., "Uha in Tanganyika Territory," *Geographical Journal* (1925).

Hartwig, G.W., *The Art of Survival in East Africa: The Kerebe and Long-Distance Trade, 1800–1895* (London: Africana Pub. Co., 1976).

————, "Demographic Considerations in East Africa During the Nineteenth Century," *International Journal of African Historical Studies* 12.4 (1979).

Iliffe, John, "The Effects of the Maji Maji Rebellion of 1905–1906 on German Occupation Policy in East Africa," in Prosser Gifford and William Roger Louis (eds.), *Britain and Germany in Africa: Imperial Rivalry and Colonial Rule* (New Haven, CT: Yale University Press, 1967).

————, *A Modern History of Tanganyika* (Cambridge, UK: Cambridge University Press, 1979).

————, *Tanganyika Under German Rule, 1905–1912* (London: Cambridge University Press, 1969).

Jervis, T.S., "A History of *Robusta* Coffee in Bukoba," *Tanganyika Notes and Records* 8 (1939).

Kakaira, D., "Histoire d'Uzinza," Mwanza, 1948, White Fathers Archive, doc. 851.

Katoke, Israel, *The Karagwe Kingdom: A History of the Abanyambo of North Western Tanzania, c. 1400–1915* (Nairobi: East African Publishing House, 1975).

———— (ed.), "The Precolonial States of North-West Tanzania," *Cahiers d'histoire mondiale* 13.3, 13.4, 14.2 (1971–1972).

Kjekshus, Helge, *Ecology Control and Economic Development in East African History: The Case of Tanganyika, 1850–1950* (London: James Curry, 1977).

Lapioche, Jean-Baptiste, "Le Buhaya et Son Histoire," White Fathers Archives, Rome, 1938.

Lapioche, R.P., "Notes sur le Buhaya," White Fathers Archives, Rome, 1917, doc. 850.

Leakey, Administrator (title), "Historical Note," *District Book of Kasulu*, S.O.A.S. Archives, London, 1929.

Louis, William Roger, *Great Britain and Germany's Lost Colonies, 1914–1919* (Oxford: Clarendon Press, 1967).

Mbwiliza, J.F., "The Hoe and the Stick: A Political Economy of the Heru Kingdom, c. 1750–1900," in Centre de Civilisation Burundaise, *La Civilisation ancienne des peuples des Grands Lacs*.

Meyer, Hans, *Die Eisenbahnen im tropischen Afrika* (Leipzig: Duncker & Humblot, 1902).

Mors, Otto, "Geschichte der Bahaya," *Anthropos*, Freiburg (1957).

Müller, Fritz Ferdinand, *Deutschland, Zanzibar, Ostafrika; Geschichte einer deutschen Kolonialeroberung, 1884–1890* (Berlin: Rütten & Loening, 1959).

Rehse, Hermann, *Kiziba, Land und Leute: Eine Monographie* (Stuttgart: Strecker & Schröder, 1910).

Reining, Priscilla, "Haya Land Tenure: Landholding and Tenancy," *Anthropological Quarterly* 35.2 (1962).

Richter, Franz, "Der Bezirk Bukoba," *Mitteilungen aus den deutschen Schutzgebieten* (1899).

————, "Einige weitere ethnographische Notizen über den Bezirk Bukoba" and "Notizen über Lebensweise, Zeitrechnung, Industrie und Handwerk der Bewohnwer des Bezirks Bukoba," *Mitteilungen aus den deutschen Schutzgebieten* 13 (1900).

Roberts, Andrew, "A Bibliography of Primary Sources for Tanzania, 1799–1899," *Tanzania Notes and Records* 73 (1974).

———, "Nyamwezi Trade," in Richard Gray and David Birmingham (eds.), *Precolonial African Trade: Essays on Trade in Central and Eastern Africa Before 1900* (London: Oxford University Press, 1970).

Schmidt, Peter R., *Historical Archaeology: A Structural Approach in an African Culture* (Westport, CT: Greenwood Press, 1978).

Struck, B. "Bermerkungen über die 'Mbandwa' des Zwischenseengebiets," *Zeitschrift für Ethnologie* 3–4 (1911).

Stuhlmann, Franz, *Handwerk und Industrie in Ostafrika; Kulturgeschichtliche Betrachtungen* (Hamburg: L. Friederichsen & Co., 1910).

———, *Mit Emin Pascha ins Herz von Afrika* (Berlin: D. Reimer, 1894).

Sundkler, Bengt, *Bara Bukoba: Church and Community in Tanzania* (London: C. Hurst, 1980).

Sutton, John and Andrew Roberts, "Uvinza and Its Salt Industry," *Azania* 3 (1968).

Tawney, J.J., "Ugabire: A Feudal Custom Amongst the Waha," *Tanganyika Notes and Records* 17 (1944).

Thiel, R.P. van, "Buzinza unter der Dynastie der Bahinda," *Anthropos* 6 (1911).

Van Sambeek, J., *Croyances et coutumes des Baha* (Kabanga, 1950), vol. 2.

Vix, A., "Beitrag zur Ethnologie des Zwischenseengebietes von deutsch Ostafrika," *Zeitschrift für Ethnologie* 3–4 (1911).

Specialized Periodicals

Africa-Tervuren

Anthropos

Cahiers d'études africaines, Clio en Afrique (an electronic magazine, http:/www.up.univ-mrs.fr/~wclio-af)

Culture et société (Bujumbura)

Enquêtes et documents d'histoire (Louvain-la-Neuve)

Etudes Rwandaise (Butare)

Journal des africanistes

Journal of African History (London)

History in Africa (Madison)

International Journal of African Historical Studies (Boston)

Mitteilungen von Forschungs-Reisenden und Gelehrten aus den deutschen Schutzgebieten (Berlin)

Revue canadienne des études africaines/Canadian Journal of African Studies (Montreal)

Revue française d'histoire d'outre-mer

Uganda Journal (Kampala)

Appendices

Demographic Situation c. 1900

Kingdom	Population	Area meters²	Population density
Buganda	1,000,000	28,700	35
Bunyoro	110,000	13,800	8
Nkore	400,000	9,200	45
Rwanda	1,500,000	26,000	58
Burundi	1,500,000	27,000	55
Buha	200,000	25,000	8
Bushi	250,000	20,000	12
Bushubi	10,000	2,000	5
Kiziba	35,000	1,100	32
Kyamutwara	23,000	350	66
Kyanja	80,000	2,200	36
Bugabo	16,000	250	64
Karagwe	26,000	8,700	3
Ihangiro	60,000	3,000	20
Rusubi	300,000	7,800	38

Dynastic lists

	Kyamutwara	Karagwe	Kiziba	Kyamutwara Kyanja	Ihangiro	Buzinza	Gisaka	Bugesera	Rwanda
	Nkango dynasty	*Hinda dynasty*	*Bito dynasty*	*Hinda dynasty*	*Hinda dynasty*	*Hinda dynasty*	*Gesera dynasty*	*Hondogo dynasty*	*Nyiginya dynasty*
							KIMENYI	NSORO Sankunda	RUGANZU Bwimba
1500		RUHINDA	KIBI	RUHINDA		KAYANGO	KABUNDA		CYIRIMA Rugwe
		? NTARE Mihingo-etayomba	? ISHAMURA	?		?	KIMENYI Shumbusho	NSORO Sangano	KIGERI Mukobanya; MIBAMBWE Mutabazi
		RUHINDA; NTARE; KAREMERA Ndagara	WANNUMI; MATWI; MAGEMBE Kitonkire	NYARUBAMBA; KAREMERA; BWOGI; KAREMERA	NYARUBAMBA; RUHINDA Kayango; NTARE	RUHINDA; NTARE Muganganzara	MUTUMINKA		YUHI Gahima; NDAHIRO Cyamatare
1600		RUHINDA				KABURA	NTAHO	NSORO Rwayitare	RUGANZU Ndori
		NTARE	MUZINGA Nyakashoke	RUKAMBYA Gihume	?	KARAMBO	?		MUTARA Semugeshi
		RUSATIRA	MWIGARA	RUGOMORA Mahe		KATOBAHA; KINWA			
		MEHINGA	BURUNGU		MURAMIRA Kikongera	KYENDANZIGU	KIMENYI Rwahashya		KIGERI Nyamubeshera
1700			MAGEMBE Kagaruki	KAHIGI Kasita	Buto	NYAMURASA	KWEZI; RUREGEYA	NSORO Sabukeye	MIBAMBWE Gisanura; YUHI Mazimpaka
	MUTASHABA	KAREMERA Rwizagenda		NKWENGE	NYARUBAMBA Kicumbu	KABURA Nyaboreza		NSORO Nyabarega	KAREMERA Rwaka
		RUZENGA	MBONEKO Hangi	KARUMUNA Rugomora	MUGUNDA	KYENDAZIGU Kisamba	BAZIMYA		CYIRIMA Rujugira
	?	NTARE Kitabanyoro	NYARWANGU	MBOGI Mpangukano	KAHIGI	KAKARAZA	KIMENYI Getura	NSORO Kabano	KIGERI Ndabarasa
		RUHINDA	RUHANGARAZI	KAREMERA Mwiru	NYARUBAMBA	MWIHAHABI			
1800	RUSHUMA	NDAGARA	RUTAJWAHA; BURUNGU Kakindi	KINYONI	RUHINDA	NTARE Muhire RUHINDA; Muhangakyaro		NSORO Nyamugeta	MIBAMBWE Sentabyo
	KITEKERE								YUHI Gahindiro
		RUMANYIKWA	KIBI	RUGOMORA	NTARE	RUSIMBYA			MUTARA Rwogira
						ISEKANYERE			
	KAITABA		RUHANGAZARI			RWOMA; MANKORONGO			KIGERI Rwabugiri
	MUKOTANI	KAYENJE NDAGARA	MUTATEMBWA	KAHIGI	NYARUBAMBA	LUTUKAWA; KASUSURA			
1900	BWAHAMA	NTARE Kyobia	MUTAHANGARWA			RUDINGIZA; MULEKWA			MIBAMBWE Rutalindwa
	MUNTU		MBONEKO	KALEMERA Alfred	RUHINDA	NTARE KAZINDONGO			YUHI Musinga
	RWAIJUMBA	RUMANYIKWA Daudi	MUTAKUBWA William	BWOGI		MUSIBA			MUTARA Rudahigwa
	RUGABANDANA	RUHINDA deposed in 1962	RUTINWA Nestor						KIGERI deposed in 1961
						Rusubi Buzinza			

Genealogical chart of East African dynasties.

Nkore	Bunyoro	Buganda	Buhavu	Ijwi	Bushi Ngweshe	Kaziba	Burundi	South Buha	
Hinda dynasty	Bito dynasty	Matrilineal alternate	Sibula dynasty	Sibula dynasty			Ganwa dynasty	Kimbiri dynasty	
RUHINDA	RUKIDI	KINTU / CHWA / KIMERA							
NKUBA	OCAKI / OYO NYIMBA	TEMBO / KIGALA							
NYAIKA	WINYI	KIYIMBA							1500
NTARE Nyabugaro	OLIMI	KIYIMA NAKIBINGE					NTARE Karemera		
RUSHANGO	NYABONGO	MULONDO / JEMBA					?		
NTARE	WYNYI	SUNA							
		SEKAMANYA							1600
NTARE	OLIMI	KIMBUGWE / KATEREGA					NTARE Kibogora	KIMENYI	
KASASIRA	NYARWA	MUTEBI					MUTAGA Nyamubi	NTARE	
		JUKO			KAGWESHE	CHIVULA			
	CWAMALI	KAYEMBA					?	?	
KITERA RUMONGYE MIRINDI	MASAMBA	TEBANDEKE / NDAWULA			MUHIVE	MBWIJE		RUHINDA	
	KYEBAMBE						NTARE RUSHATSI		1700
NTARE Kitabanyoro	WINYI	KAGULU / KIKULWE			KASERERE	NGWINA	MWEZI	MAZIGA	
								MASIMBA	
MACWA	NYAIKA KYEBAMBE	MAWANDA	?		WEZA	BIREMERA	MUTAGA Senyamwiza	KIVUNANGOMA	
RWABIRERE		MWANGA NAMUGALA KYABAGGU			BICHINGA	MUKENGE		NTARE	
GAHAYA	OLIMI		KAMEROGOSA				MWAMBUTSA Mbariza	KANYONI	
RWEBISHENGYE	DUHAGA	JUNJU SEMAKOKIRO		KABWIKA	CHIRIMWENTALE	MBWIJE		RWASA	1800
	OLIMI KYEBAMBE	KAMANYA	MPAKA	MWENDANGA	KWIBUKA	KABONWA	NTARE Rugamba		
GASYONGA								NTARE	
MUTAMBUKA	NYABONGO KABOYO OLIMI	SUNA	NSIBULA Bahole		RUGENGE LUSHAMBA	KARHENDE			
NTARE	KAMURASI NYAIKA	MUTESA MWANGA		KABEGO				KANYONI	
GAHAYA	KABAREGA KITAHIMBWA	NTARE	NTARE		LIRANGWE	MUKENGE	MWEZI Gisabo		
	DUHAGA / DAUDI Kasagama	DAUDI CWA		NDOGOSA	RUHONGEKA	MADJIRI		NTARE RWASA	1900
GASYONGA +1967	WINYI Tito +1962	MUTESA deposed in 1966	LUSHOMBO	BERA	MAFUNDWE	KABONWA	MUTAGA Mbikije		
	KAMURASI Rukidi +1965			NTAMBUKA					
				MUHAMIRIZA	MUHIGIRWA	CHIMANYE	MWAMBUTSA Bangiricenge		
		MUTEBI Ronald			NDATABAYE		NTARE Ndizeye deposed in 1966		
	Bunyoro Toro							Bushingo Heru	

Maps

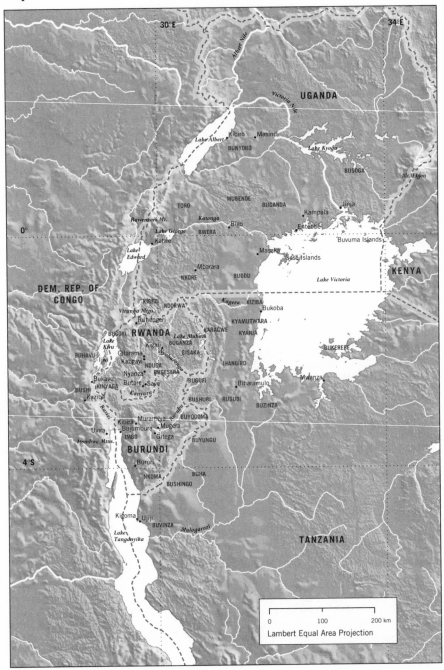

The Great Lakes Region

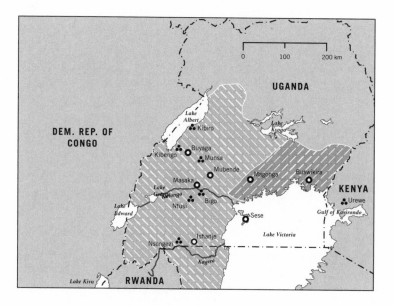

Archeology and traditions of the northern Great Lakes region

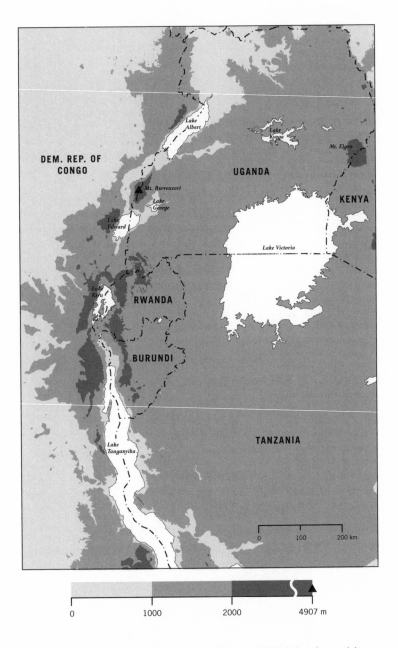

Elevation (in meters) [Data: GTOPO30 global 30-second digital elevation model, U.S. Geological Survey EROS Data Center]

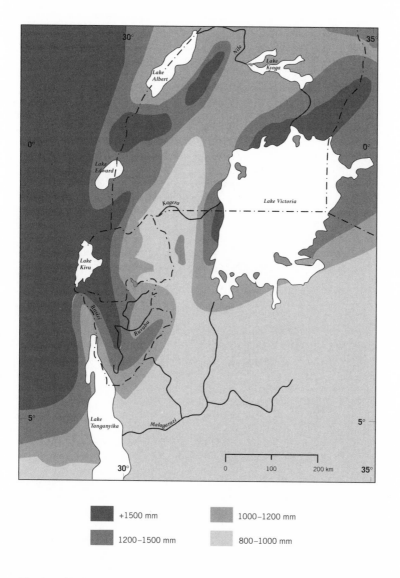

Climate and hydrography: annual rainfall

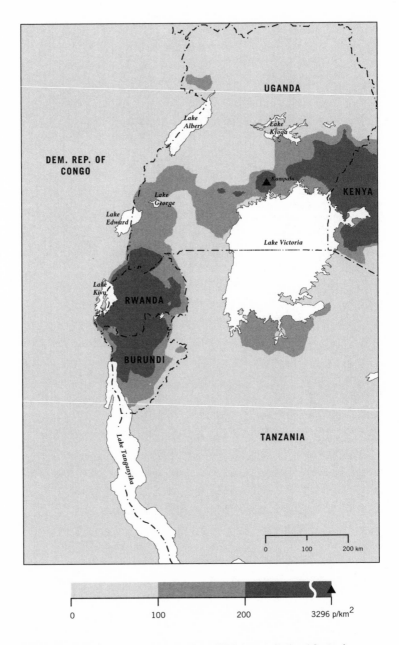

Population density (people per sq km) [Data: GPW dataset, National Center for Geographic Information and Analysis, Santa Barbara]

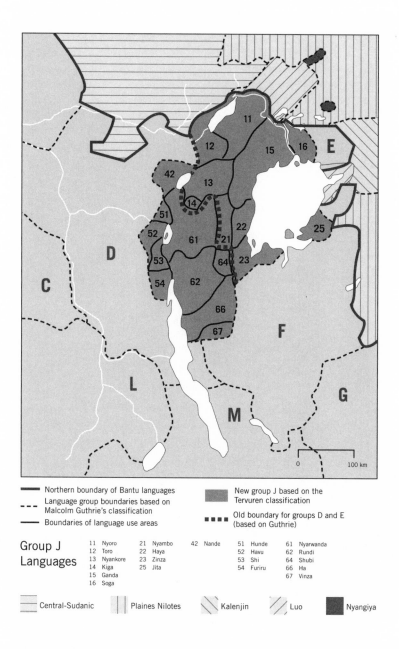

Northern boundary of Bantu languages
Language group boundaries based on Malcolm Guthrie's classification
Boundaries of language use areas

New group J based on the Tervuren classification
Old boundary for groups D and E (based on Guthrie)

**Group J
Languages**

11 Nyoro	21 Nyambo	42 Nande	51 Hunde	61 Nyarwanda
12 Toro	22 Haya		52 Havu	62 Rundi
13 Nyankore	23 Zinza		53 Shi	64 Shubi
14 Kiga	25 Jita		54 Furiru	66 Ha
15 Ganda				67 Vinza
16 Soga				

Central-Sudanic   Plaines Nilotes   Kalenjin   Luo   Nyangiya

Language distribution [Sources: M. Guthrie, *The Classification of Bantu Languages* (London: Oxford University Press, 1967); A. Coupez et al, "Classification d'un échantillon de langues bantoues d'après la lexicostatistique," in *Africana Linguistica* vol. 6 (Tervuren: Musée Royal de l'Afrique Centrale, 1975)]

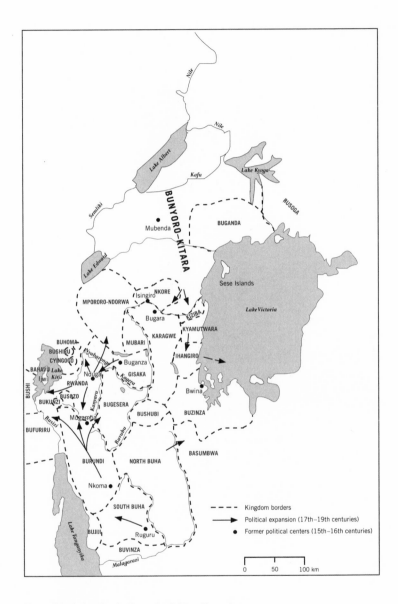

The political situation in the early eighteenth century

The Great Lakes kingdoms in the late nineteenth century

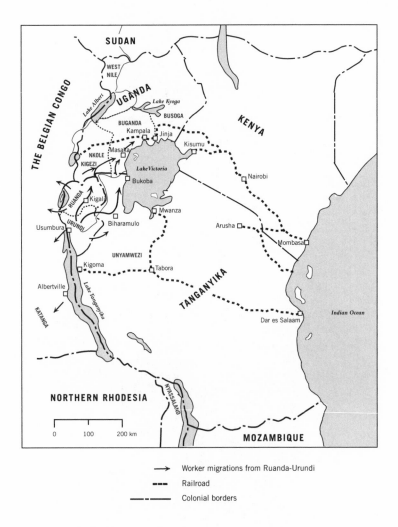

	Worker migrations from Ruanda-Urundi
---	Railroad
—·—·—	Colonial borders

East Africa in the mid-twentieth century

Name Index

Place Index

Designed by Bruce Mau with Julie Fry
Typeset by Archetype
Printed and bound by Maple-Vail on Sebago acid-free paper

DATE DUE